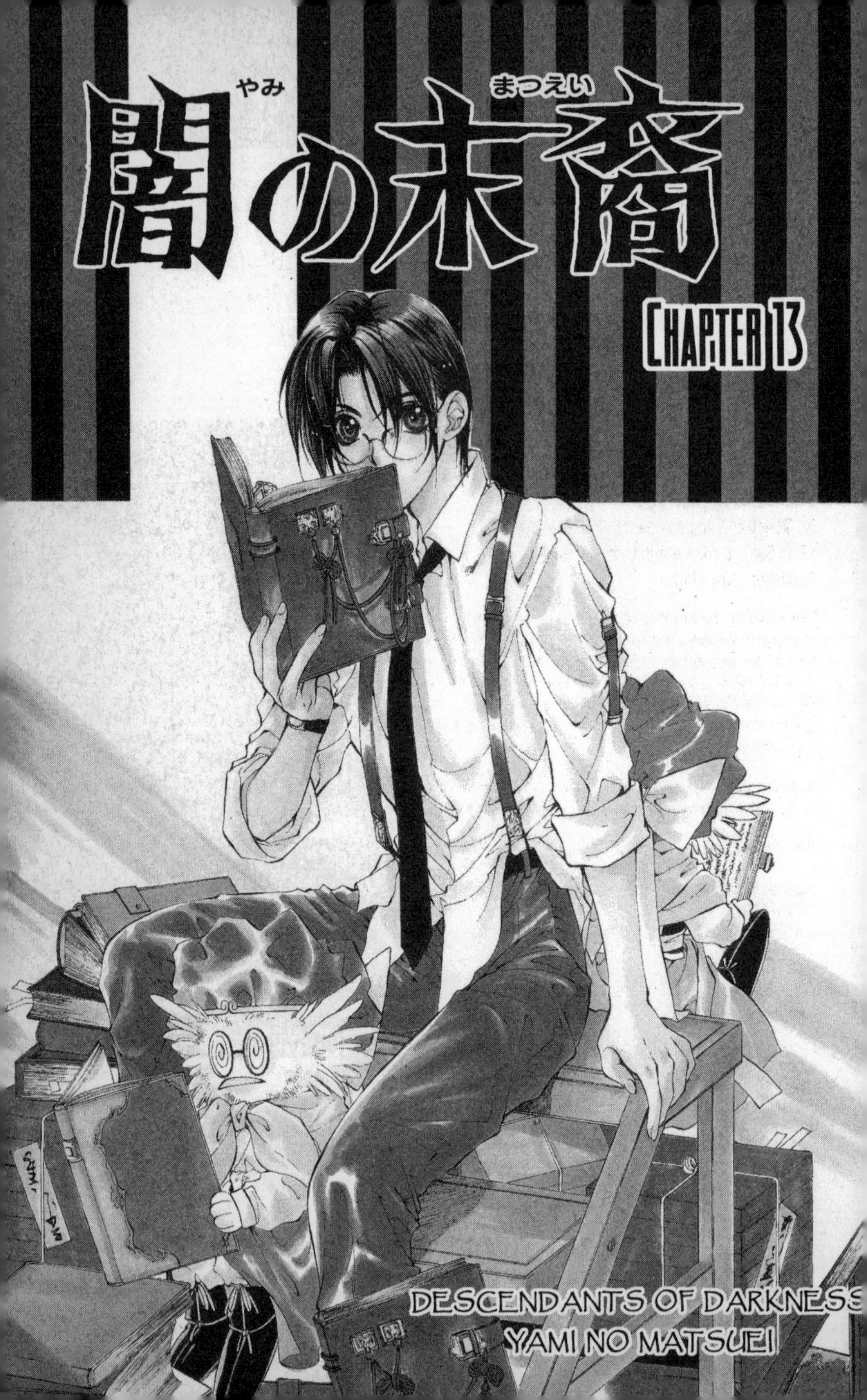

やみ まつえい
闇の末裔
CHAPTER 13
DESCENDANTS OF DARKNESS
YAMI NO MATSUEI

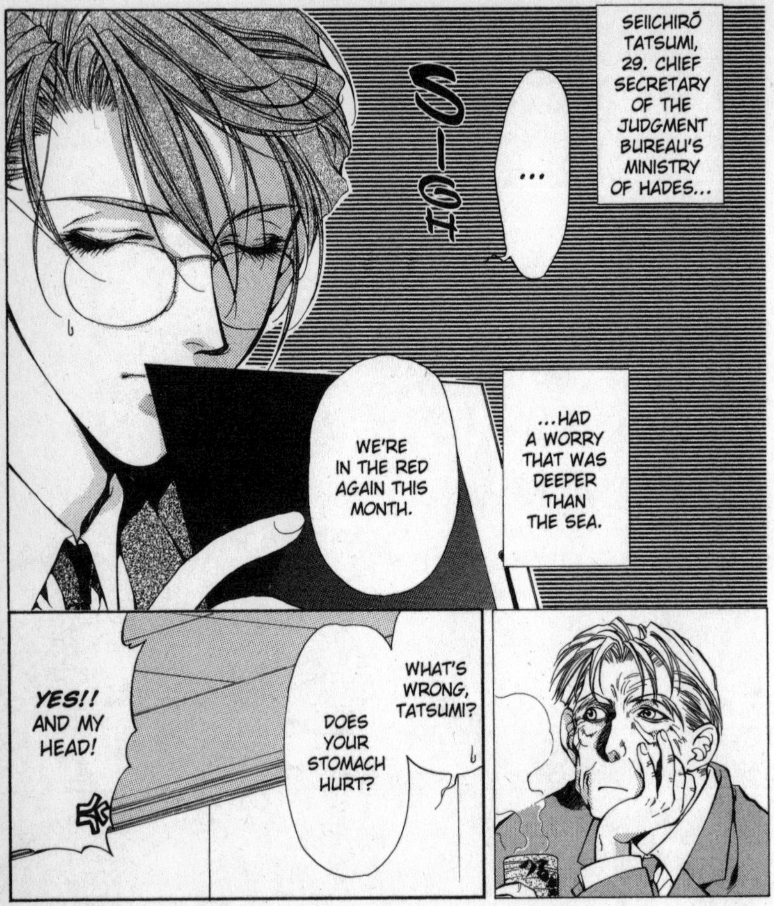
SEIICHIRŌ TATSUMI, 29. CHIEF SECRETARY OF THE JUDGMENT BUREAU'S MINISTRY OF HADES...
S-I-G-H
...
...HAD A WORRY THAT WAS DEEPER THAN THE SEA.
WE'RE IN THE RED AGAIN THIS MONTH.
WHAT'S WRONG, TATSUMI? DOES YOUR STOMACH HURT?
YES!! AND MY HEAD!

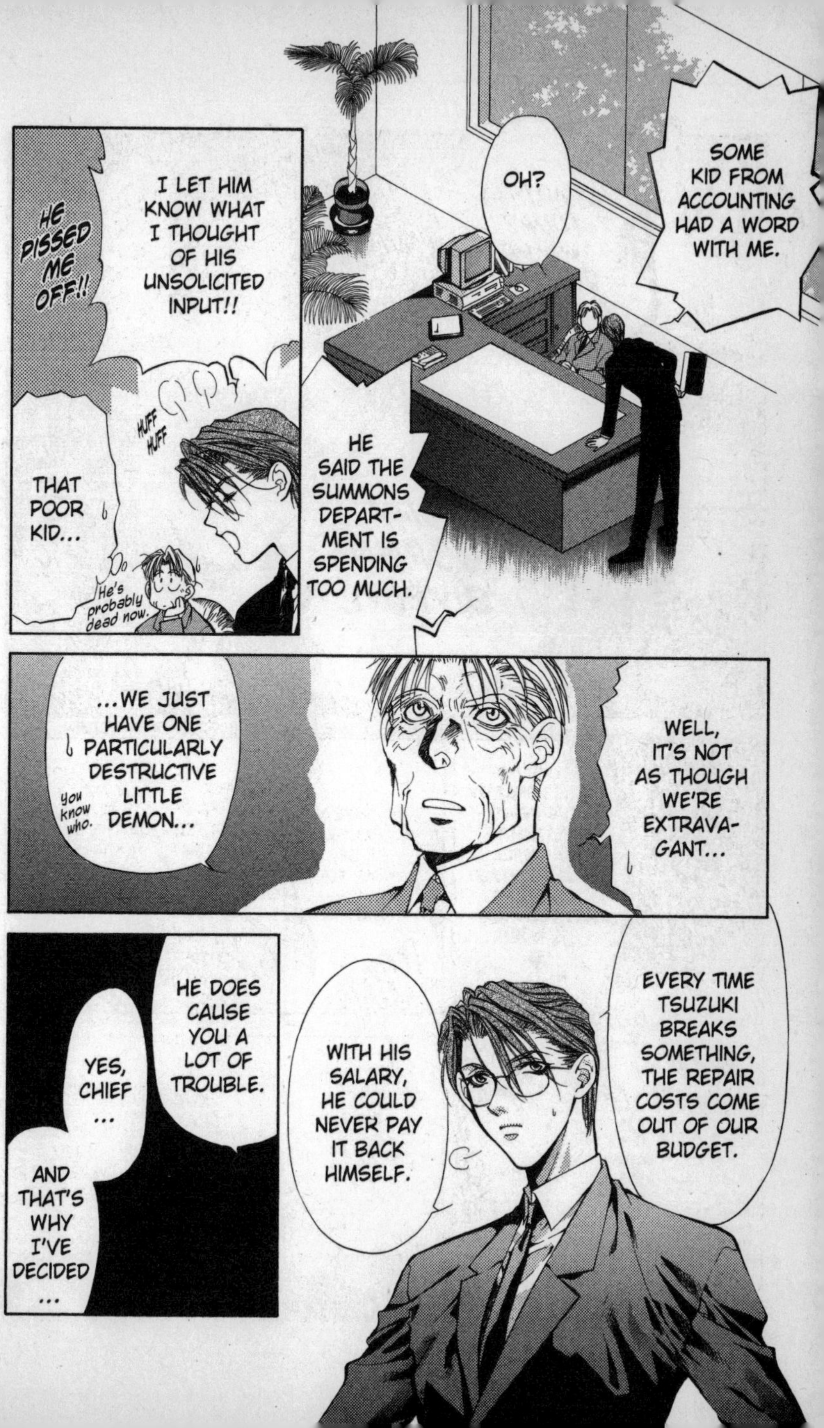
SOME KID FROM ACCOUNTING HAD A WORD WITH ME.
OH?
HE SAID THE SUMMONS DEPART-MENT IS SPENDING TOO MUCH.
I LET HIM KNOW WHAT I THOUGHT OF HIS UNSOLICITED INPUT!!
HE PISSED ME OFF!!
HUFF HUFF
THAT POOR KID...
He's probably dead now.
WELL, IT'S NOT AS THOUGH WE'RE EXTRAVA-GANT...
...WE JUST HAVE ONE PARTICULARLY DESTRUCTIVE LITTLE DEMON...
You know who.
EVERY TIME TSUZUKI BREAKS SOMETHING, THE REPAIR COSTS COME OUT OF OUR BUDGET.
WITH HIS SALARY, HE COULD NEVER PAY IT BACK HIMSELF.
HE DOES CAUSE YOU A LOT OF TROUBLE.
YES, CHIEF ...
AND THAT'S WHY I'VE DECIDED ...

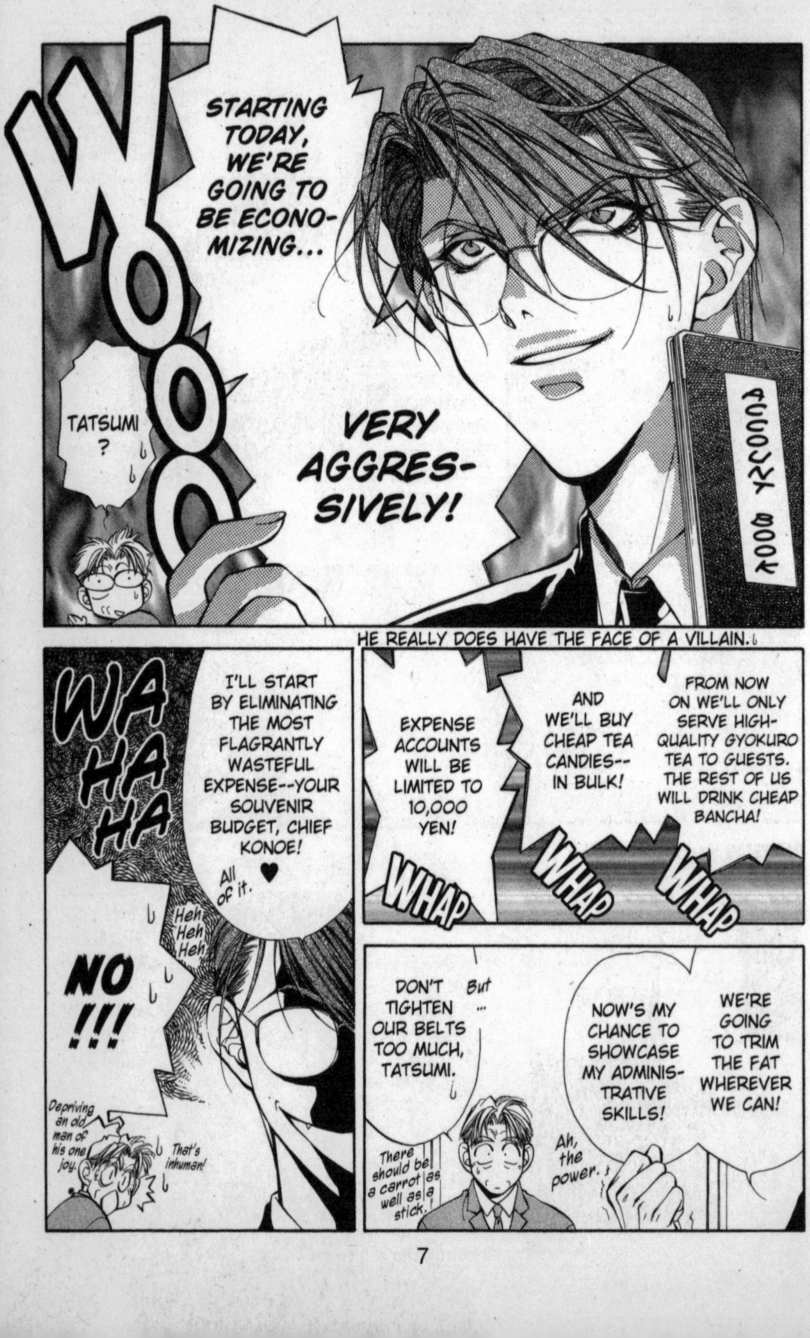
STARTING TODAY, WE'RE GOING TO BE ECONOMIZING...
VERY AGGRESSIVELY!
ACCOUNT BOOK
WOOOO
TATSUMI ?
HE REALLY DOES HAVE THE FACE OF A VILLAIN.
FROM NOW ON WE'LL ONLY SERVE HIGH-QUALITY GYOKURO TEA TO GUESTS. THE REST OF US WILL DRINK CHEAP BANCHA!
AND WE'LL BUY CHEAP TEA CANDIES-- IN BULK!
EXPENSE ACCOUNTS WILL BE LIMITED TO 10,000 YEN!
WHAP
WHAP
WHAP
WE'RE GOING TO TRIM THE FAT WHEREVER WE CAN!
NOW'S MY CHANCE TO SHOWCASE MY ADMINISTRATIVE SKILLS!
Ah, the power.
But ...
DON'T TIGHTEN OUR BELTS TOO MUCH, TATSUMI.
There should be a carrot as well as a stick.
I'LL START BY ELIMINATING THE MOST FLAGRANTLY WASTEFUL EXPENSE--YOUR SOUVENIR BUDGET, CHIEF KONOE!
All of it. ♥
WA HA HA HA
Heh Heh Heh
NO !!!
Depriving an old man of his one joy.
That's inhuman!

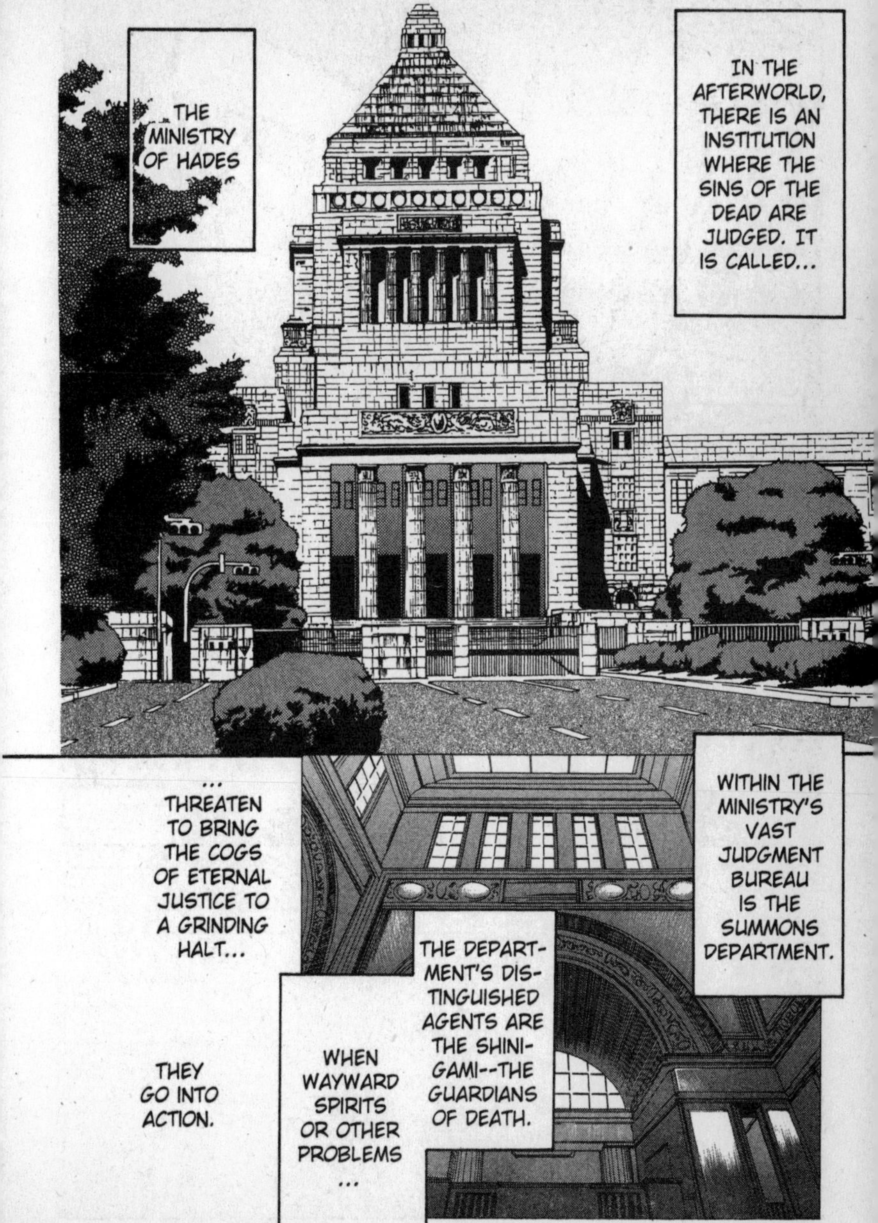
IN THE AFTERWORLD, THERE IS AN INSTITUTION WHERE THE SINS OF THE DEAD ARE JUDGED. IT IS CALLED...
THE MINISTRY OF HADES
WITHIN THE MINISTRY'S VAST JUDGMENT BUREAU IS THE SUMMONS DEPARTMENT.
THE DEPARTMENT'S DISTINGUISHED AGENTS ARE THE SHINIGAMI--THE GUARDIANS OF DEATH.
WHEN WAYWARD SPIRITS OR OTHER PROBLEMS ...
... THREATEN TO BRING THE COGS OF ETERNAL JUSTICE TO A GRINDING HALT...
THEY GO INTO ACTION.

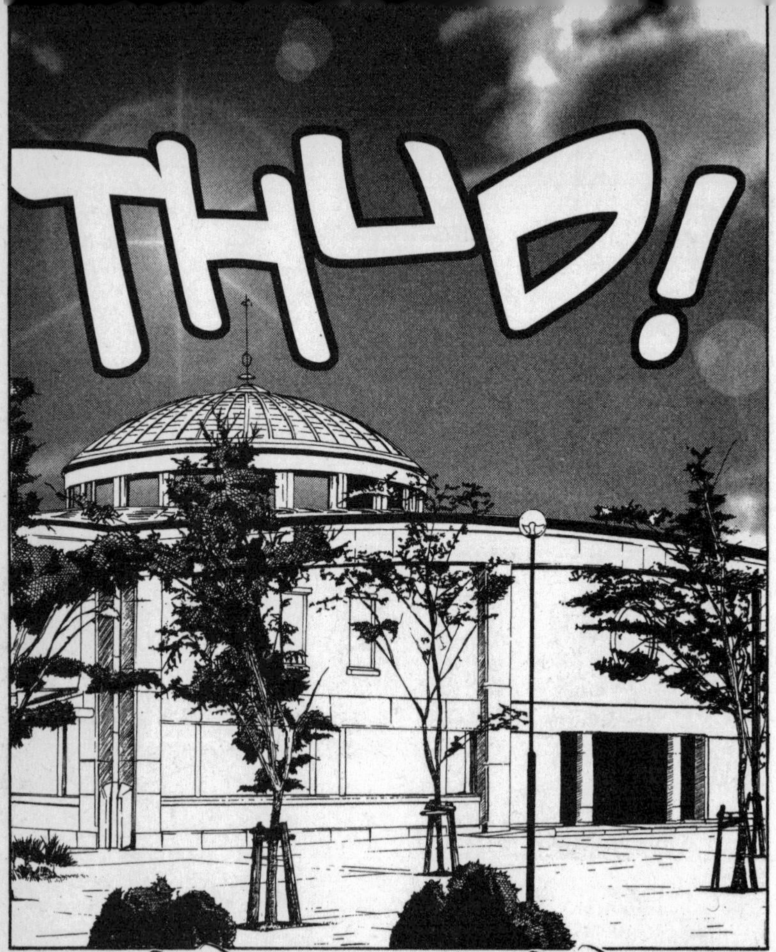
THUD!

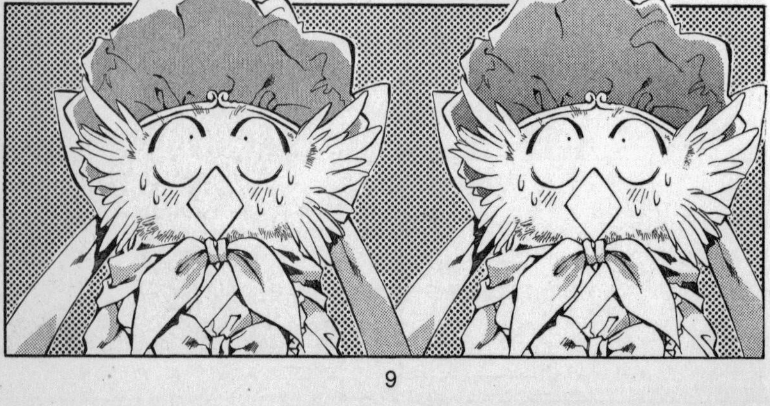

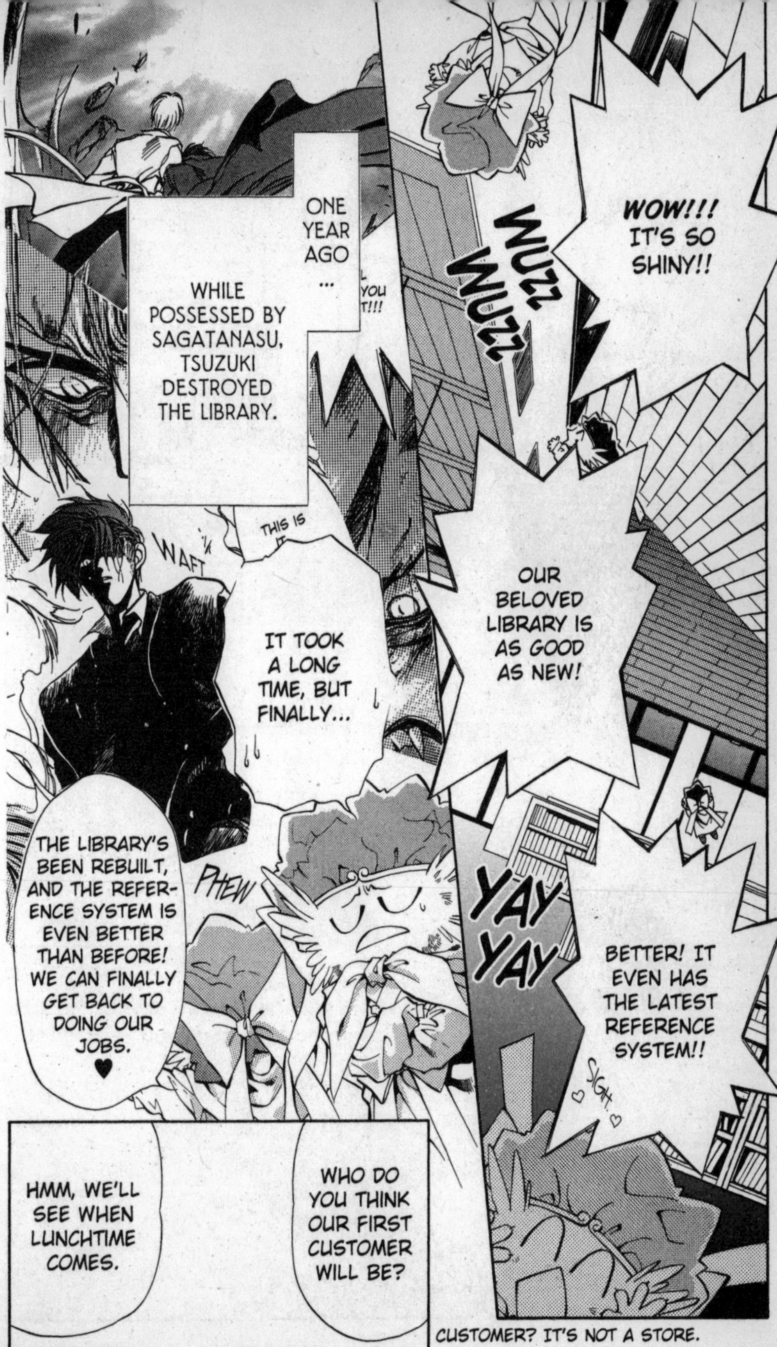
WOW!!! IT'S SO SHINY!!
WUZZ WUZZ
ONE YEAR AGO ...
WHILE POSSESSED BY SAGATANASU, TSUZUKI DESTROYED THE LIBRARY.
OUR BELOVED LIBRARY IS AS GOOD AS NEW!
THIS IS
WAFT
IT TOOK A LONG TIME, BUT FINALLY...
YAY YAY
BETTER! IT EVEN HAS THE LATEST REFERENCE SYSTEM!!
SIGH.
THE LIBRARY'S BEEN REBUILT, AND THE REFER-ENCE SYSTEM IS EVEN BETTER THAN BEFORE! WE CAN FINALLY GET BACK TO DOING OUR JOBS. ♥
PHEW
WHO DO YOU THINK OUR FIRST CUSTOMER WILL BE?
HMM, WE'LL SEE WHEN LUNCHTIME COMES.

CUSTOMER? IT'S NOT A STORE.

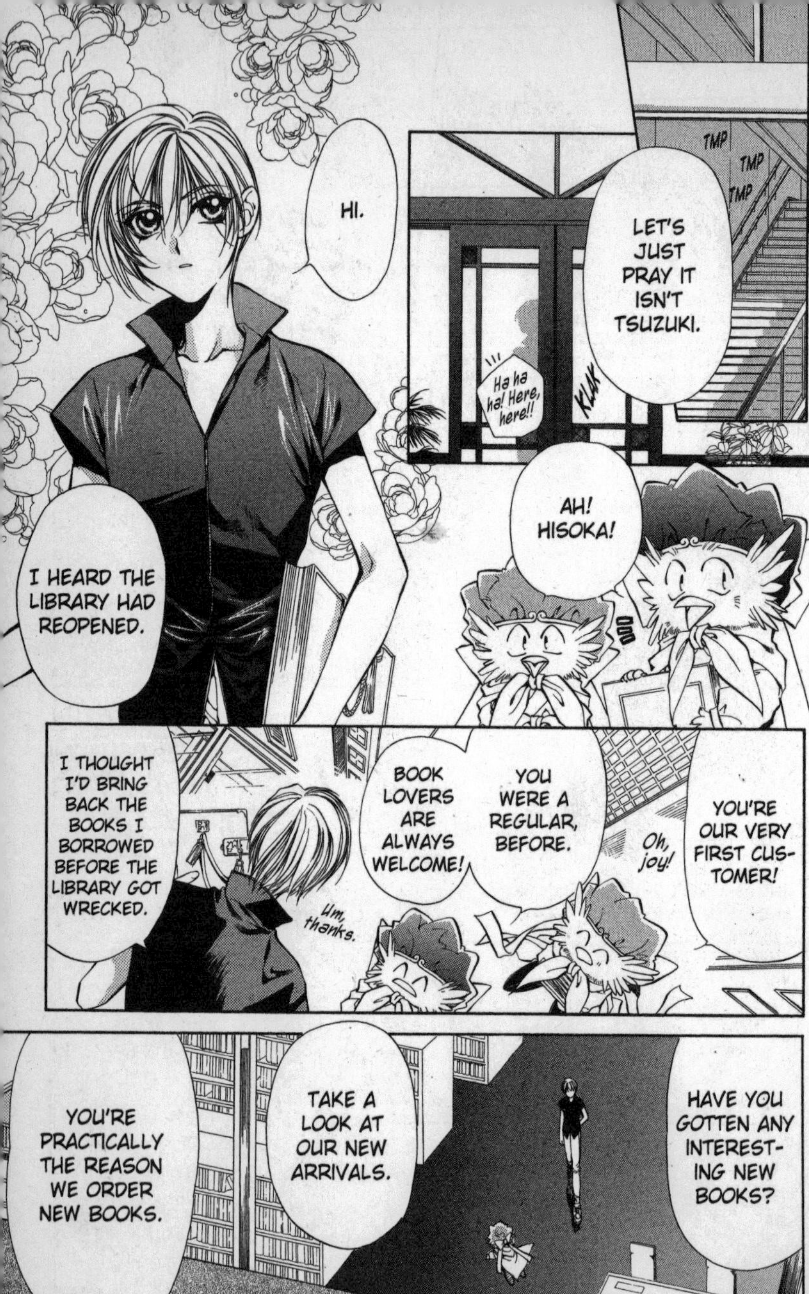
TMP
TMP
TMP
LET'S JUST PRAY IT ISN'T TSUZUKI.
KLAK
Ha ha ha! Here, here!!
AH! HISOKA!
HI.
I HEARD THE LIBRARY HAD REOPENED.
YOU'RE OUR VERY FIRST CUS-TOMER!
Oh, joy!
YOU WERE A REGULAR, BEFORE.
BOOK LOVERS ARE ALWAYS WELCOME!
I THOUGHT I'D BRING BACK THE BOOKS I BORROWED BEFORE THE LIBRARY GOT WRECKED.
Um, thanks.
HAVE YOU GOTTEN ANY INTEREST-ING NEW BOOKS?
TAKE A LOOK AT OUR NEW ARRIVALS.
YOU'RE PRACTICALLY THE REASON WE ORDER NEW BOOKS.

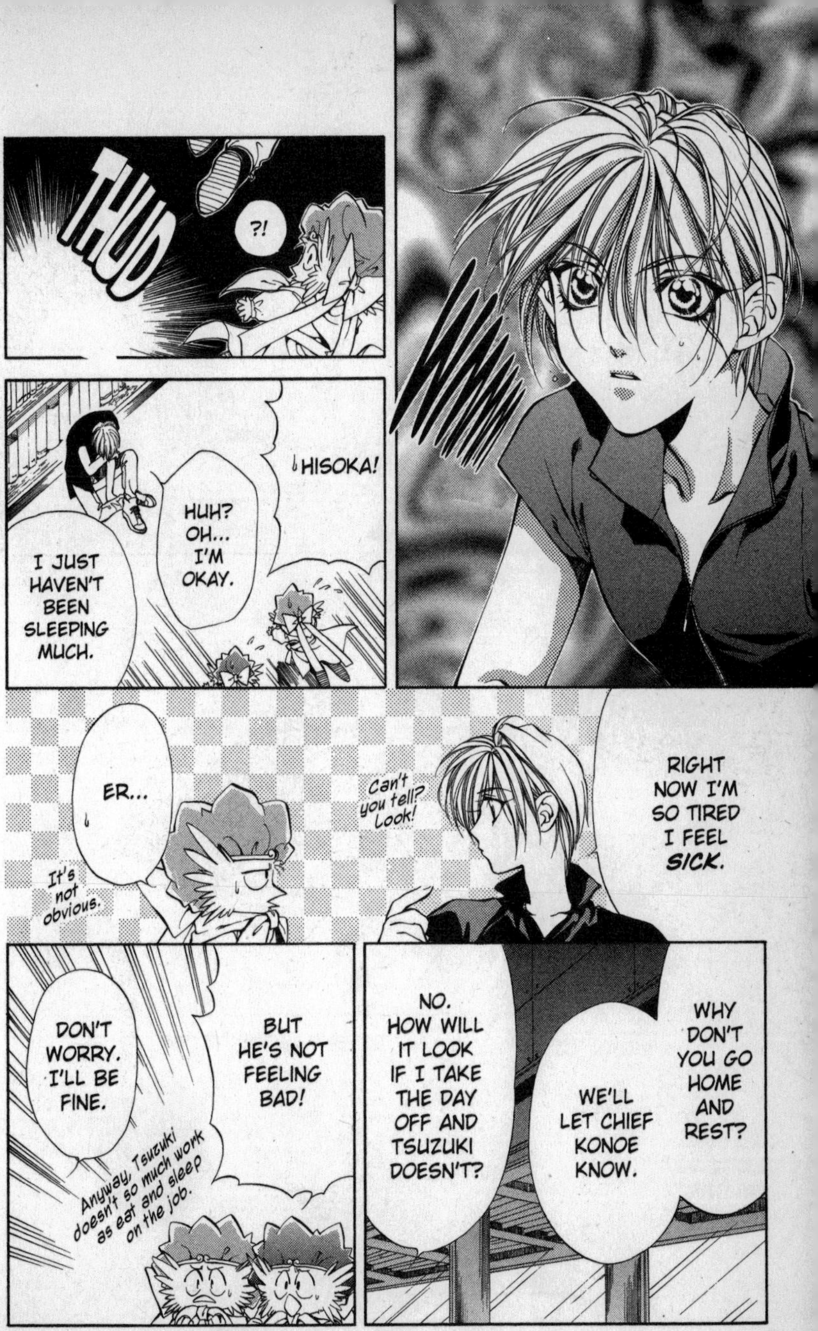
THUD
?!
HISOKA!
HUH? OH... I'M OKAY.
I JUST HAVEN'T BEEN SLEEPING MUCH.
RIGHT NOW I'M SO TIRED I FEEL SICK.
Can't you tell? Look!
ER...
It's not obvious.
WHY DON'T YOU GO HOME AND REST?
WE'LL LET CHIEF KONOE KNOW.
NO. HOW WILL IT LOOK IF I TAKE THE DAY OFF AND TSUZUKI DOESN'T?
BUT HE'S NOT FEELING BAD!
DON'T WORRY. I'LL BE FINE.
Anyway, Tsuzuki doesn't so much work as eat and sleep on the job.

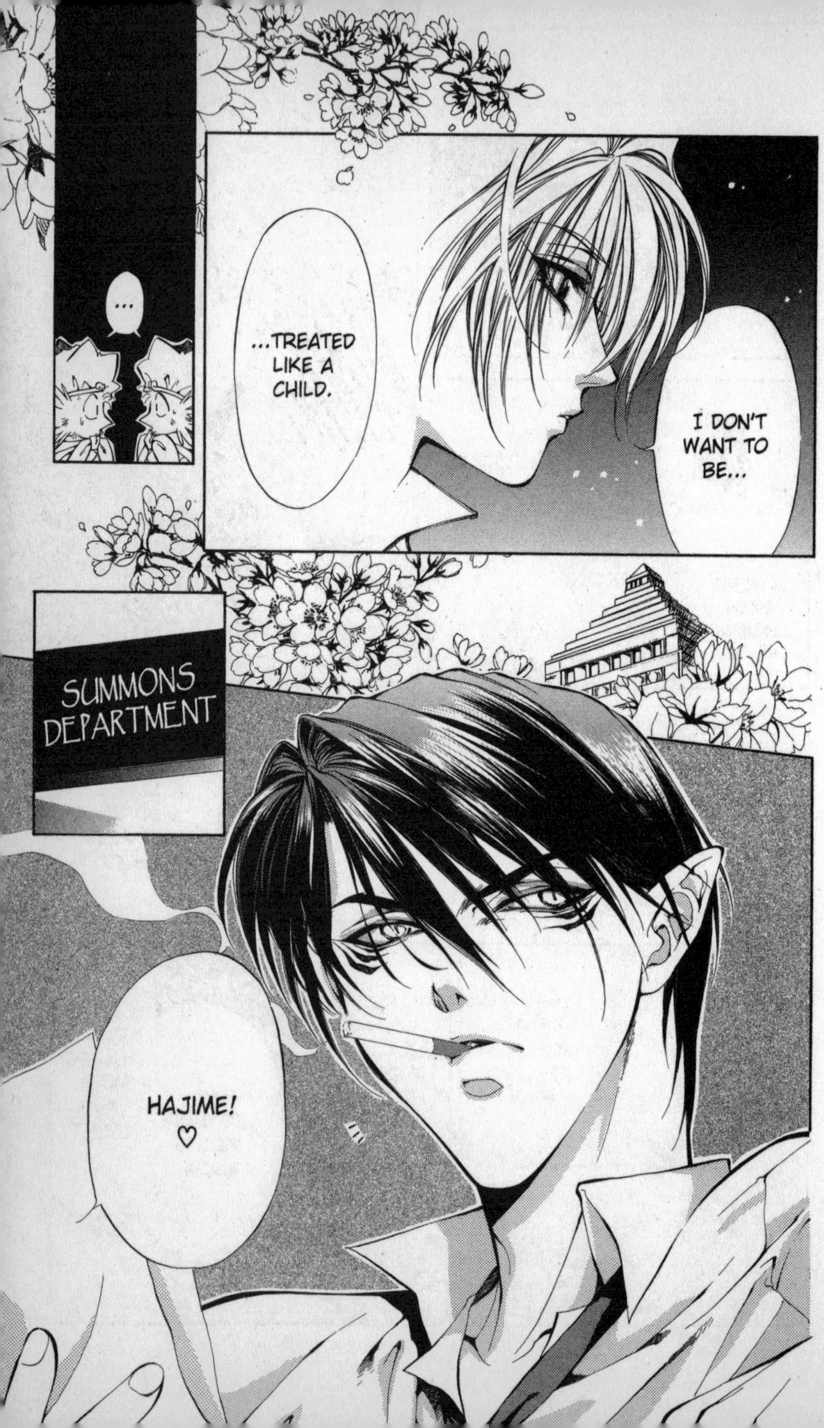
I DON'T WANT TO BE...
...TREATED LIKE A CHILD.
...
SUMMONS DEPARTMENT
HAJIME! ♡

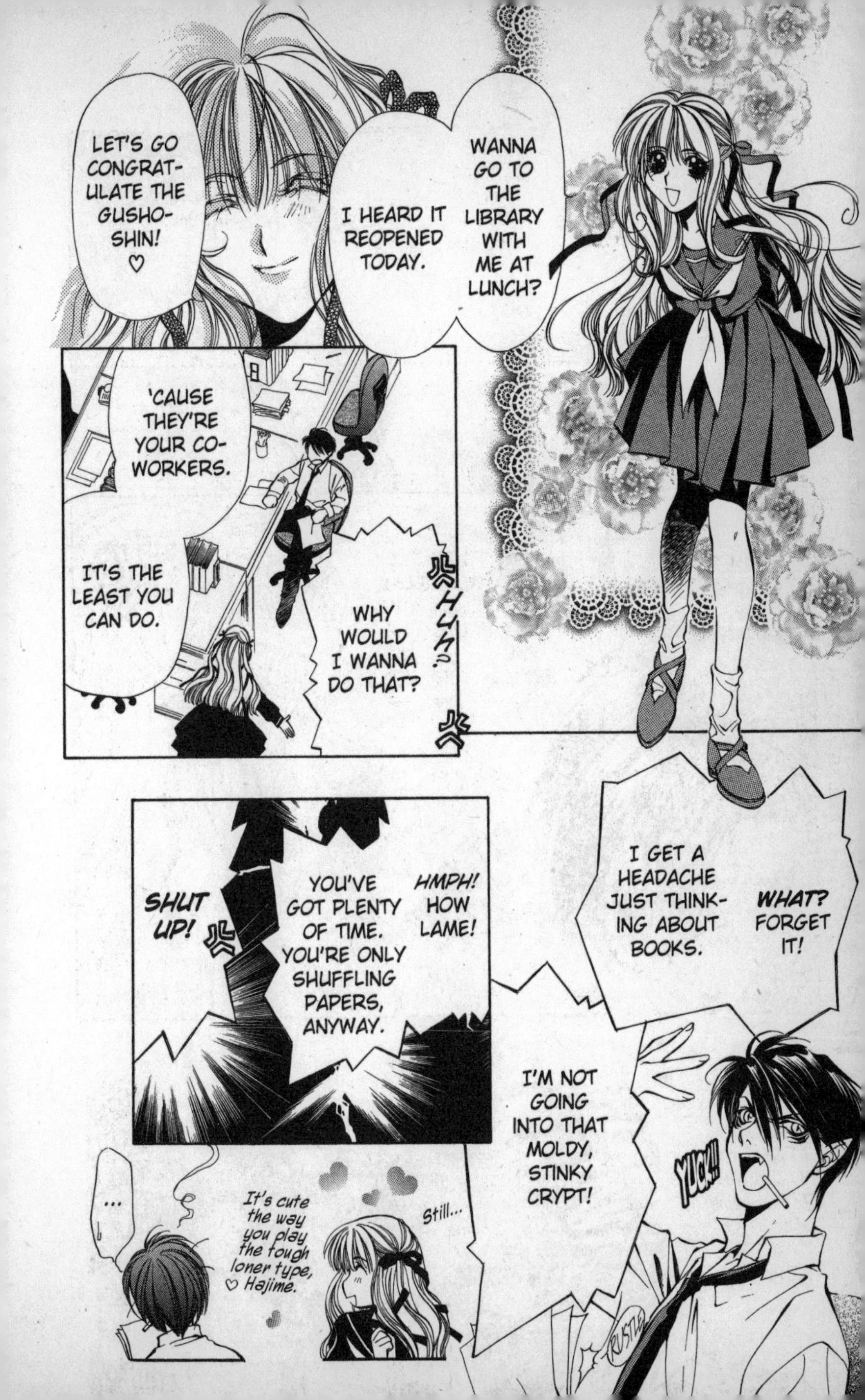
WANNA GO TO THE LIBRARY WITH ME AT LUNCH?
I HEARD IT REOPENED TODAY.
LET'S GO CONGRATULATE THE GUSHO-SHIN! ♡
WHY WOULD I WANNA DO THAT?
HUH?
'CAUSE THEY'RE YOUR CO-WORKERS.
IT'S THE LEAST YOU CAN DO.
WHAT? FORGET IT!
I GET A HEADACHE JUST THINKING ABOUT BOOKS.
YUCK!!
I'M NOT GOING INTO THAT MOLDY, STINKY CRYPT!
RUSTLE
HMPH! HOW LAME!
YOU'VE GOT PLENTY OF TIME. YOU'RE ONLY SHUFFLING PAPERS, ANYWAY.
SHUT UP!
Still...
It's cute the way you play the tough loner type, ♡ Hajime.
...

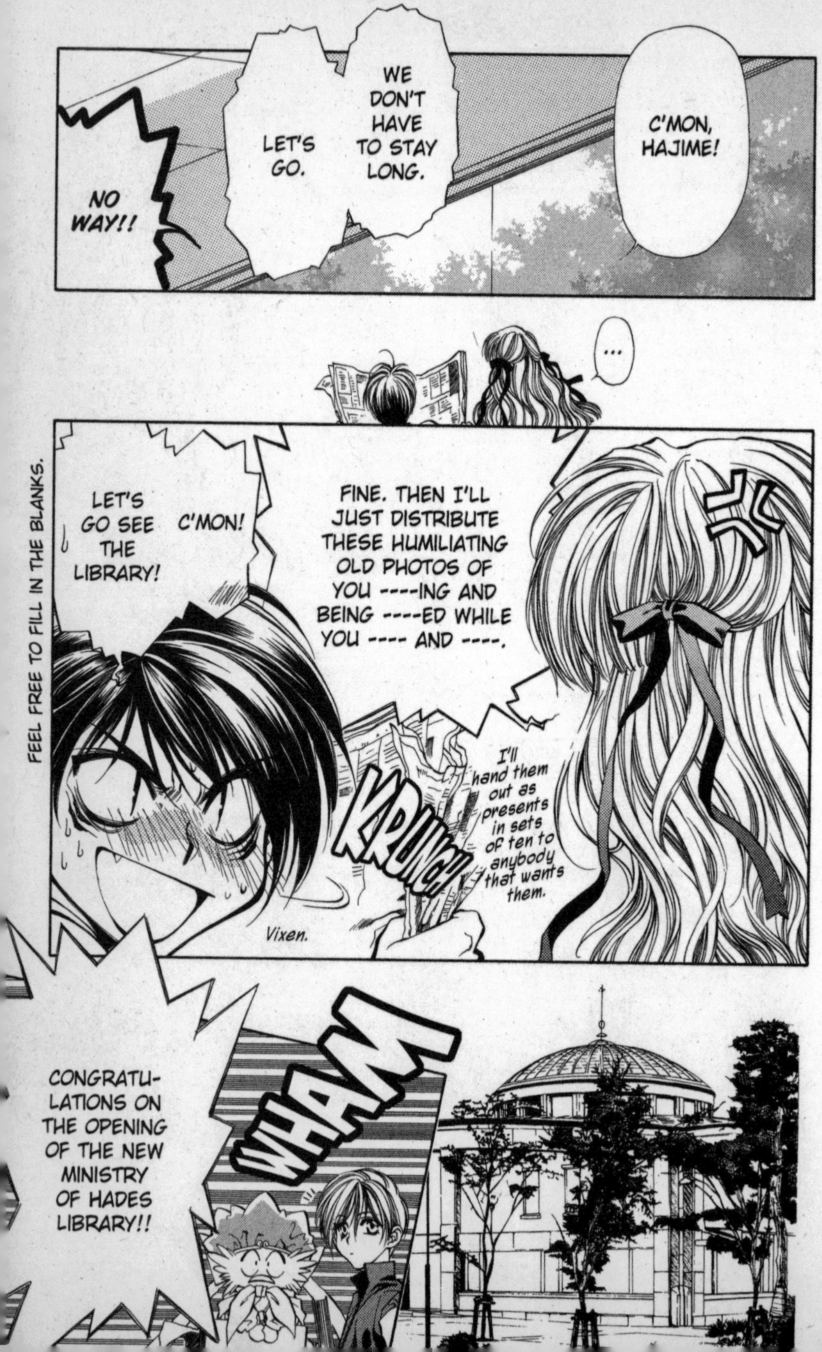

C'MON, HAJIME!
WE DON'T HAVE TO STAY LONG.
LET'S GO.
NO WAY!!
...
FINE. THEN I'LL JUST DISTRIBUTE THESE HUMILIATING OLD PHOTOS OF YOU ----ING AND BEING ----ED WHILE YOU ---- AND ----.
I'll hand them out as presents in sets of ten to anybody that wants them.
KRUNCH
Vixen.
C'MON!
LET'S GO SEE THE LIBRARY!
FEEL FREE TO FILL IN THE BLANKS.
WHAM
CONGRATULATIONS ON THE OPENING OF THE NEW MINISTRY OF HADES LIBRARY!!

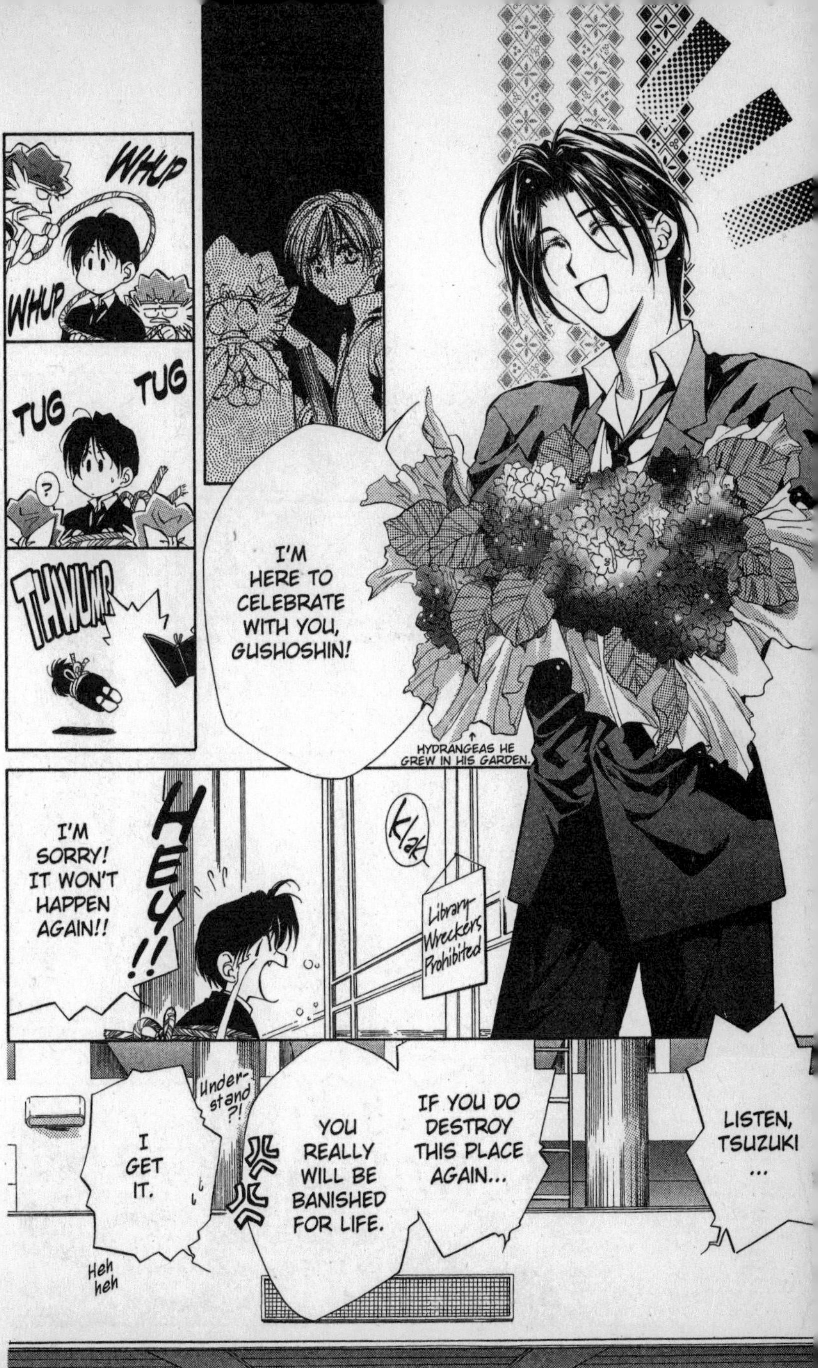
I'M HERE TO CELEBRATE WITH YOU, GUSHOSHIN!
HYDRANGEAS HE GREW IN HIS GARDEN.
WHUP
WHUP
TUG
TUG
?
THWUMP
Klak
Library-Wreckers Prohibited
HEY!!
I'M SORRY! IT WON'T HAPPEN AGAIN!!
LISTEN, TSUZUKI ...
IF YOU DO DESTROY THIS PLACE AGAIN...
YOU REALLY WILL BE BANISHED FOR LIFE.
Understand?!
I GET IT.
Heh heh

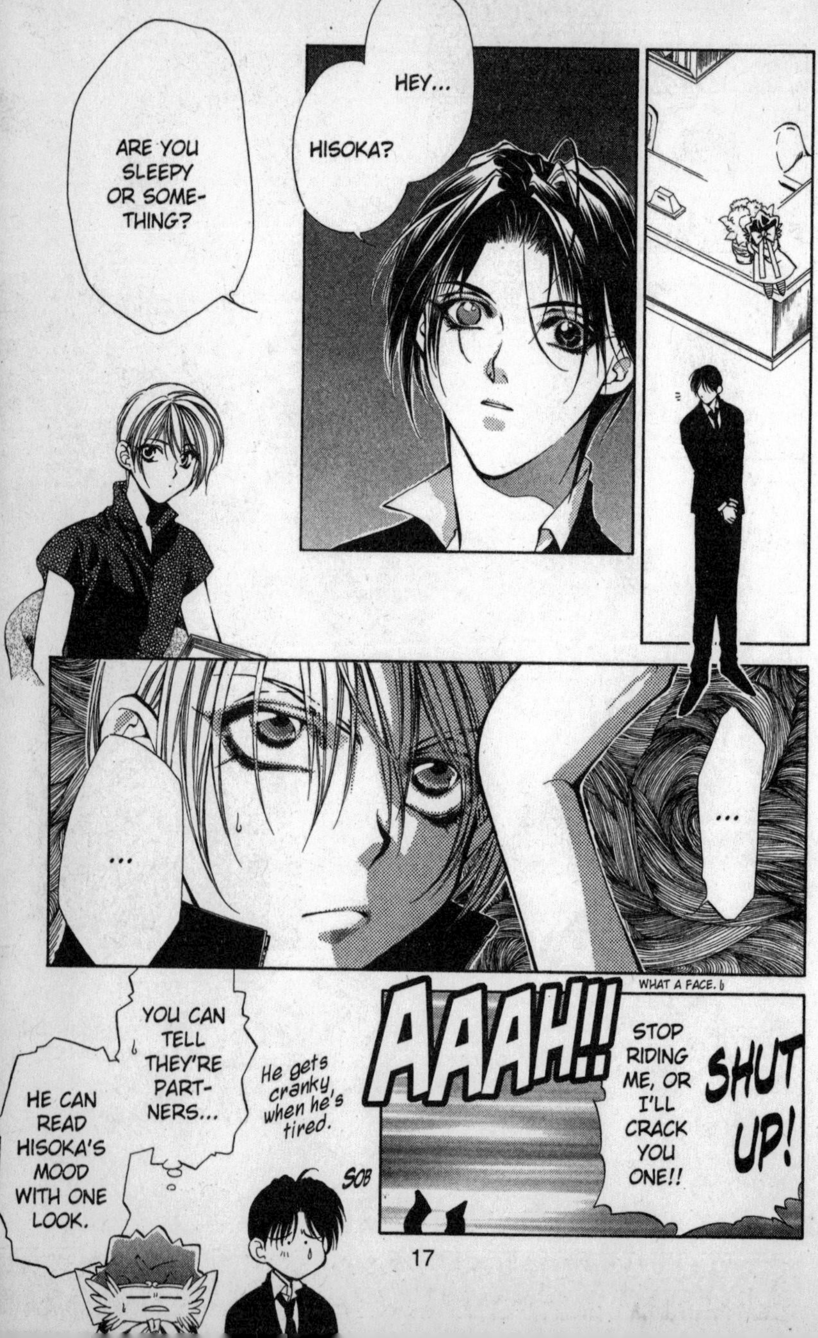
HEY... HISOKA?
ARE YOU SLEEPY OR SOME-THING?
...
...
WHAT A FACE.
SHUT UP!
STOP RIDING ME, OR I'LL CRACK YOU ONE!!
AAAH!!
SOB
YOU CAN TELL THEY'RE PART-NERS...
He gets cranky when he's tired.
HE CAN READ HISOKA'S MOOD WITH ONE LOOK.

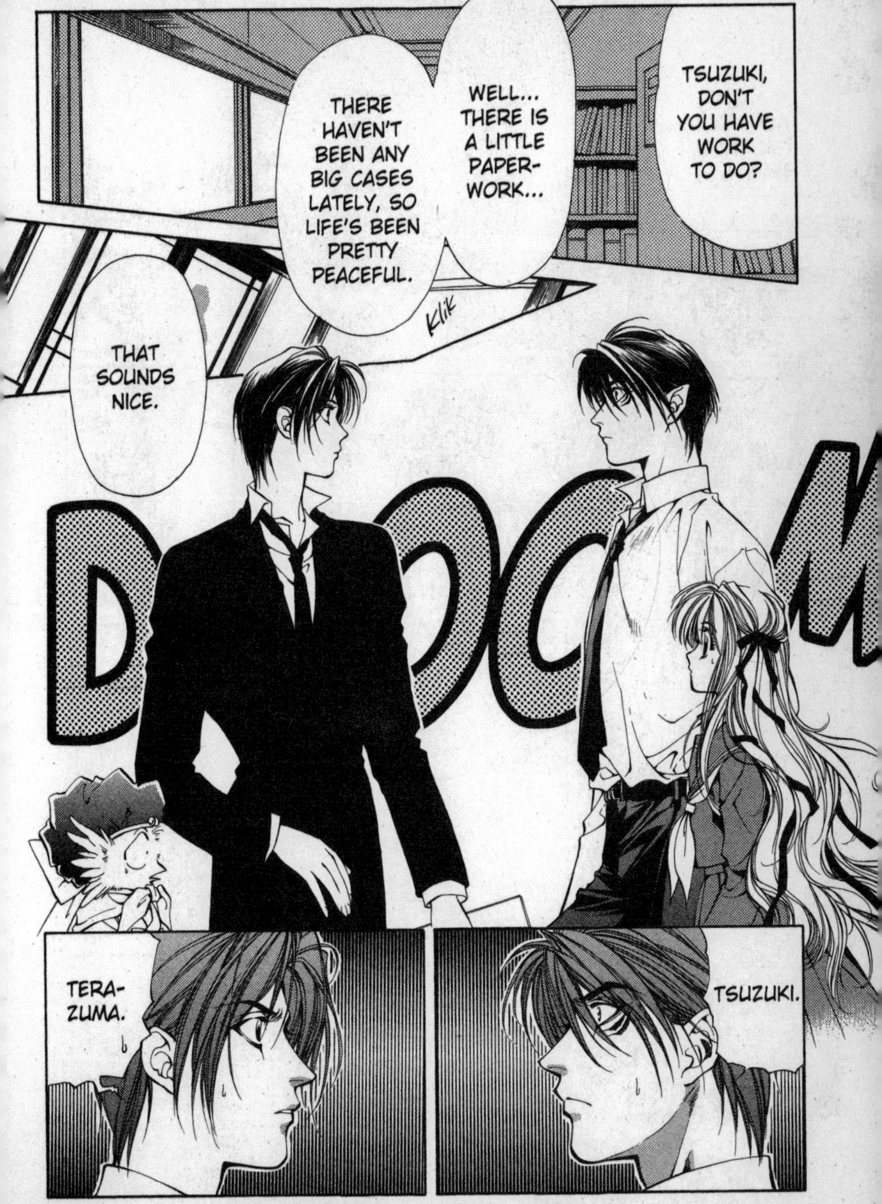
TSUZUKI, DON'T YOU HAVE WORK TO DO?
WELL... THERE IS A LITTLE PAPER-WORK...
THERE HAVEN'T BEEN ANY BIG CASES LATELY, SO LIFE'S BEEN PRETTY PEACEFUL.
Klik
THAT SOUNDS NICE.
DOOM
TSUZUKI.
TERA-ZUMA.

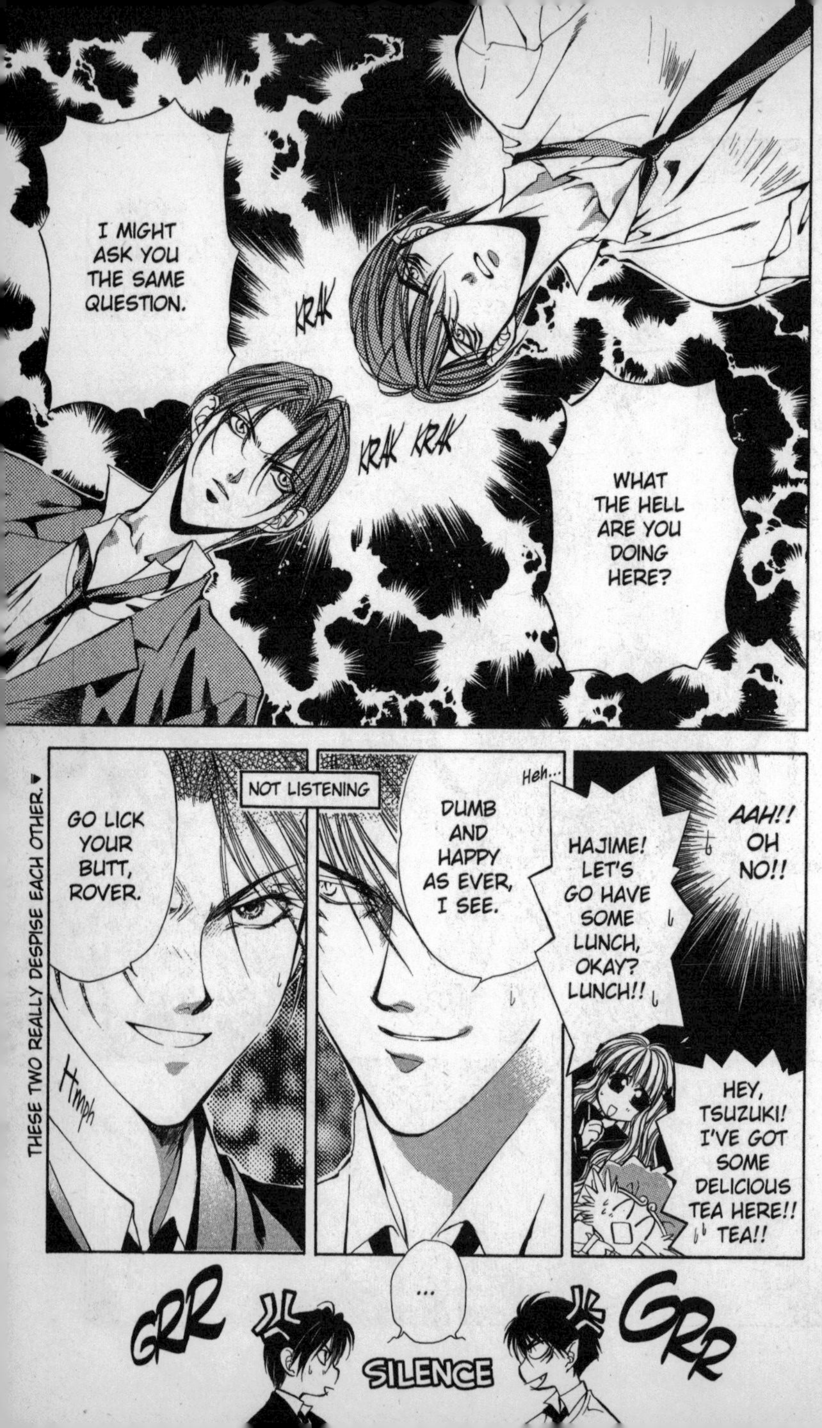
WHAT THE HELL ARE YOU DOING HERE?
KRAK
KRAK KRAK
I MIGHT ASK YOU THE SAME QUESTION.
AAH!! OH NO!!
HAJIME! LET'S GO HAVE SOME LUNCH, OKAY? LUNCH!!
HEY, TSUZUKI! I'VE GOT SOME DELICIOUS TEA HERE!! TEA!!
Heh...
DUMB AND HAPPY AS EVER, I SEE.
NOT LISTENING
GO LICK YOUR BUTT, ROVER.
Hmph
THESE TWO REALLY DESPISE EACH OTHER. ♥
GRR
...
SILENCE
GRR

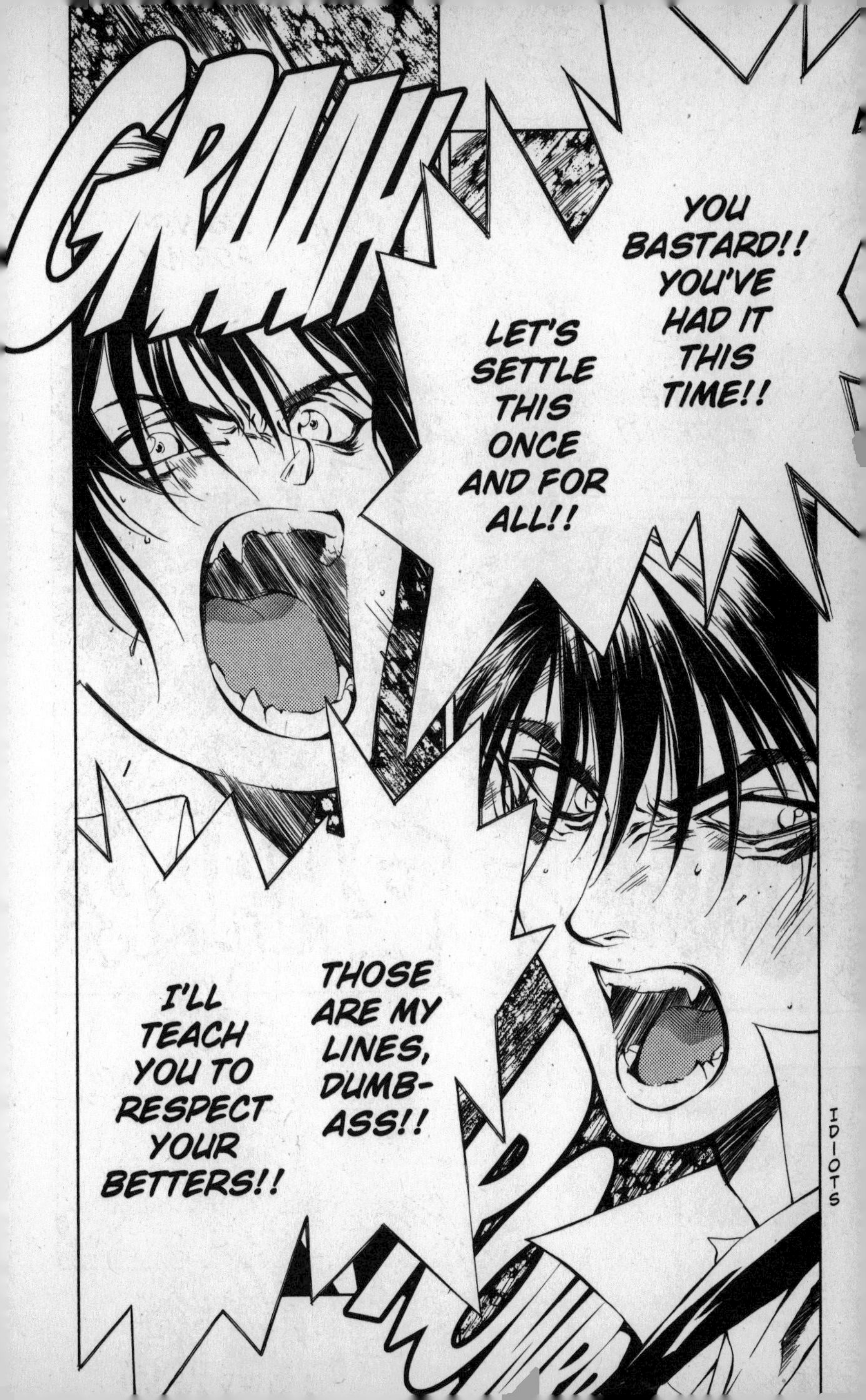
YOU BASTARD!! YOU'VE HAD IT THIS TIME!!
LET'S SETTLE THIS ONCE AND FOR ALL!!
THOSE ARE MY LINES, DUMB-ASS!!
I'LL TEACH YOU TO RESPECT YOUR BETTERS!!
IDIOTS

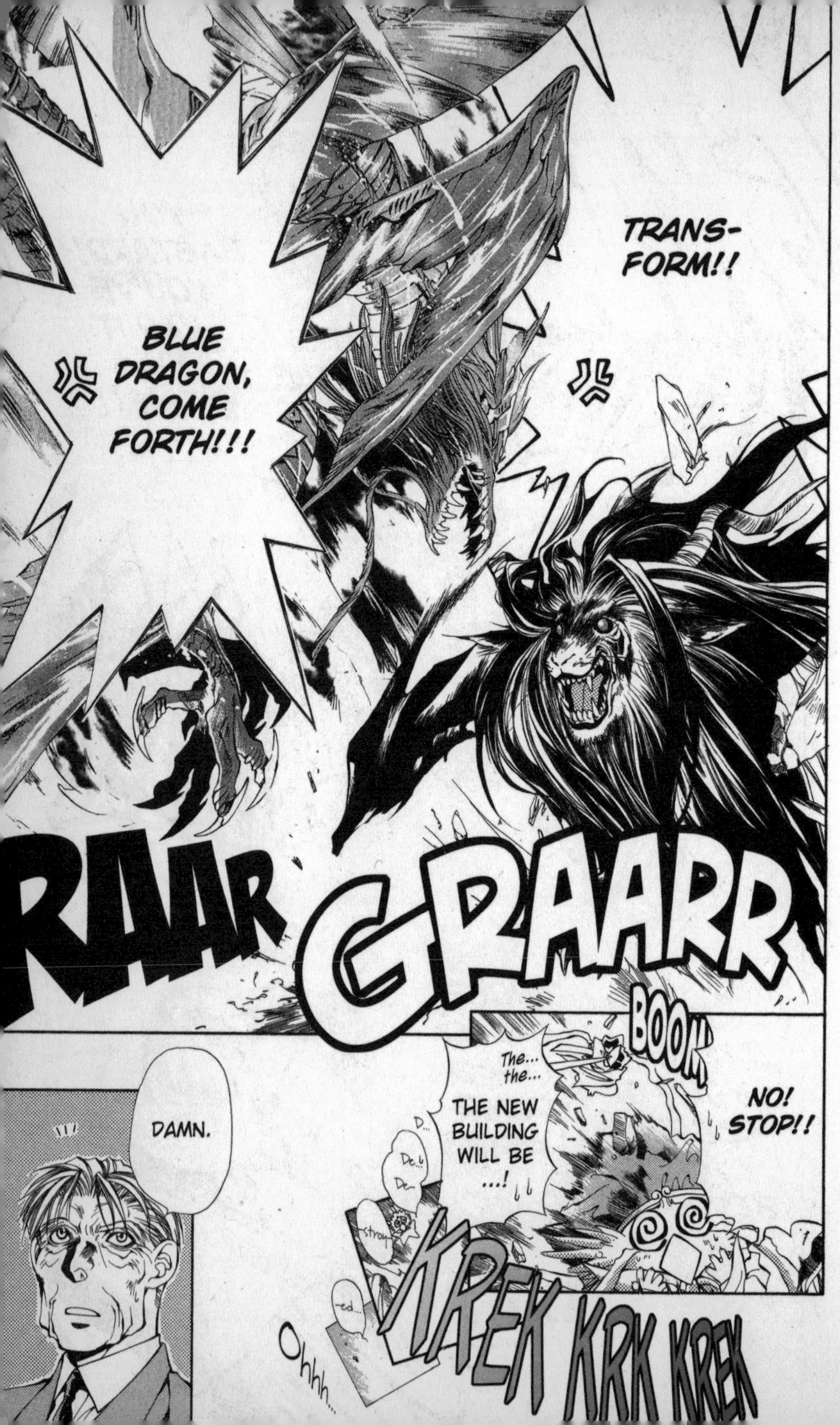
TRANS-
FORM!!
BLUE DRAGON, COME FORTH!!!
GRAARR
RAAAR
BOOM
NO! STOP!!
The... the...
THE NEW BUILDING WILL BE ...!
D...
De...
De-
-stroy-
-ed...
KREK KRK KREK
Ohhh...
DAMN.

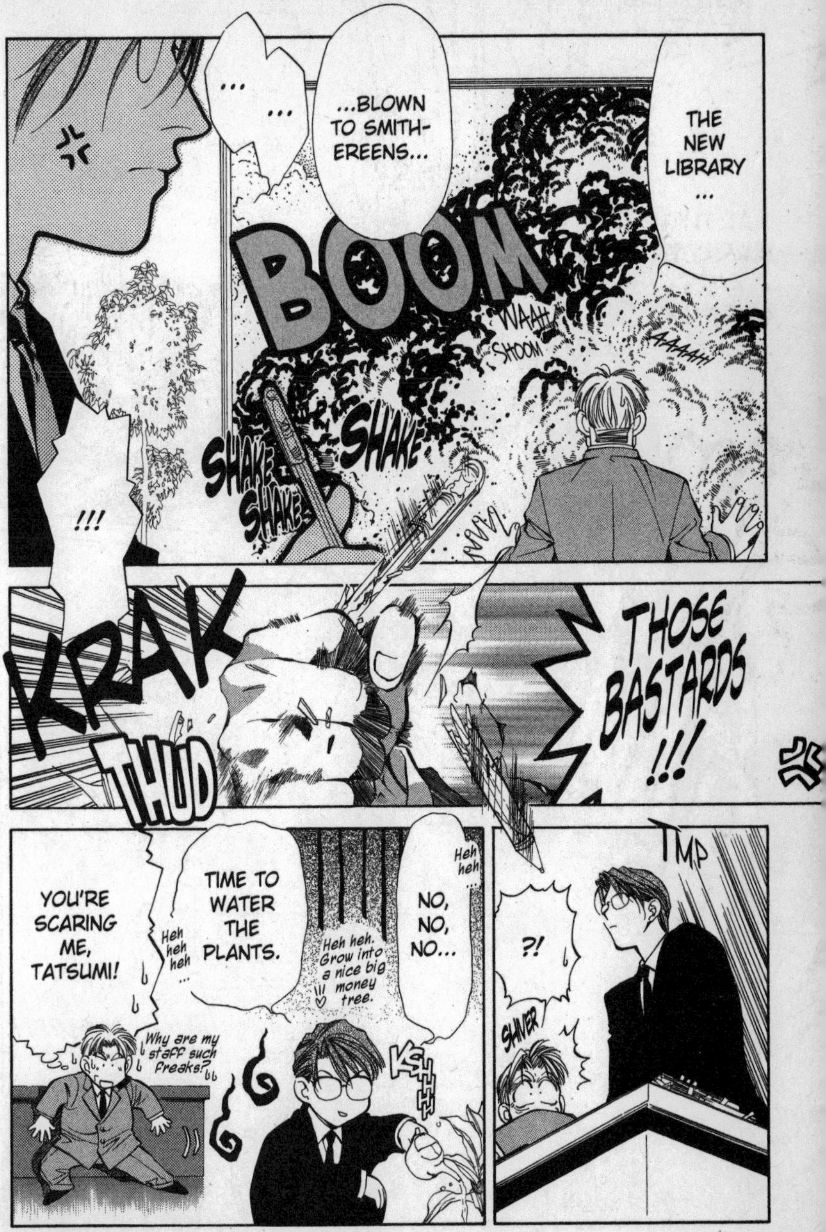
THE NEW LIBRARY ...
...BLOWN TO SMITHEREENS...
...
...
BOOM
WAAH
SHOOM
AAAAHH
SHAKE
SHAKE
SHAKE
!!!
THOSE BASTARDS!!!
KRAK
THUD
TMP
?!
SHIVER
Heh heh ...
NO, NO, NO...
TIME TO WATER THE PLANTS.
Heh heh. Grow into a nice big money tree.
KSHHH
Heh heh heh ...
YOU'RE SCARING ME, TATSUMI!
Why are my staff such freaks?

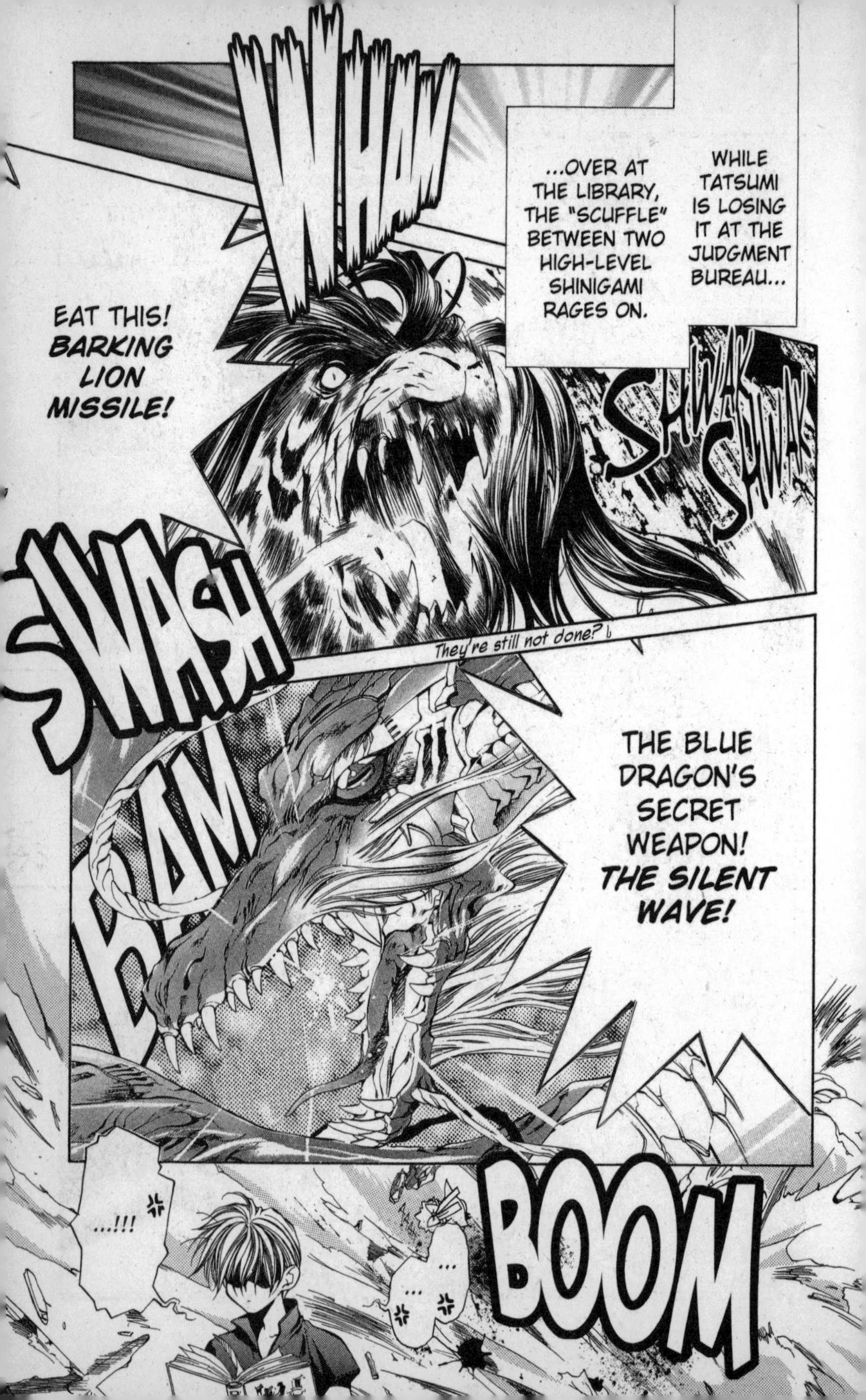
WHILE TATSUMI IS LOSING IT AT THE JUDGMENT BUREAU...
...OVER AT THE LIBRARY, THE "SCUFFLE" BETWEEN TWO HIGH-LEVEL SHINIGAMI RAGES ON.
WHAM
SHWAK SHWAK
EAT THIS! BARKING LION MISSILE!
SWASH
They're still not done?
THE BLUE DRAGON'S SECRET WEAPON! THE SILENT WAVE!
BAM
BOOM
...
...
...!!!

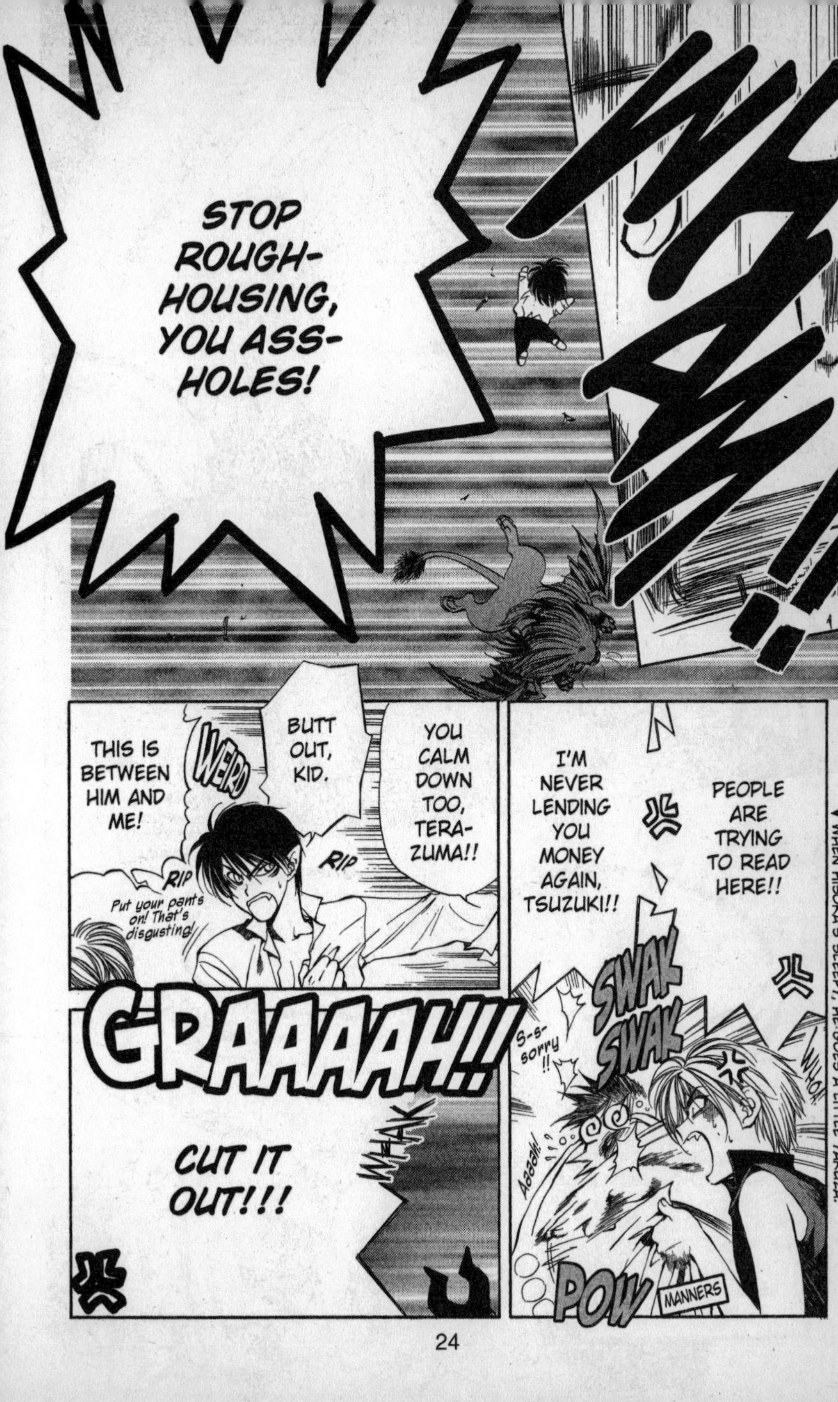
WHAM!!
STOP ROUGH-HOUSING, YOU ASS-HOLES!
PEOPLE ARE TRYING TO READ HERE!!
I'M NEVER LENDING YOU MONEY AGAIN, TSUZUKI!!
SWAK SWAK
WHO!
S-s-sorry!!
Aaaah!
POW
MANNERS
YOU CALM DOWN TOO, TERA-ZUMA!!
BUTT OUT, KID.
WEIRD
THIS IS BETWEEN HIM AND ME!
RIP
RIP
Put your pants on! That's disgusting!
GRAAAAH!!
WHAK
CUT IT OUT!!!

▼WHEN HISOKA'S SLEEPY, HE GOES A LITTLE YAKUZA.

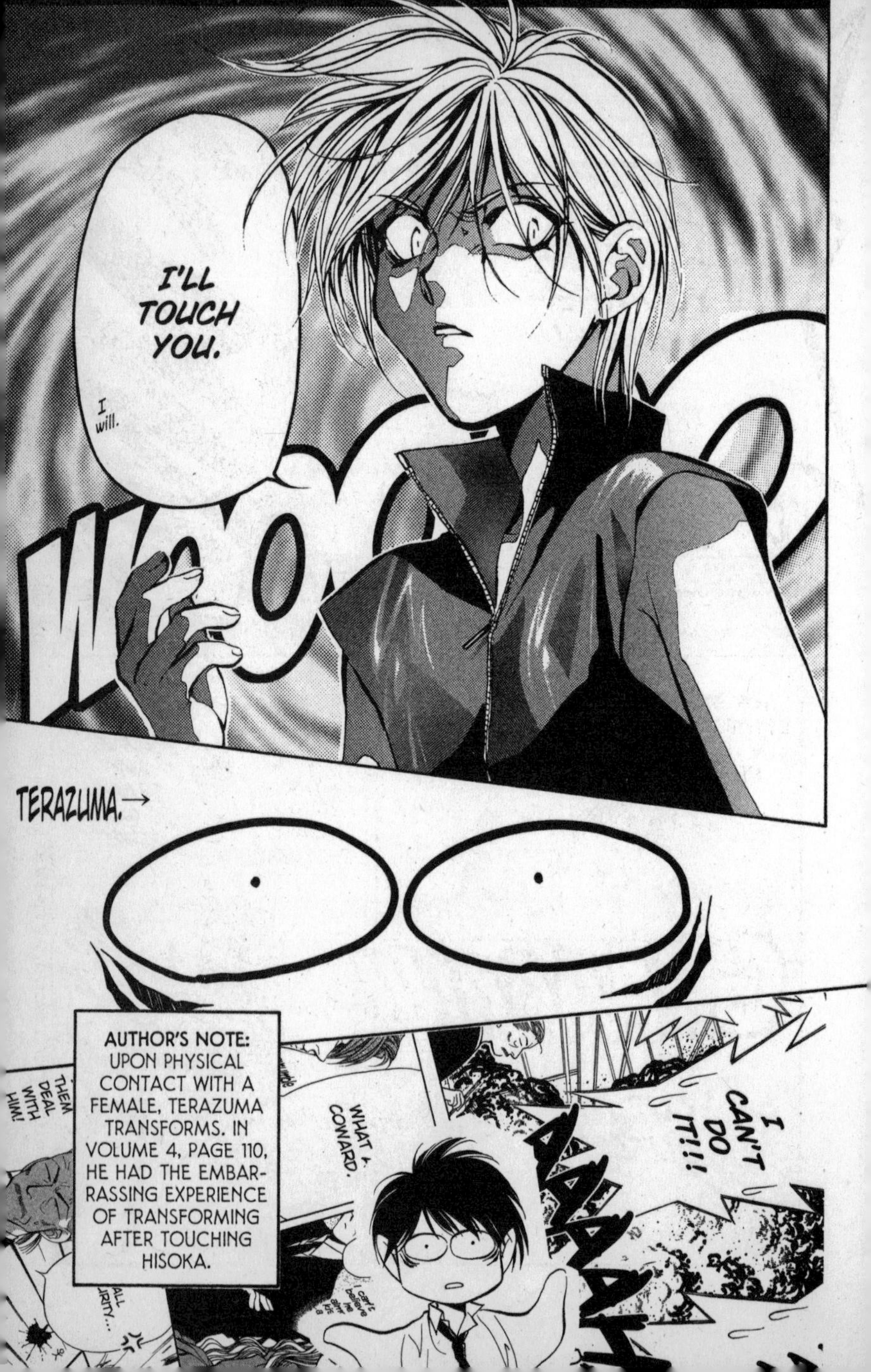
I'LL TOUCH YOU.
I will.
TERAZUMA.→
I CAN'T DO IT!!!
WHAT A COWARD.
THEN DEAL WITH HIM!
AUTHOR'S NOTE: UPON PHYSICAL CONTACT WITH A FEMALE, TERAZUMA TRANSFORMS. IN VOLUME 4, PAGE 110, HE HAD THE EMBARRASSING EXPERIENCE OF TRANSFORMING AFTER TOUCHING HISOKA.

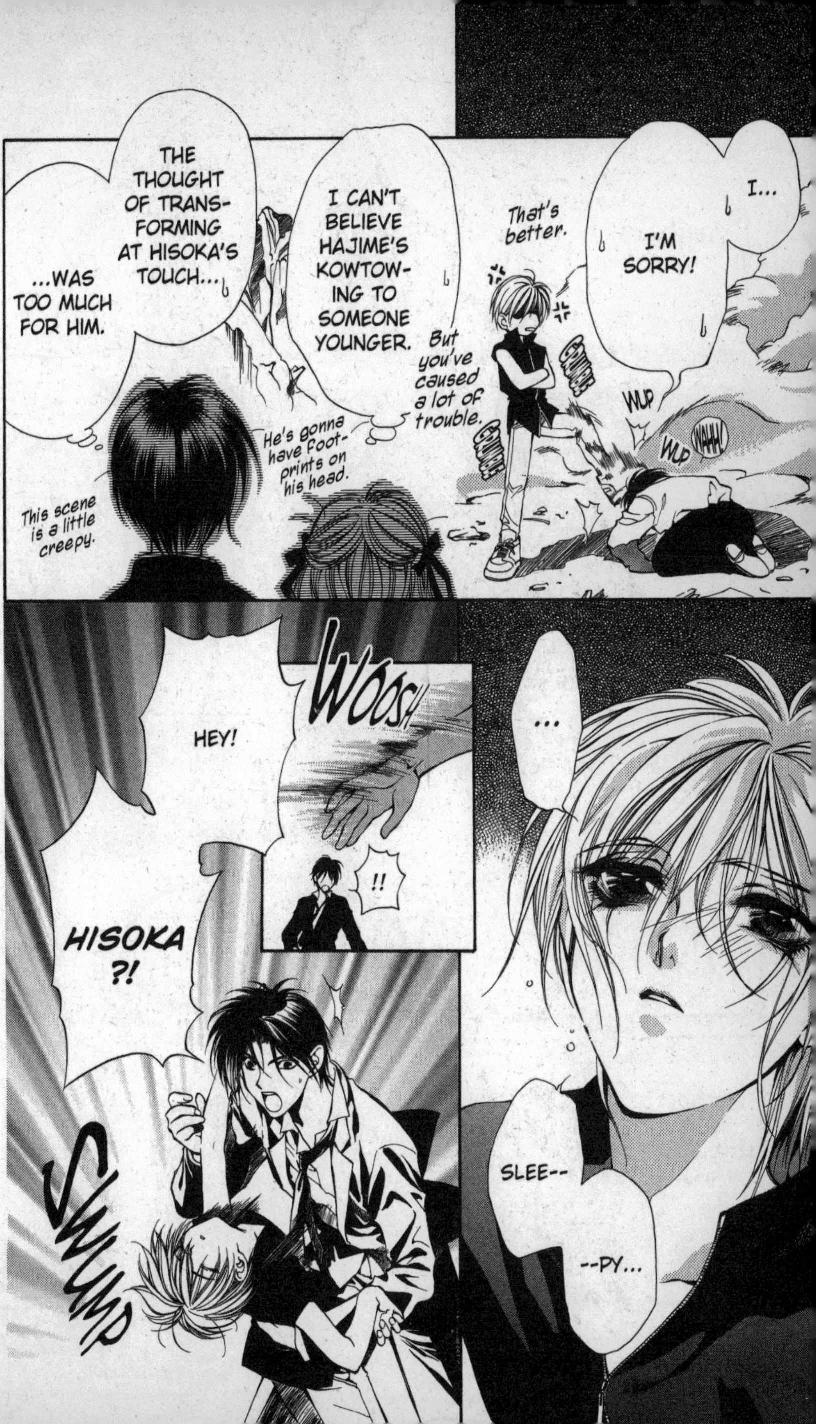
I...
I'M SORRY!
That's better.
But you've caused a lot of trouble.
WUP
WUP
WAHH!
I CAN'T BELIEVE HAJIME'S KOWTOWING TO SOMEONE YOUNGER.
He's gonna have footprints on his head.
THE THOUGHT OF TRANSFORMING AT HISOKA'S TOUCH...
...WAS TOO MUCH FOR HIM.
This scene is a little creepy.
...
SLEE--
--PY...
WOOSH
HEY!
!!
HISOKA ?!
SWUMP

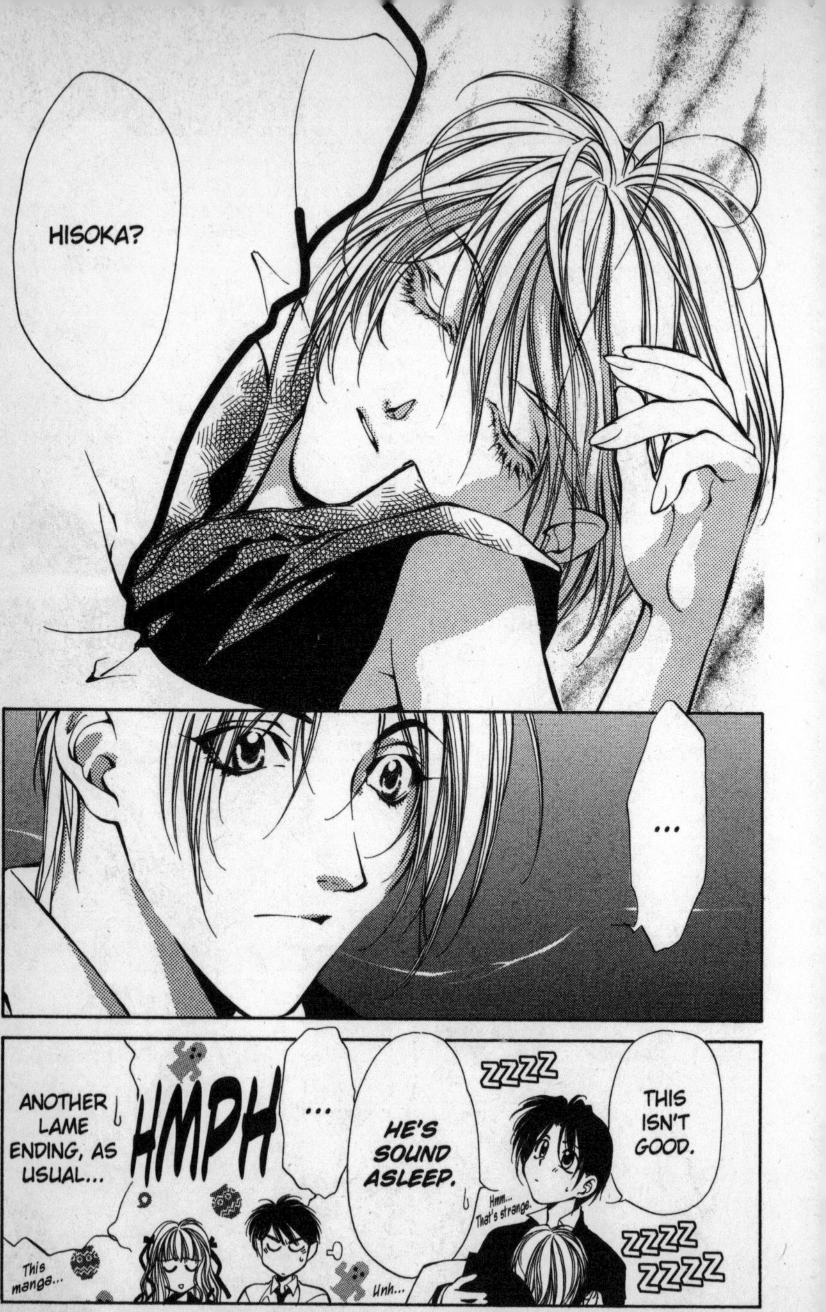
HISOKA?
...
THIS ISN'T GOOD.
ZZZZ
ZZZZ ZZZZ
Hmm... That's strange.
HE'S SOUND ASLEEP.
Unh...
...
HMPH
ANOTHER LAME ENDING, AS USUAL...
This manga...

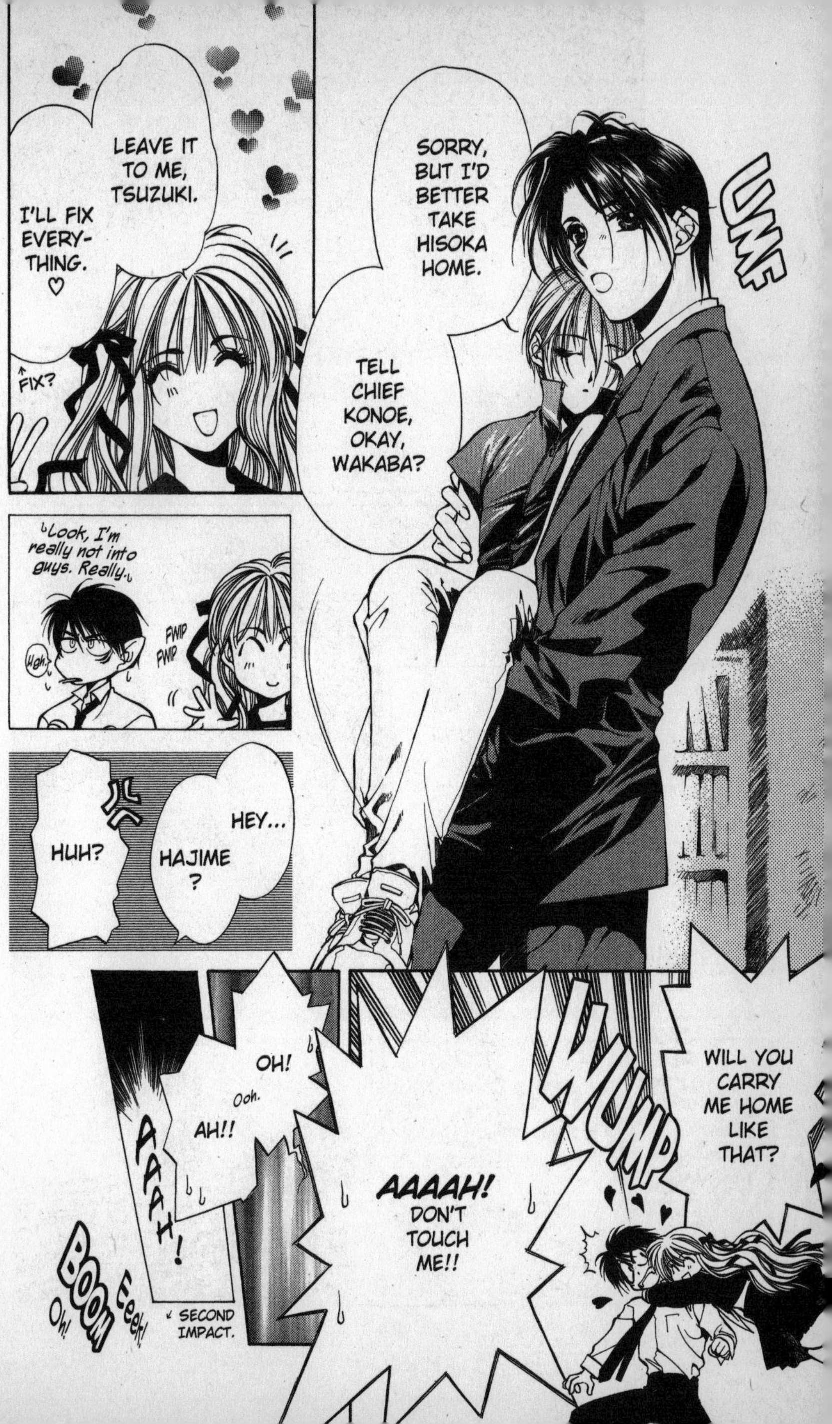
UMF
SORRY, BUT I'D BETTER TAKE HISOKA HOME.
TELL CHIEF KONOE, OKAY, WAKABA?
LEAVE IT TO ME, TSUZUKI.
I'LL FIX EVERY-THING. ♡
FIX?
Look, I'm really not into guys. Really.
Ugh.
FWIP FWIP
HEY... HAJIME?
HUH?
WILL YOU CARRY ME HOME LIKE THAT?
WUMP
AAAAH! DON'T TOUCH ME!!
OH!
Ooh.
AH!!
AAAAH!
SECOND IMPACT.
BOOM
Eeek!
Oh!

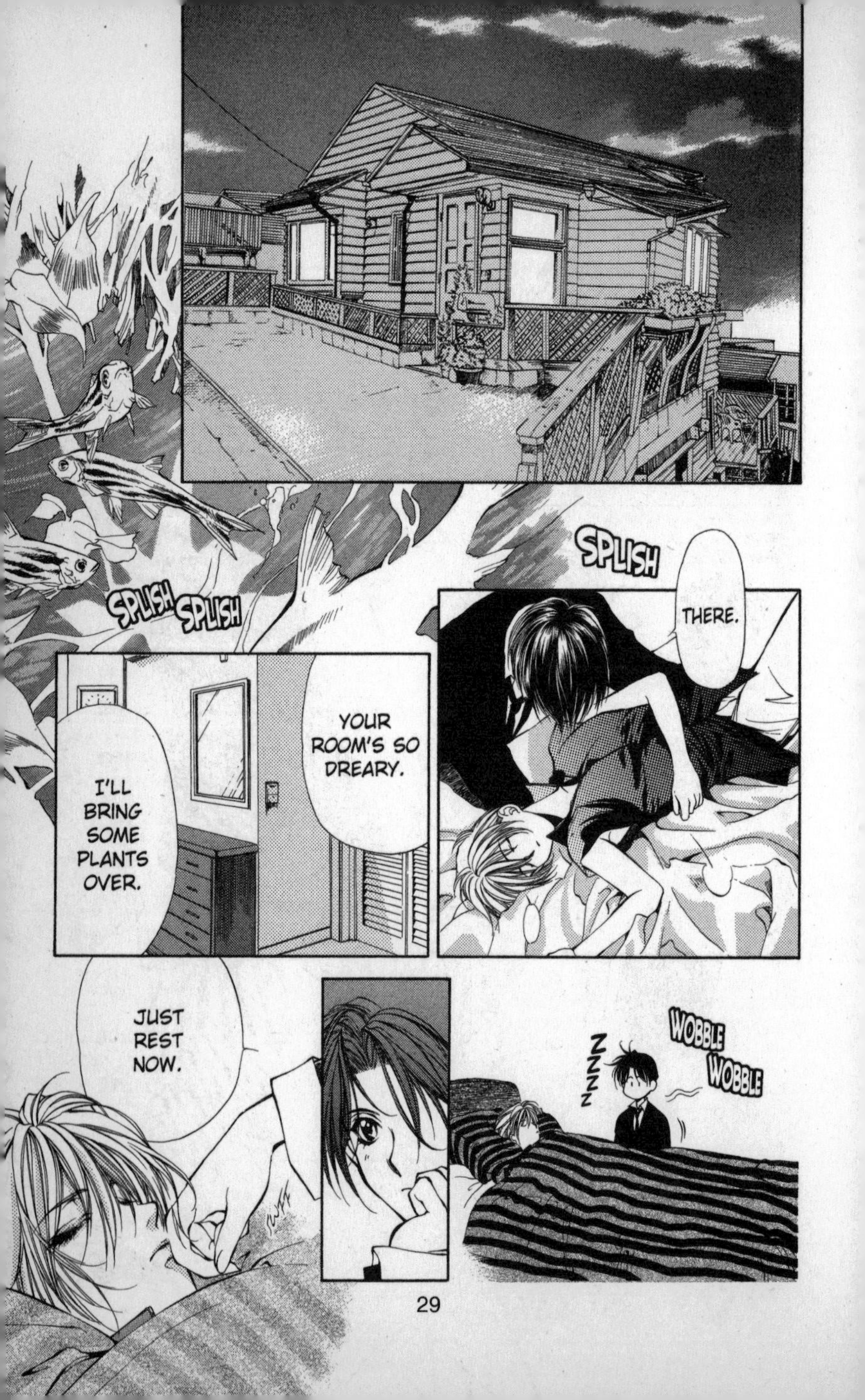
SPLISH
THERE.
SPLISH SPLISH
YOUR ROOM'S SO DREARY.
I'LL BRING SOME PLANTS OVER.
WOBBLE WOBBLE
ZZZZ
JUST REST NOW.

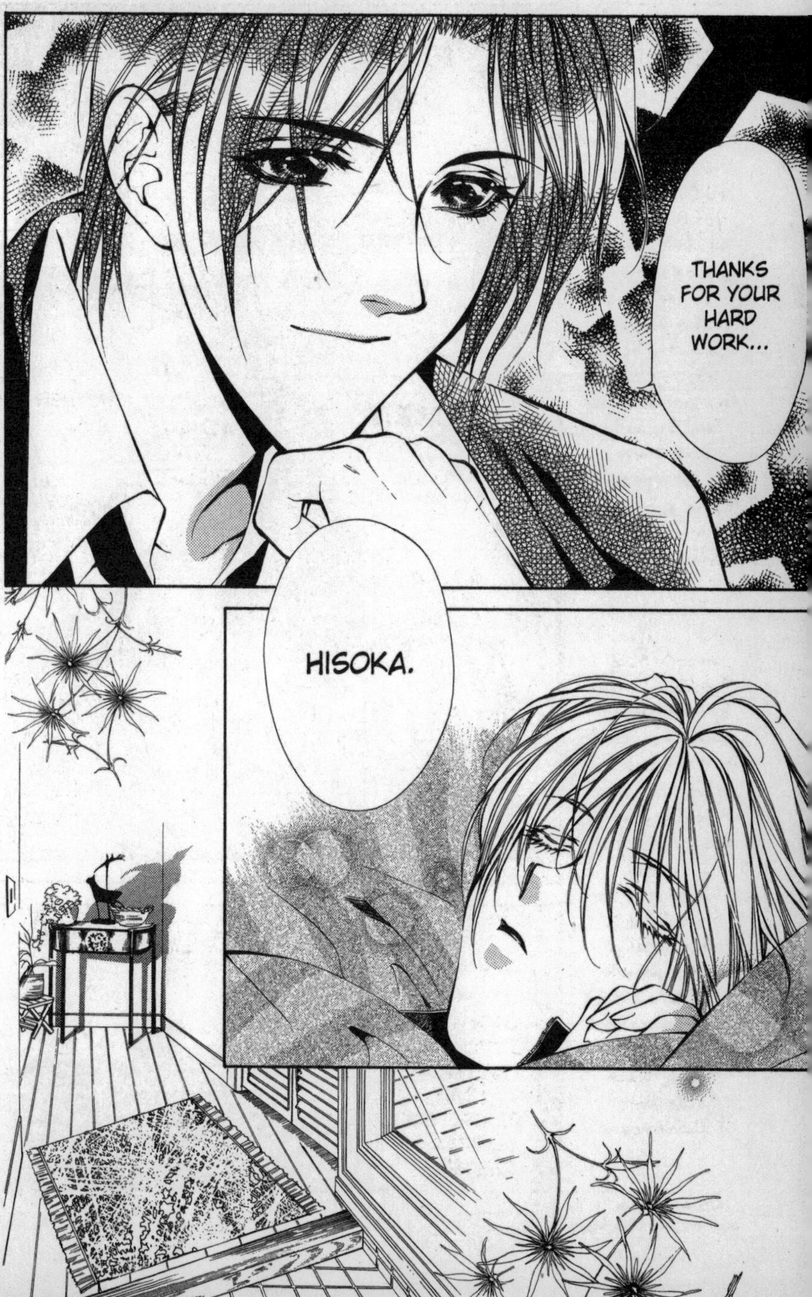
THANKS FOR YOUR HARD WORK...
HISOKA.

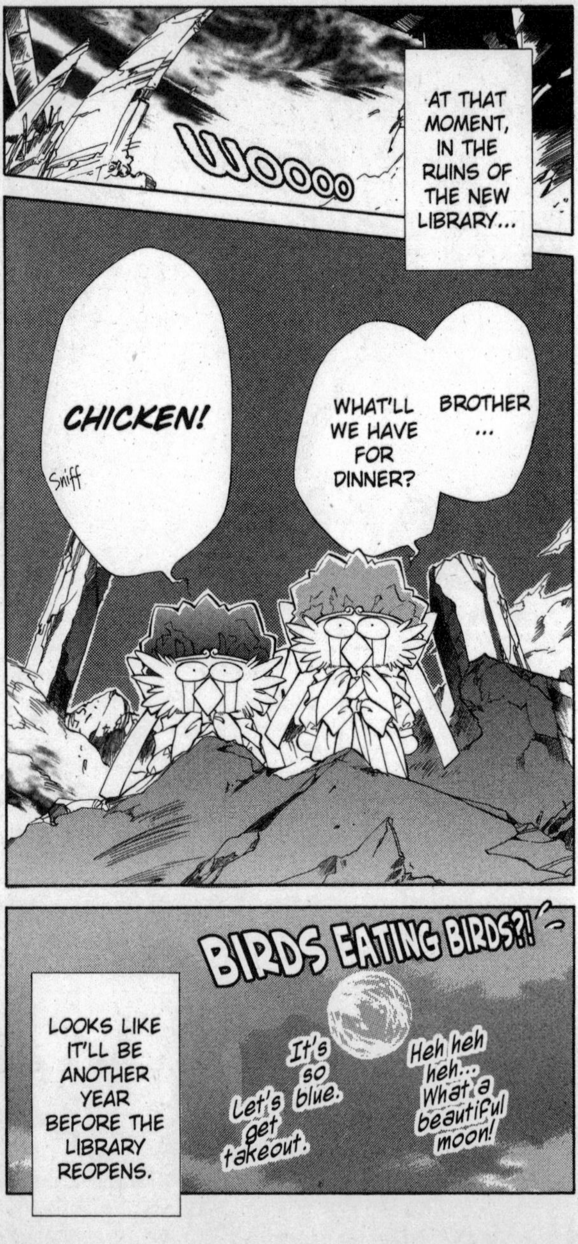
AT THAT MOMENT, IN THE RUINS OF THE NEW LIBRARY...
WOOOO
BROTHER ...
WHAT'LL WE HAVE FOR DINNER?
CHICKEN!
Sniff
BIRDS EATING BIRDS?!
Heh heh heh... What a beautiful moon!
It's so blue.
Let's get takeout.
LOOKS LIKE IT'LL BE ANOTHER YEAR BEFORE THE LIBRARY REOPENS.

Hello, Matsushita here bringing you Descendants of Darkness volume 6. I hope you're enjoying it. In addition to the Okinawa story, this book also contains two shorter tales. Well, I usually write these quarter pages by hand, but this time I had to type it. There's no time to hand-write it. Well, that's not exactly true. But when I write by hand I worry that the lines will slant, so I decided to do it this way. And now, a word about the letters I receive... I'm going to use this volume to write detailed lessons on how to write a letter, so if you're planning on writing to me, please follow them. Thank you.

Lesson 1: How to address the envelope

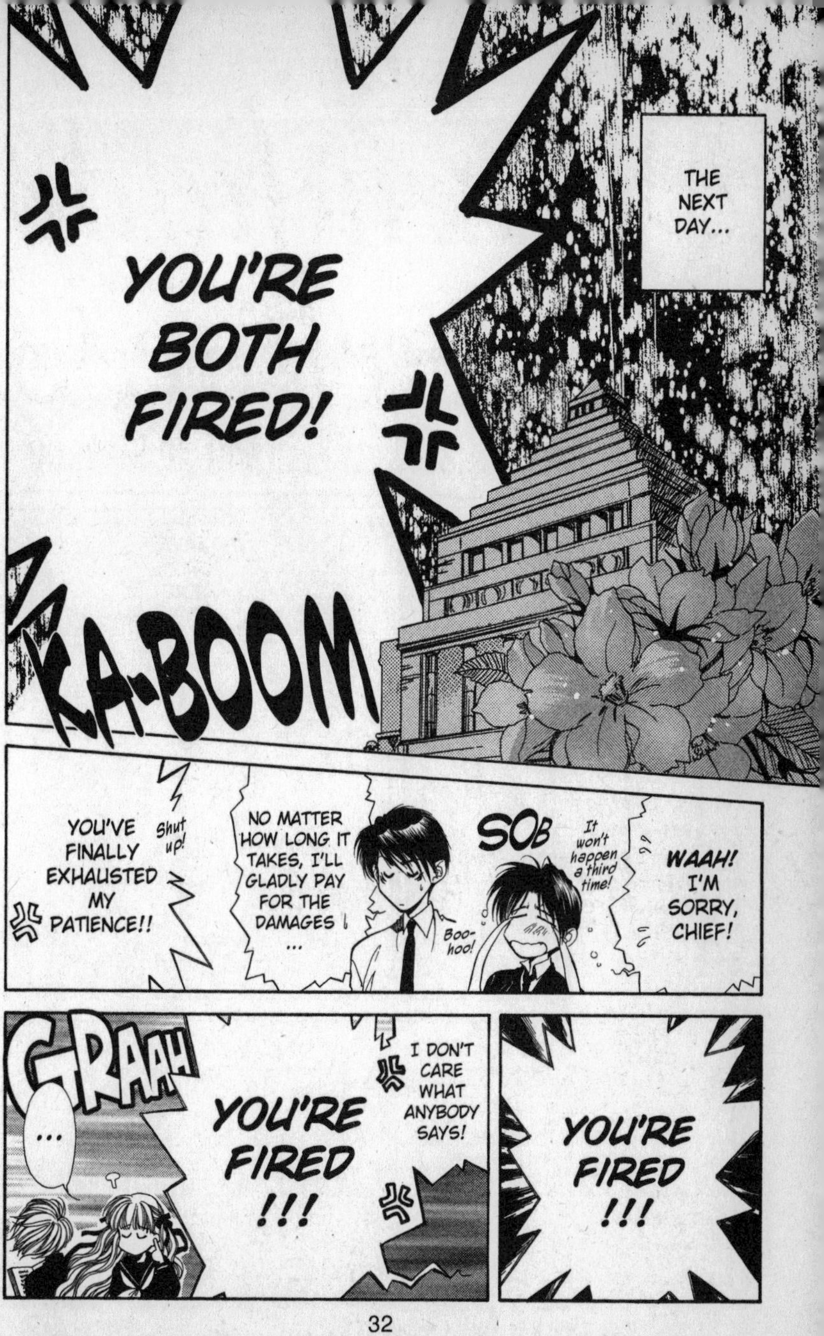
THE NEXT DAY...
YOU'RE BOTH FIRED!
KA-BOOM
WAAH! I'M SORRY, CHIEF!
It won't happen a third time!
SOB
Boo-hoo!
NO MATTER HOW LONG IT TAKES, I'LL GLADLY PAY FOR THE DAMAGES ...
Shut up!
YOU'VE FINALLY EXHAUSTED MY PATIENCE!!
YOU'RE FIRED !!!
I DON'T CARE WHAT ANYBODY SAYS!
YOU'RE FIRED !!!
GRAAH
...

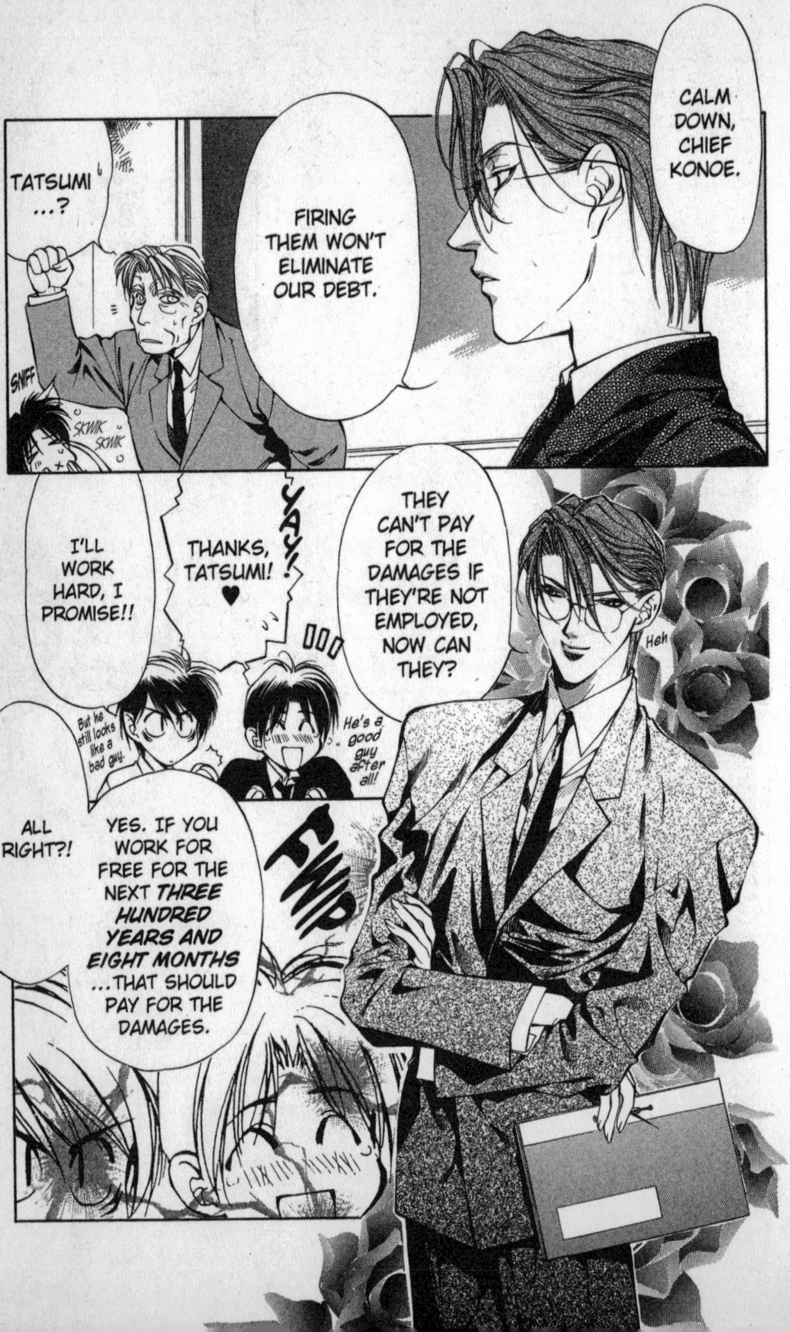
CALM DOWN, CHIEF KONOE.
FIRING THEM WON'T ELIMINATE OUR DEBT.
TATSUMI ...?
SNIFF
SKWIK SKWIK
THEY CAN'T PAY FOR THE DAMAGES IF THEY'RE NOT EMPLOYED, NOW CAN THEY?
Heh
YAY!!
THANKS, TATSUMI! ♥
I'LL WORK HARD, I PROMISE!!
He's a good guy after all!
But he still looks like a bad guy.
YES. IF YOU WORK FOR FREE FOR THE NEXT *THREE HUNDRED YEARS AND EIGHT MONTHS* ...THAT SHOULD PAY FOR THE DAMAGES.
FWIP
ALL RIGHT?!

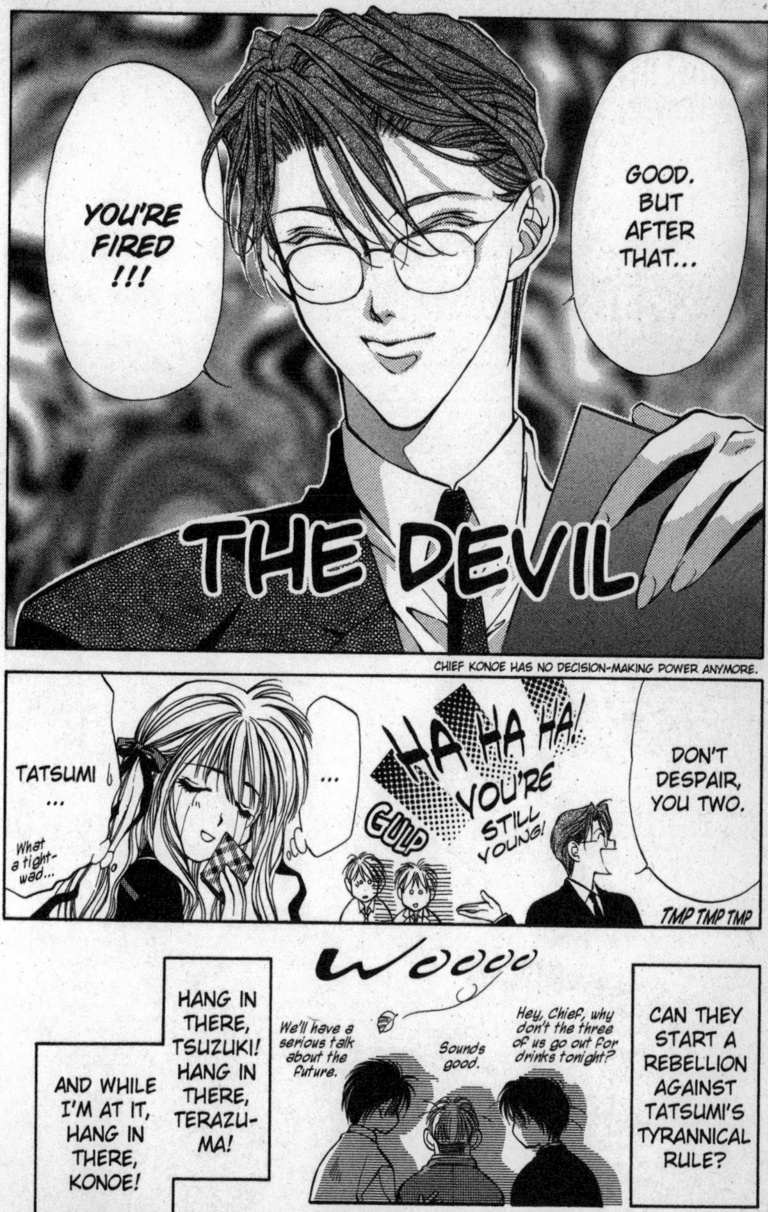
GOOD. BUT AFTER THAT...
YOU'RE FIRED!!!
THE DEVIL
CHIEF KONOE HAS NO DECISION-MAKING POWER ANYMORE.
DON'T DESPAIR, YOU TWO.
TMP TMP TMP
HA HA HA! YOU'RE STILL YOUNG!
GULP
...
TATSUMI ...
What a tight-wad...
CAN THEY START A REBELLION AGAINST TATSUMI'S TYRANNICAL RULE?
Woooo
Hey, Chief, why don't the three of us go out for drinks tonight?
Sounds good.
We'll have a serious talk about the future.
HANG IN THERE, TSUZUKI! HANG IN THERE, TERAZUMA!
AND WHILE I'M AT IT, HANG IN THERE, KONOE!

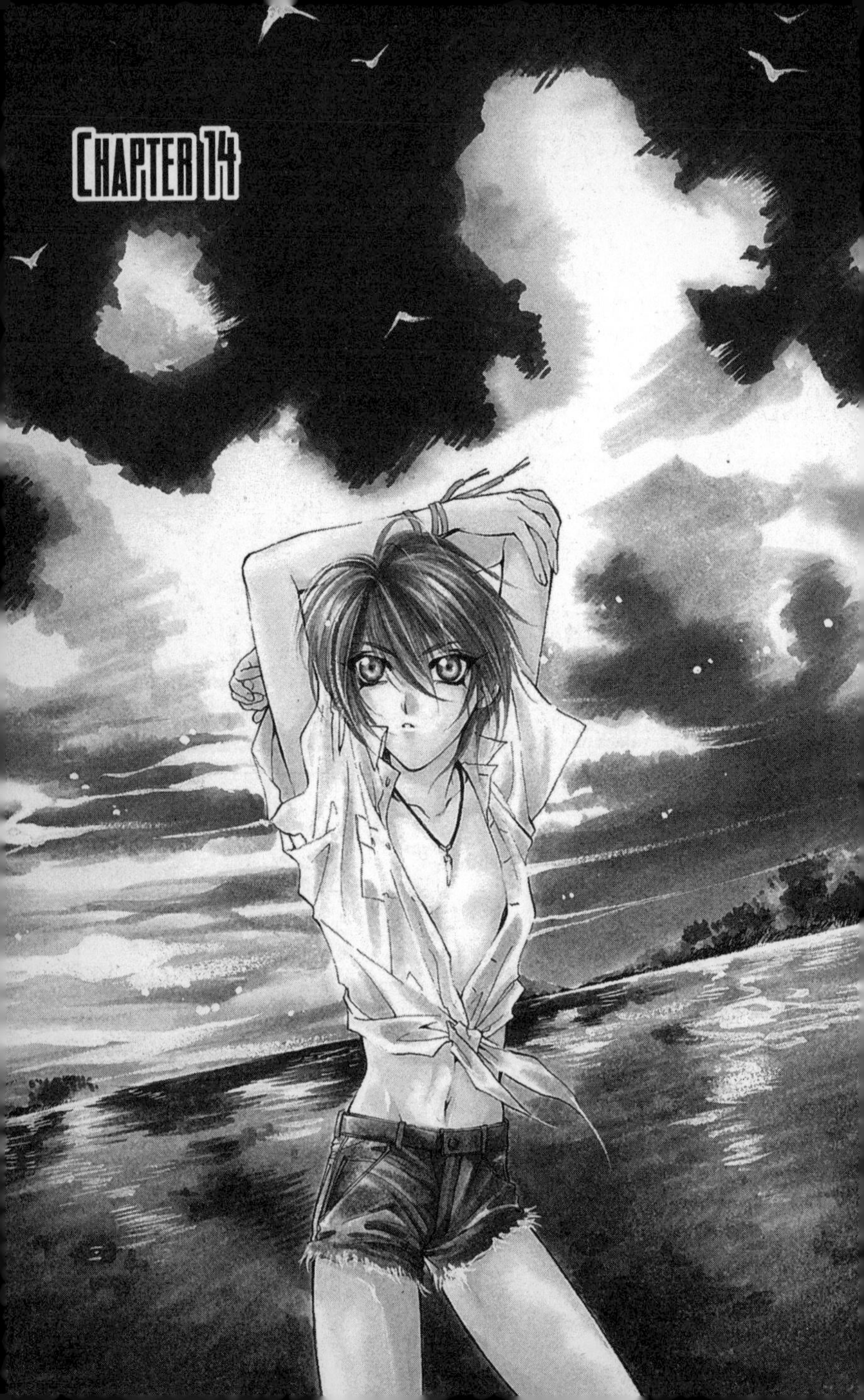
CHAPTER 14

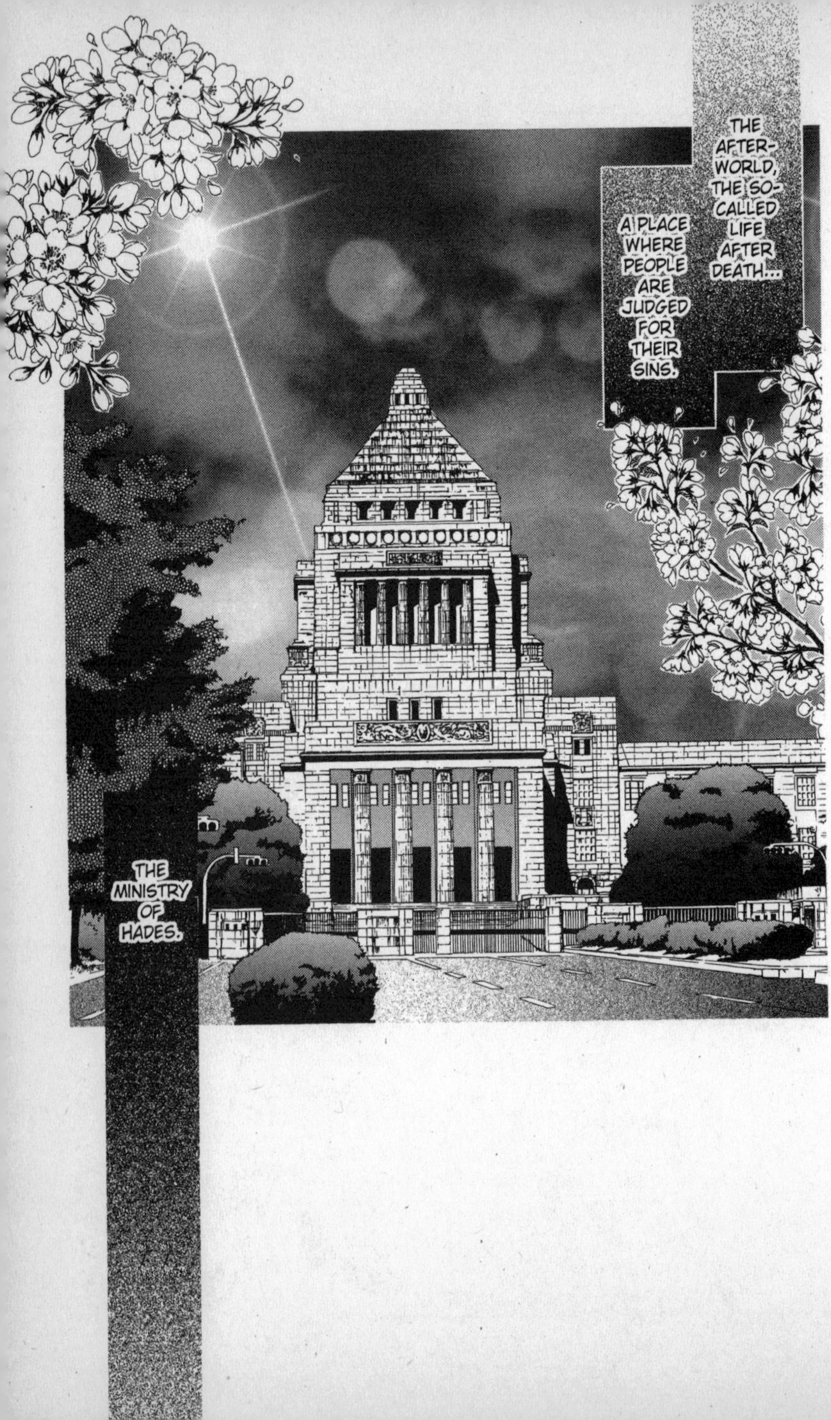
THE AFTER-WORLD, THE SO-CALLED LIFE AFTER DEATH...
A PLACE WHERE PEOPLE ARE JUDGED FOR THEIR SINS.
THE MINISTRY OF HADES.

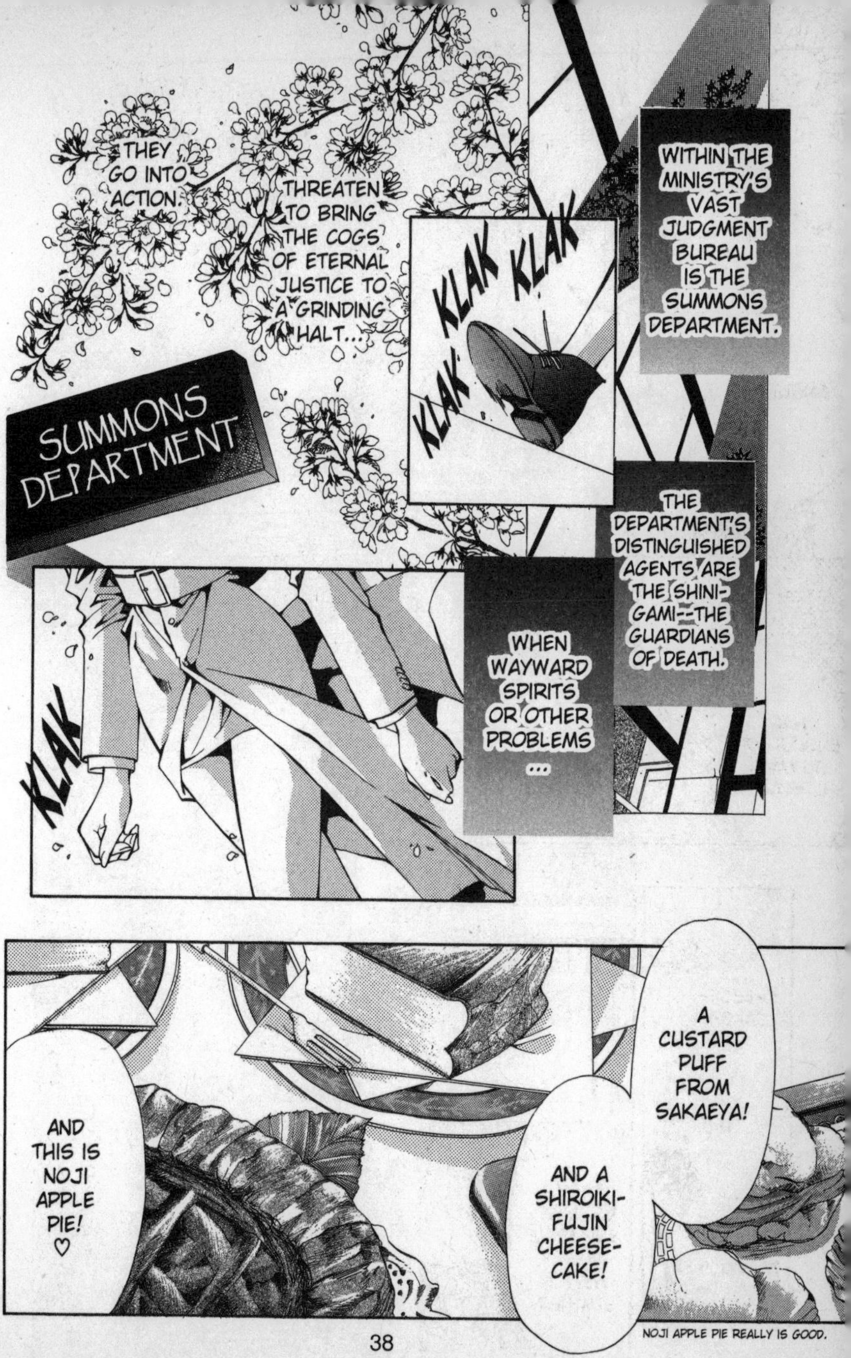
WITHIN THE MINISTRY'S VAST JUDGMENT BUREAU IS THE SUMMONS DEPARTMENT.
KLAK KLAK KLAK
SUMMONS DEPARTMENT
THE DEPARTMENT'S DISTINGUISHED AGENTS ARE THE SHINI-GAMI--THE GUARDIANS OF DEATH.
WHEN WAYWARD SPIRITS OR OTHER PROBLEMS ...
THREATEN TO BRING THE COGS OF ETERNAL JUSTICE TO A GRINDING HALT...
THEY GO INTO ACTION.
KLAK
A CUSTARD PUFF FROM SAKAEYA!
AND A SHIROIKI-FUJIN CHEESE-CAKE!
AND THIS IS NOJI APPLE PIE! ♡

NOJI APPLE PIE REALLY IS GOOD.

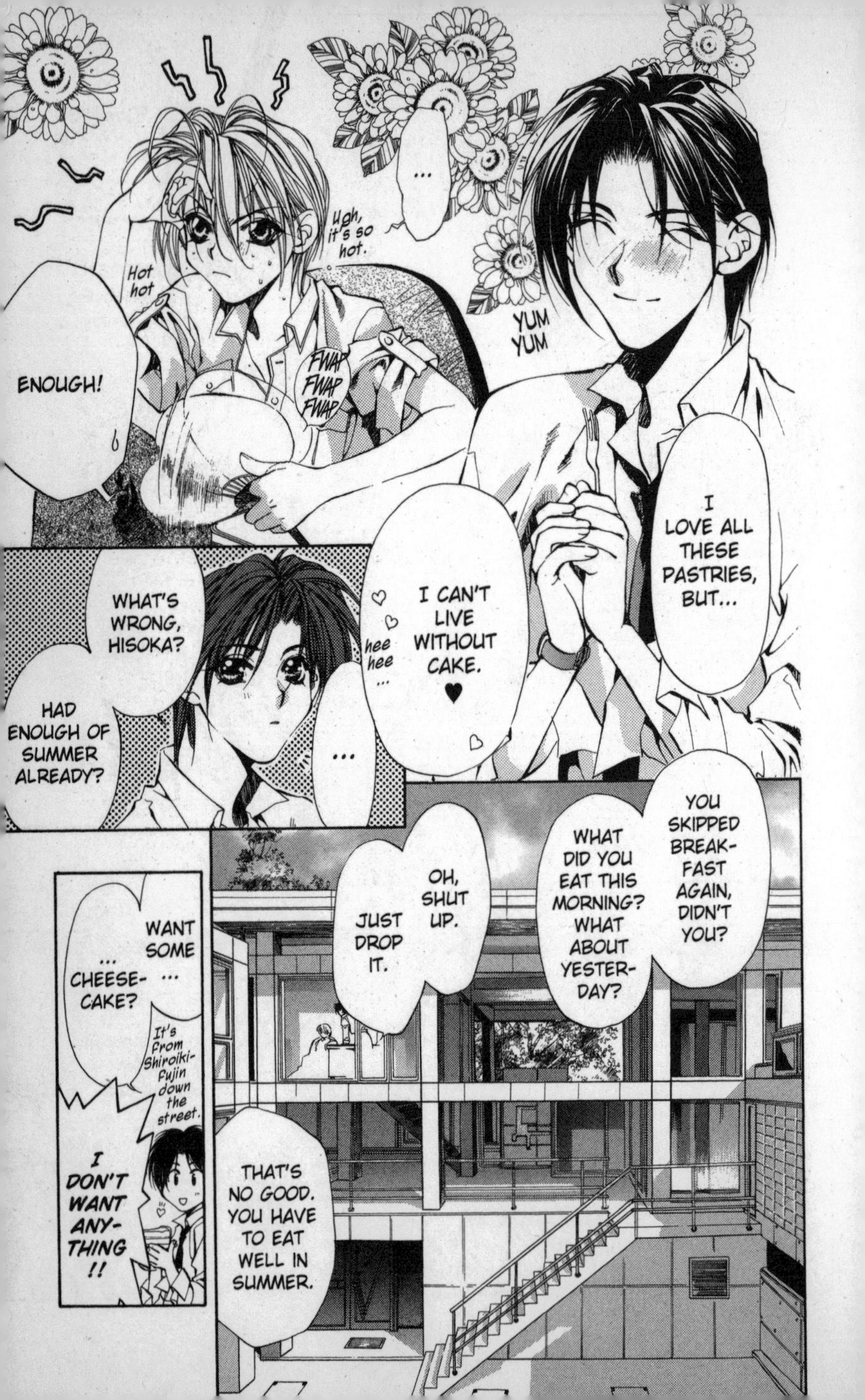
YUM YUM
...
Ugh, it's so hot.
Hot hot
FWAP FWAP FWAP
ENOUGH!
I LOVE ALL THESE PASTRIES, BUT...
I CAN'T LIVE WITHOUT CAKE. ♥
hee hee ...
...
WHAT'S WRONG, HISOKA?
HAD ENOUGH OF SUMMER ALREADY?
YOU SKIPPED BREAK-FAST AGAIN, DIDN'T YOU?
WHAT DID YOU EAT THIS MORNING? WHAT ABOUT YESTER-DAY?
OH, SHUT UP.
JUST DROP IT.
THAT'S NO GOOD. YOU HAVE TO EAT WELL IN SUMMER.
WANT SOME ... ... CHEESE-CAKE?
It's from Shiroiki-Fujin down the street.
I DON'T WANT ANY-THING!!

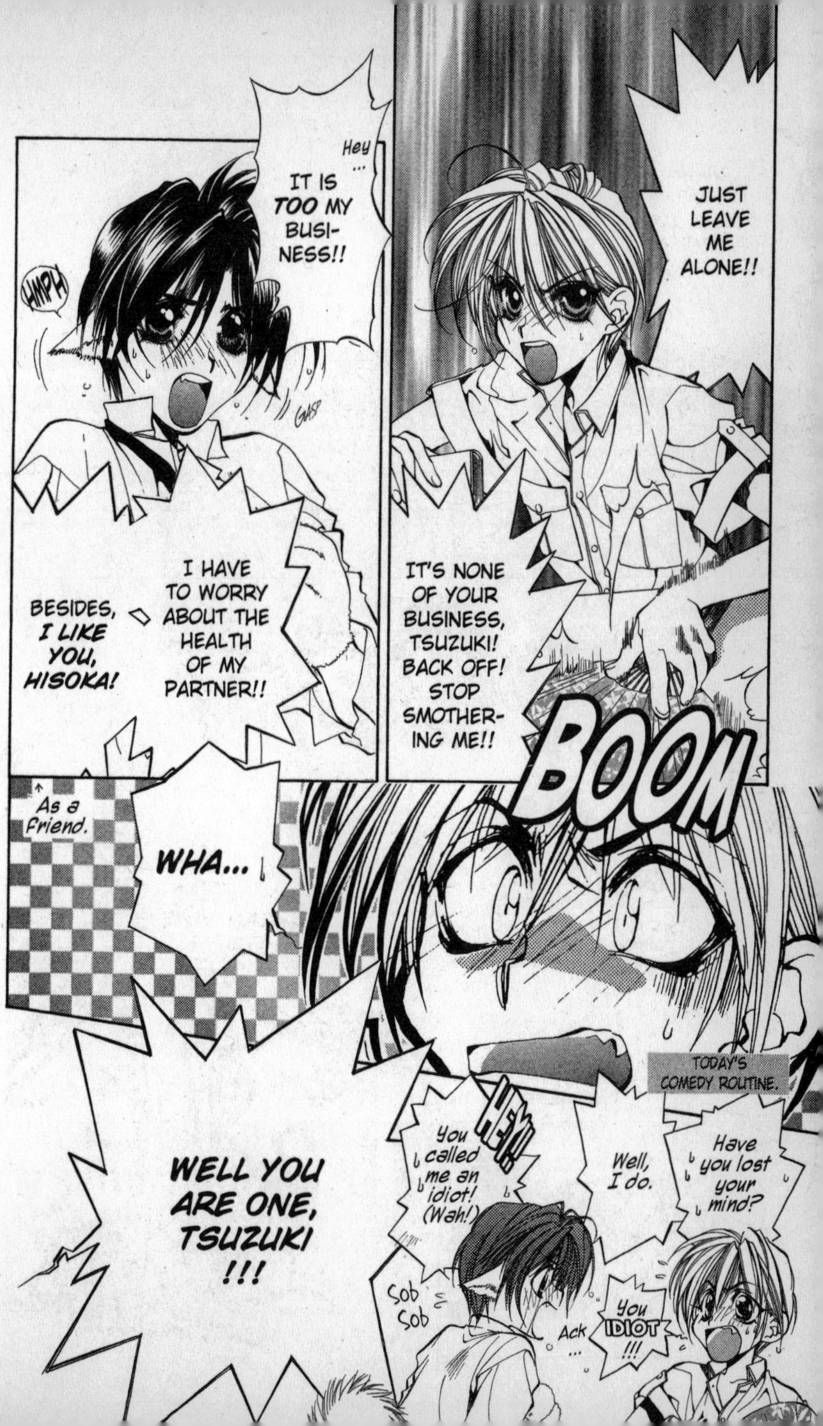
JUST LEAVE ME ALONE!!
IT'S NONE OF YOUR BUSINESS, TSUZUKI! BACK OFF! STOP SMOTHERING ME!!
Hey ...
IT IS TOO MY BUSINESS!!
HMPH
GASP
I HAVE TO WORRY ABOUT THE HEALTH OF MY PARTNER!!
BESIDES, I LIKE YOU, HISOKA!
BOOM
WHA...
As a friend.
TODAY'S COMEDY ROUTINE.
Have you lost your mind?
Well, I do.
HEY!!
You called me an idiot! (Wah!)
WELL YOU ARE ONE, TSUZUKI !!!
You IDIOT !!!
Ack ...
Sob Sob

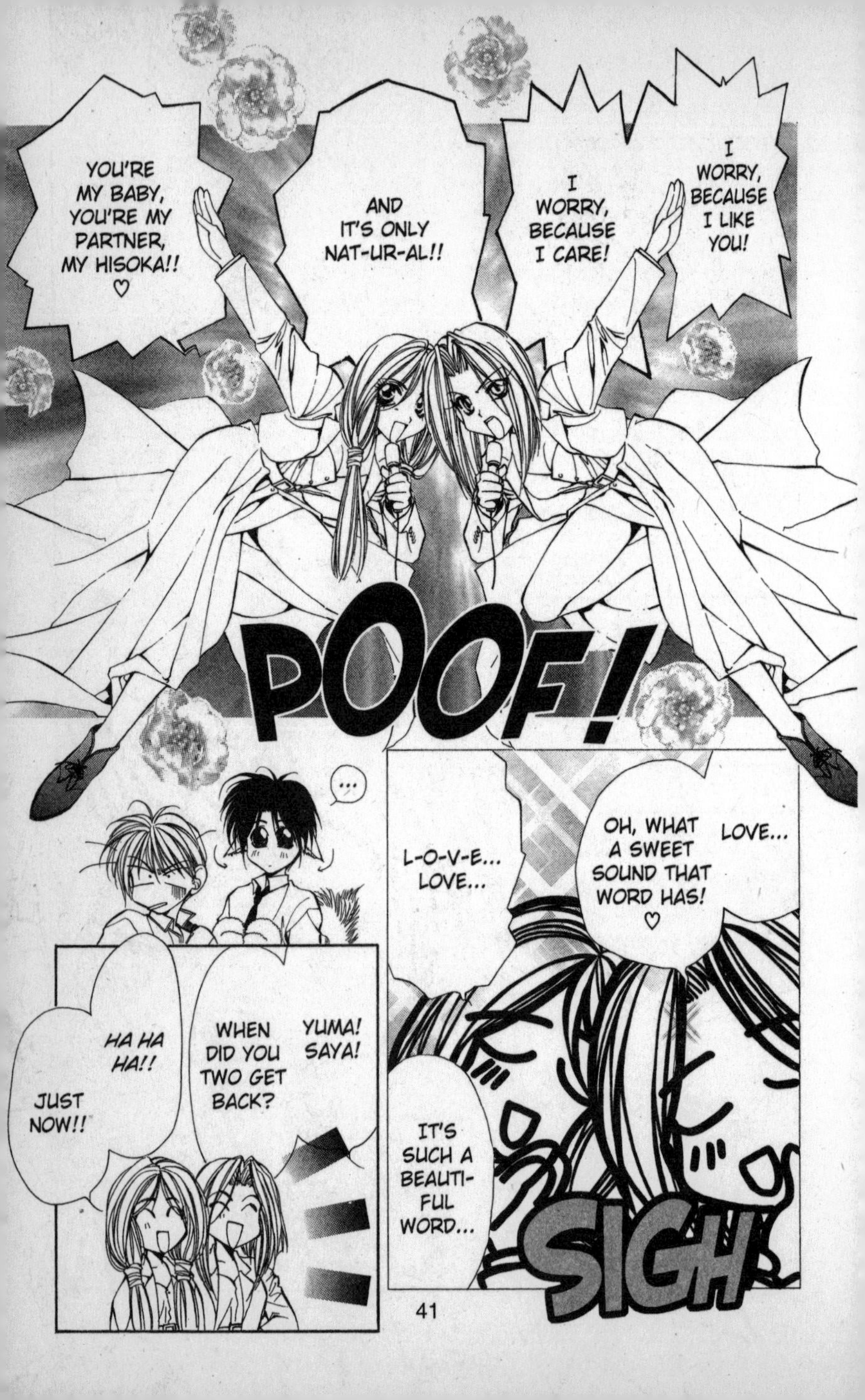
I WORRY, BECAUSE I LIKE YOU!
I WORRY, BECAUSE I CARE!
AND IT'S ONLY NAT-UR-AL!!
YOU'RE MY BABY, YOU'RE MY PARTNER, MY HISOKA!! ♡
POOF!
LOVE...
OH, WHAT A SWEET SOUND THAT WORD HAS! ♡
L-O-V-E... LOVE...
IT'S SUCH A BEAUTI-FUL WORD...
SIGH
...
YUMA! SAYA!
WHEN DID YOU TWO GET BACK?
HA HA HA!!
JUST NOW!!

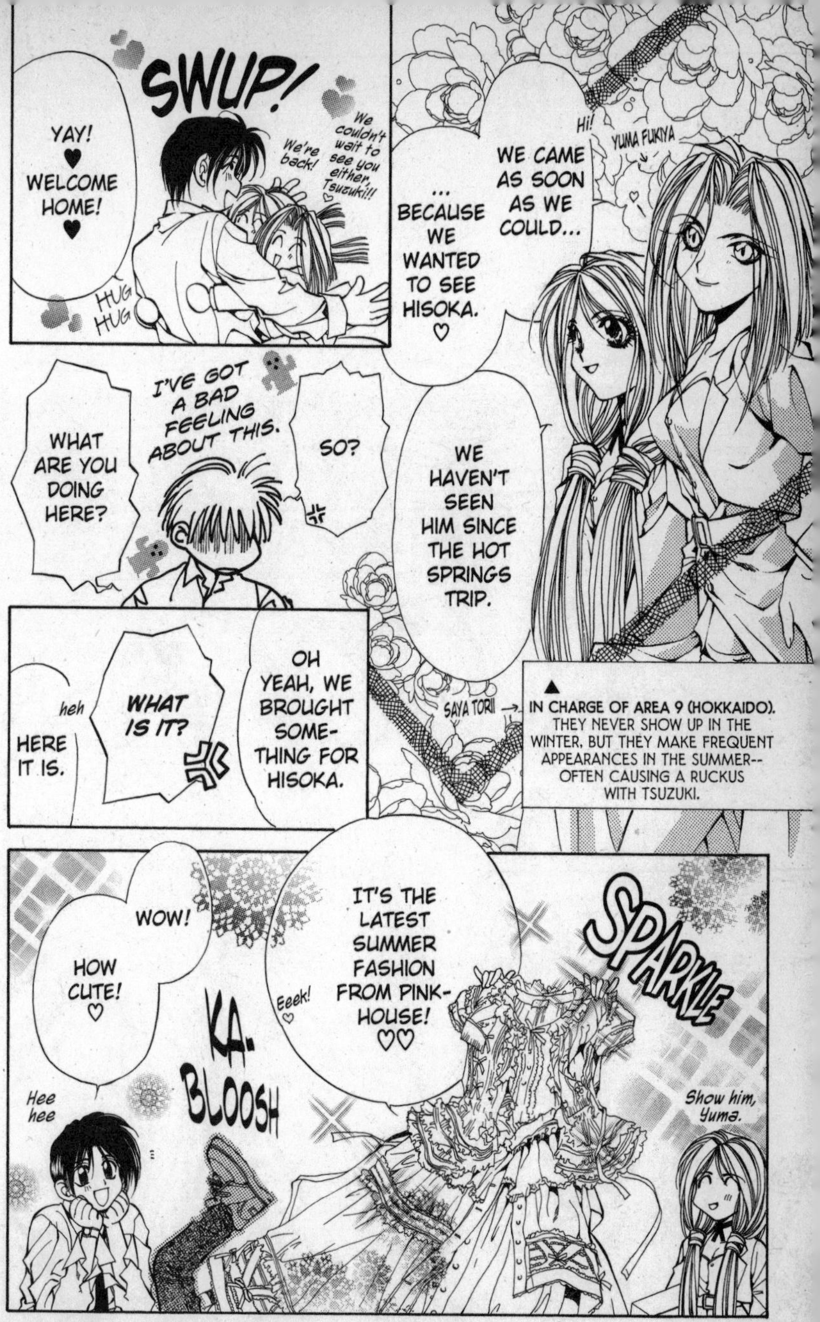

Hi!
WE CAME AS SOON AS WE COULD...
... BECAUSE WE WANTED TO SEE HISOKA. ♡
YUMA FUKIYA
WE HAVEN'T SEEN HIM SINCE THE HOT SPRINGS TRIP.
SAYA TORII
▲ IN CHARGE OF AREA 9 (HOKKAIDO). THEY NEVER SHOW UP IN THE WINTER, BUT THEY MAKE FREQUENT APPEARANCES IN THE SUMMER-- OFTEN CAUSING A RUCKUS WITH TSUZUKI.
SWUP!
We couldn't wait to see you either, Tsuzuki!! ♡
We're back!
YAY! ♥ WELCOME HOME! ♥
HUG HUG
SO?
I'VE GOT A BAD FEELING ABOUT THIS.
WHAT ARE YOU DOING HERE?
OH YEAH, WE BROUGHT SOME-THING FOR HISOKA.
WHAT IS IT?
heh
HERE IT IS.
SPARKLE
IT'S THE LATEST SUMMER FASHION FROM PINK-HOUSE! ♡♡
Show him, Yuma.
Eeek! ♡
KA. BLOOSH
WOW!
HOW CUTE! ♡
Hee hee

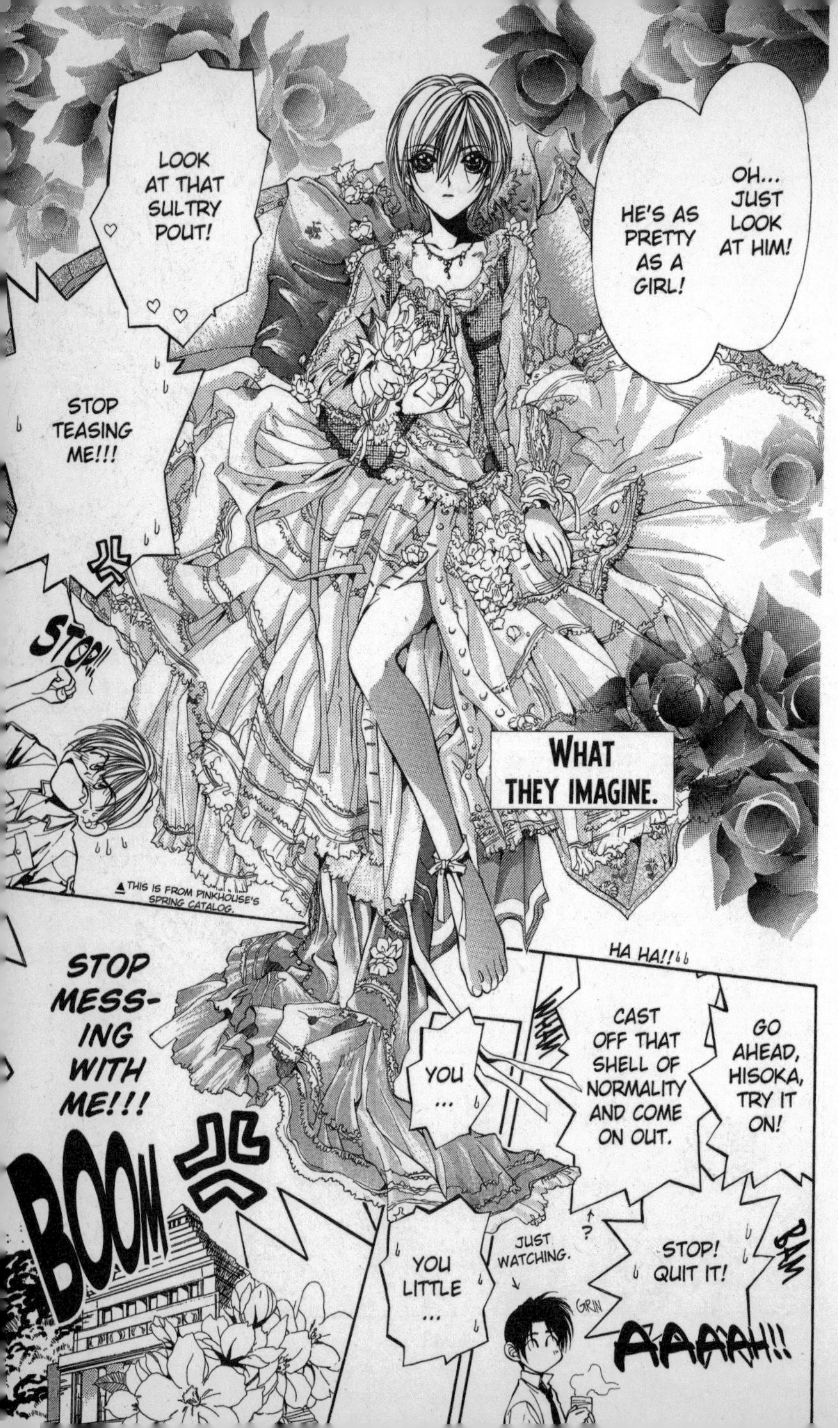
OH... JUST LOOK AT HIM!
HE'S AS PRETTY AS A GIRL!
LOOK AT THAT SULTRY POUT!
WHAT THEY IMAGINE.
STOP TEASING ME!!!
STOP!!
THIS IS FROM PINKHOUSE'S SPRING CATALOG.
HA HA!!
GO AHEAD, HISOKA, TRY IT ON!
CAST OFF THAT SHELL OF NORMALITY AND COME ON OUT.
YOU ...
STOP MESS-ING WITH ME!!!
BOOM
BAM
STOP! QUIT IT!
AAAAH!!
GRIN
?
JUST WATCHING.
YOU LITTLE ...

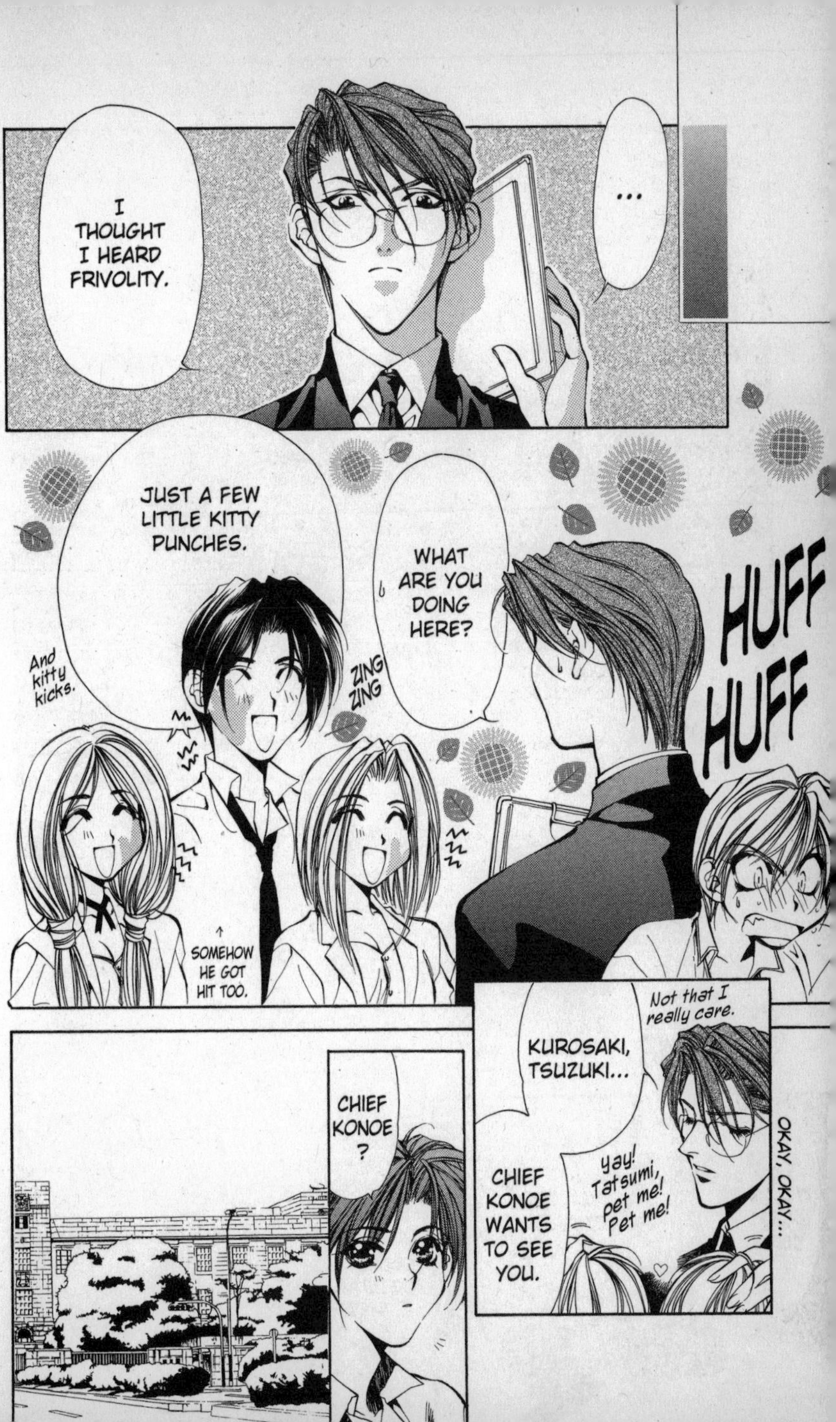
...
I THOUGHT I HEARD FRIVOLITY.
HUFF HUFF
WHAT ARE YOU DOING HERE?
ZING ZING
JUST A FEW LITTLE KITTY PUNCHES.
And kitty kicks.
SOMEHOW HE GOT HIT TOO.
OKAY, OKAY...
Not that I really care.
KUROSAKI, TSUZUKI...
CHIEF KONOE WANTS TO SEE YOU.
yay! Tatsumi, pet me! Pet me!
CHIEF KONOE?

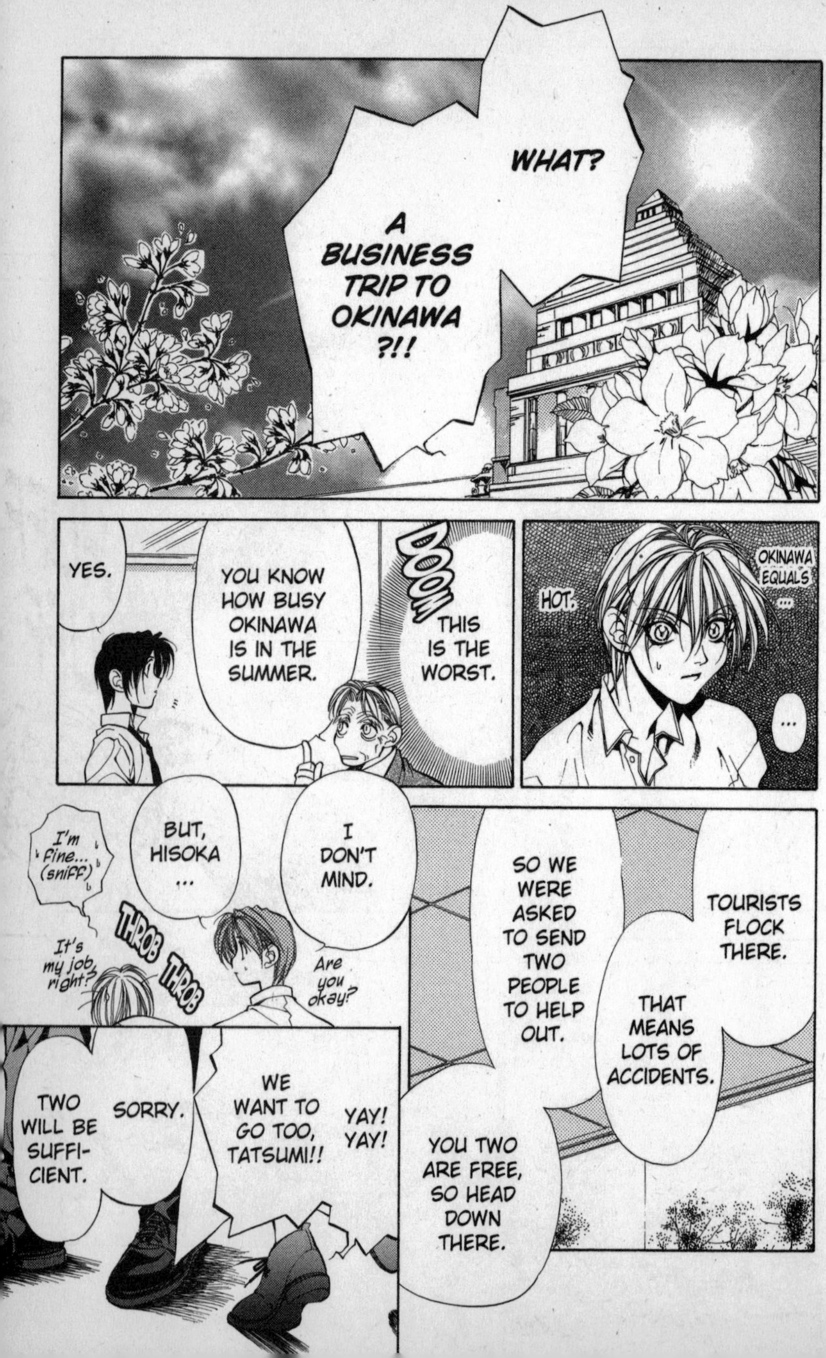
WHAT?
A BUSINESS TRIP TO OKINAWA ?!!
OKINAWA EQUALS ...
HOT.
...
DOOM
THIS IS THE WORST.
YOU KNOW HOW BUSY OKINAWA IS IN THE SUMMER.
YES.
TOURISTS FLOCK THERE.
THAT MEANS LOTS OF ACCIDENTS.
SO WE WERE ASKED TO SEND TWO PEOPLE TO HELP OUT.
YOU TWO ARE FREE, SO HEAD DOWN THERE.
I DON'T MIND.
Are you okay?
BUT, HISOKA ...
THROB THROB
It's my job right?
I'm fine... (sniff)
YAY! YAY!
WE WANT TO GO TOO, TATSUMI!!
SORRY.
TWO WILL BE SUFFI-CIENT.

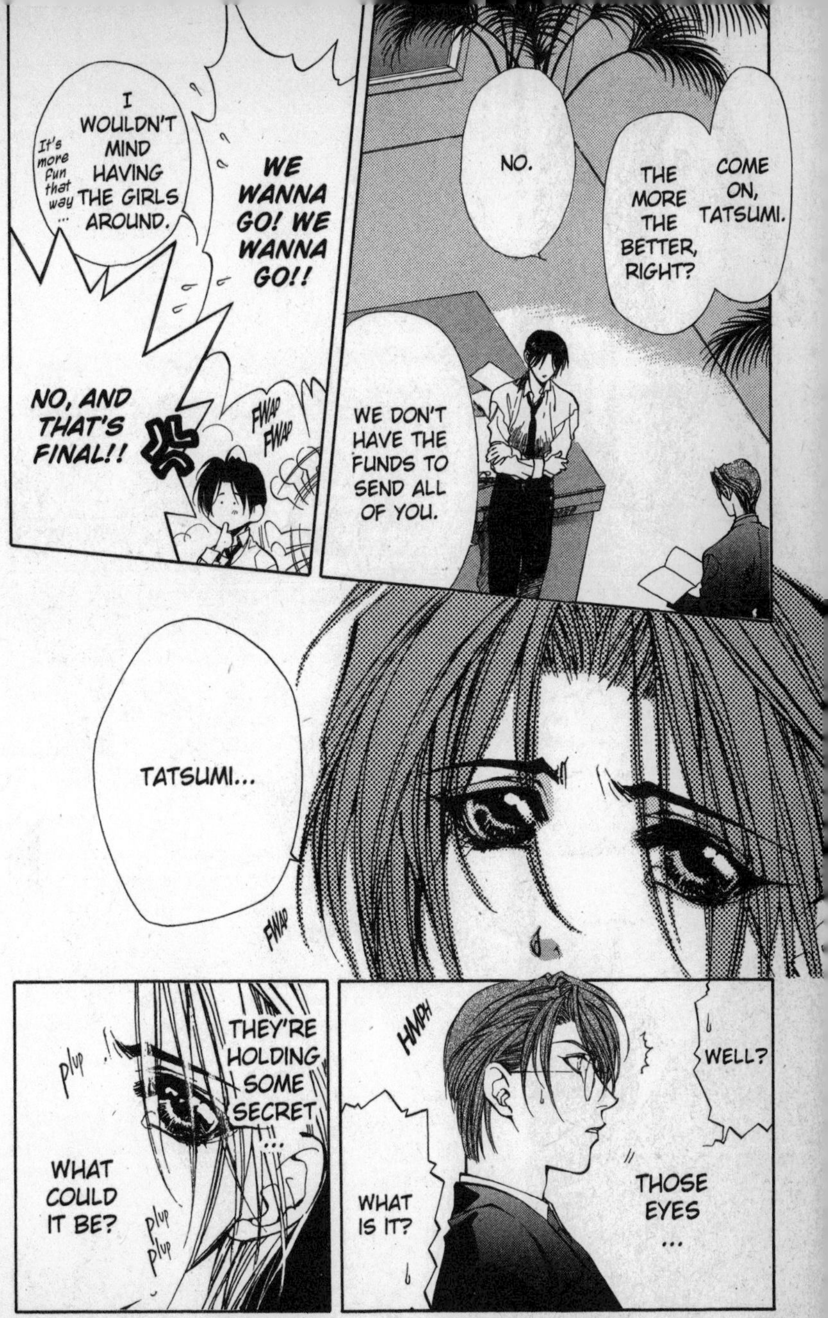
COME ON, TATSUMI.
THE MORE THE BETTER, RIGHT?
NO.
WE DON'T HAVE THE FUNDS TO SEND ALL OF YOU.
WE WANNA GO! WE WANNA GO!!
I WOULDN'T MIND HAVING THE GIRLS AROUND.
It's more fun that way...
FWAP FWAP
NO, AND THAT'S FINAL!!
TATSUMI...
FWAP
WELL?
HMPH
THOSE EYES...
WHAT IS IT?
THEY'RE HOLDING SOME SECRET...
plup
WHAT COULD IT BE?
plup plup

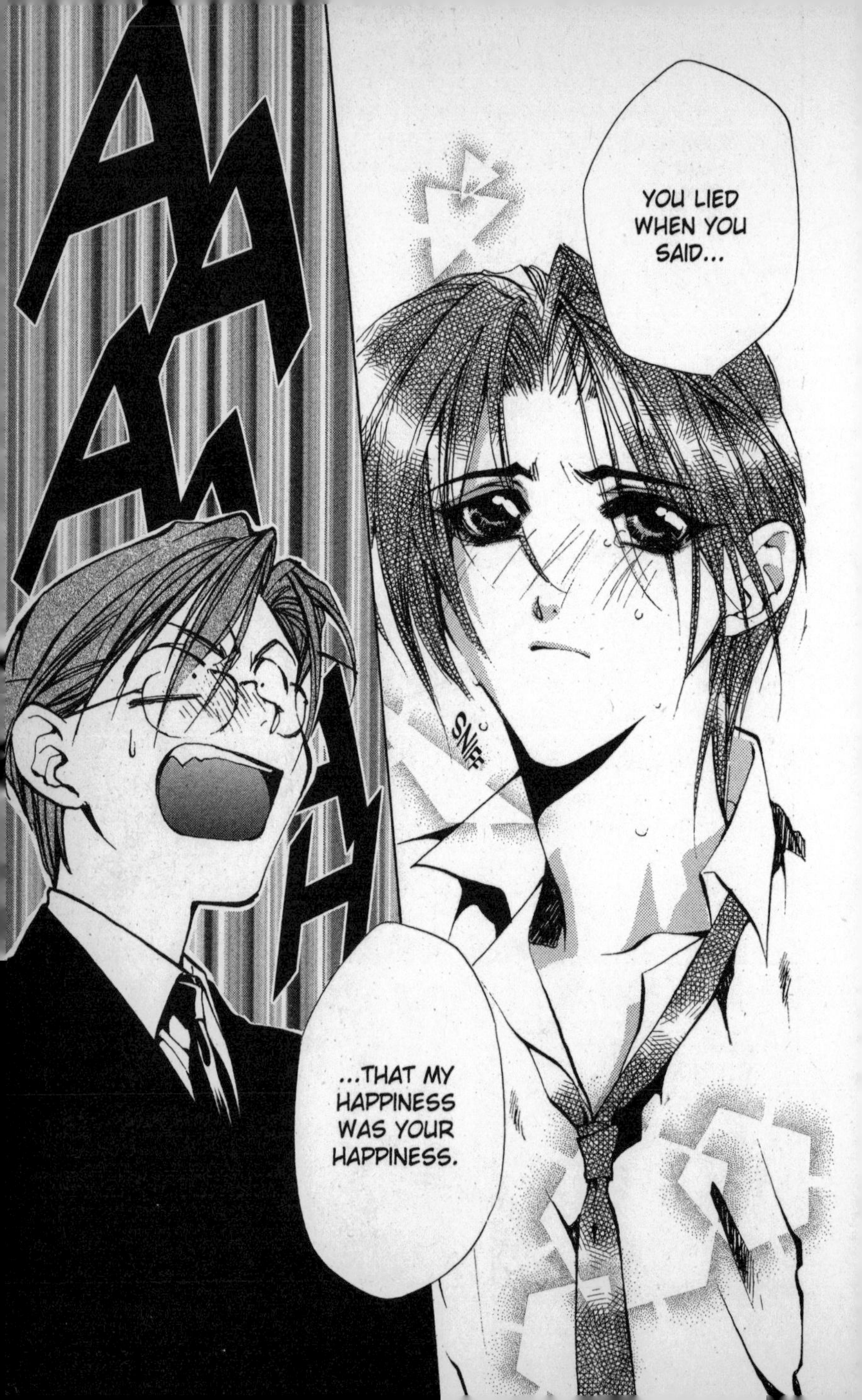
YOU LIED WHEN YOU SAID...
AAAAH
SNIFF
...THAT MY HAPPINESS WAS YOUR HAPPINESS.

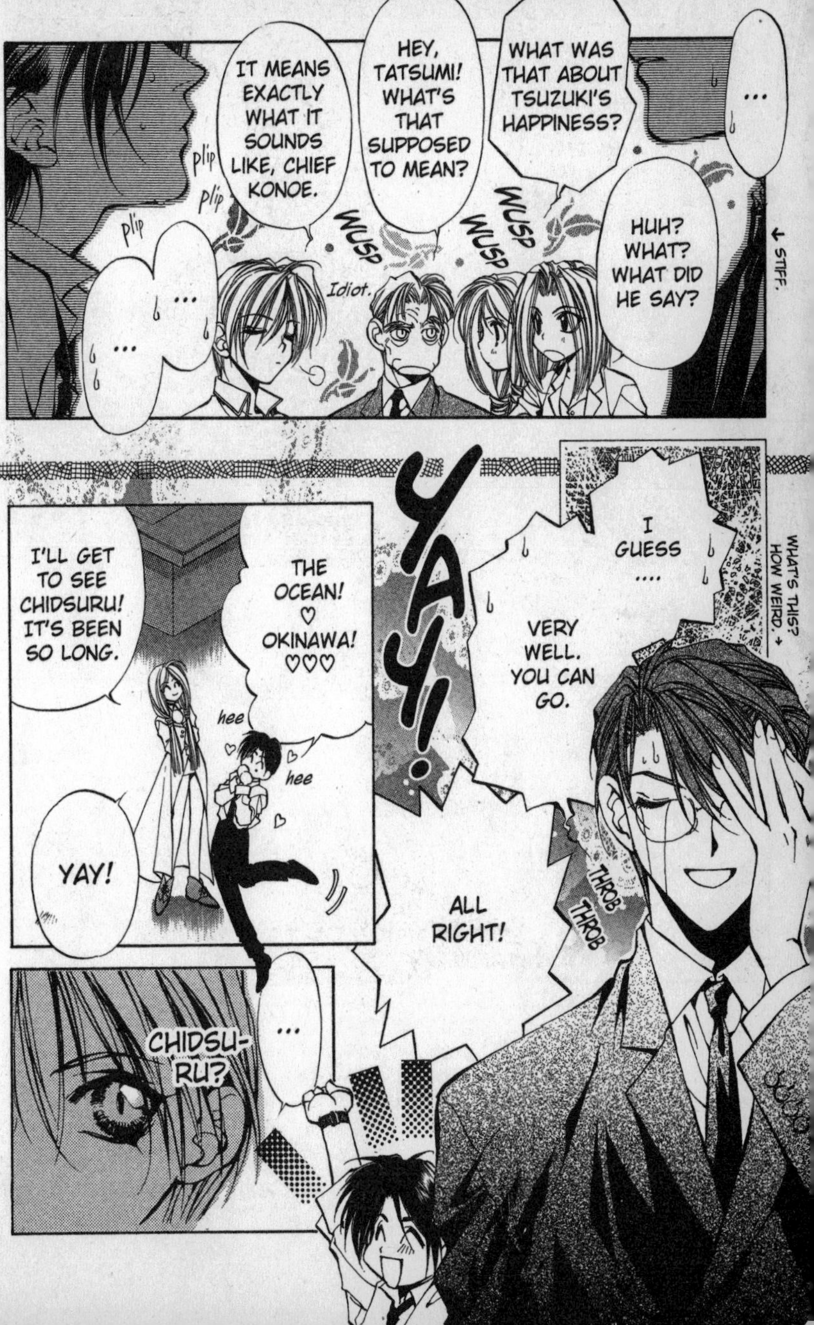
...
← STIFF.
WHAT WAS THAT ABOUT TSUZUKI'S HAPPINESS?
HUH? WHAT? WHAT DID HE SAY?
WUSP WUSP
HEY, TATSUMI! WHAT'S THAT SUPPOSED TO MEAN?
WUSP
Idiot.
IT MEANS EXACTLY WHAT IT SOUNDS LIKE, CHIEF KONOE.
plip plip plip
... ...
WHAT'S THIS? HOW WEIRD. →
I GUESS ....
VERY WELL. YOU CAN GO.
THROB THROB
ALL RIGHT!
YAY!
THE OCEAN! ♡ OKINAWA! ♡♡♡
I'LL GET TO SEE CHIDSURU! IT'S BEEN SO LONG.
hee hee
YAY!
...
CHIDSU-RU?

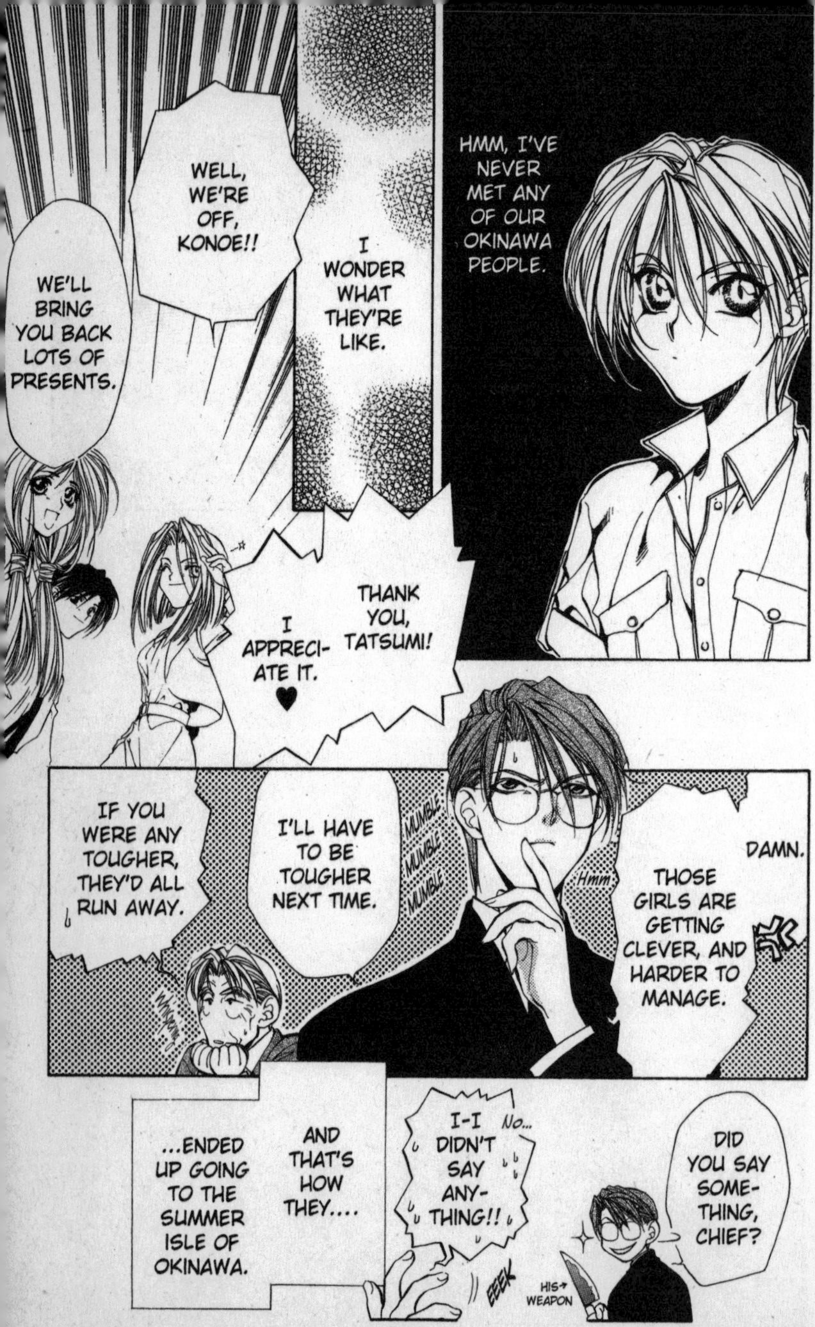
HMM, I'VE NEVER MET ANY OF OUR OKINAWA PEOPLE.
I WONDER WHAT THEY'RE LIKE.
WELL, WE'RE OFF, KONOE!!
WE'LL BRING YOU BACK LOTS OF PRESENTS.
THANK YOU, TATSUMI!
I APPRECI-ATE IT. ♥
DAMN.
THOSE GIRLS ARE GETTING CLEVER, AND HARDER TO MANAGE.
Hmm.
MUMBLE MUMBLE MUMBLE
I'LL HAVE TO BE TOUGHER NEXT TIME.
IF YOU WERE ANY TOUGHER, THEY'D ALL RUN AWAY.
DID YOU SAY SOME-THING, CHIEF?
HIS WEAPON
I-I DIDN'T SAY ANY-THING!!
No...
EEEK
AND THAT'S HOW THEY....
...ENDED UP GOING TO THE SUMMER ISLE OF OKINAWA.

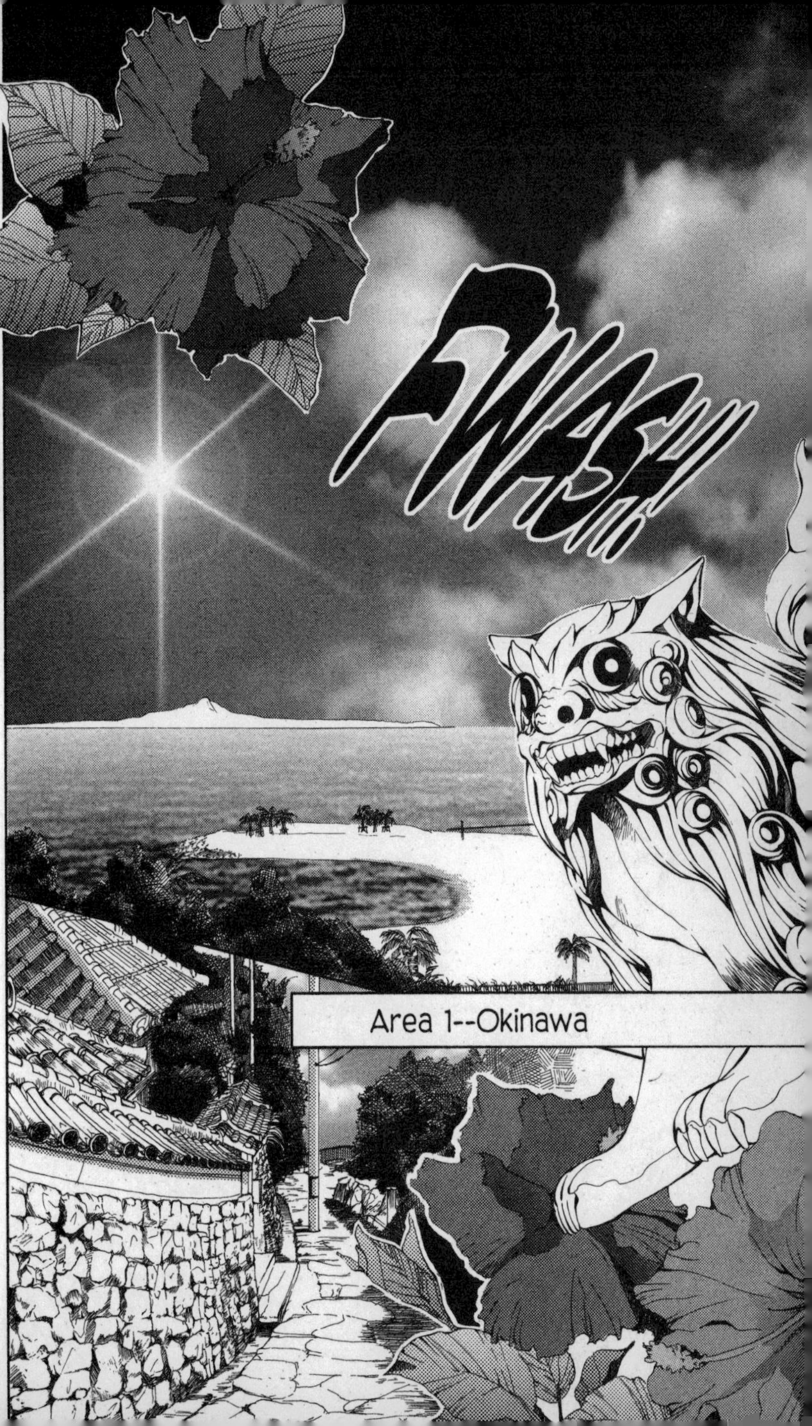
FWASH!!
Area 1--Okinawa

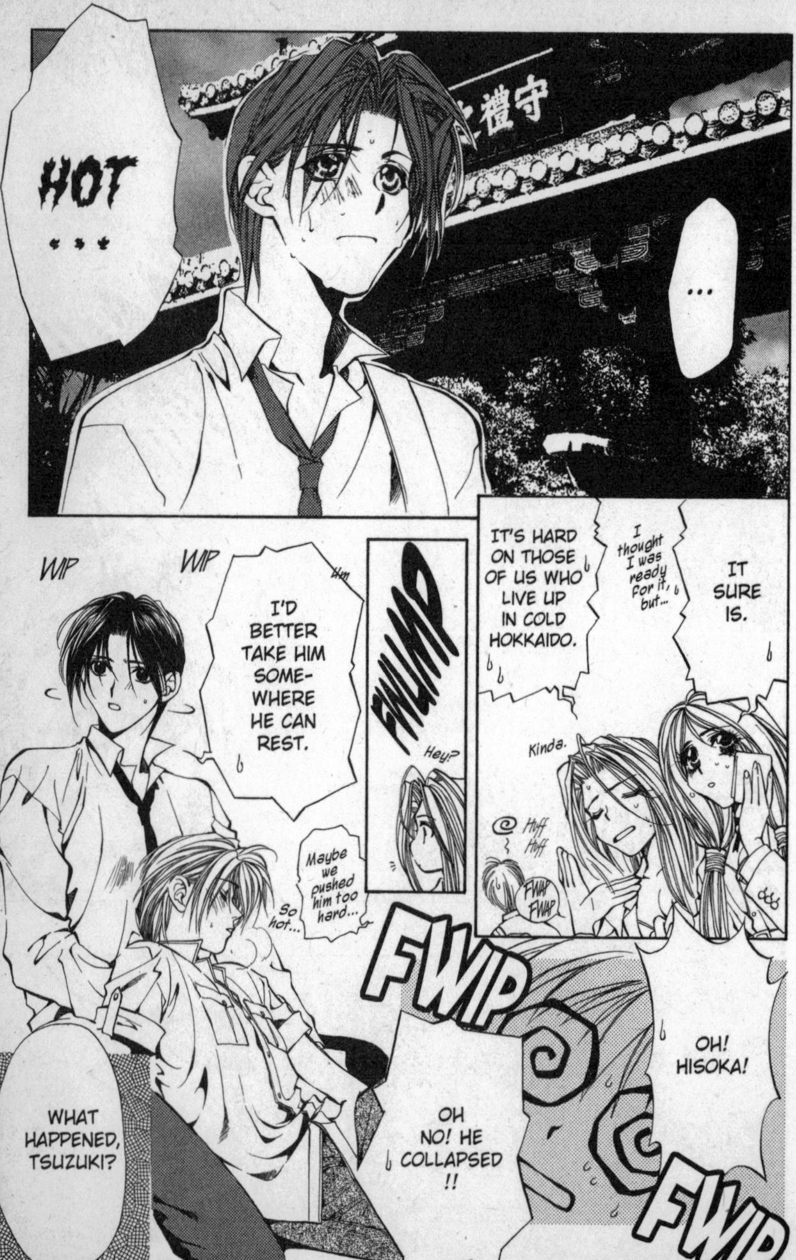
...
HOT
IT SURE IS.
I thought I was ready for it, but...
IT'S HARD ON THOSE OF US WHO LIVE UP IN COLD HOKKAIDO.
Kinda.
Huff Huff
FWAP FWAP
FWUMP
Hey?
Maybe we pushed him too hard...
I'D BETTER TAKE HIM SOME-WHERE HE CAN REST.
WIP WIP
So hot...
OH! HISOKA!
FWIP
FWIP
OH NO! HE COLLAPSED!!
WHAT HAPPENED, TSUZUKI?

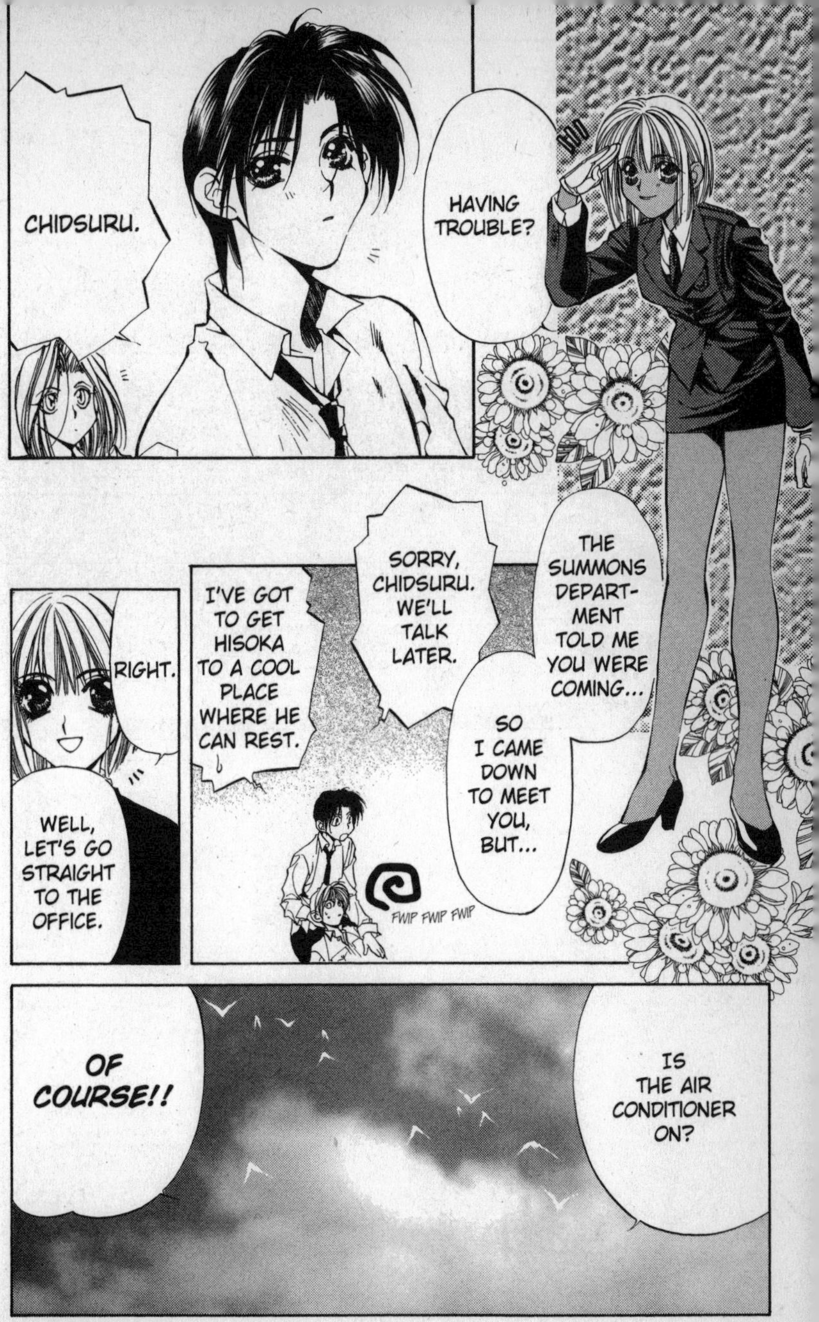
HAVING TROUBLE?
THE SUMMONS DEPART-MENT TOLD ME YOU WERE COMING...
SO I CAME DOWN TO MEET YOU, BUT...
CHIDSURU.
SORRY, CHIDSURU. WE'LL TALK LATER.
I'VE GOT TO GET HISOKA TO A COOL PLACE WHERE HE CAN REST.
FWIP FWIP FWIP
RIGHT.
WELL, LET'S GO STRAIGHT TO THE OFFICE.
IS THE AIR CONDITIONER ON?
OF COURSE!!

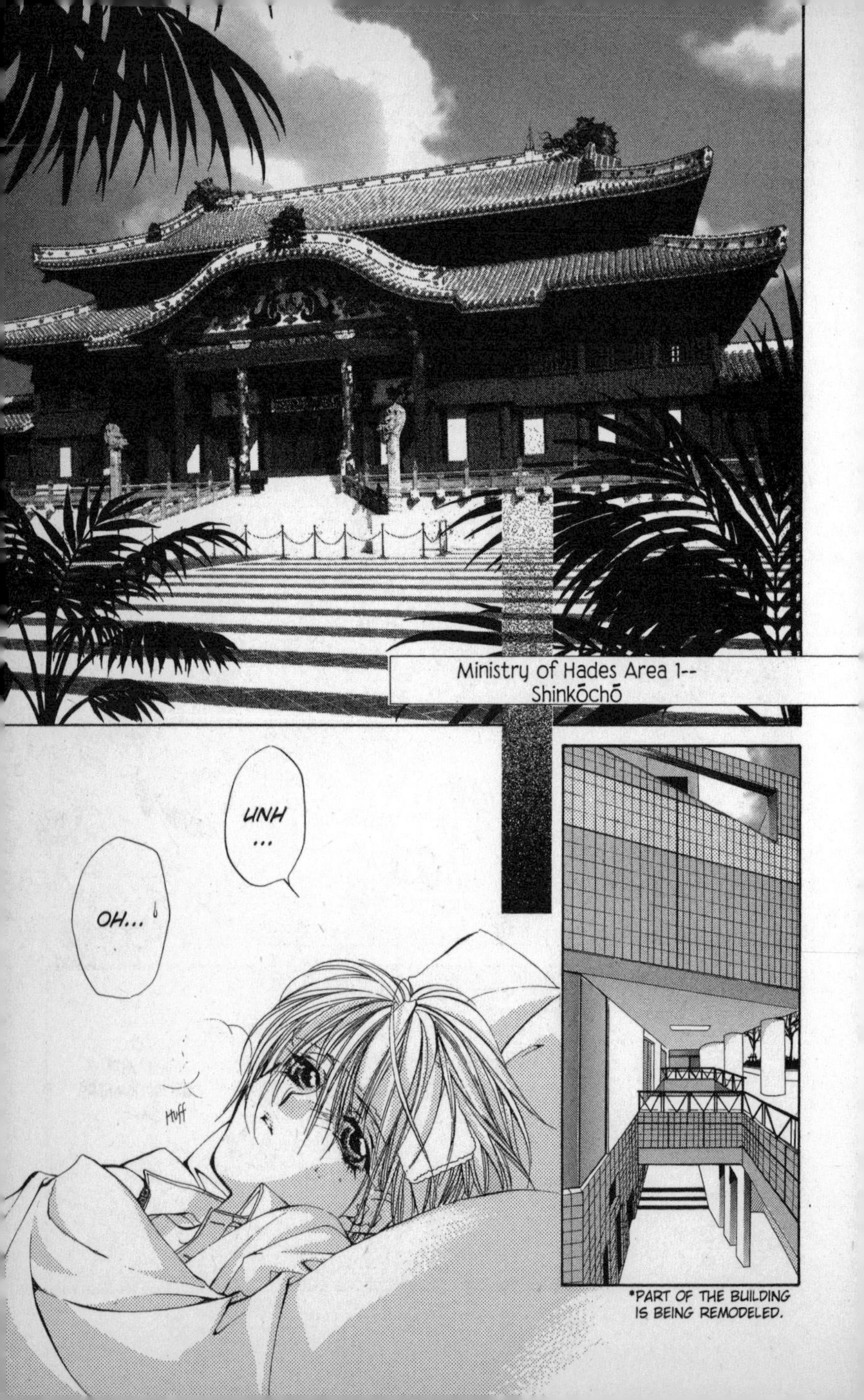
Ministry of Hades Area 1-- Shinkōchō
*PART OF THE BUILDING IS BEING REMODELED.
UNH ...
OH...
Huff

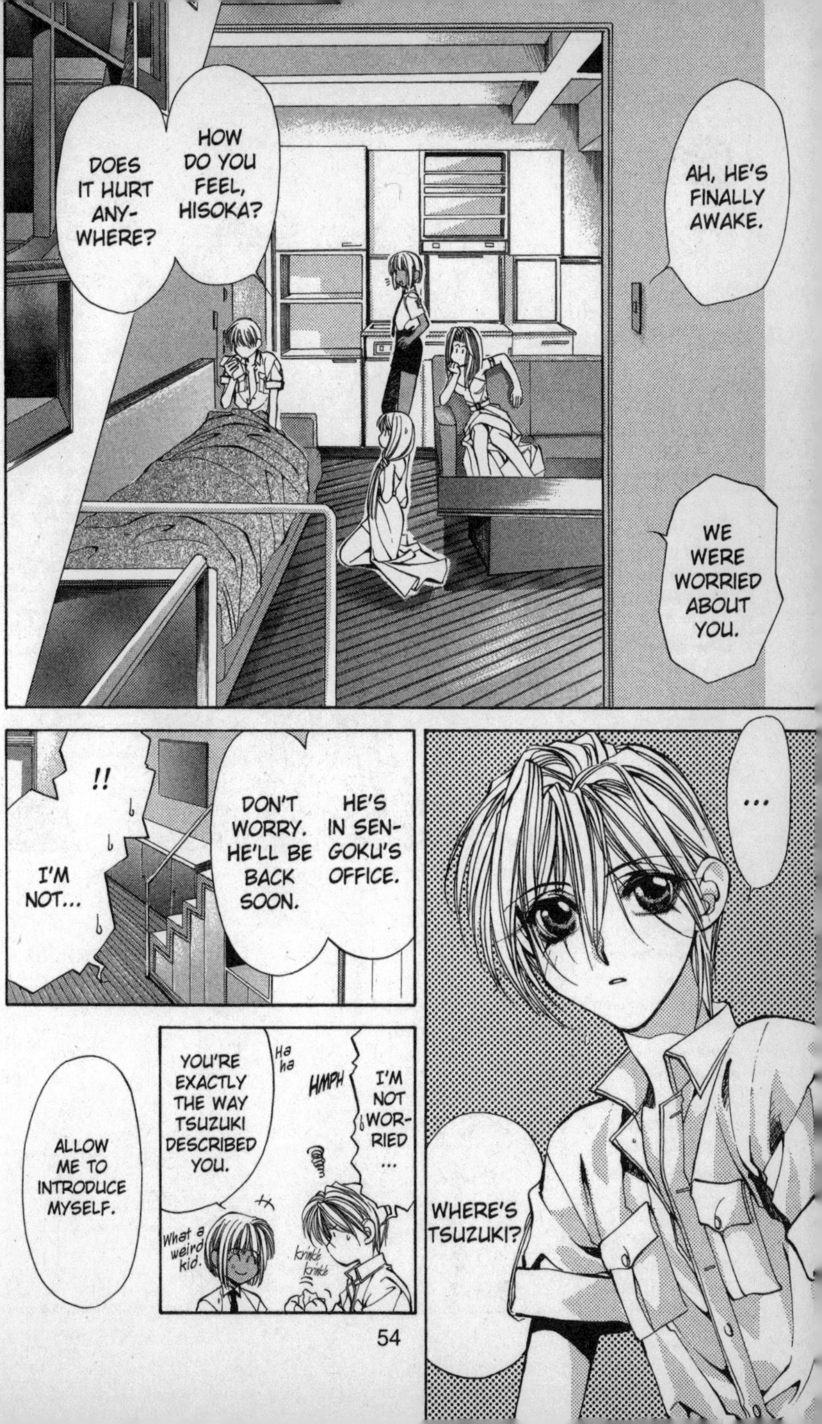
AH, HE'S FINALLY AWAKE.
WE WERE WORRIED ABOUT YOU.
HOW DO YOU FEEL, HISOKA?
DOES IT HURT ANY-WHERE?
...
WHERE'S TSUZUKI?
HE'S IN SEN-GOKU'S OFFICE.
DON'T WORRY. HE'LL BE BACK SOON.
!!
I'M NOT...
I'M NOT WOR-RIED ...
HMPH
Ha ha
YOU'RE EXACTLY THE WAY TSUZUKI DESCRIBED YOU.
What a weird kid.
krinkle krinkle
ALLOW ME TO INTRODUCE MYSELF.

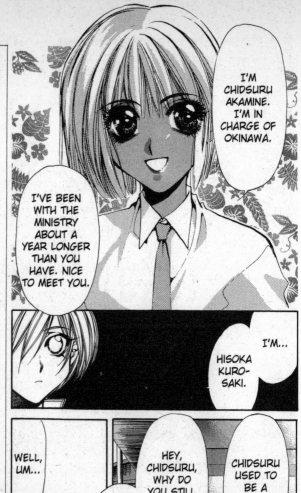

I'M CHIDSURU AKAMINE. I'M IN CHARGE OF OKINAWA.
I'VE BEEN WITH THE MINISTRY ABOUT A YEAR LONGER THAN YOU HAVE. NICE TO MEET YOU.
I'M...
HISOKA KURO-SAKI.
CHIDSURU USED TO BE A POLICE-WOMAN.
HEY, CHIDSURU, WHY DO YOU STILL WEAR THAT UNIFORM?
THE SUMMONS DEPARTMENT DOESN'T HAVE A DRESS CODE, BUT YOU STICK OUT IN THAT.
WELL, UM...

Lesson 1:
How to address
the envelope

Let me start by saying this:

THE USE OF PENCIL IS STRICTLY FORBIDDEN.

Even though I've asked people not to write in pencil, some people still do it. A reader informed me that writing a letter in pencil shows a lack of respect for the recipient. Even grade school students should follow this rule. Pencil is really hard to read.

On the back of the envelope, be sure to write your name and address. As long as you've written it there, you don't need to write it on the inside. I'm sorry, but I won't open envelopes that don't have a return name and address on them.

These are very basic rules so I hope you will follow them.

Lesson 2: The contents of the letter

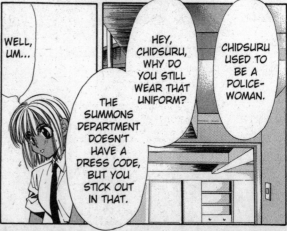

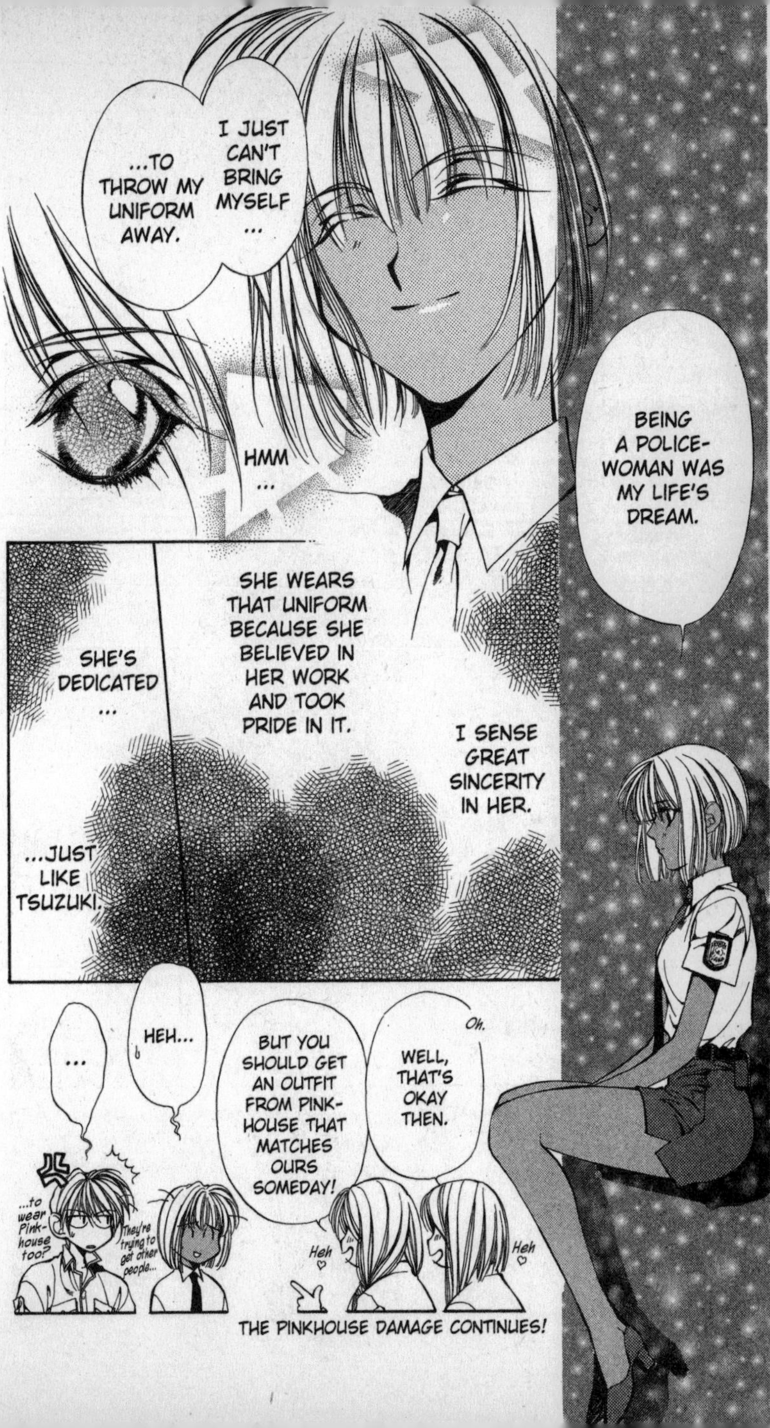
BEING A POLICE-WOMAN WAS MY LIFE'S DREAM.
I JUST CAN'T BRING MYSELF ...
...TO THROW MY UNIFORM AWAY.
HMM ...
SHE WEARS THAT UNIFORM BECAUSE SHE BELIEVED IN HER WORK AND TOOK PRIDE IN IT.
I SENSE GREAT SINCERITY IN HER.
SHE'S DEDICATED ...
...JUST LIKE TSUZUKI.
Oh.
WELL, THAT'S OKAY THEN.
BUT YOU SHOULD GET AN OUTFIT FROM PINK-HOUSE THAT MATCHES OURS SOMEDAY!
Heh ♡
Heh ♡
HEH...
...
They're trying to get other people...
...to wear Pink-house too?
THE PINKHOUSE DAMAGE CONTINUES!

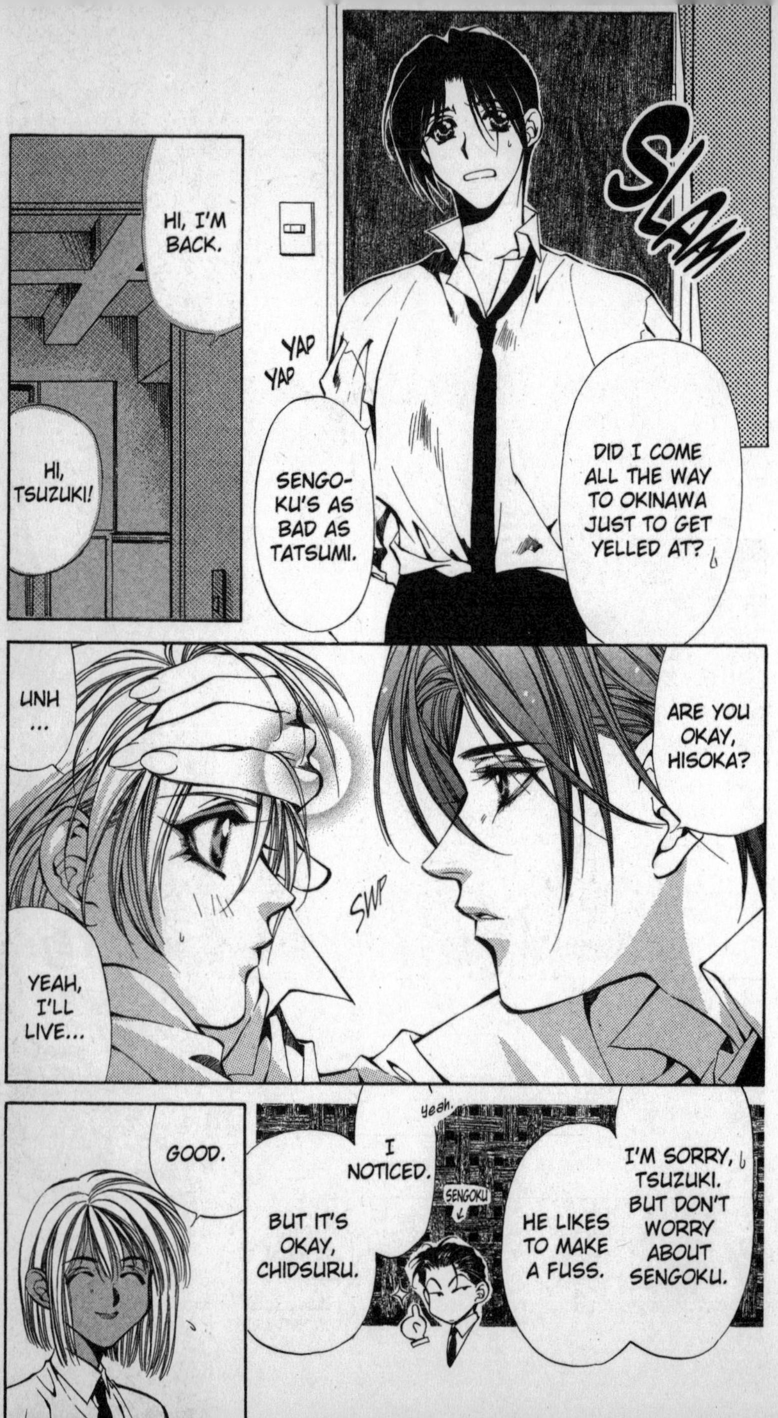
SLAM
DID I COME ALL THE WAY TO OKINAWA JUST TO GET YELLED AT?
YAP YAP
SENGO-KU'S AS BAD AS TATSUMI.
HI, I'M BACK.
HI, TSUZUKI!
ARE YOU OKAY, HISOKA?
UNH ...
SWP
YEAH, I'LL LIVE...
I'M SORRY, TSUZUKI. BUT DON'T WORRY ABOUT SENGOKU.
HE LIKES TO MAKE A FUSS.
SENGOKU
yeah.
I NOTICED.
BUT IT'S OKAY, CHIDSURU.
GOOD.

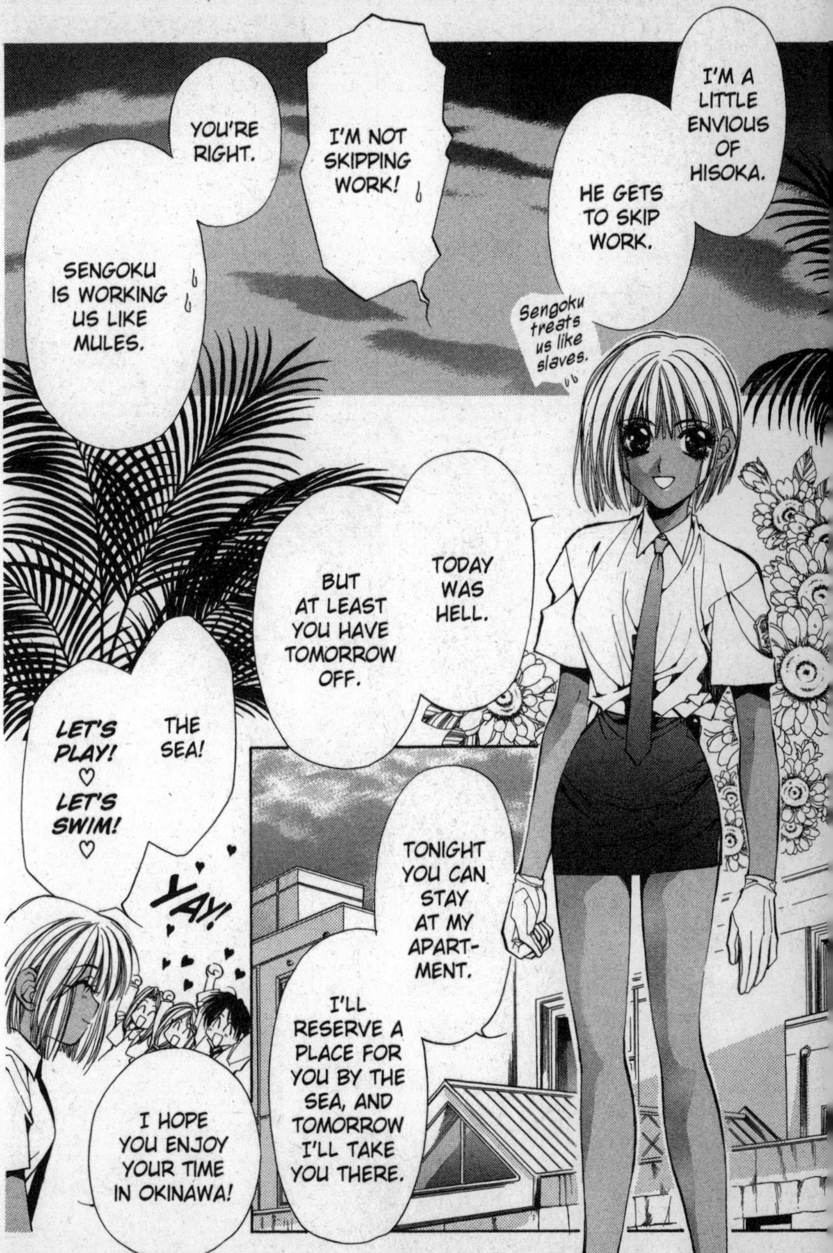
I'M A LITTLE ENVIOUS OF HISOKA.
HE GETS TO SKIP WORK.
Sengoku treats us like slaves.
I'M NOT SKIPPING WORK!
YOU'RE RIGHT.
SENGOKU IS WORKING US LIKE MULES.
TODAY WAS HELL.
BUT AT LEAST YOU HAVE TOMORROW OFF.
THE SEA!
LET'S PLAY! ♡ LET'S SWIM! ♡
YAY!
TONIGHT YOU CAN STAY AT MY APARTMENT.
I'LL RESERVE A PLACE FOR YOU BY THE SEA, AND TOMORROW I'LL TAKE YOU THERE.
I HOPE YOU ENJOY YOUR TIME IN OKINAWA!

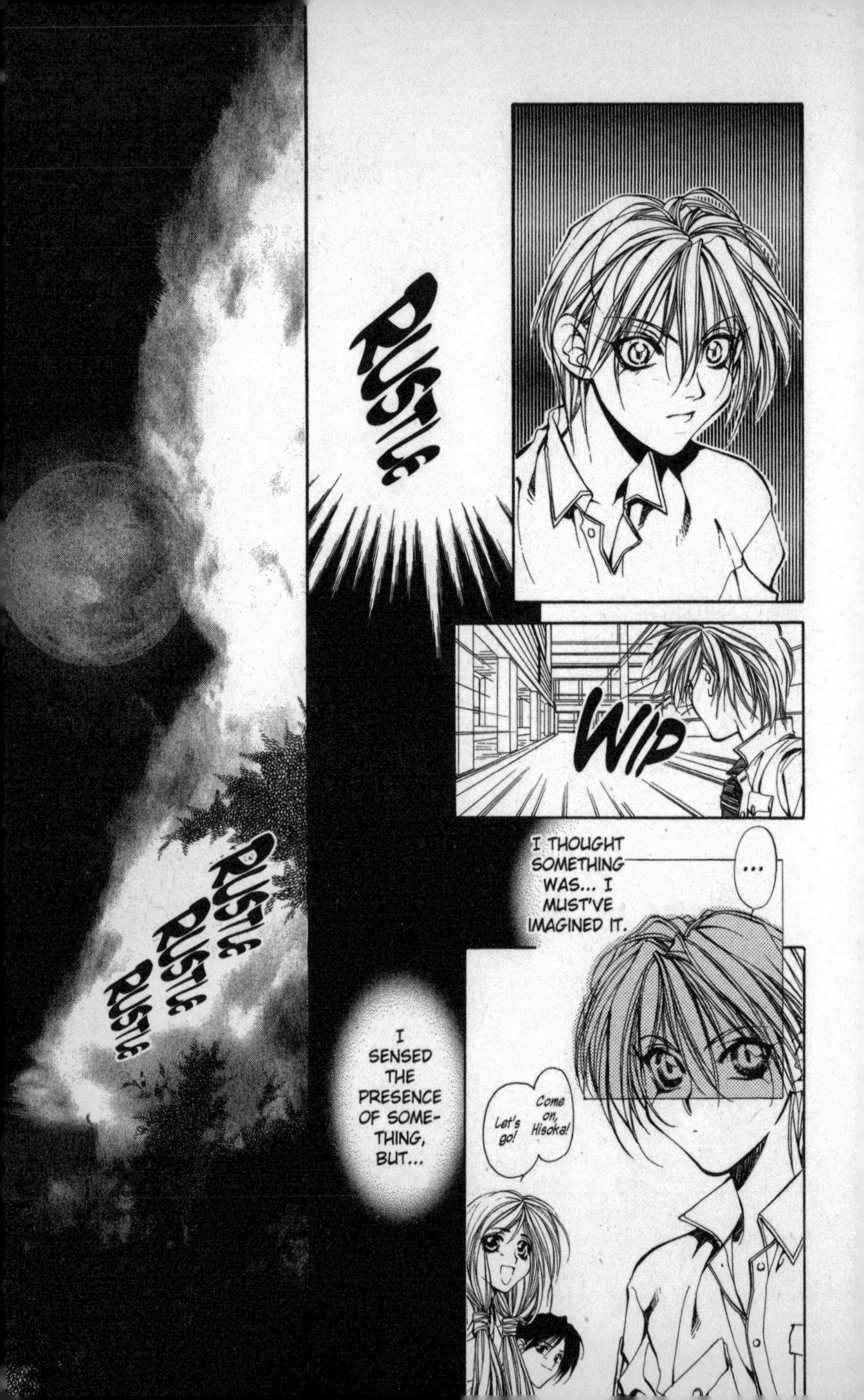
RUSTLE
WIP
...
I THOUGHT SOMETHING WAS... I MUST'VE IMAGINED IT.
Come on, Hisoka!
Let's go!
I SENSED THE PRESENCE OF SOME-THING, BUT...
RUSTLE RUSTLE RUSTLE

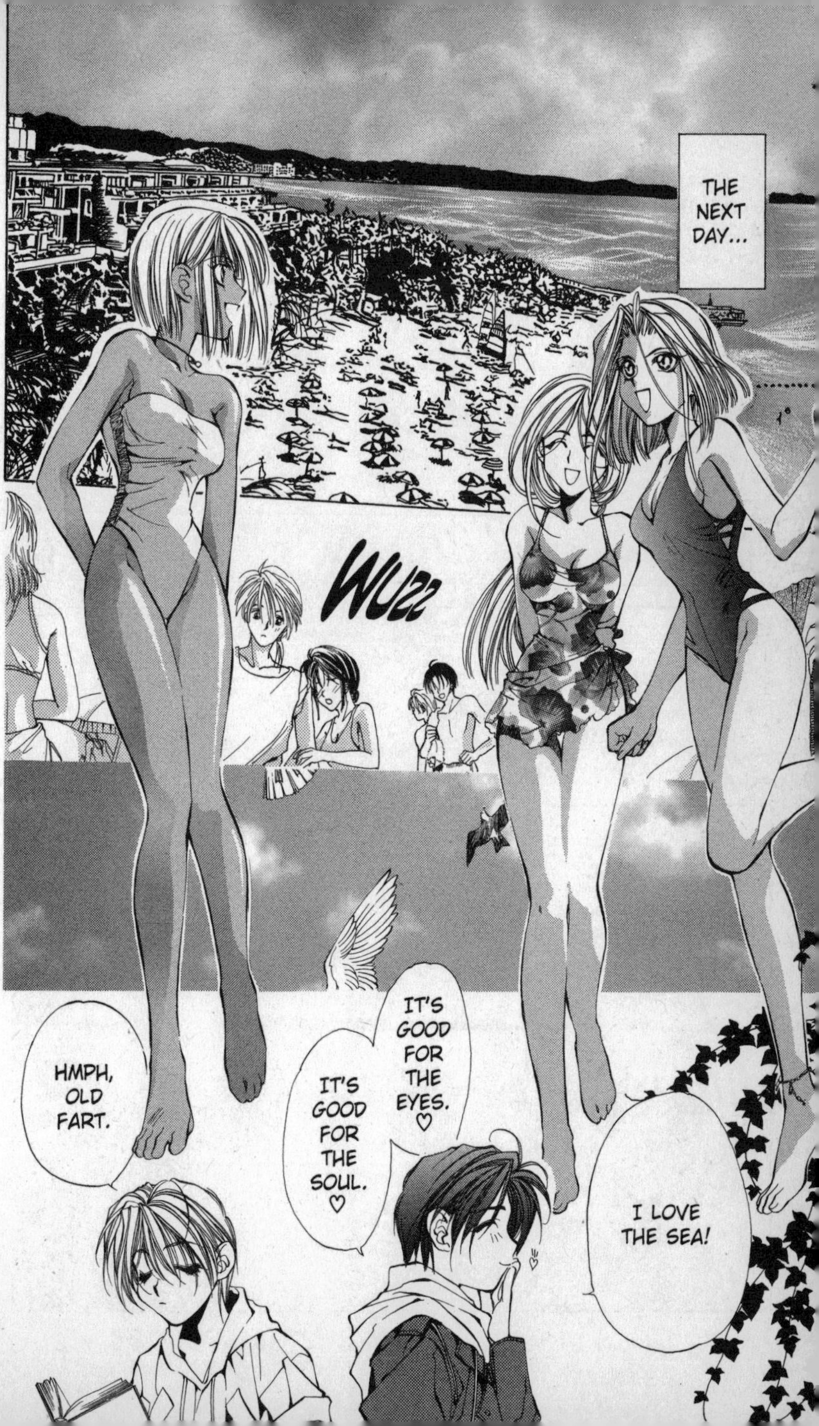
THE NEXT DAY...
WUZZ
I LOVE THE SEA!
IT'S GOOD FOR THE EYES. ♡
IT'S GOOD FOR THE SOUL. ♡
HMPH, OLD FART.

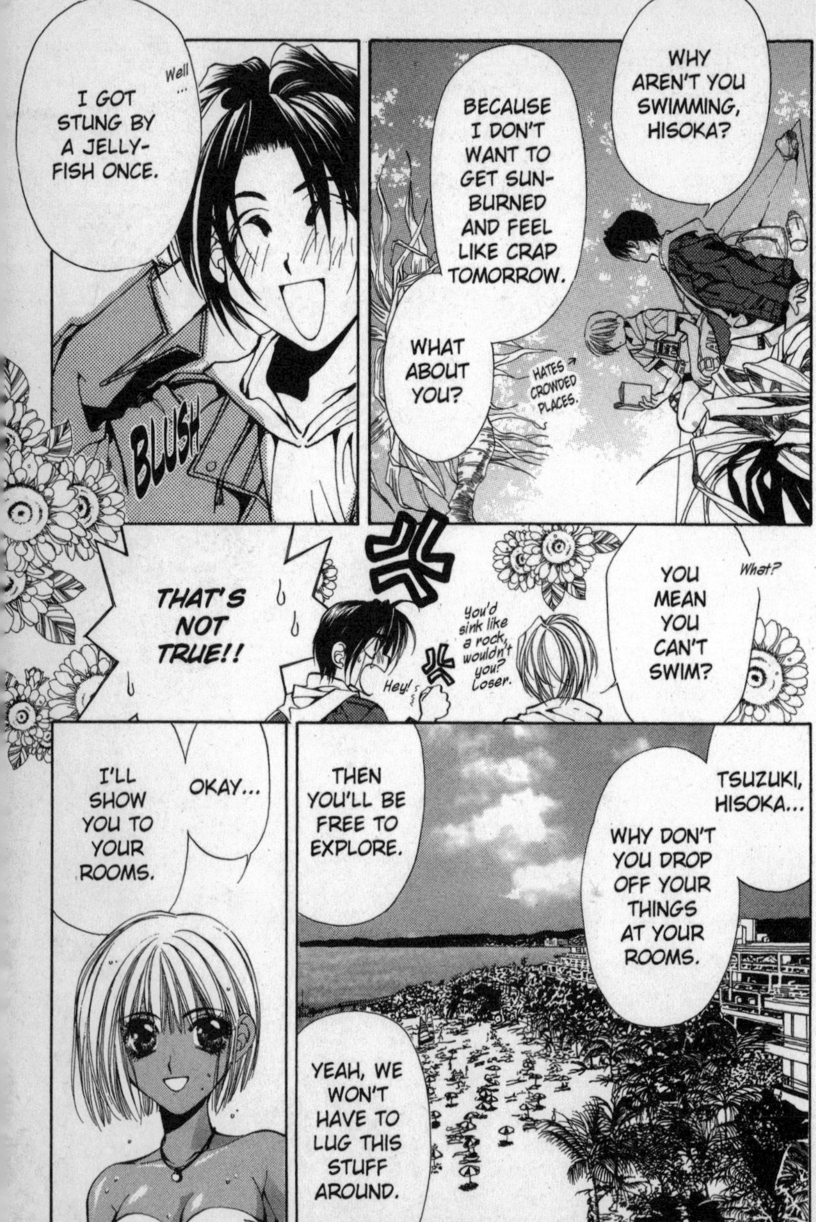
WHY AREN'T YOU SWIMMING, HISOKA?
BECAUSE I DON'T WANT TO GET SUN-BURNED AND FEEL LIKE CRAP TOMORROW.
HATES CROWDED PLACES.
WHAT ABOUT YOU?
Well...
I GOT STUNG BY A JELLY-FISH ONCE.
BLUSH
What?
YOU MEAN YOU CAN'T SWIM?
You'd sink like a rock, wouldn't you? Loser.
Hey!
THAT'S NOT TRUE!!
TSUZUKI, HISOKA...
WHY DON'T YOU DROP OFF YOUR THINGS AT YOUR ROOMS.
THEN YOU'LL BE FREE TO EXPLORE.
YEAH, WE WON'T HAVE TO LUG THIS STUFF AROUND.
OKAY...
I'LL SHOW YOU TO YOUR ROOMS.

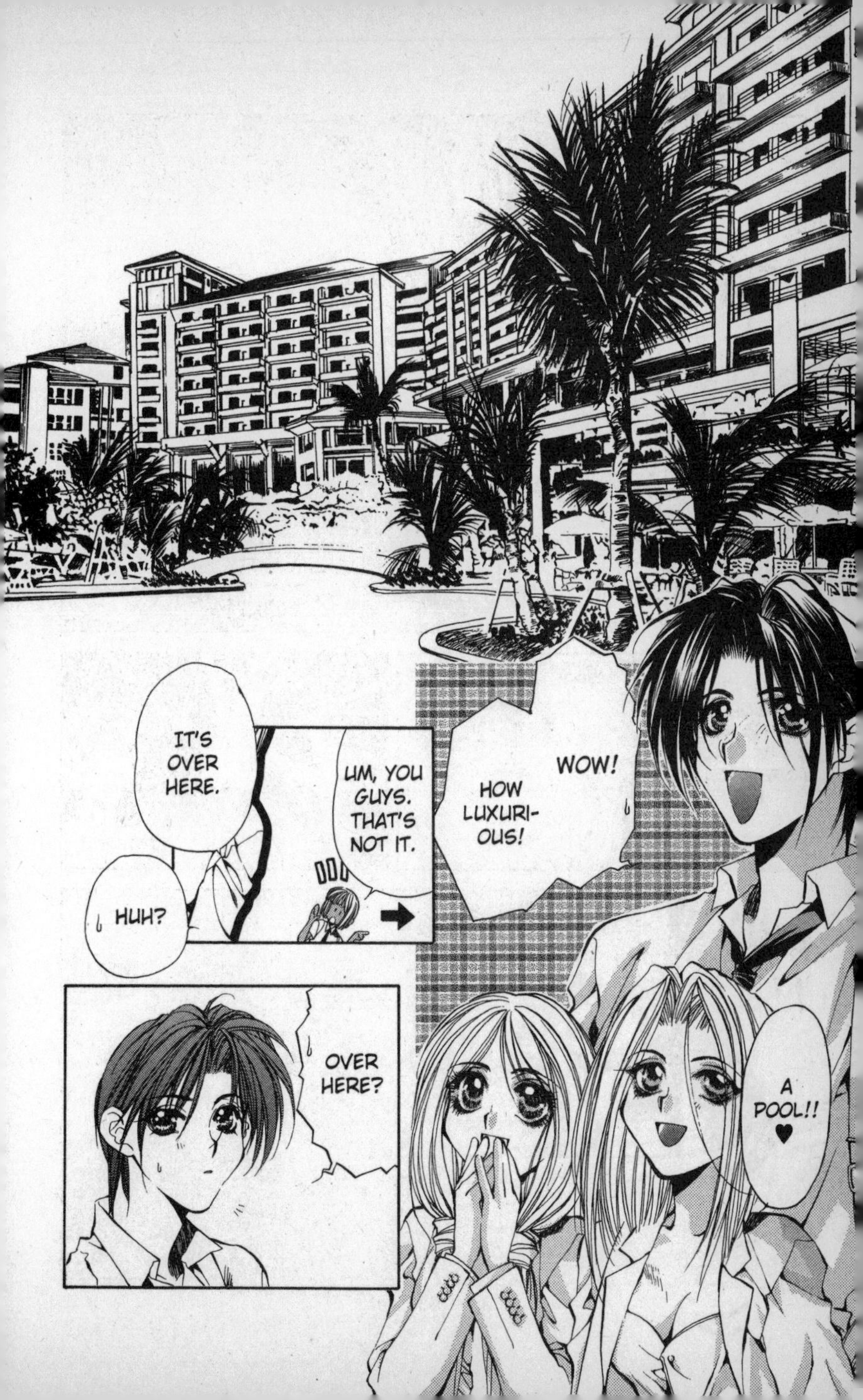
WOW!
HOW LUXURI-OUS!
A POOL!! ♥
UM, YOU GUYS. THAT'S NOT IT.
IT'S OVER HERE.
HUH?
OVER HERE?

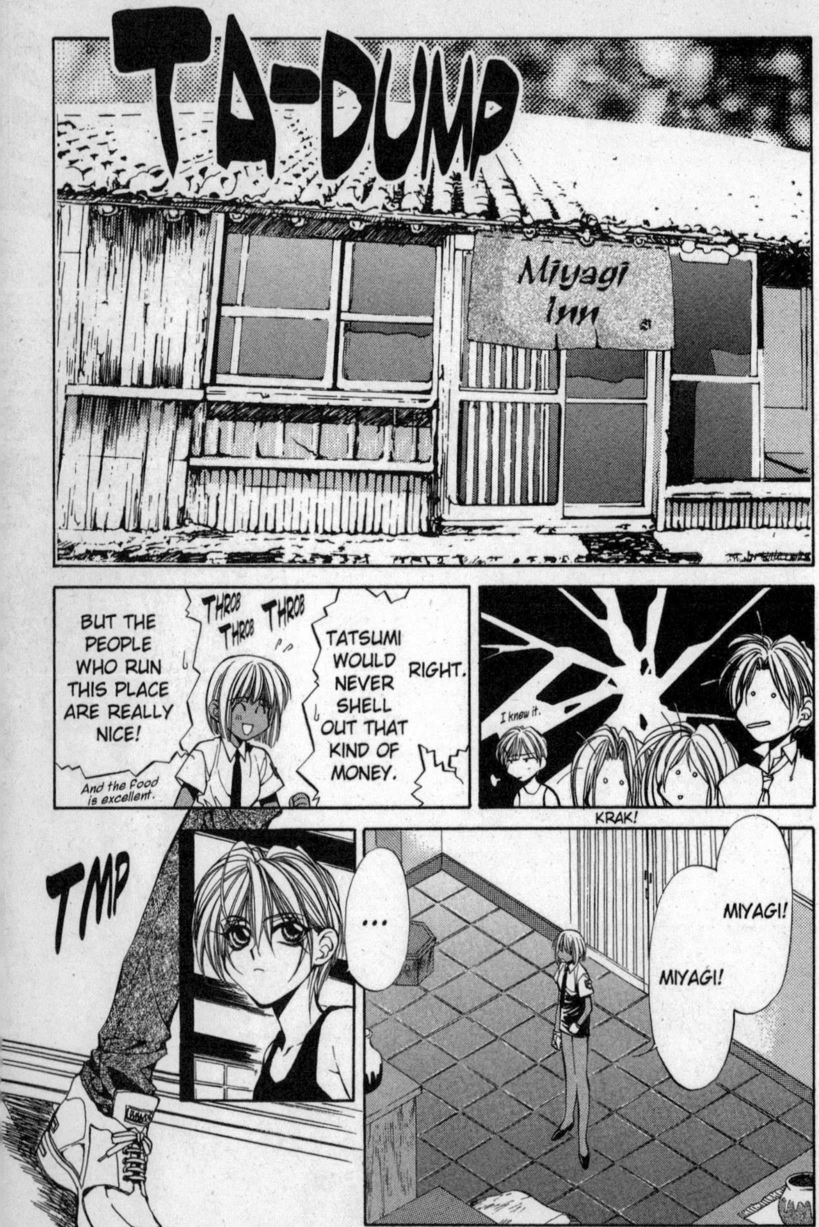
TA-DUMP
Miyagi Inn
I knew it.
KRAK!
RIGHT.
TATSUMI WOULD NEVER SHELL OUT THAT KIND OF MONEY.
THROB THROB THROB
BUT THE PEOPLE WHO RUN THIS PLACE ARE REALLY NICE!
And the food is excellent.
MIYAGI!
MIYAGI!
THE LOBBY IS EMPTY.
...
TMP

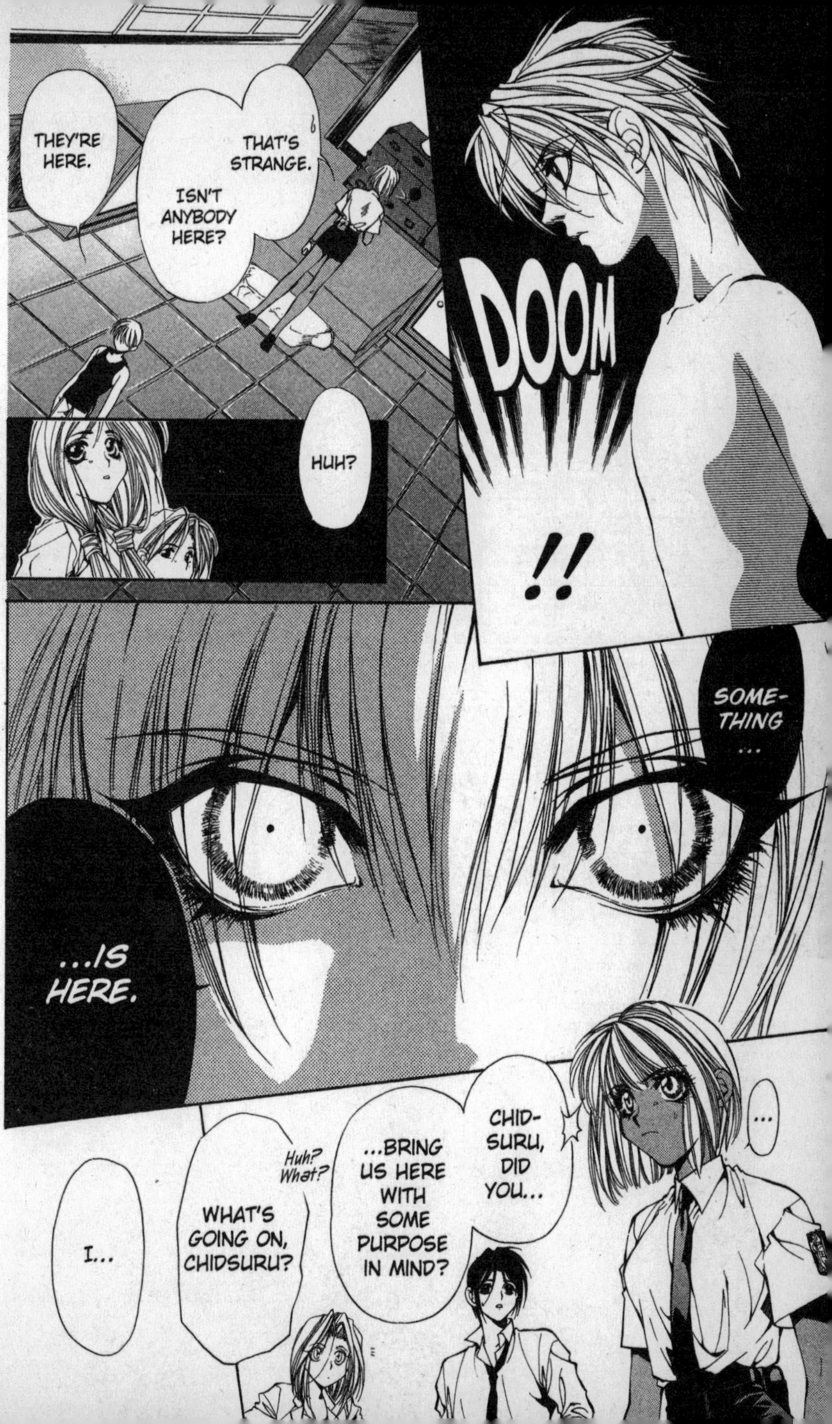
DOOM
!!
THAT'S STRANGE.
ISN'T ANYBODY HERE?
THEY'RE HERE.
HUH?
SOME-THING...
...IS HERE.
...
CHID-SURU, DID YOU...
...BRING US HERE WITH SOME PURPOSE IN MIND?
Huh? What?
WHAT'S GOING ON, CHIDSURU?
I...

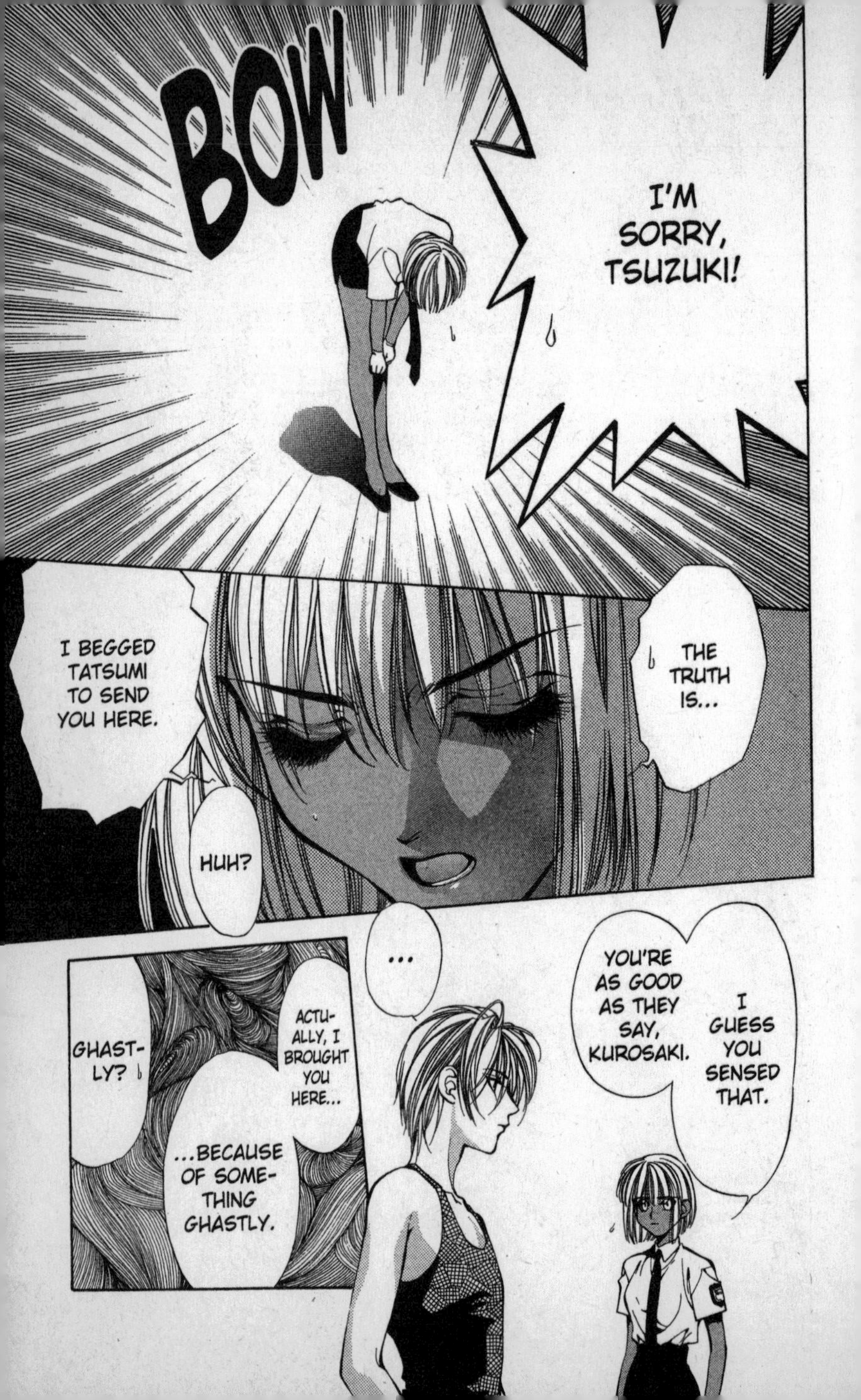
BOW
I'M SORRY, TSUZUKI!
THE TRUTH IS...
I BEGGED TATSUMI TO SEND YOU HERE.
HUH?
I GUESS YOU SENSED THAT.
YOU'RE AS GOOD AS THEY SAY, KUROSAKI.
...
ACTU-ALLY, I BROUGHT YOU HERE...
...BECAUSE OF SOME-THING GHASTLY.
GHAST-LY?

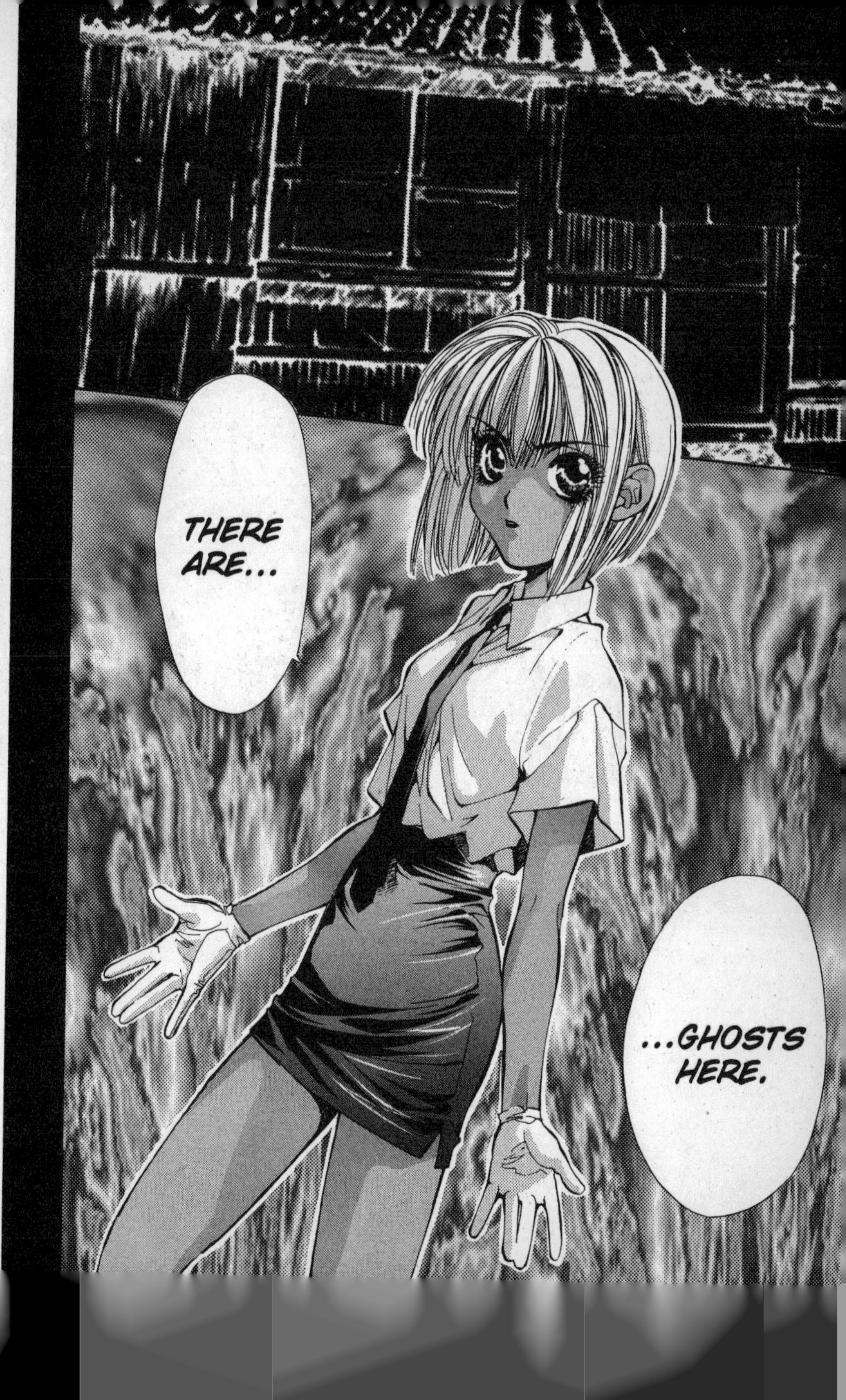
THERE ARE...
...GHOSTS HERE.

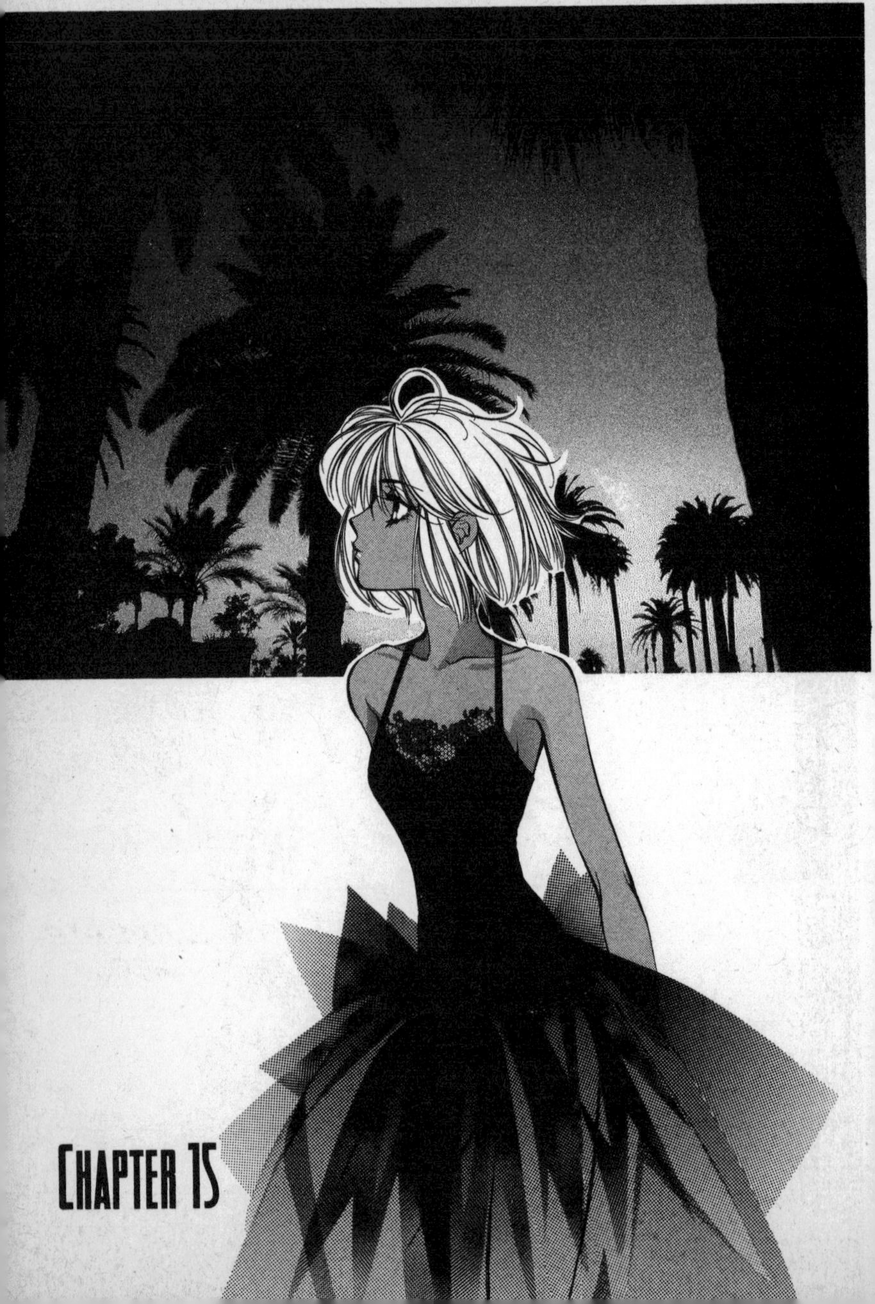
CHAPTER 15

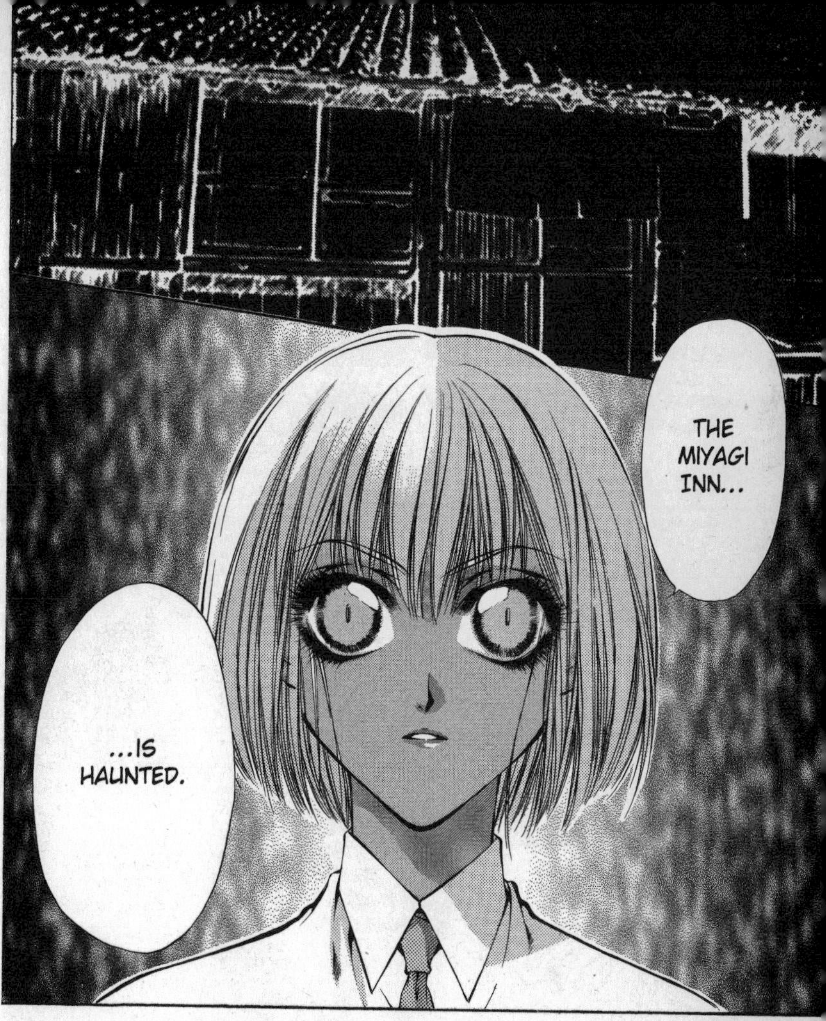
THE MIYAGI INN...
...IS HAUNTED.

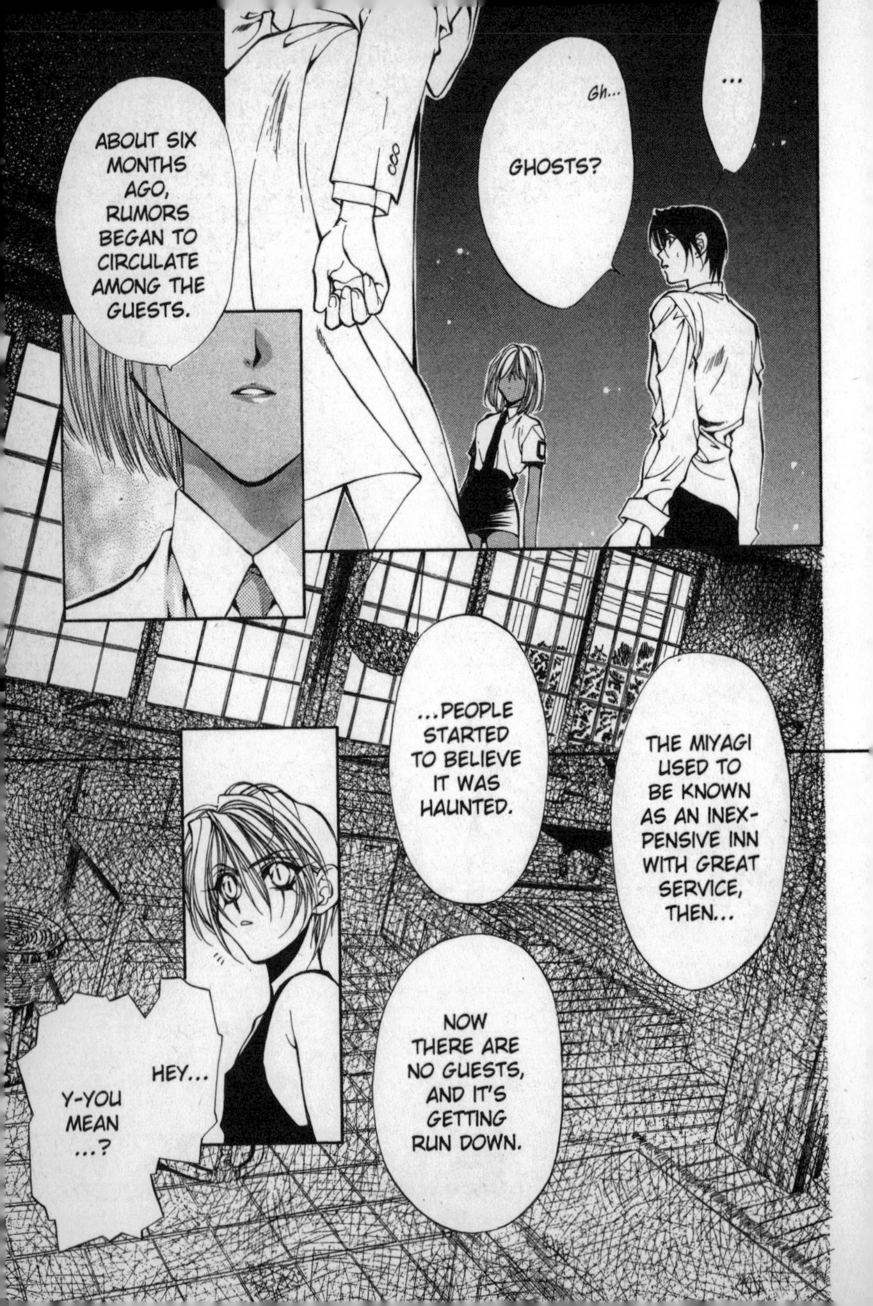
...
Gh...
GHOSTS?
ABOUT SIX MONTHS AGO, RUMORS BEGAN TO CIRCULATE AMONG THE GUESTS.
THE MIYAGI USED TO BE KNOWN AS AN INEX-PENSIVE INN WITH GREAT SERVICE, THEN...
...PEOPLE STARTED TO BELIEVE IT WAS HAUNTED.
NOW THERE ARE NO GUESTS, AND IT'S GETTING RUN DOWN.
HEY...
Y-YOU MEAN ...?

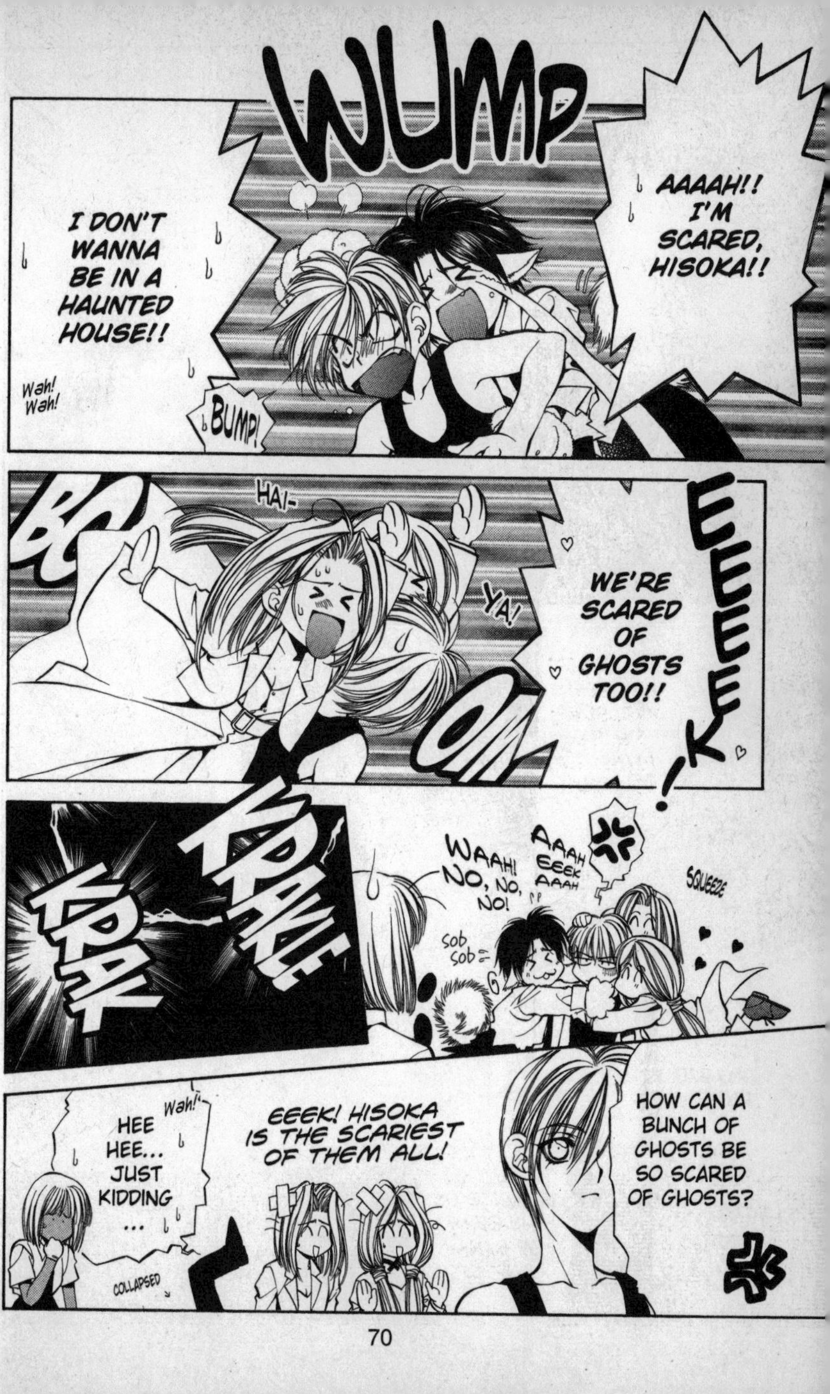
WUMP
AAAAH!! I'M SCARED, HISOKA!!
I DON'T WANNA BE IN A HAUNTED HOUSE!!
BUMP!
Wah! Wah!
EEEEEK!
WE'RE SCARED OF GHOSTS TOO!!
YA!
HAI-
BO
OM
SQUEEZE
AAAH EEEK AAAH
WAAH! NO, NO, NO!
Sob sob
KRAKLE
KRAK
HOW CAN A BUNCH OF GHOSTS BE SO SCARED OF GHOSTS?
EEEK! HISOKA IS THE SCARIEST OF THEM ALL!
Wah!
HEE HEE... JUST KIDDING ...
COLLAPSED

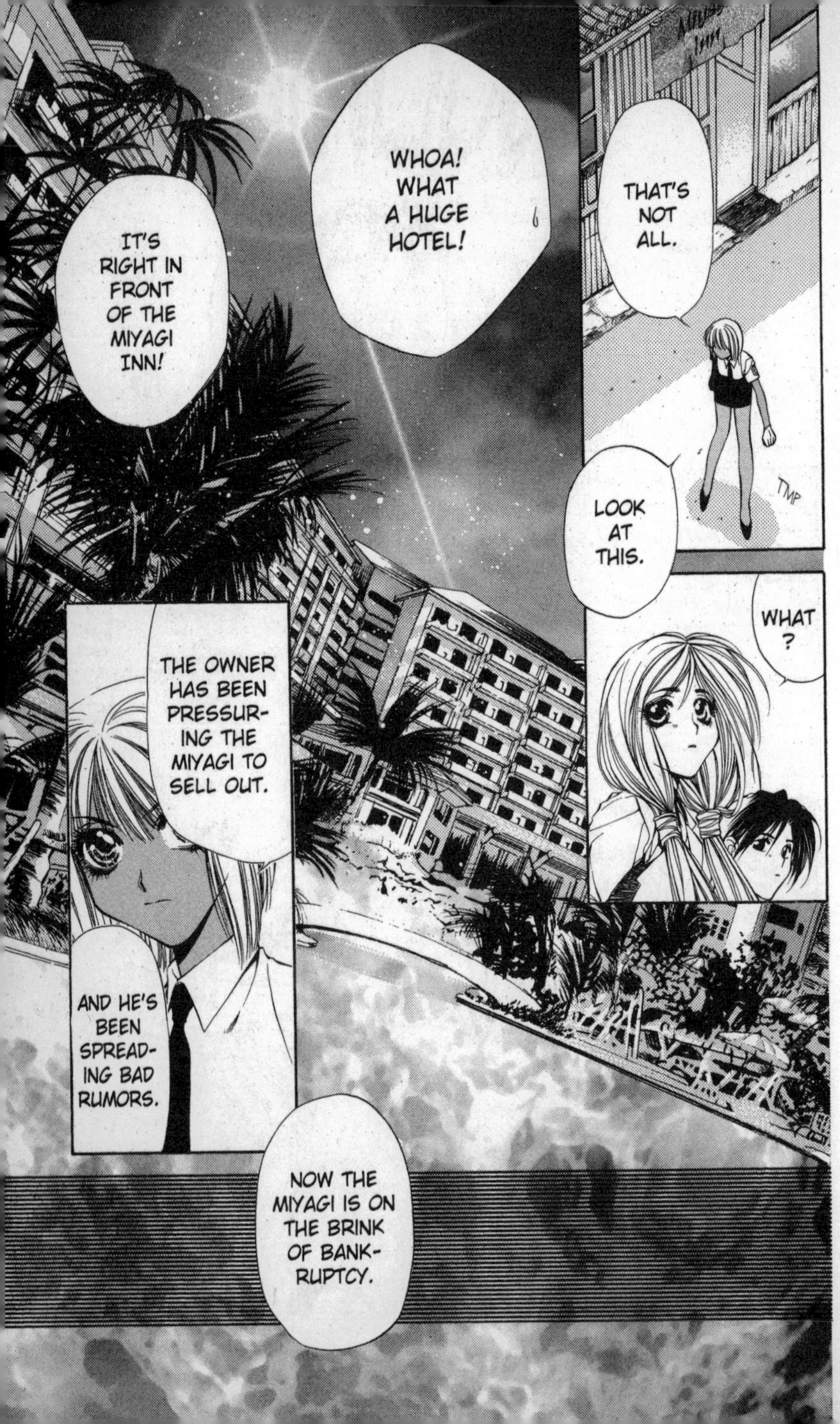
THAT'S NOT ALL.
TMP
LOOK AT THIS.
WHAT?
WHOA! WHAT A HUGE HOTEL!
IT'S RIGHT IN FRONT OF THE MIYAGI INN!
THE OWNER HAS BEEN PRESSURING THE MIYAGI TO SELL OUT.
AND HE'S BEEN SPREADING BAD RUMORS.
NOW THE MIYAGI IS ON THE BRINK OF BANKRUPTCY.

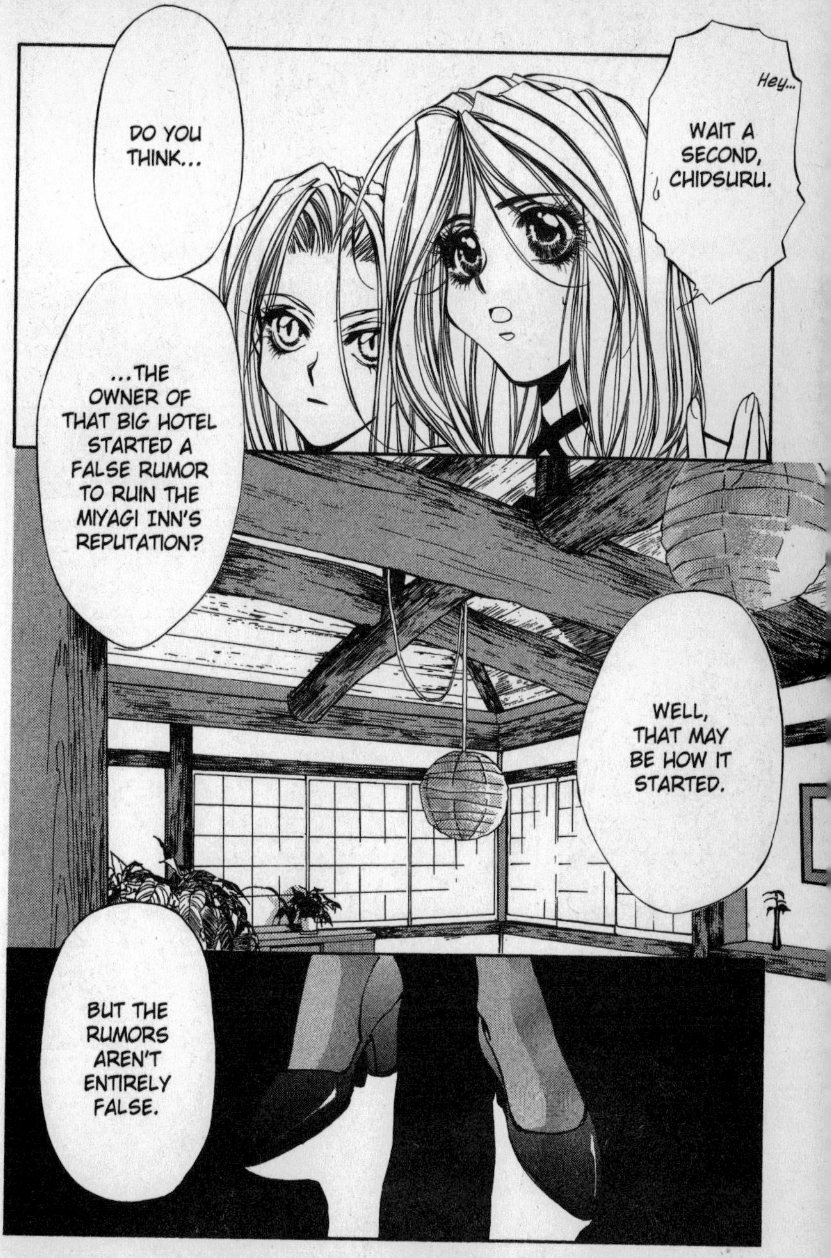
Hey...
WAIT A SECOND, CHIDSURU.
DO YOU THINK...
...THE OWNER OF THAT BIG HOTEL STARTED A FALSE RUMOR TO RUIN THE MIYAGI INN'S REPUTATION?
WELL, THAT MAY BE HOW IT STARTED.
BUT THE RUMORS AREN'T ENTIRELY FALSE.

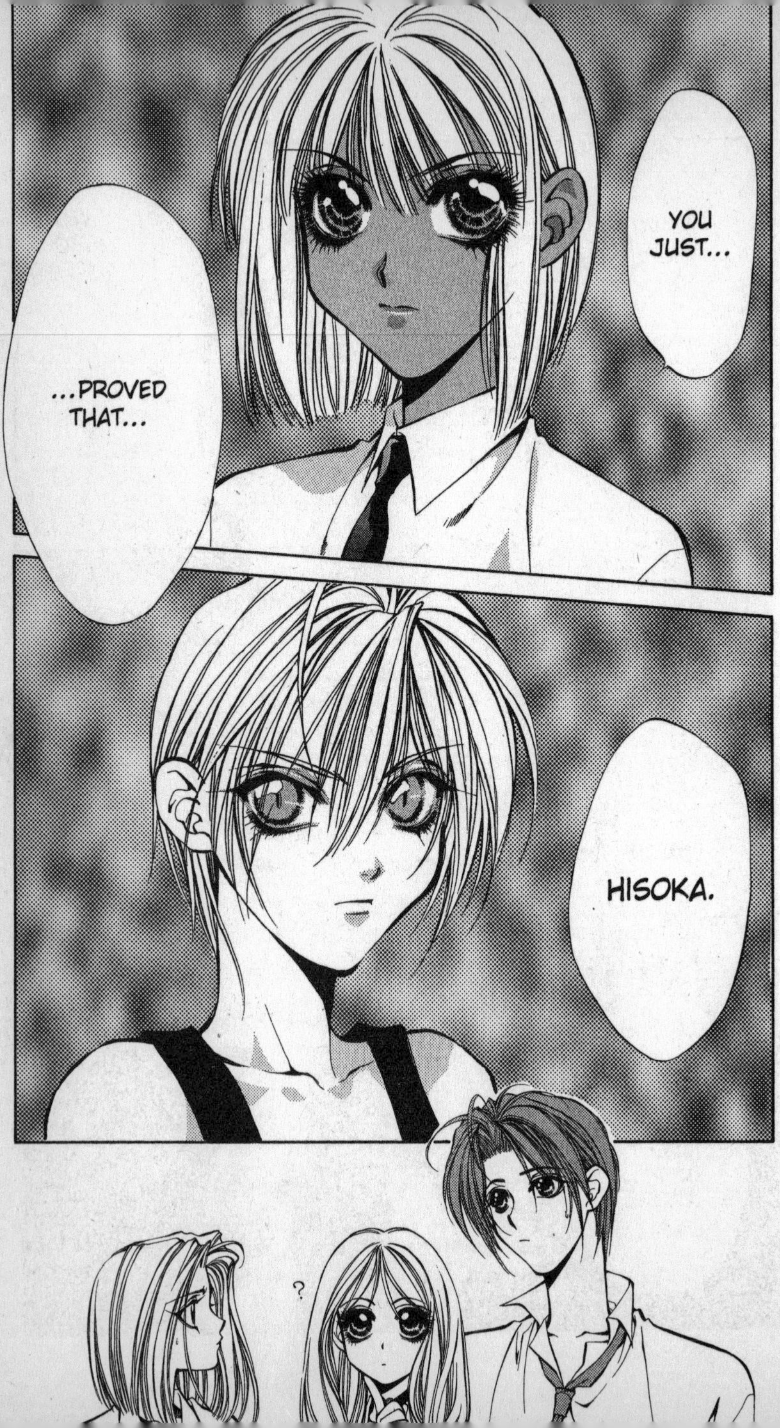
YOU JUST...
...PROVED THAT...
HISOKA.
?

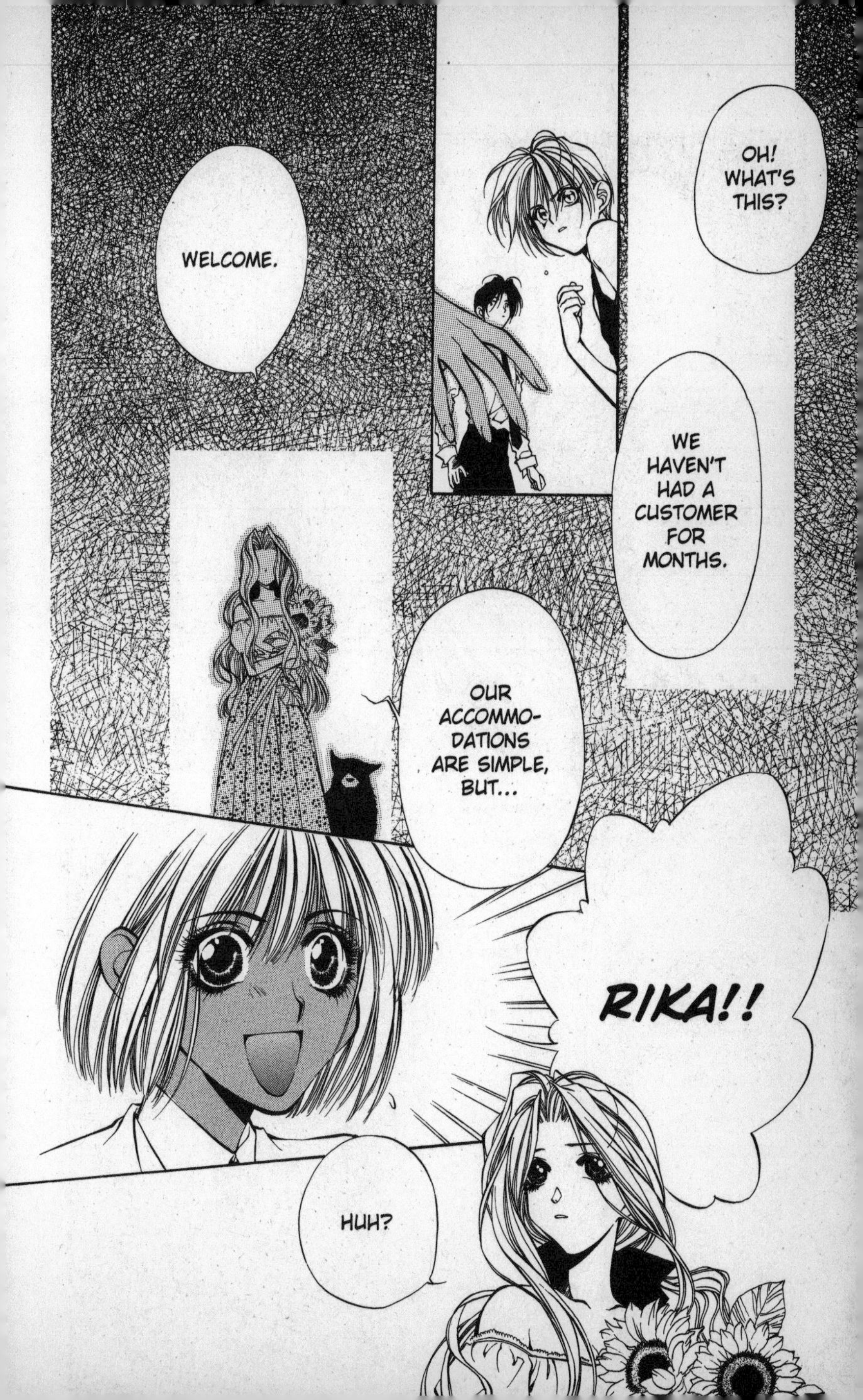
OH! WHAT'S THIS?
WELCOME.
WE HAVEN'T HAD A CUSTOMER FOR MONTHS.
OUR ACCOMMODATIONS ARE SIMPLE, BUT...
RIKA!!
HUH?

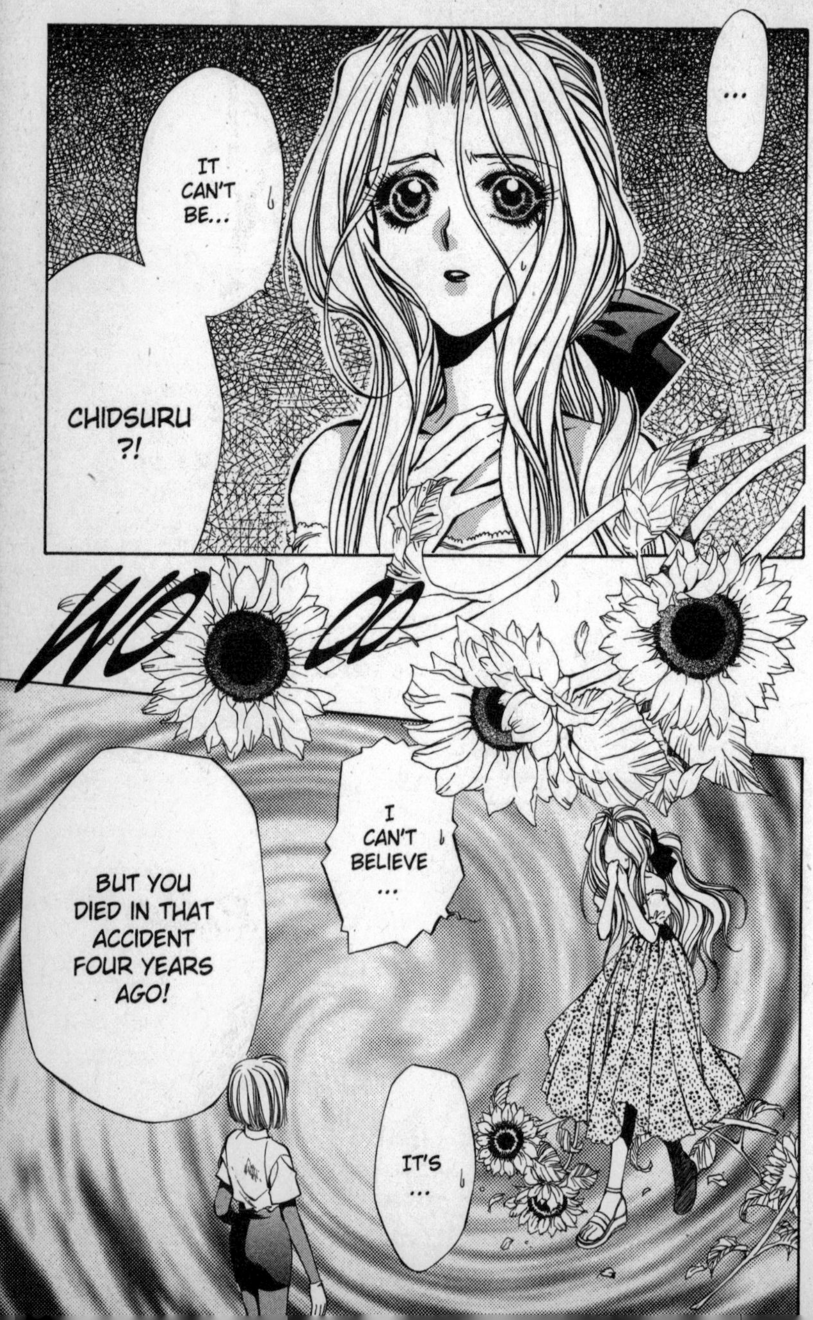
...
IT CAN'T BE...
CHIDSURU ?!
WOOO
I CAN'T BELIEVE ...
IT'S ...
BUT YOU DIED IN THAT ACCIDENT FOUR YEARS AGO!

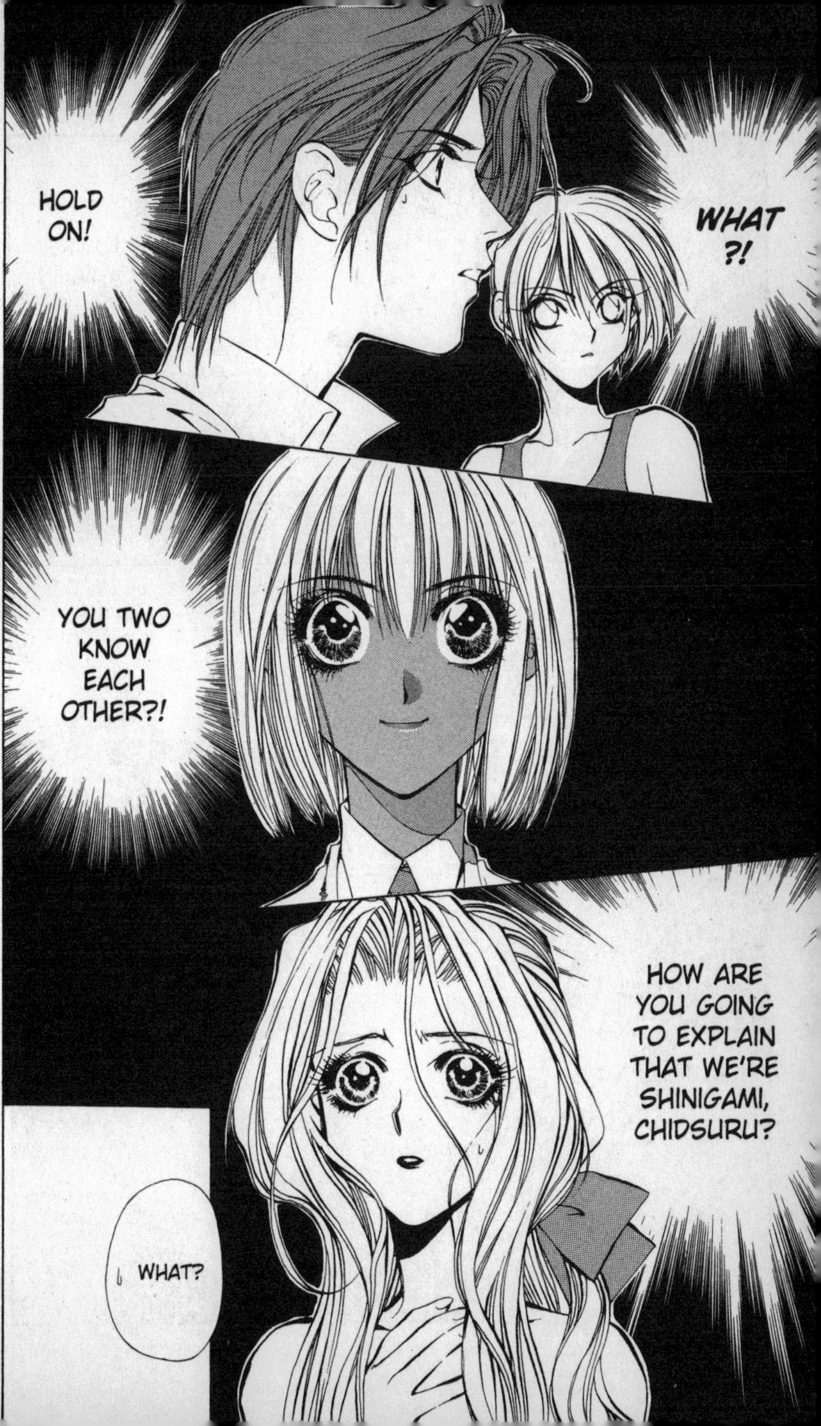
WHAT ?!
HOLD ON!
YOU TWO KNOW EACH OTHER?!
HOW ARE YOU GOING TO EXPLAIN THAT WE'RE SHINIGAMI, CHIDSURU?
WHAT?

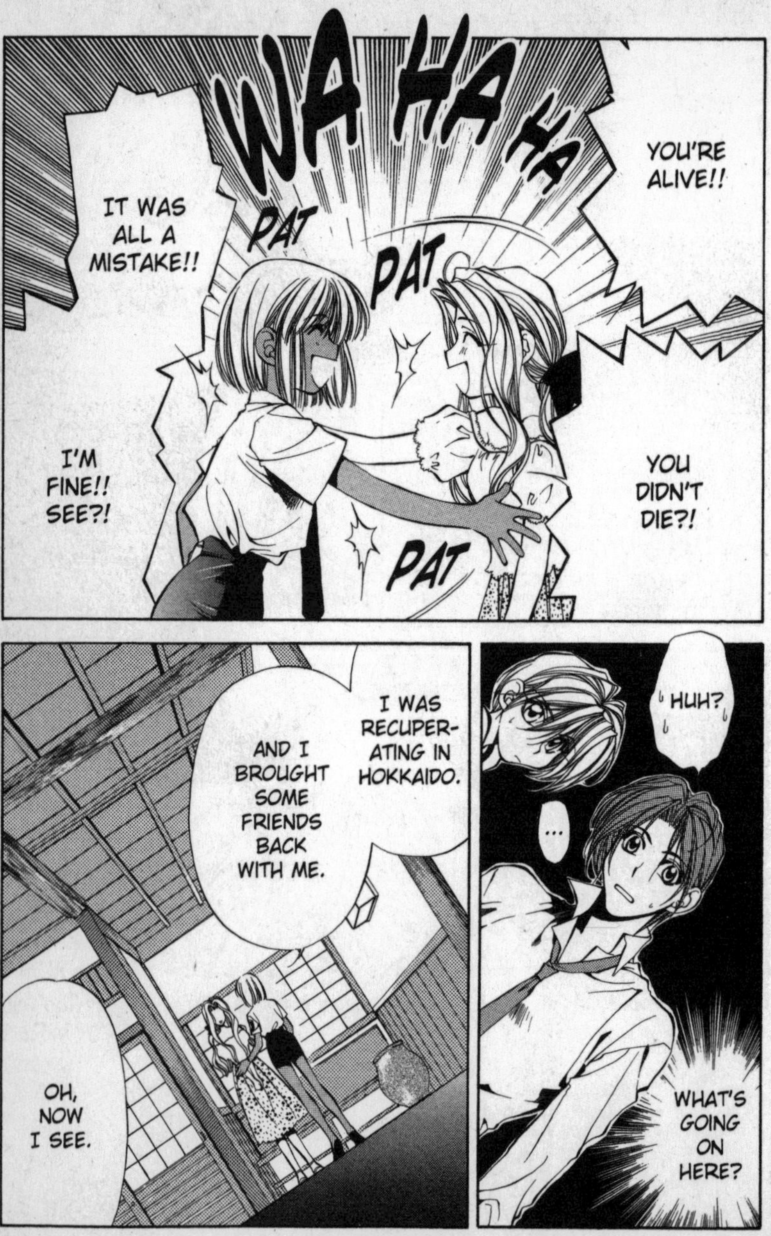
YOU'RE ALIVE!!
WA HA HA
IT WAS ALL A MISTAKE!!
PAT
PAT
YOU DIDN'T DIE?!
I'M FINE!! SEE?!
PAT
HUH?
...
WHAT'S GOING ON HERE?
I WAS RECUPER-ATING IN HOKKAIDO.
AND I BROUGHT SOME FRIENDS BACK WITH ME.
OH, NOW I SEE.

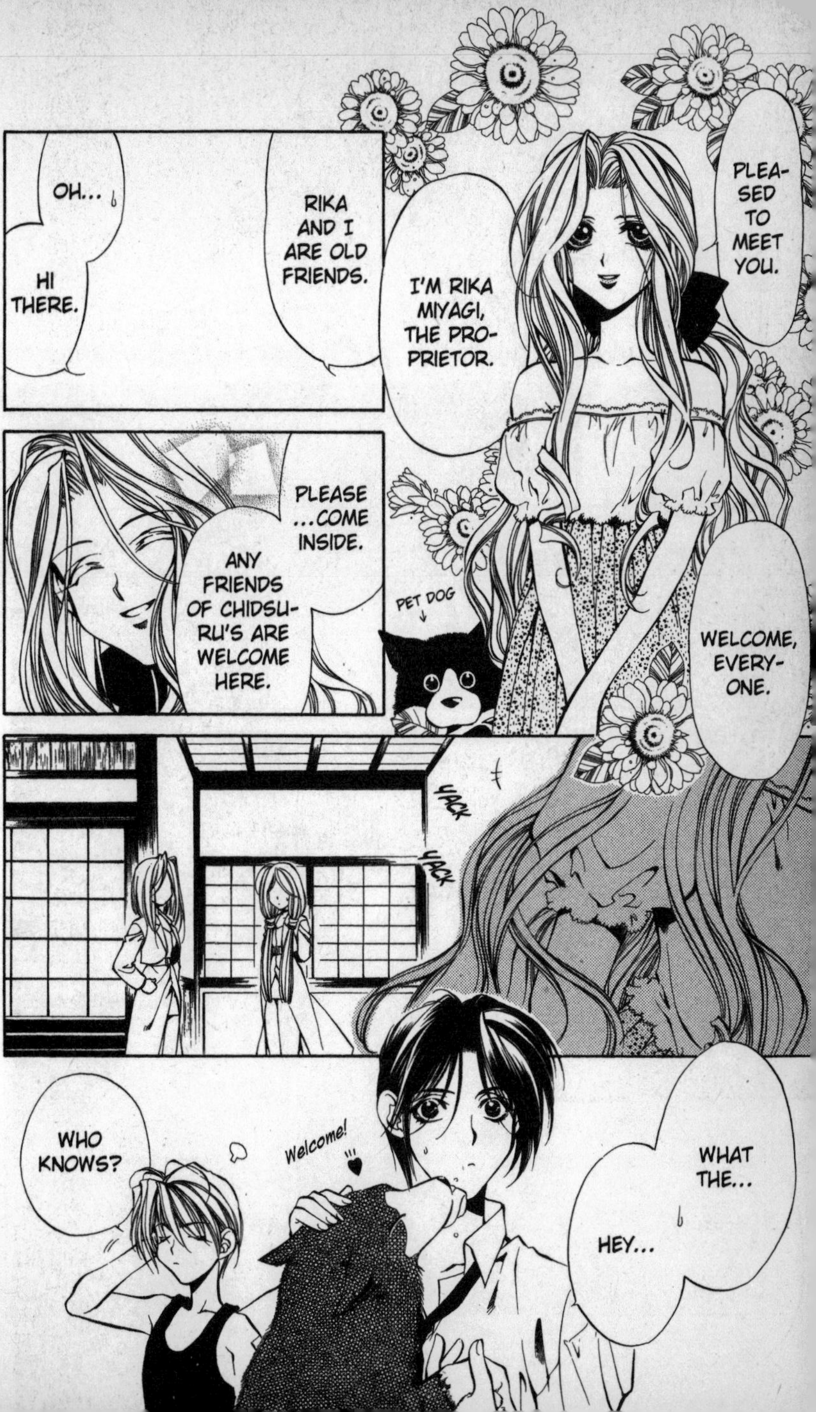
PLEA-SED TO MEET YOU.
I'M RIKA MIYAGI, THE PRO-PRIETOR.
WELCOME, EVERY-ONE.
PET DOG
RIKA AND I ARE OLD FRIENDS.
OH... HI THERE.
PLEASE ...COME INSIDE.
ANY FRIENDS OF CHIDSU-RU'S ARE WELCOME HERE.
YACK
YACK
WHAT THE... HEY...
Welcome!
WHO KNOWS?

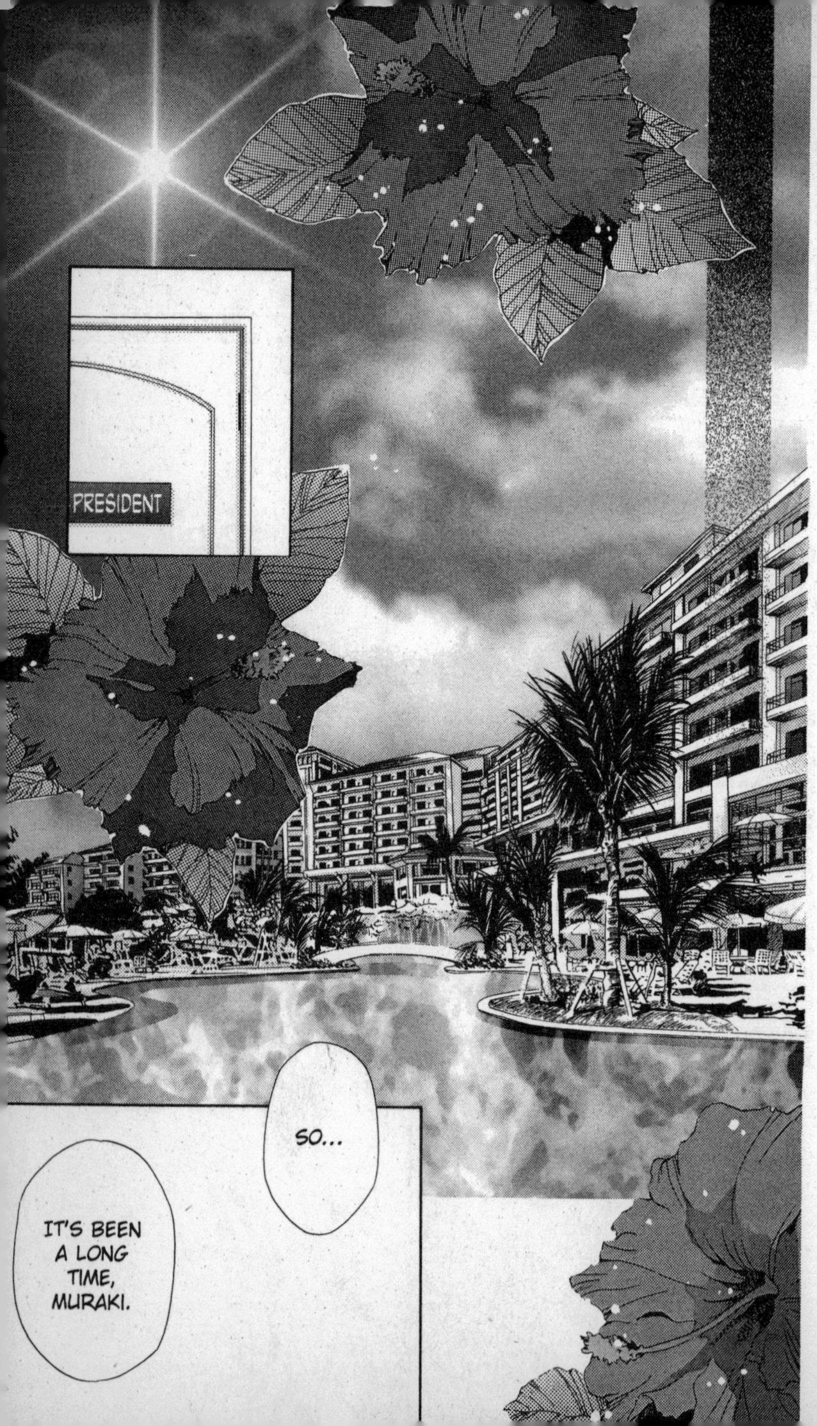
PRESIDENT
SO...
IT'S BEEN A LONG TIME, MURAKI.

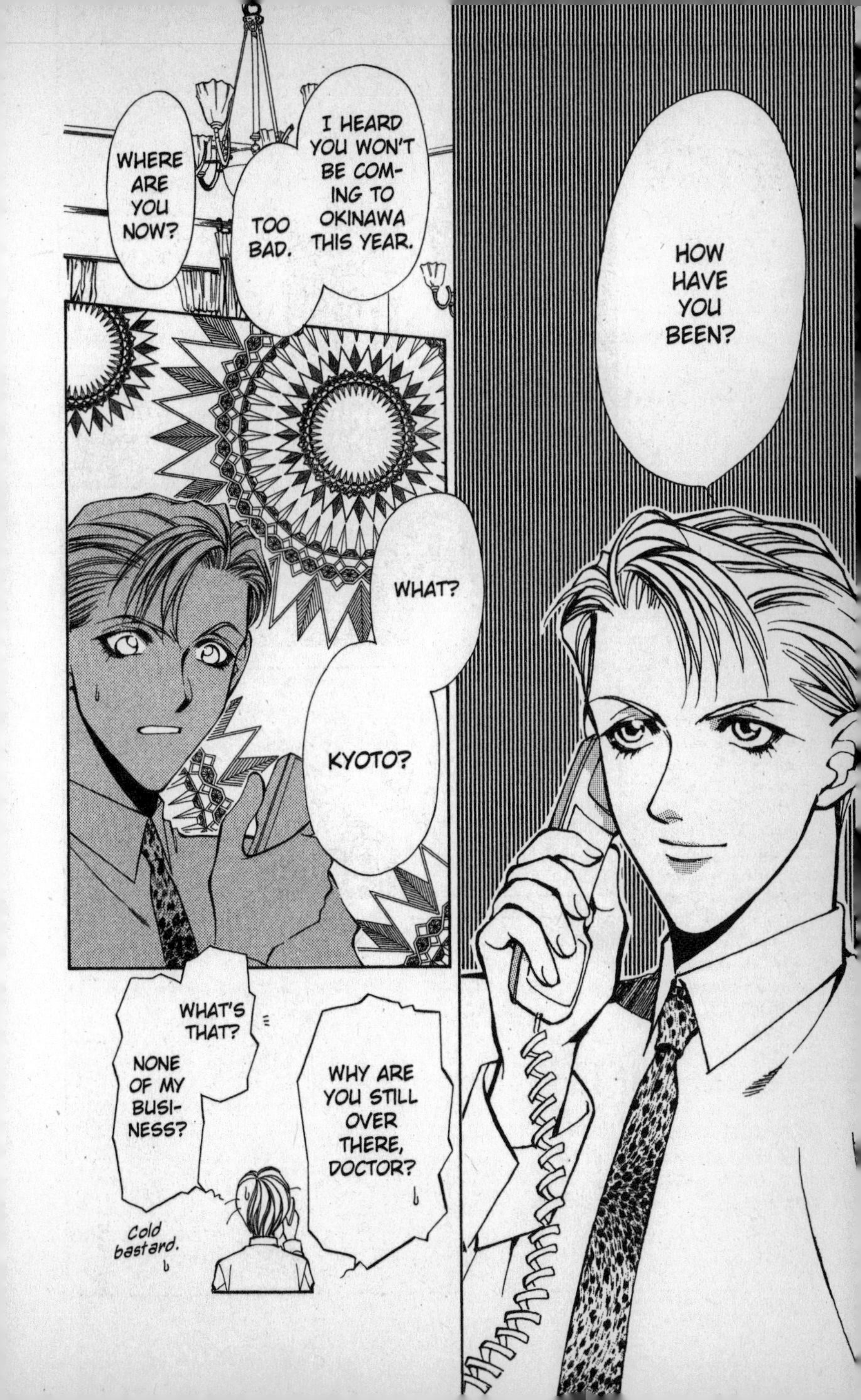
HOW HAVE YOU BEEN?
I HEARD YOU WON'T BE COMING TO OKINAWA THIS YEAR.
TOO BAD.
WHERE ARE YOU NOW?
WHAT?
KYOTO?
WHY ARE YOU STILL OVER THERE, DOCTOR?
WHAT'S THAT?
NONE OF MY BUSINESS?
Cold bastard.

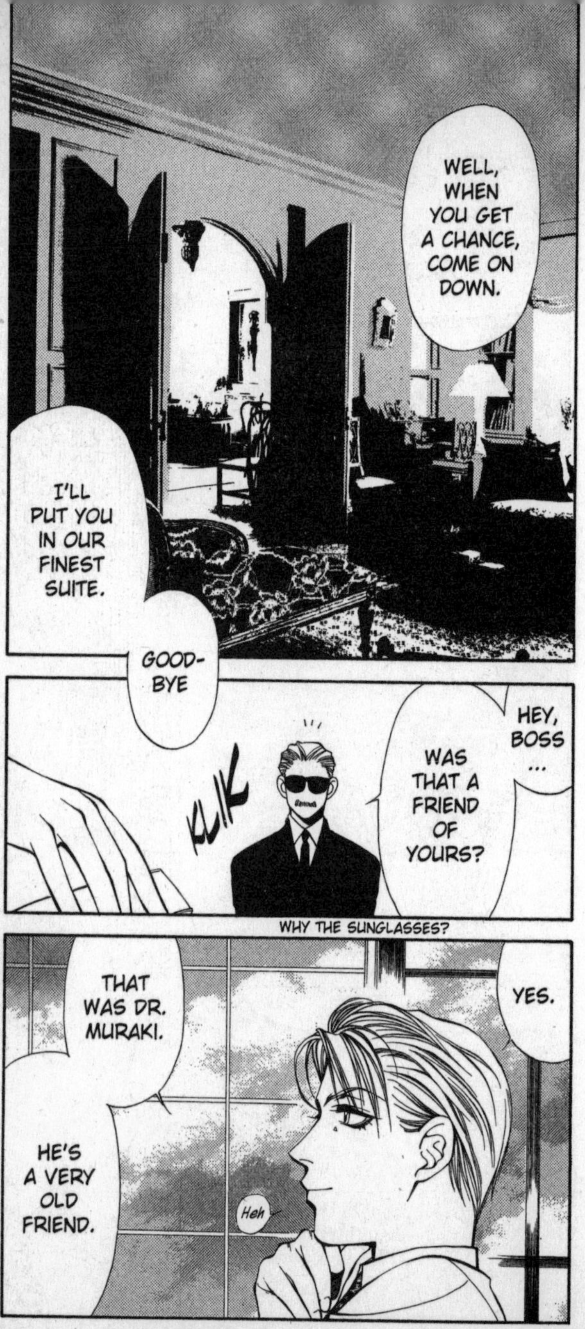
WELL, WHEN YOU GET A CHANCE, COME ON DOWN.
I'LL PUT YOU IN OUR FINEST SUITE.
GOOD-BYE
HEY, BOSS...
WAS THAT A FRIEND OF YOURS?
KLIK
WHY THE SUNGLASSES?
YES.
THAT WAS DR. MURAKI.
HE'S A VERY OLD FRIEND.
Heh

Lesson 2:
The content of the letter

The polite people who send me letters are very polite, and the rude people are terribly rude. People over the age of 20 seem to have good manners and I thoroughly enjoy their letters, but... I'd like all the students who write me to adhere to the following rules:

#1 Please make it clear to whom you are writing. (Sometimes we get very ambiguous letters.)

#2 Please be polite. Some people start their letters with, "Send me some sketches," or, "Give Hisoka a bigger role." Okay, I understand, but you're not writing to a close friend, so at least start off with "Hello" or "Dear Yoko." I want you to begin with a proper introduction. Even among friends, good manners are important, okay?

#3 Please write legibly. (Even if you have poor penmanship, do your best, and I'll be able to read it.)

Please adhere to all of the above rules when writing to me.

Lesson 3: Choosing the proper stationery

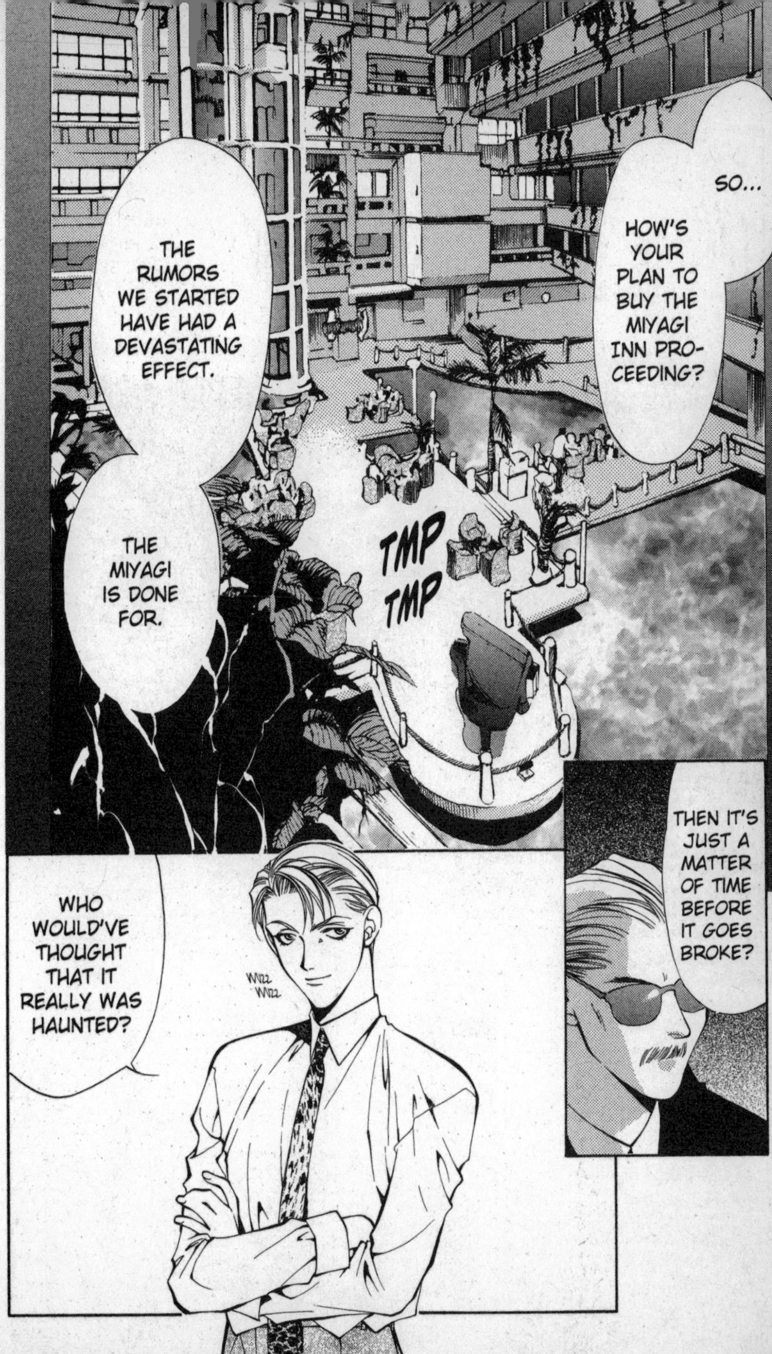
SO...
HOW'S YOUR PLAN TO BUY THE MIYAGI INN PRO-CEEDING?
THE RUMORS WE STARTED HAVE HAD A DEVASTATING EFFECT.
THE MIYAGI IS DONE FOR.
TMP TMP
THEN IT'S JUST A MATTER OF TIME BEFORE IT GOES BROKE?
WHO WOULD'VE THOUGHT THAT IT REALLY WAS HAUNTED?

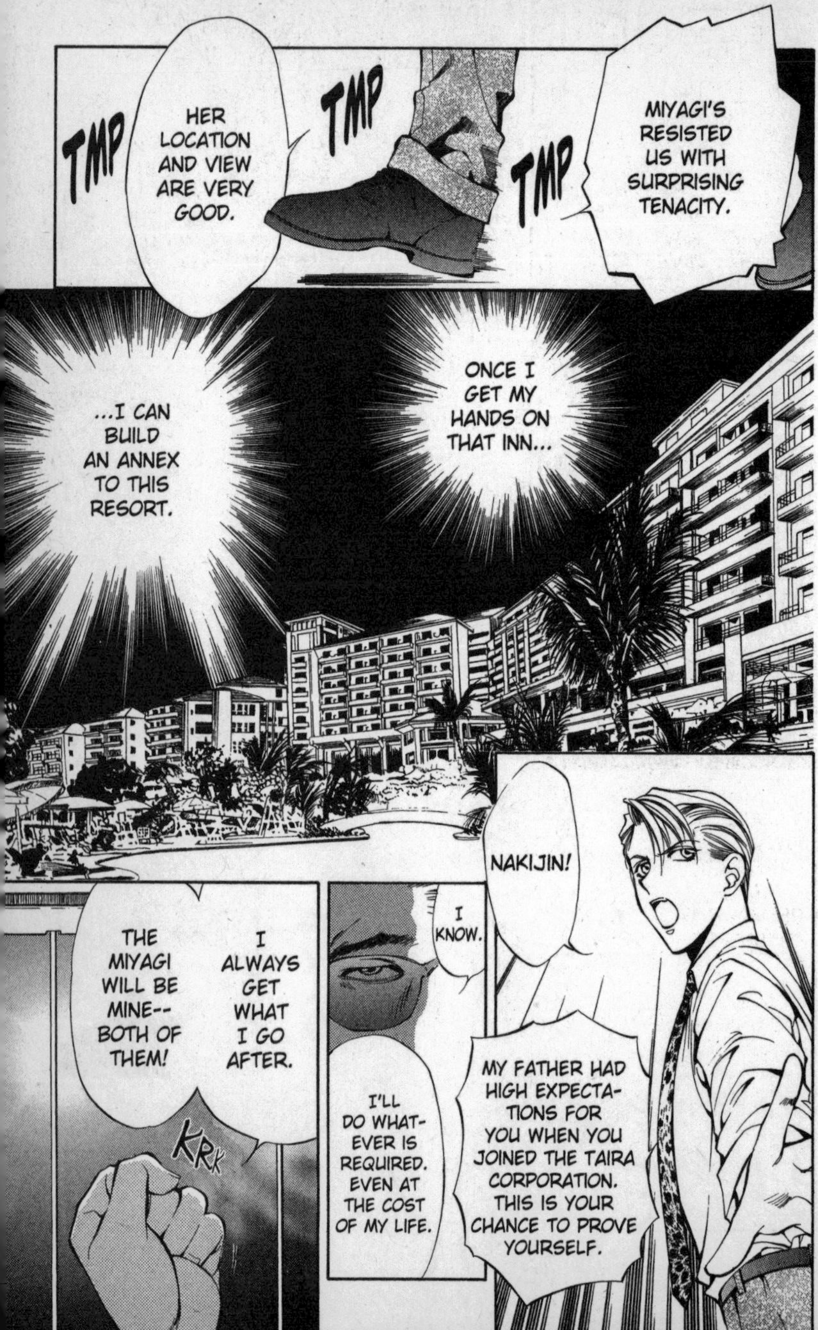
MIYAGI'S RESISTED US WITH SURPRISING TENACITY.
TMP
TMP
HER LOCATION AND VIEW ARE VERY GOOD.
TMP
ONCE I GET MY HANDS ON THAT INN...
...I CAN BUILD AN ANNEX TO THIS RESORT.
NAKIJIN!
MY FATHER HAD HIGH EXPECTATIONS FOR YOU WHEN YOU JOINED THE TAIRA CORPORATION. THIS IS YOUR CHANCE TO PROVE YOURSELF.
I KNOW.
I'LL DO WHATEVER IS REQUIRED. EVEN AT THE COST OF MY LIFE.
I ALWAYS GET WHAT I GO AFTER.
THE MIYAGI WILL BE MINE-- BOTH OF THEM!
KRK

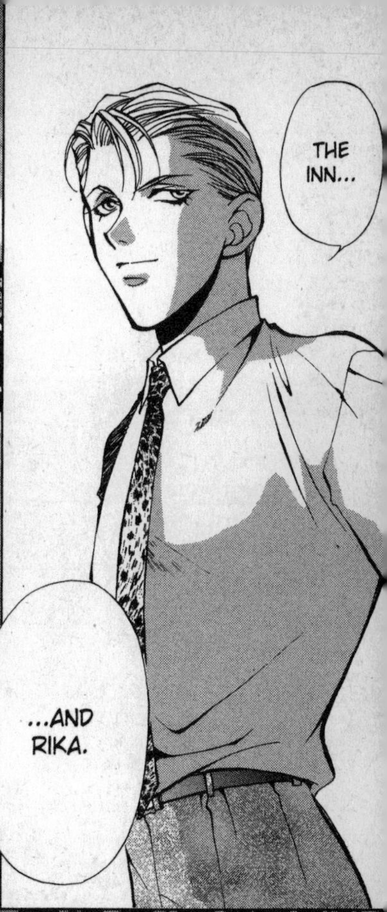
THE INN...
...AND RIKA.
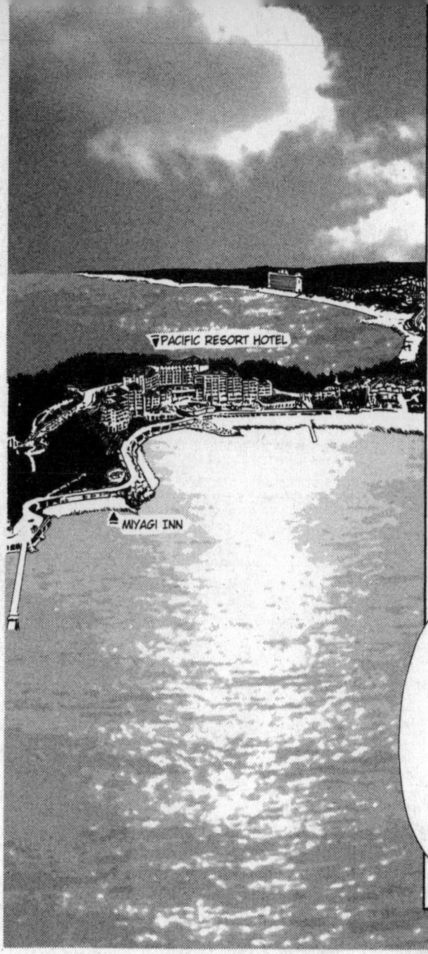
PACIFIC RESORT HOTEL
MIYAGI INN
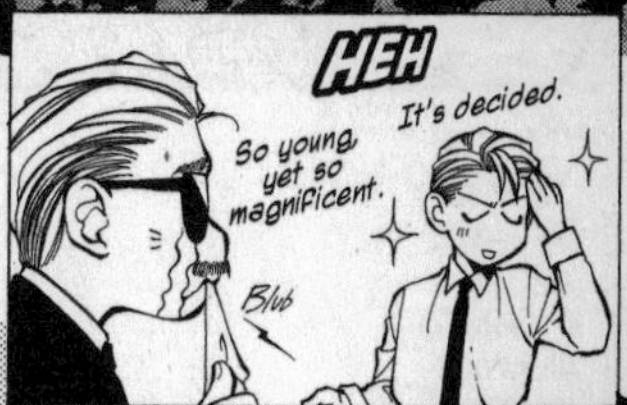
HEH
It's decided.
So young, yet so magnificent.
Blub
STUPID
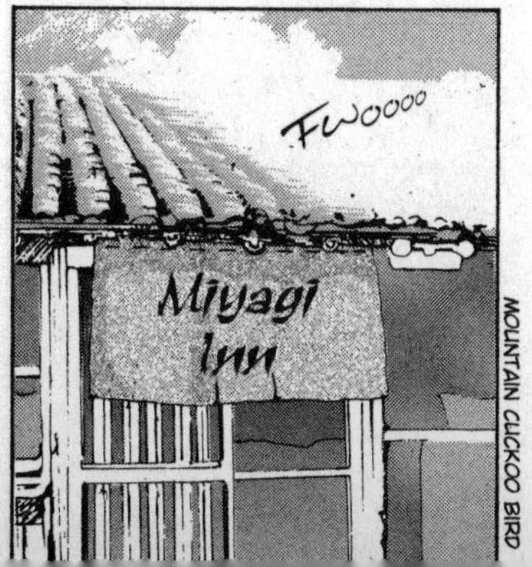
FWOOOO
Miyagi Inn
MOUNTAIN CUCKOO BIRD

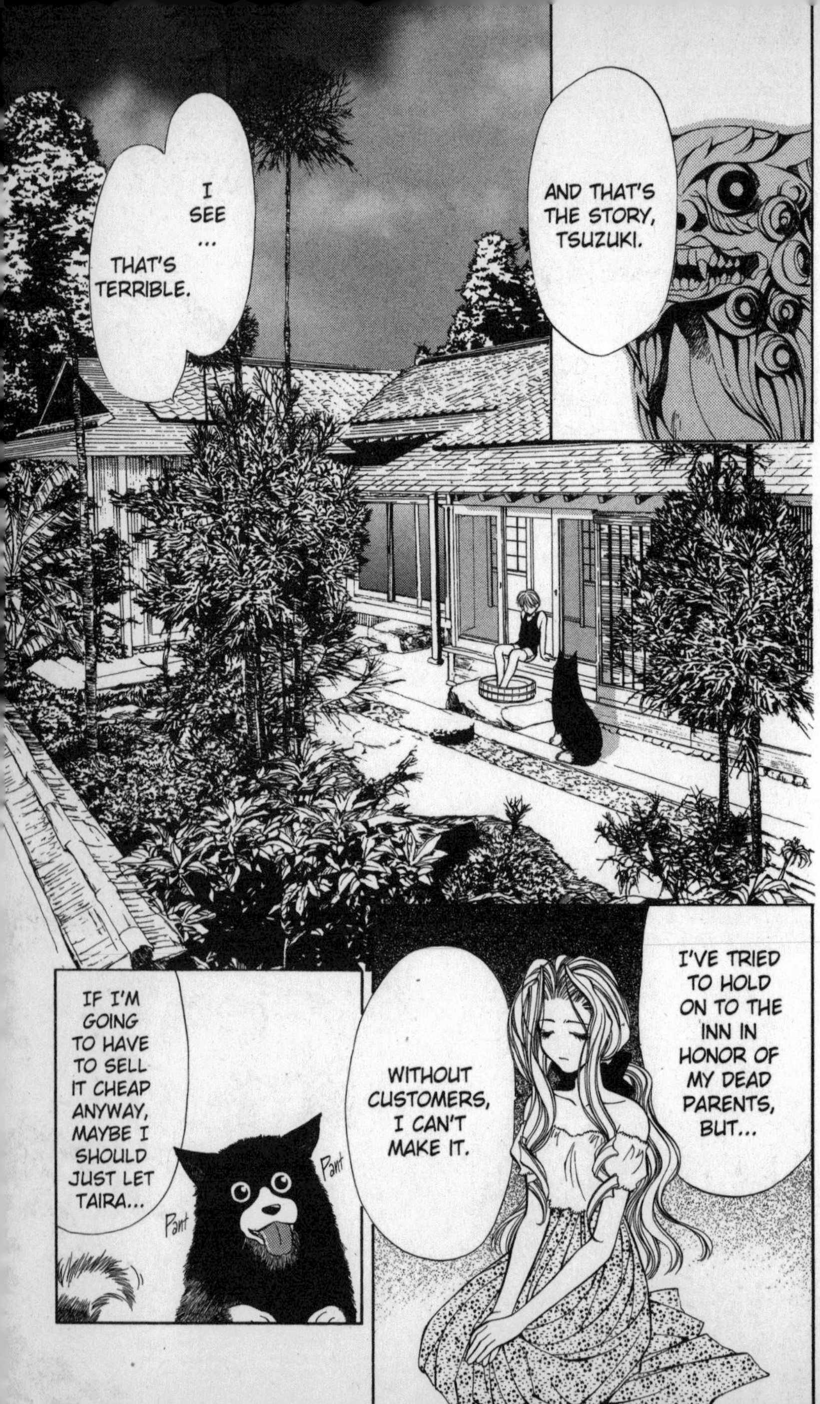
AND THAT'S THE STORY, TSUZUKI.
I SEE ... THAT'S TERRIBLE.
I'VE TRIED TO HOLD ON TO THE INN IN HONOR OF MY DEAD PARENTS, BUT...
WITHOUT CUSTOMERS, I CAN'T MAKE IT.
IF I'M GOING TO HAVE TO SELL IT CHEAP ANYWAY, MAYBE I SHOULD JUST LET TAIRA...
Pant
Pant

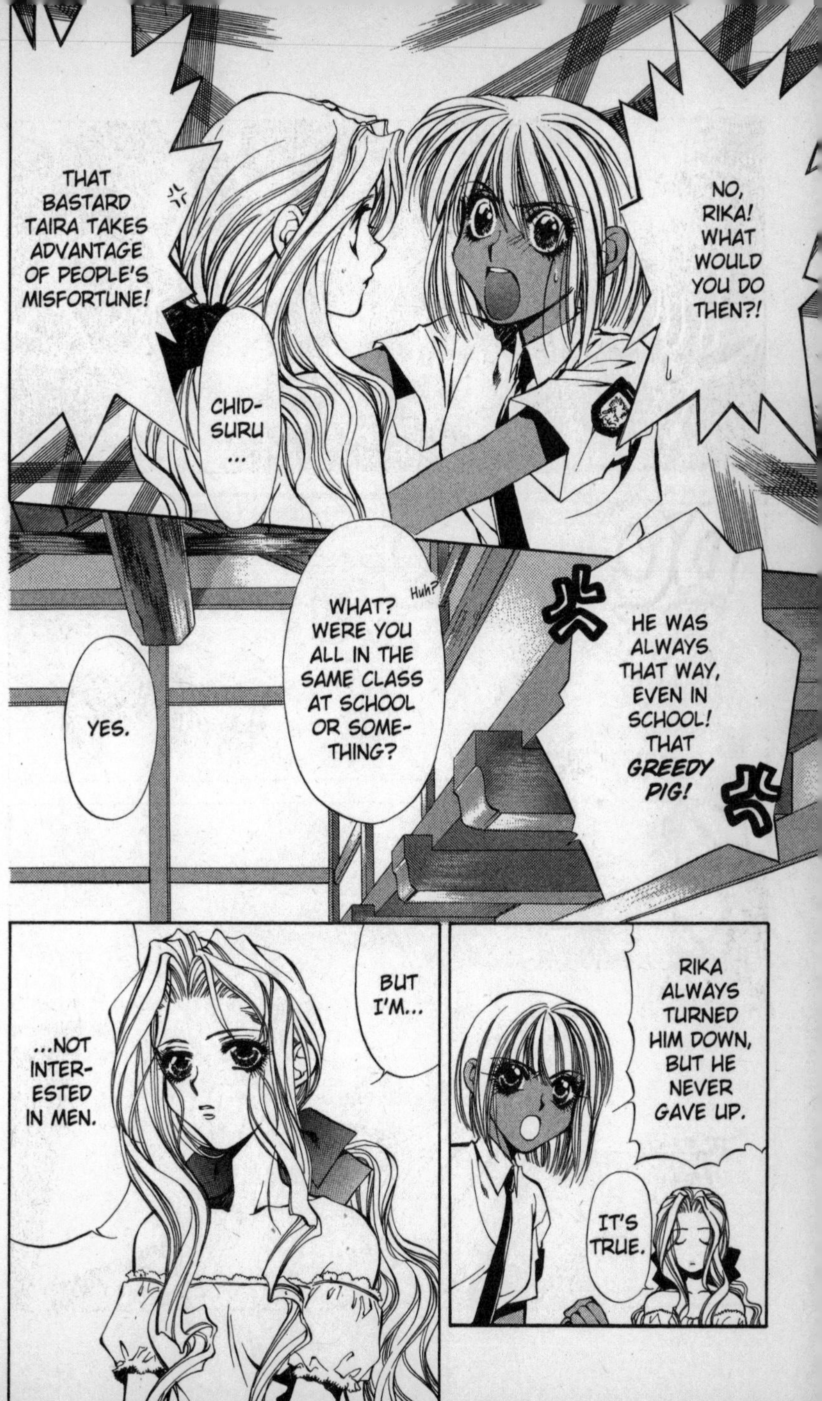
NO, RIKA! WHAT WOULD YOU DO THEN?!
THAT BASTARD TAIRA TAKES ADVANTAGE OF PEOPLE'S MISFORTUNE!
CHID-SURU ...
HE WAS ALWAYS THAT WAY, EVEN IN SCHOOL! THAT GREEDY PIG!
Huh?
WHAT? WERE YOU ALL IN THE SAME CLASS AT SCHOOL OR SOME-THING?
YES.
RIKA ALWAYS TURNED HIM DOWN, BUT HE NEVER GAVE UP.
IT'S TRUE.
BUT I'M...
...NOT INTER-ESTED IN MEN.

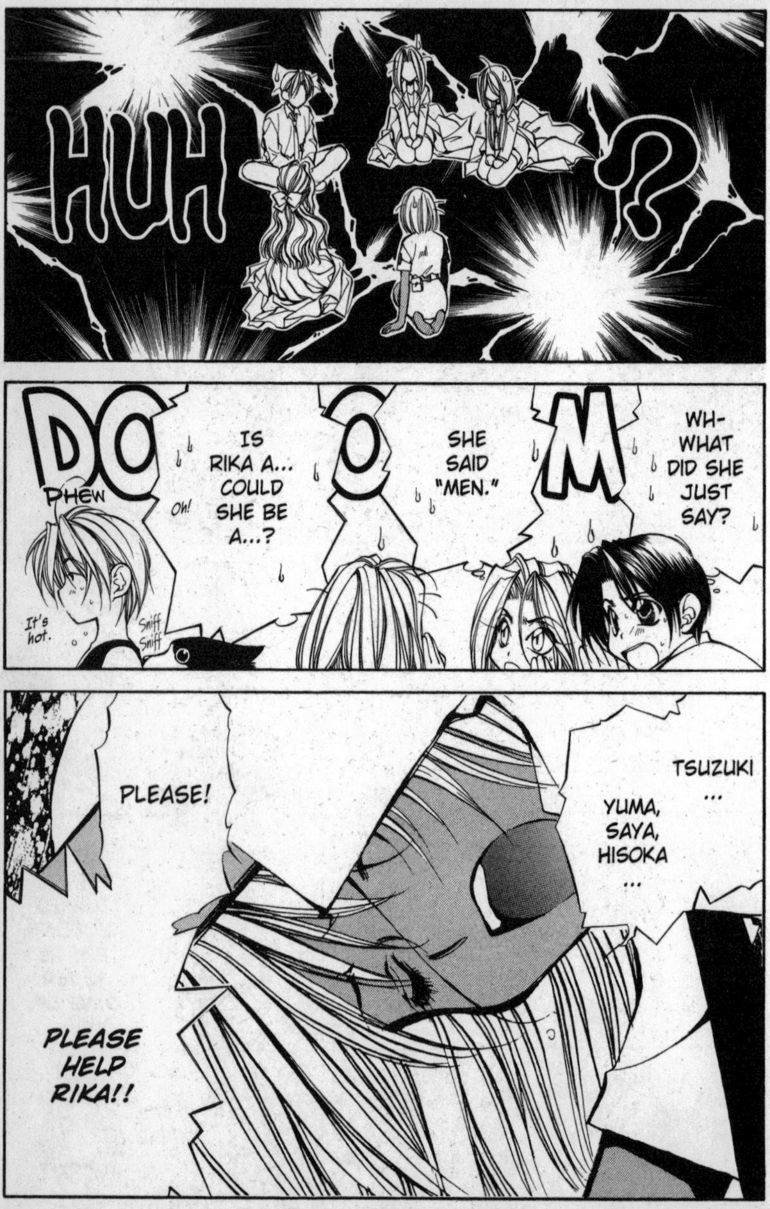
HUH
?
DO O M
WH- WHAT DID SHE JUST SAY?
SHE SAID "MEN."
IS RIKA A... COULD SHE BE A...?
Oh!
PHEW
Sniff Sniff
It's hot.
TSUZUKI ...
YUMA, SAYA, HISOKA ...
PLEASE!
PLEASE HELP RIKA!!

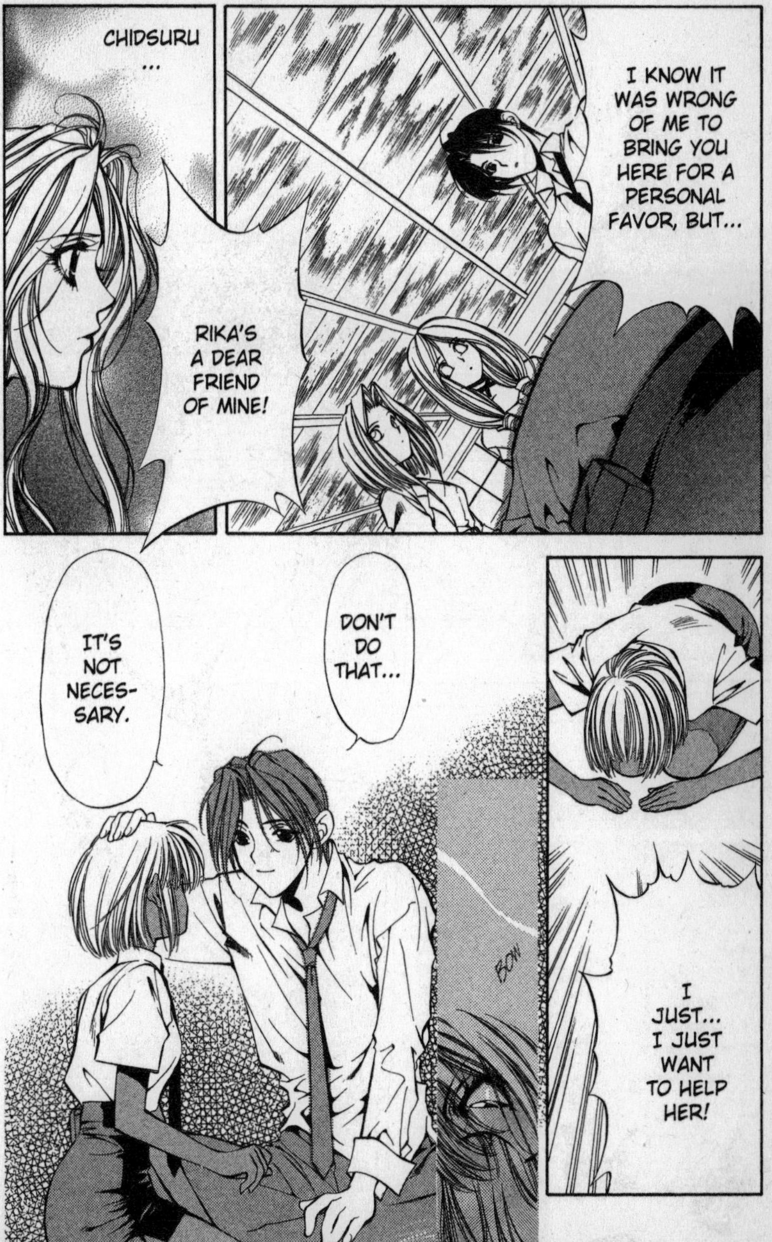
I KNOW IT WAS WRONG OF ME TO BRING YOU HERE FOR A PERSONAL FAVOR, BUT...
RIKA'S A DEAR FRIEND OF MINE!
CHIDSURU ...
BOW
I JUST... I JUST WANT TO HELP HER!
DON'T DO THAT...
IT'S NOT NECES-SARY.

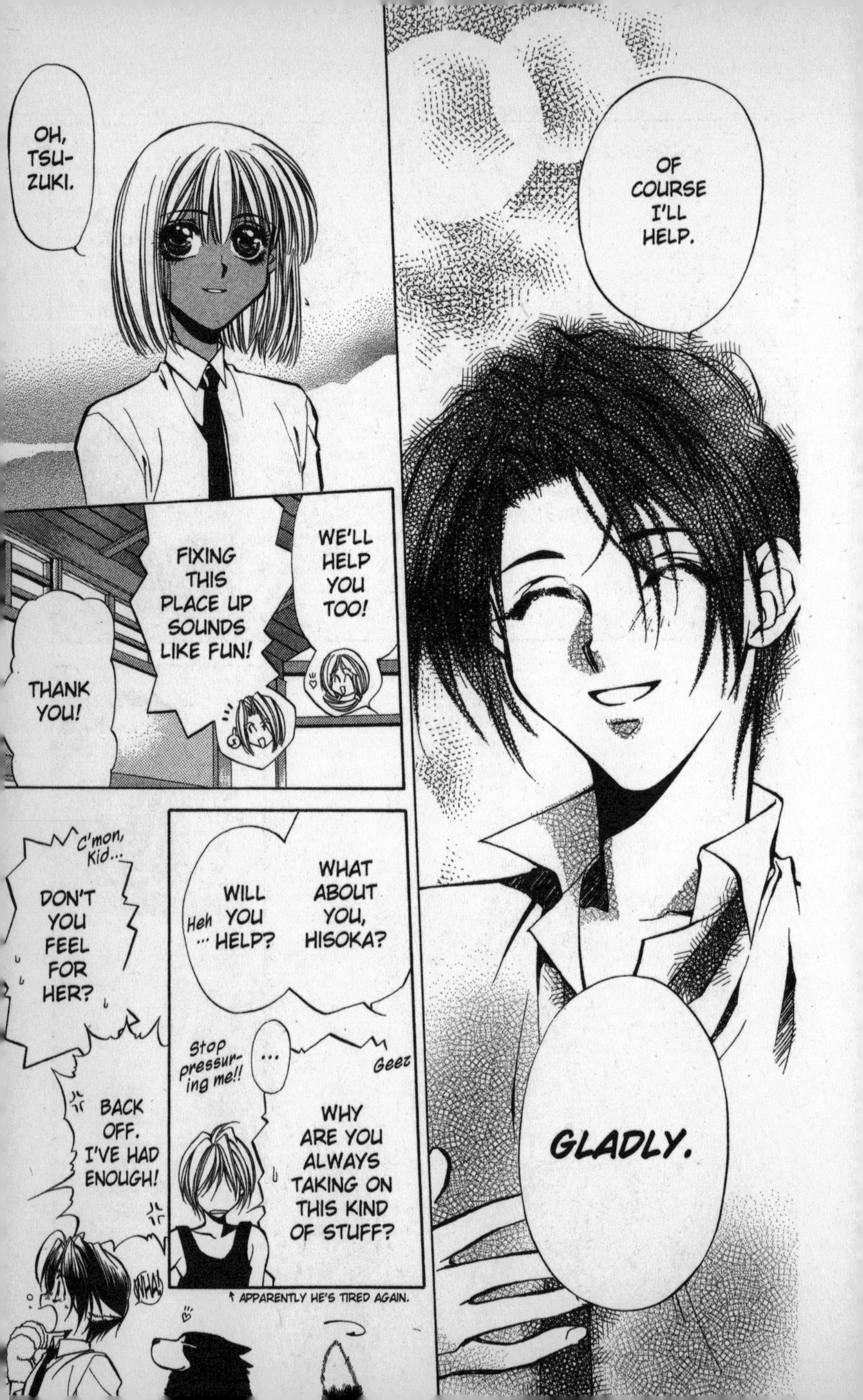
OF COURSE I'LL HELP.
GLADLY.
OH, TSU-ZUKI.
WE'LL HELP YOU TOO!
FIXING THIS PLACE UP SOUNDS LIKE FUN!
THANK YOU!
WHAT ABOUT YOU, HISOKA?
WILL YOU HELP?
Heh ...
Geez
...
WHY ARE YOU ALWAYS TAKING ON THIS KIND OF STUFF?
Stop pressuring me!!
C'mon, Kid...
DON'T YOU FEEL FOR HER?
BACK OFF. I'VE HAD ENOUGH!
WHA!
↑ APPARENTLY HE'S TIRED AGAIN.

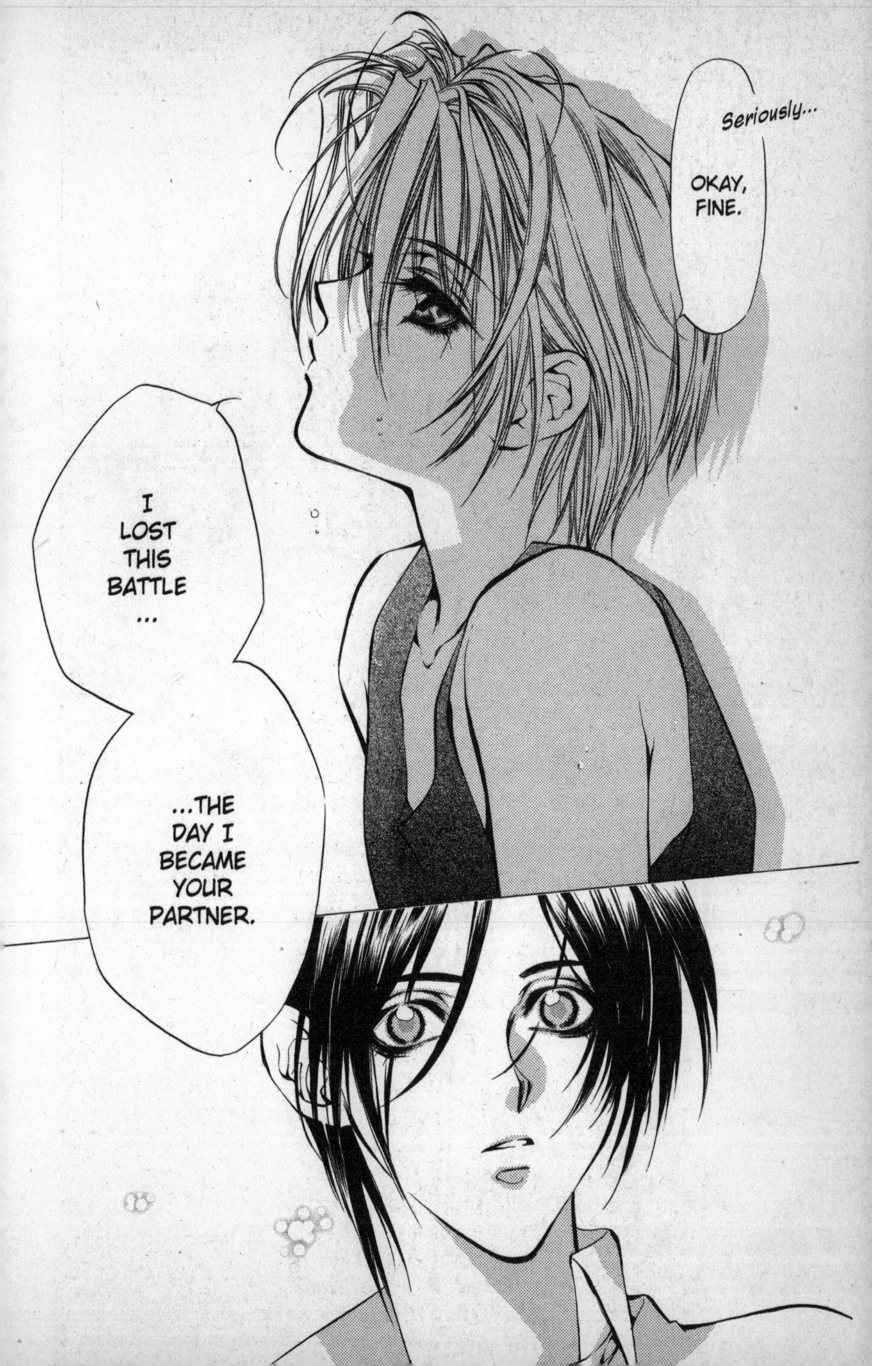
Seriously...
OKAY, FINE.
I LOST THIS BATTLE...
...THE DAY I BECAME YOUR PARTNER.

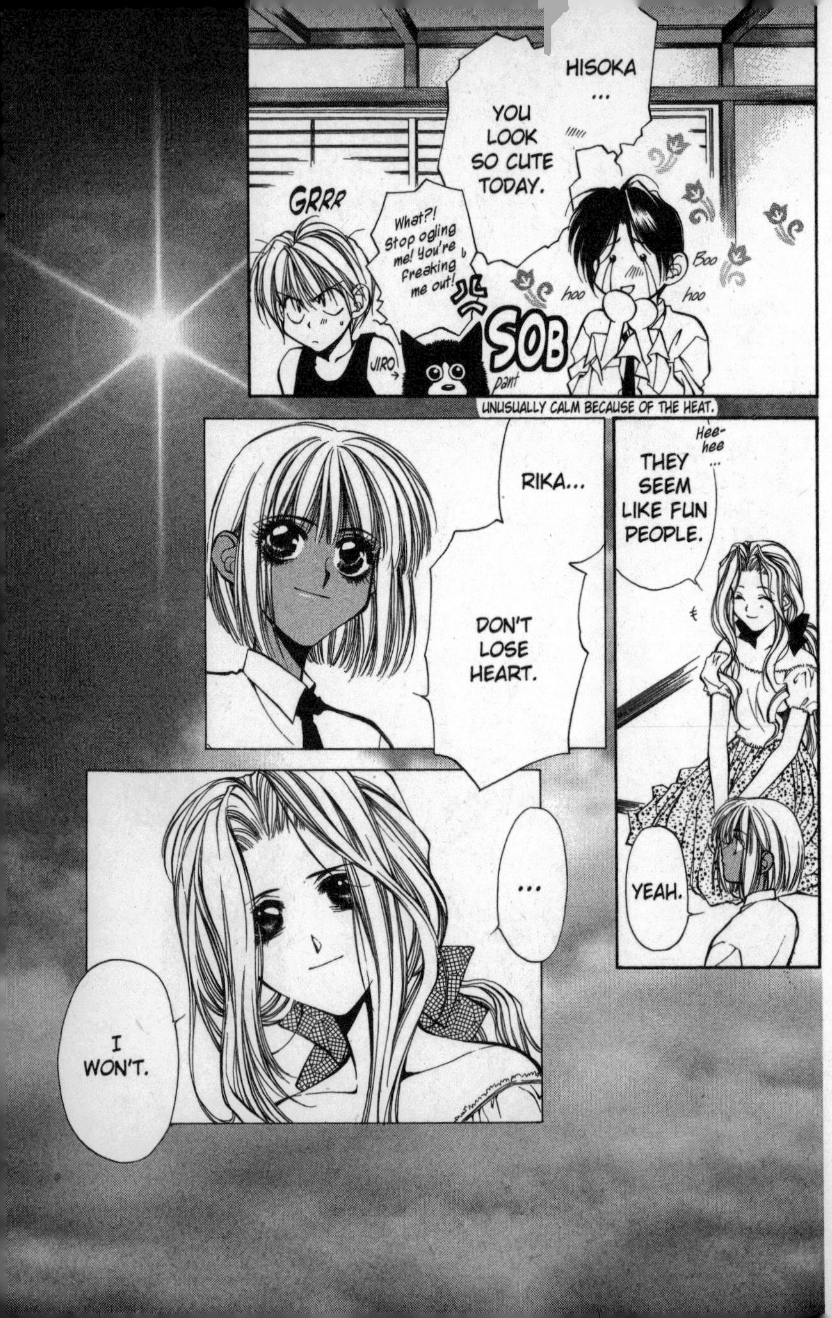
HISOKA ...
YOU LOOK SO CUTE TODAY.
Boo hoo
SOB
What?! Stop ogling me! You're freaking me out!
GRRR
JIRO
pant
UNUSUALLY CALM BECAUSE OF THE HEAT.
Hee-hee ...
THEY SEEM LIKE FUN PEOPLE.
YEAH.
RIKA...
DON'T LOSE HEART.
...
I WON'T.

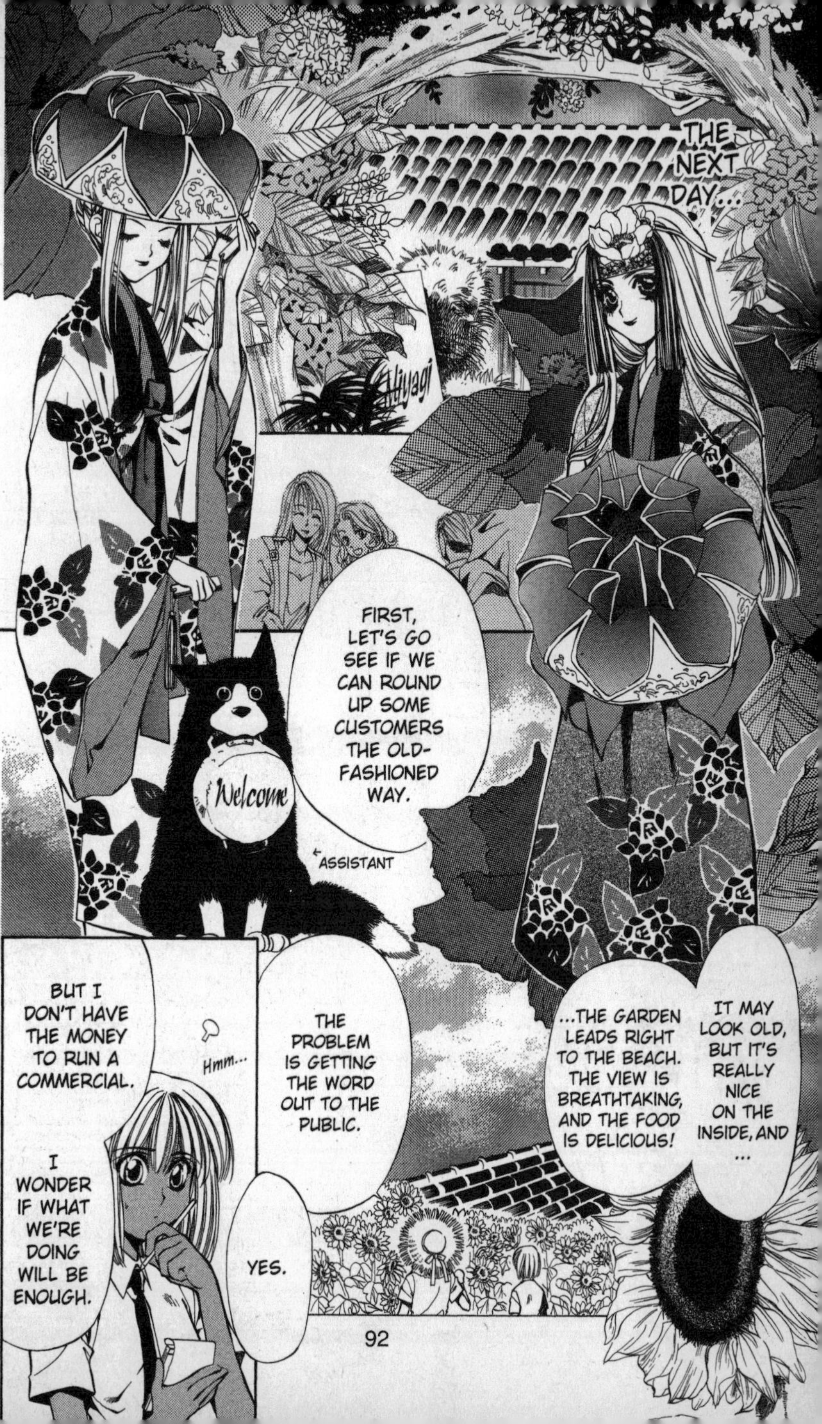

THE NEXT DAY...
Miyagi
FIRST, LET'S GO SEE IF WE CAN ROUND UP SOME CUSTOMERS THE OLD-FASHIONED WAY.
Welcome
ASSISTANT
IT MAY LOOK OLD, BUT IT'S REALLY NICE ON THE INSIDE, AND ...
...THE GARDEN LEADS RIGHT TO THE BEACH. THE VIEW IS BREATHTAKING, AND THE FOOD IS DELICIOUS!
THE PROBLEM IS GETTING THE WORD OUT TO THE PUBLIC.
YES.
Hmm...
BUT I DON'T HAVE THE MONEY TO RUN A COMMERCIAL.
I WONDER IF WHAT WE'RE DOING WILL BE ENOUGH.

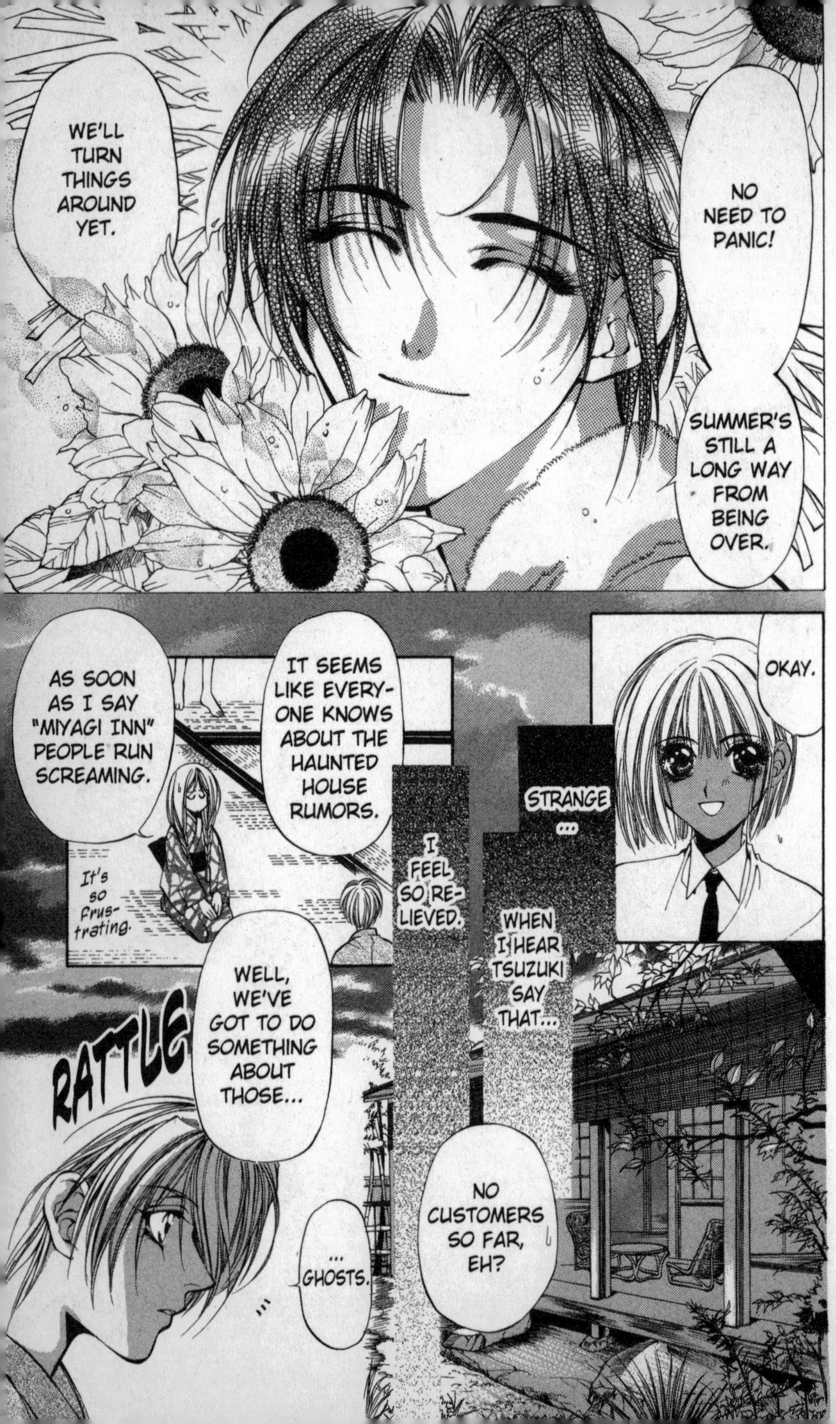
NO NEED TO PANIC!
SUMMER'S STILL A LONG WAY FROM BEING OVER.
WE'LL TURN THINGS AROUND YET.
OKAY.
STRANGE...
WHEN I HEAR TSUZUKI SAY THAT...
I FEEL SO RE-LIEVED.
NO CUSTOMERS SO FAR, EH?
IT SEEMS LIKE EVERY-ONE KNOWS ABOUT THE HAUNTED HOUSE RUMORS.
AS SOON AS I SAY "MIYAGI INN" PEOPLE RUN SCREAMING.
It's so frus-trating.
WELL, WE'VE GOT TO DO SOMETHING ABOUT THOSE...
RATTLE
... GHOSTS.

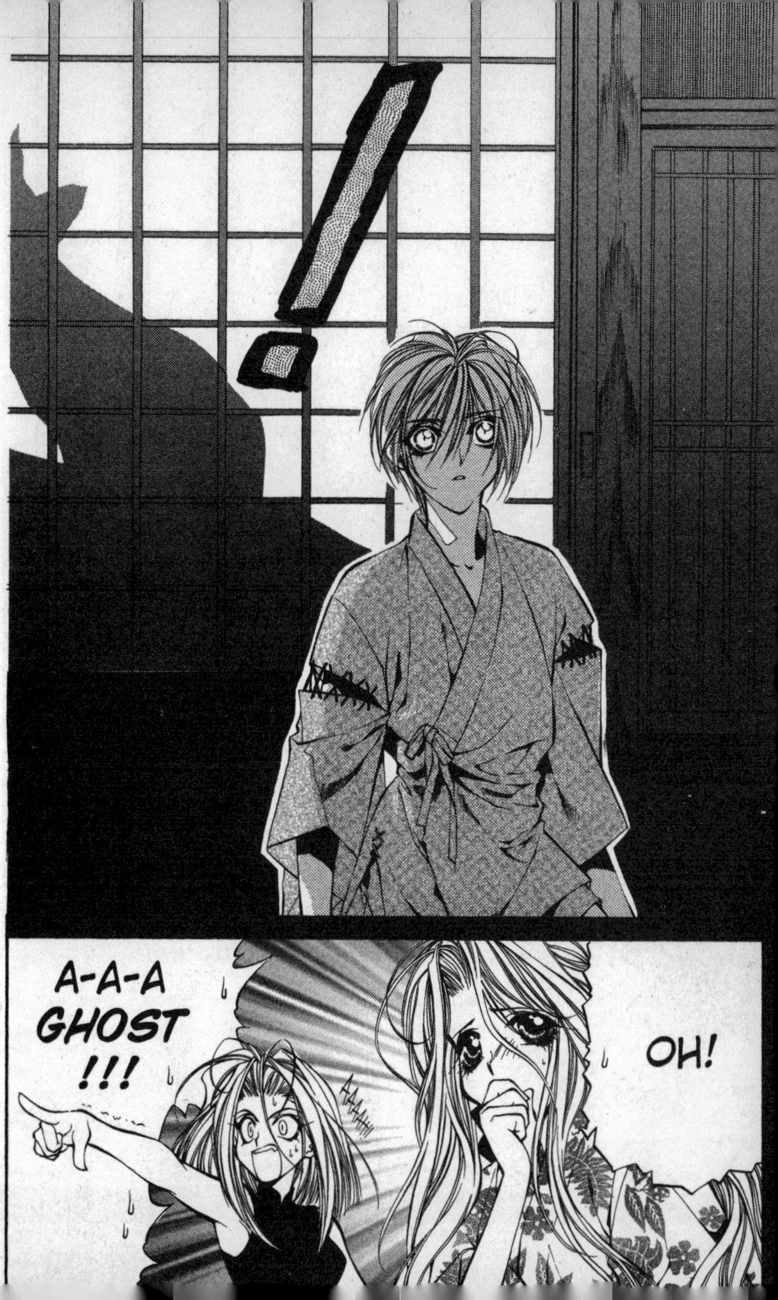
OH!
A-A-A GHOST !!!

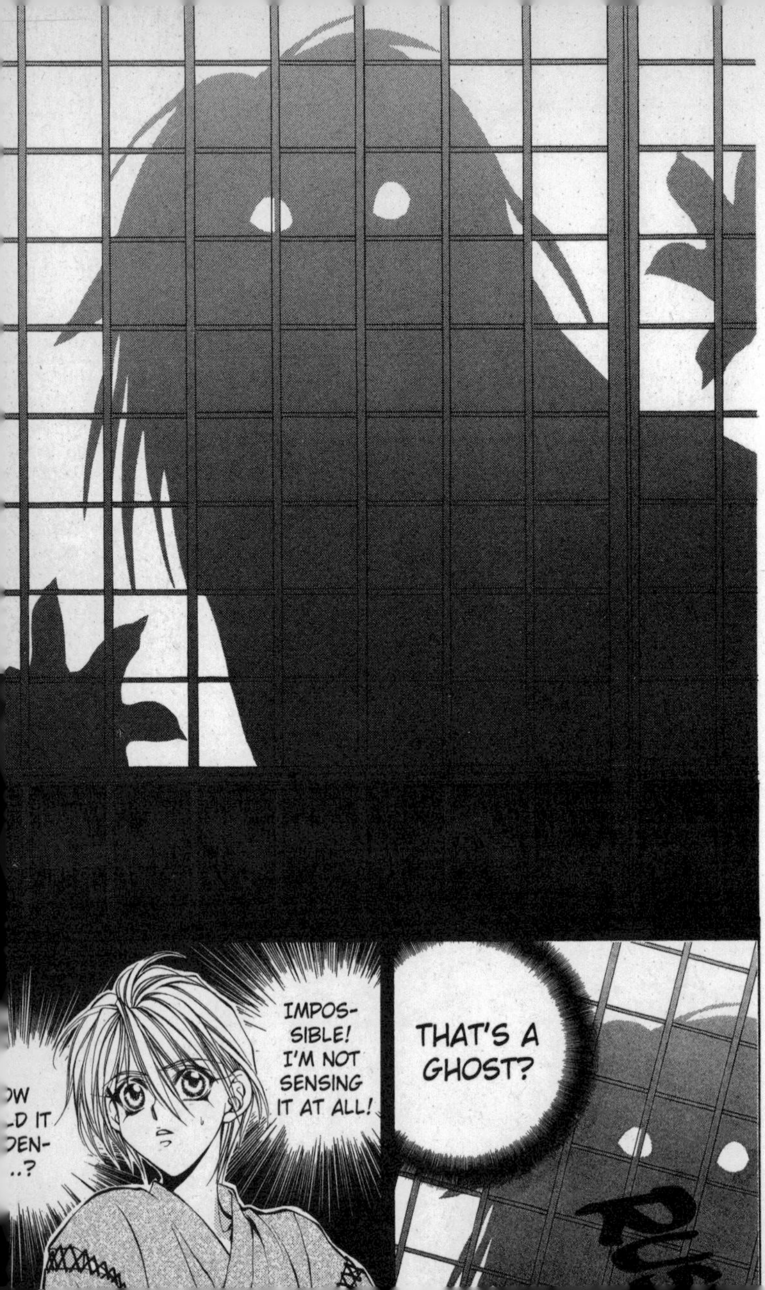
THAT'S A GHOST?
IMPOS-
SIBLE!
I'M NOT
SENSING
IT AT ALL!

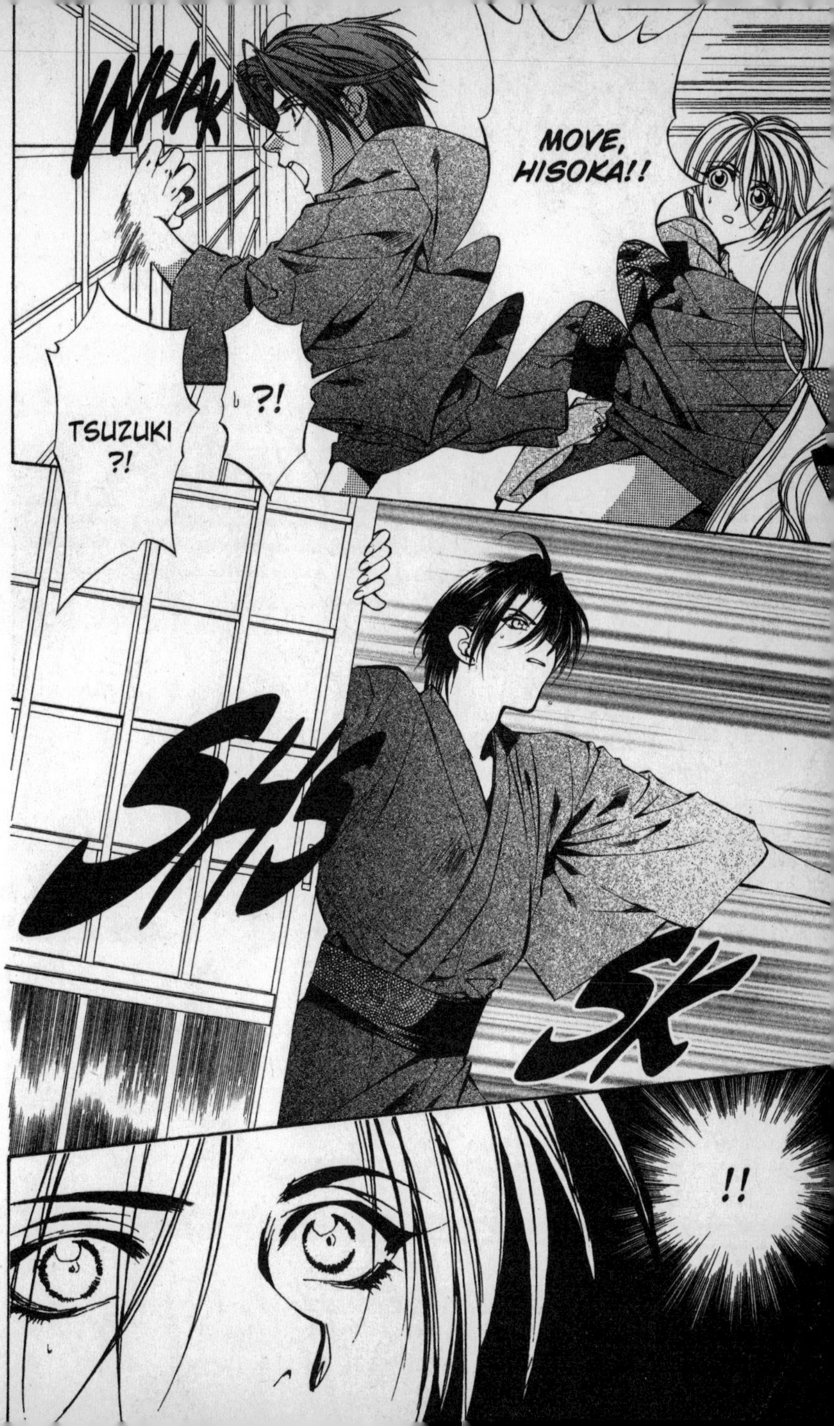
MOVE, HISOKA!!
WHAK
?!
TSUZUKI ?!
SK
SHS
!!

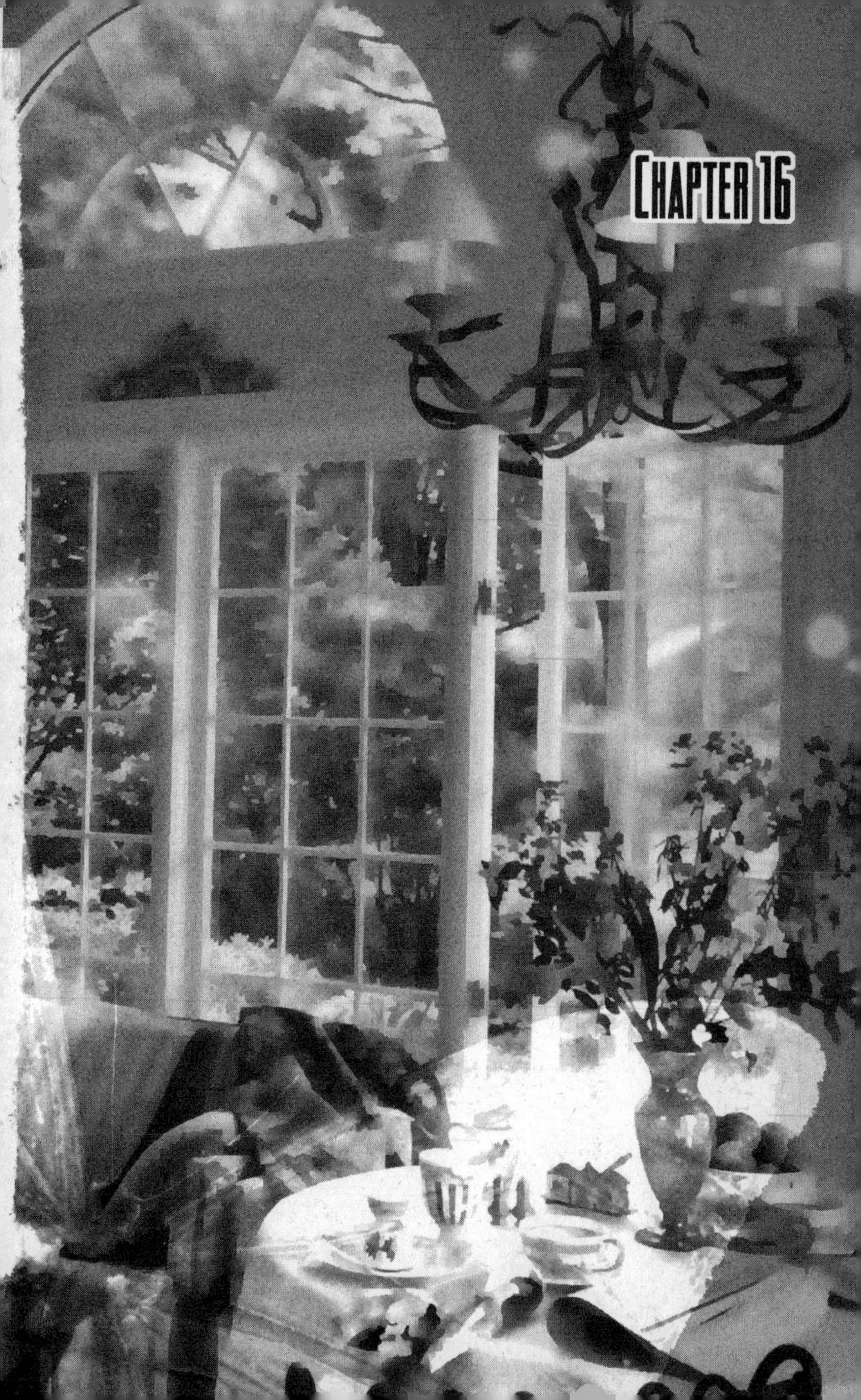
CHAPTER 16

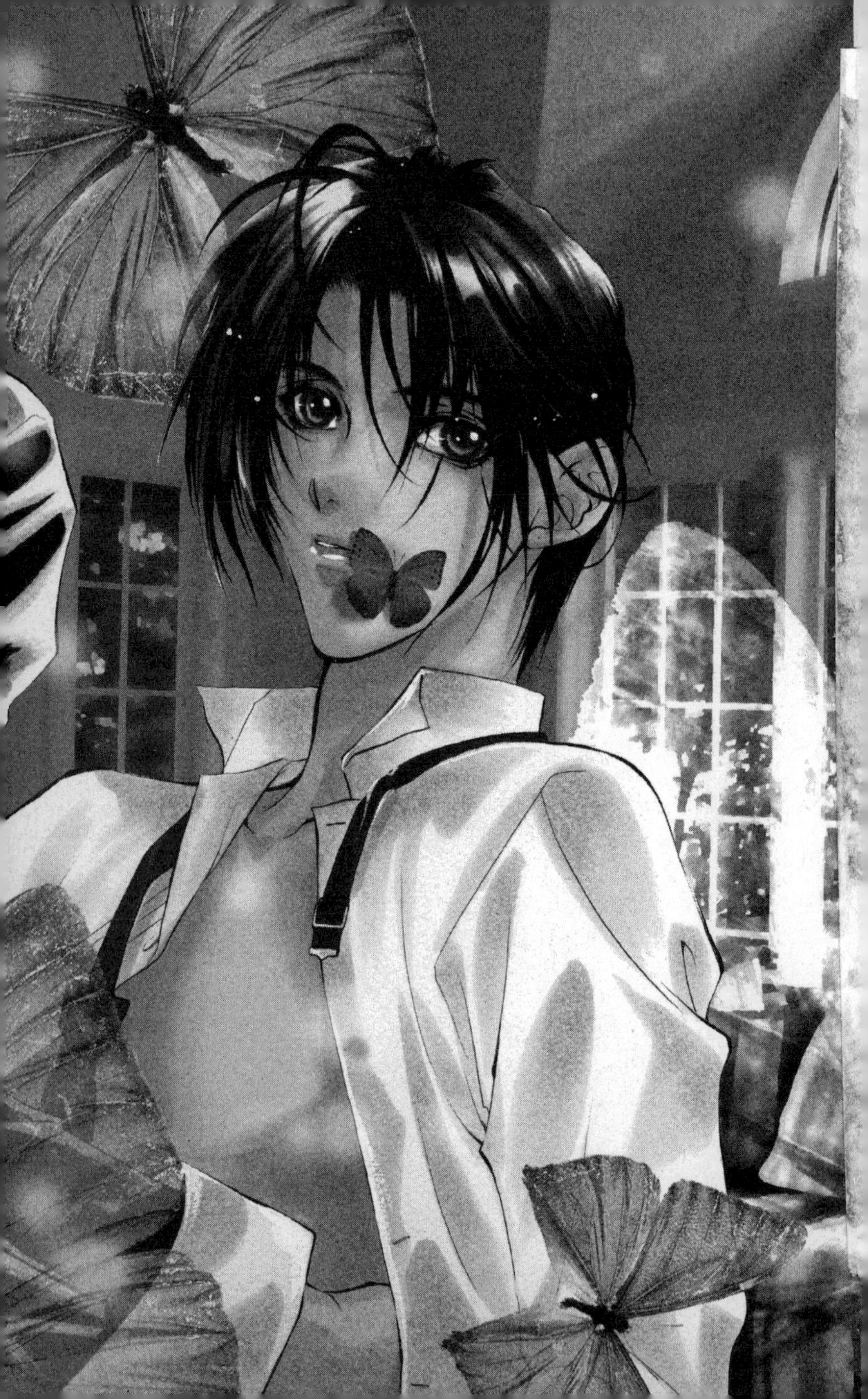

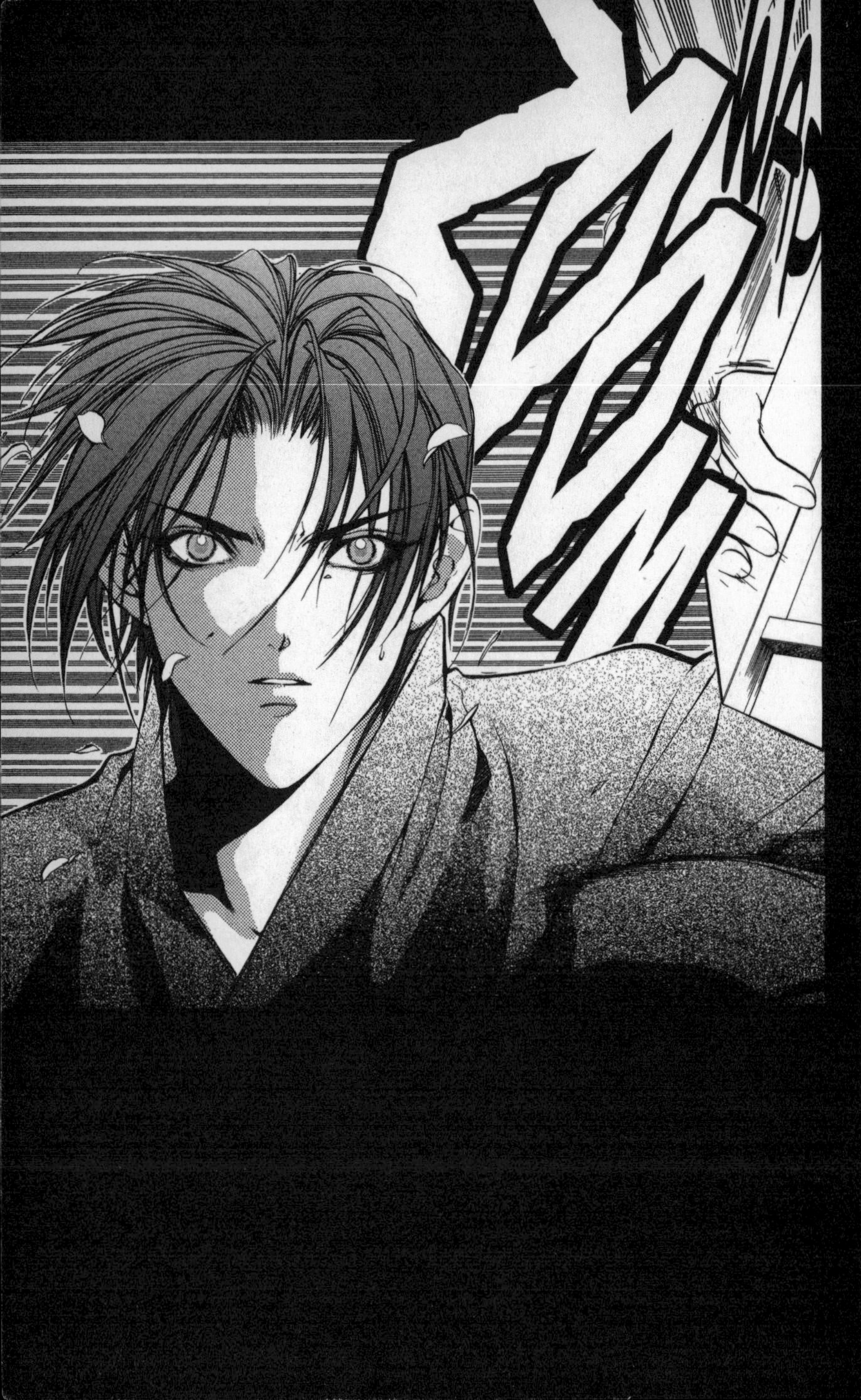

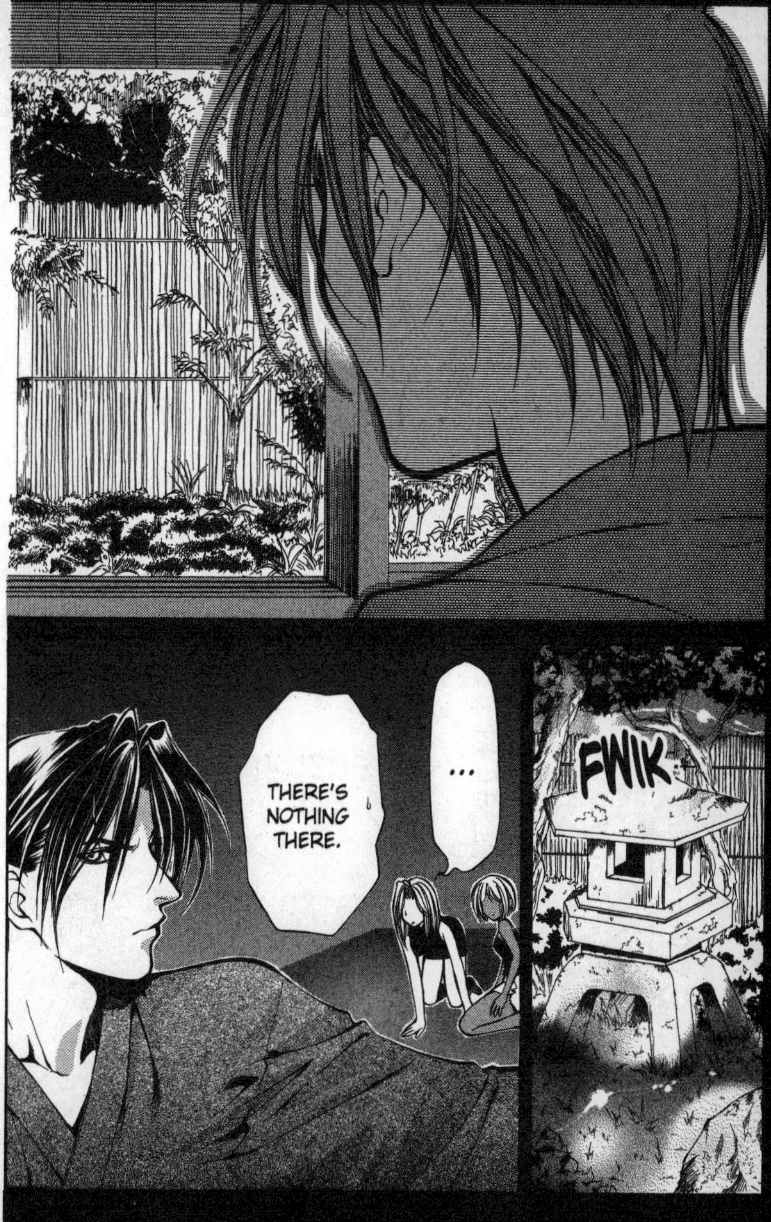
FWIK
...
THERE'S NOTHING THERE.

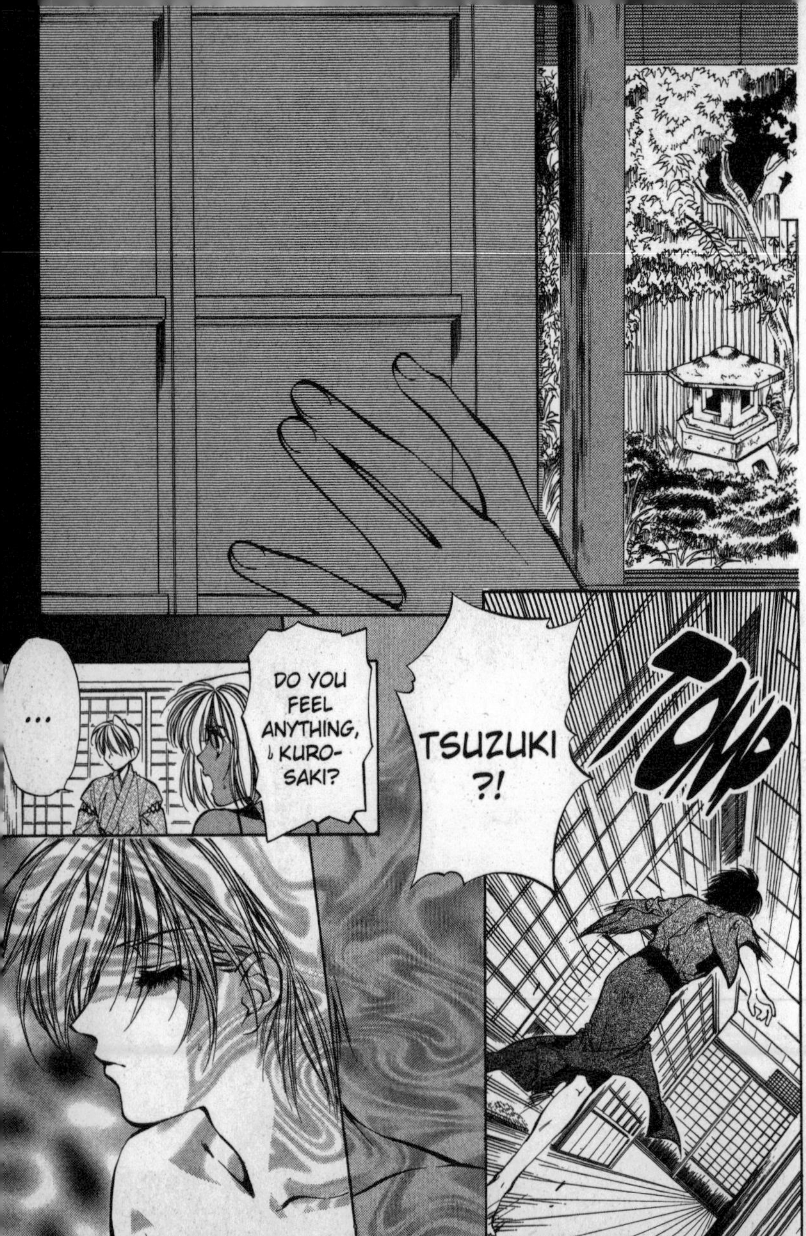
TONP
TSUZUKI ?!
DO YOU FEEL ANYTHING, KURO-SAKI?
...

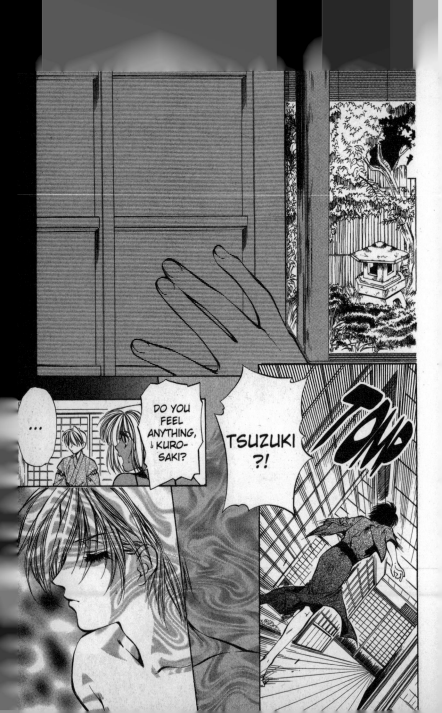

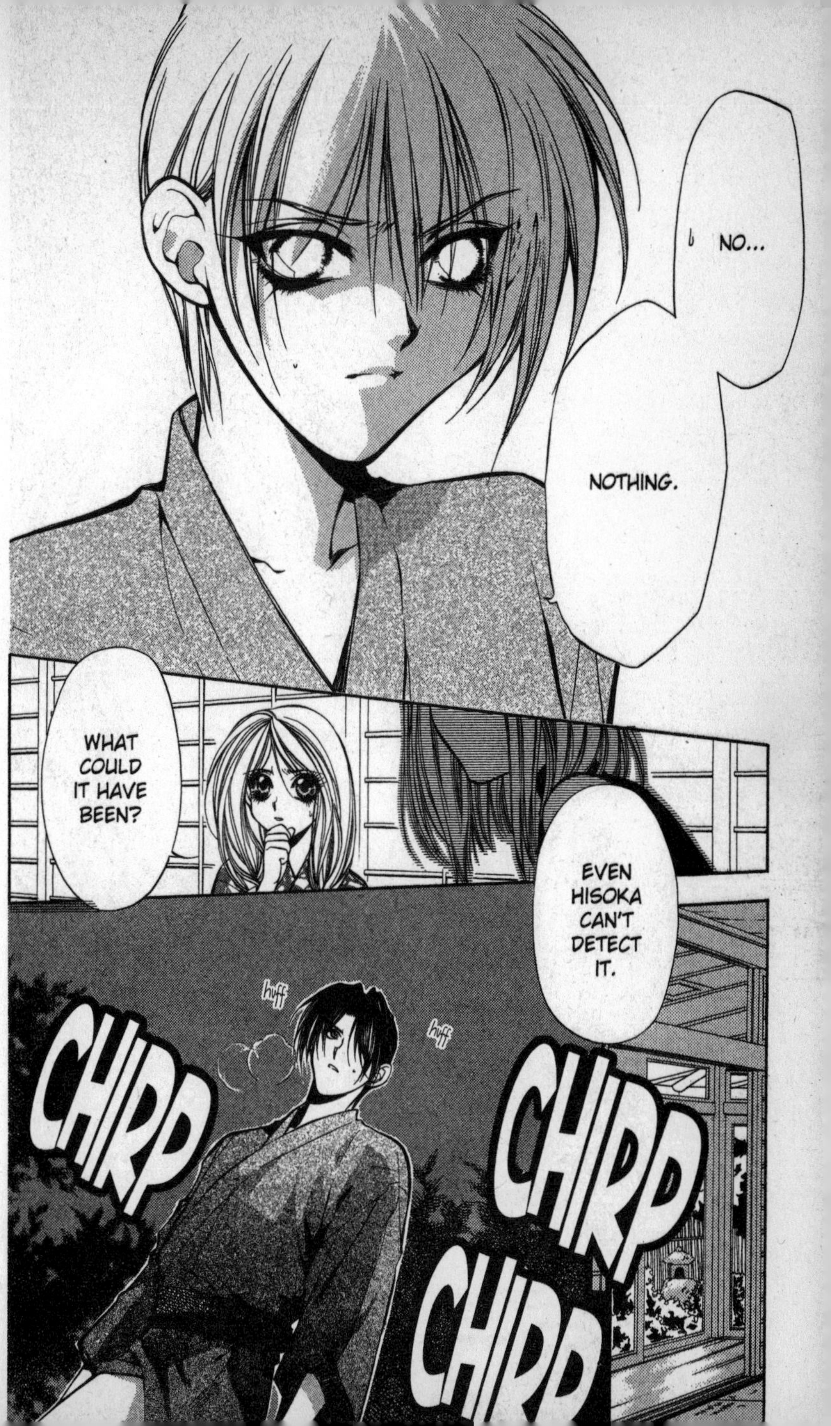
NO...
NOTHING.
EVEN HISOKA CAN'T DETECT IT.
WHAT COULD IT HAVE BEEN?
huff
huff
CHIRP
CHIRP
CHIRP

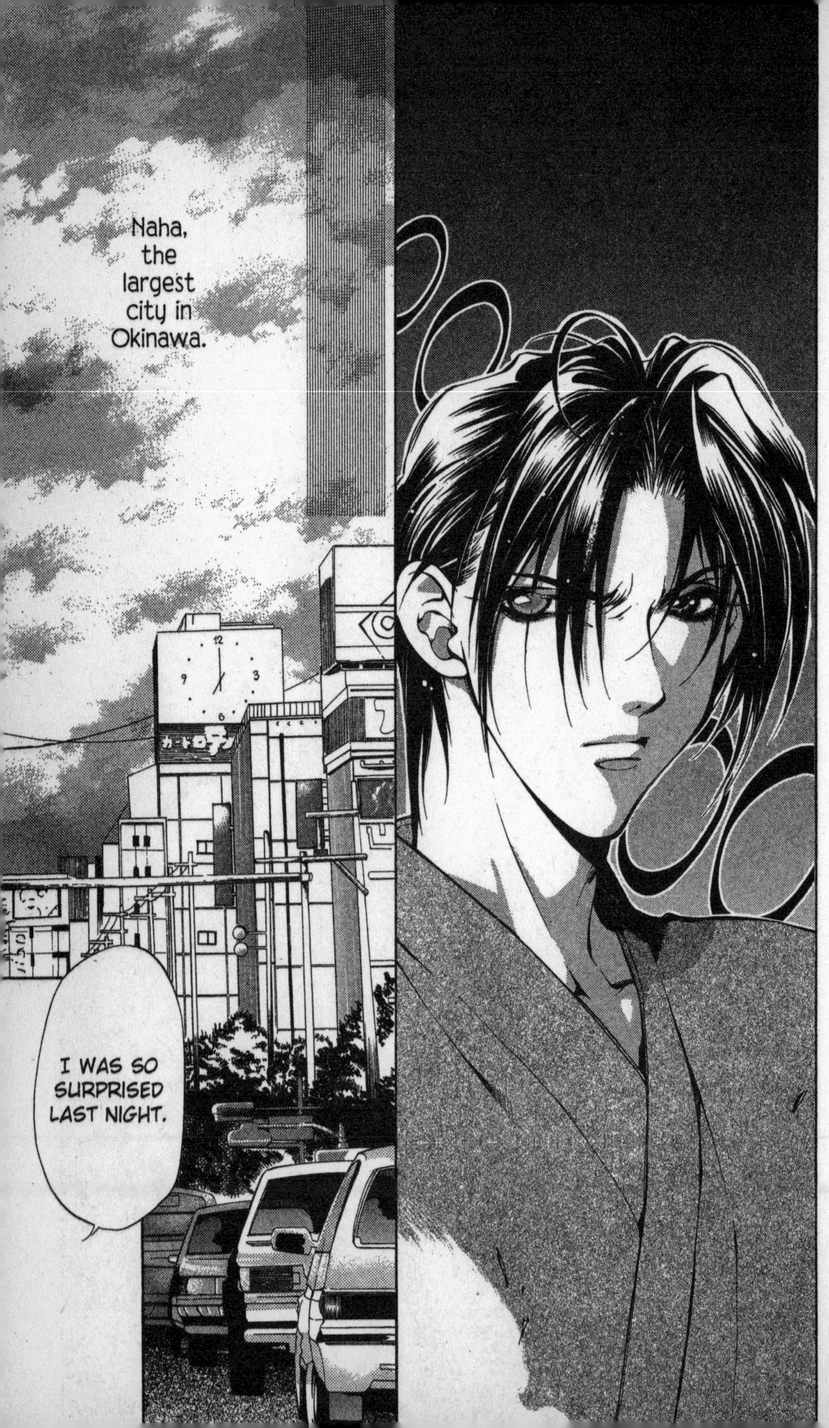
Naha, the largest city in Okinawa.
I WAS SO SURPRISED LAST NIGHT.

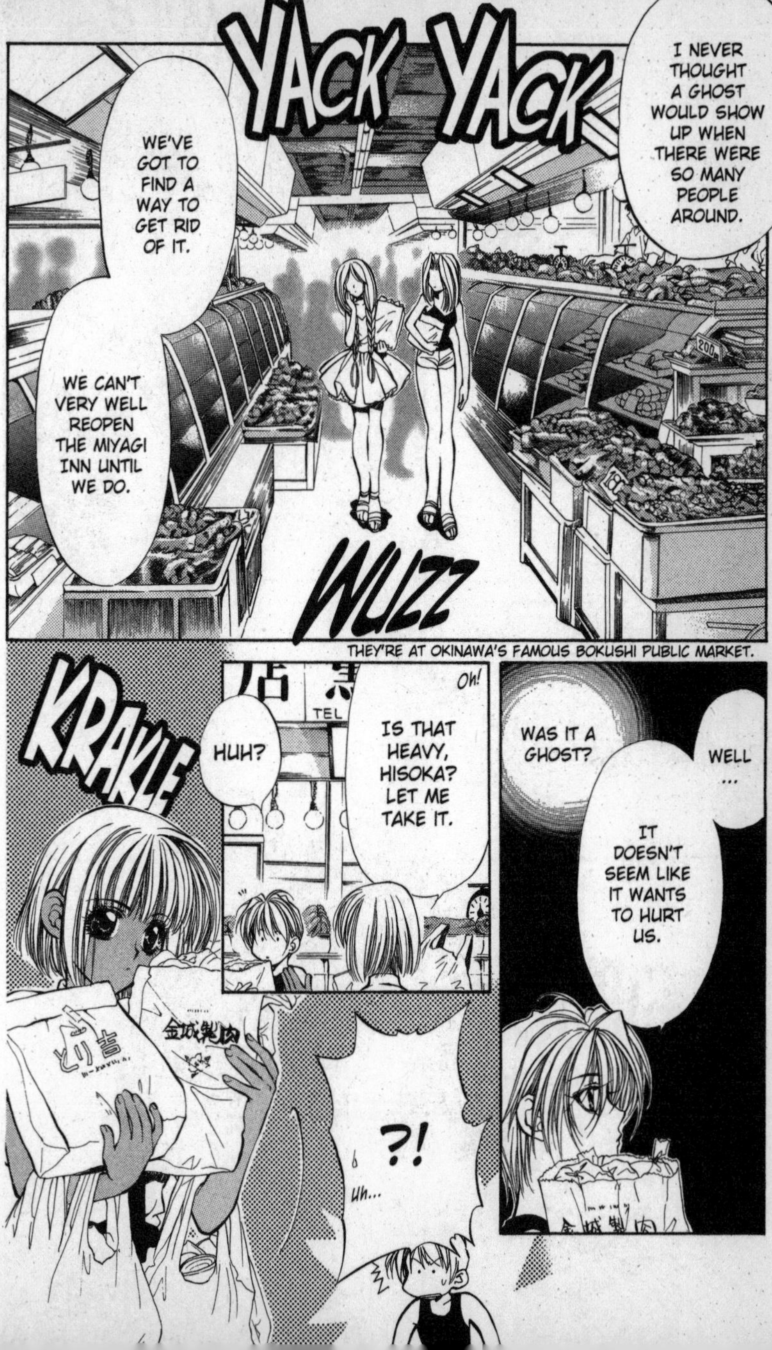
I NEVER THOUGHT A GHOST WOULD SHOW UP WHEN THERE WERE SO MANY PEOPLE AROUND.
YACK YACK
WE'VE GOT TO FIND A WAY TO GET RID OF IT.
WE CAN'T VERY WELL REOPEN THE MIYAGI INN UNTIL WE DO.
WUZZ
THEY'RE AT OKINAWA'S FAMOUS BOKUSHI PUBLIC MARKET.
WAS IT A GHOST?
WELL ...
IT DOESN'T SEEM LIKE IT WANTS TO HURT US.
Oh!
IS THAT HEAVY, HISOKA? LET ME TAKE IT.
HUH?
KRAKLE
とり吉
金城製肉
?!
uh...

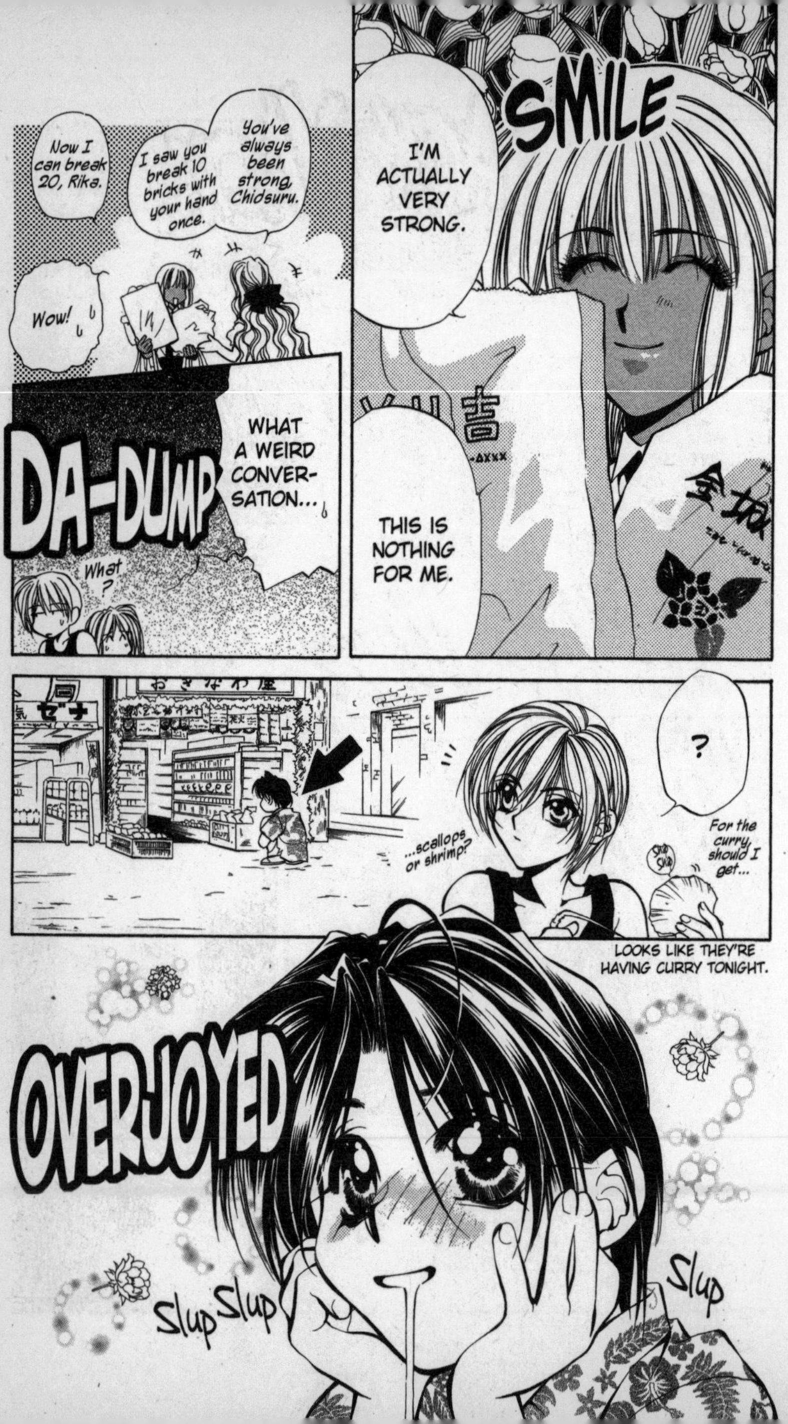
SMILE
I'M ACTUALLY VERY STRONG.
THIS IS NOTHING FOR ME.
You've always been strong, Chidsuru.
I saw you break 10 bricks with your hand once.
Now I can break 20, Rika.
Wow!
WHAT A WEIRD CONVERSATION...
DA-DUMP
What?
?
For the curry, should I get...
...scallops or shrimp?
LOOKS LIKE THEY'RE HAVING CURRY TONIGHT.
OVERJOYED
Slup
Slup
Slup

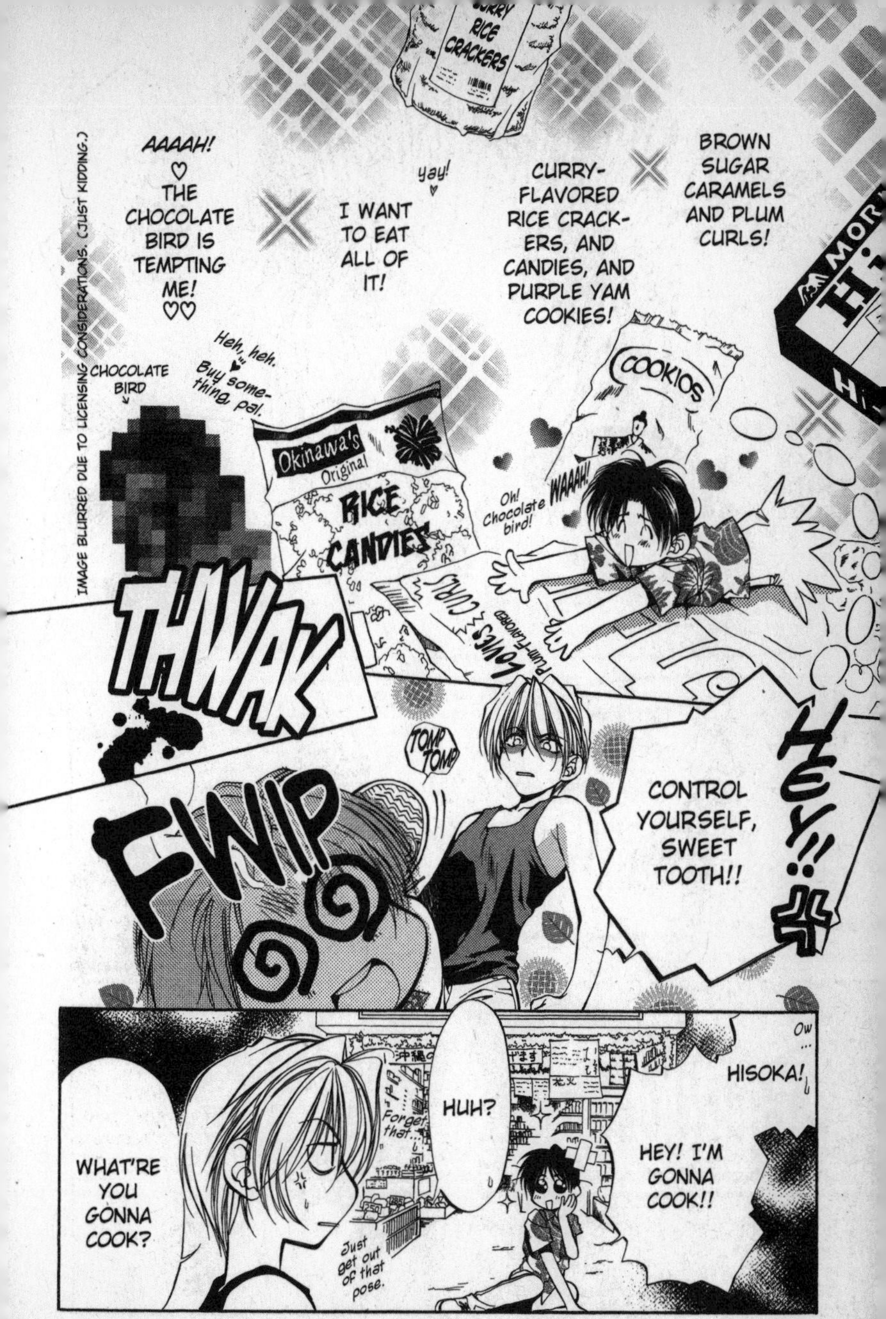
CURRY RICE CRACKERS
BROWN SUGAR CARAMELS AND PLUM CURLS!
CURRY-FLAVORED RICE CRACKERS, AND CANDIES, AND PURPLE YAM COOKIES!
I WANT TO EAT ALL OF IT!
yay! ♥
AAAAH! ♡ THE CHOCOLATE BIRD IS TEMPTING ME! ♡♡
IMAGE BLURRED DUE TO LICENSING CONSIDERATIONS. (JUST KIDDING.)
CHOCOLATE BIRD
Heh, heh. ♥ Buy something, pal.
Okinawa's Original RICE CANDIES
COOKIOS
Oh! Chocolate bird!
WAAAH!
Plum-Flavored LOVE'S CURLS
THWAK
HEY!!
CONTROL YOURSELF, SWEET TOOTH!!
TOMP TOMP
FWIP
Ow...
HISOKA!
HEY! I'M GONNA COOK!!
HUH?
Forget that...
WHAT'RE YOU GONNA COOK?
Just get out of that pose.

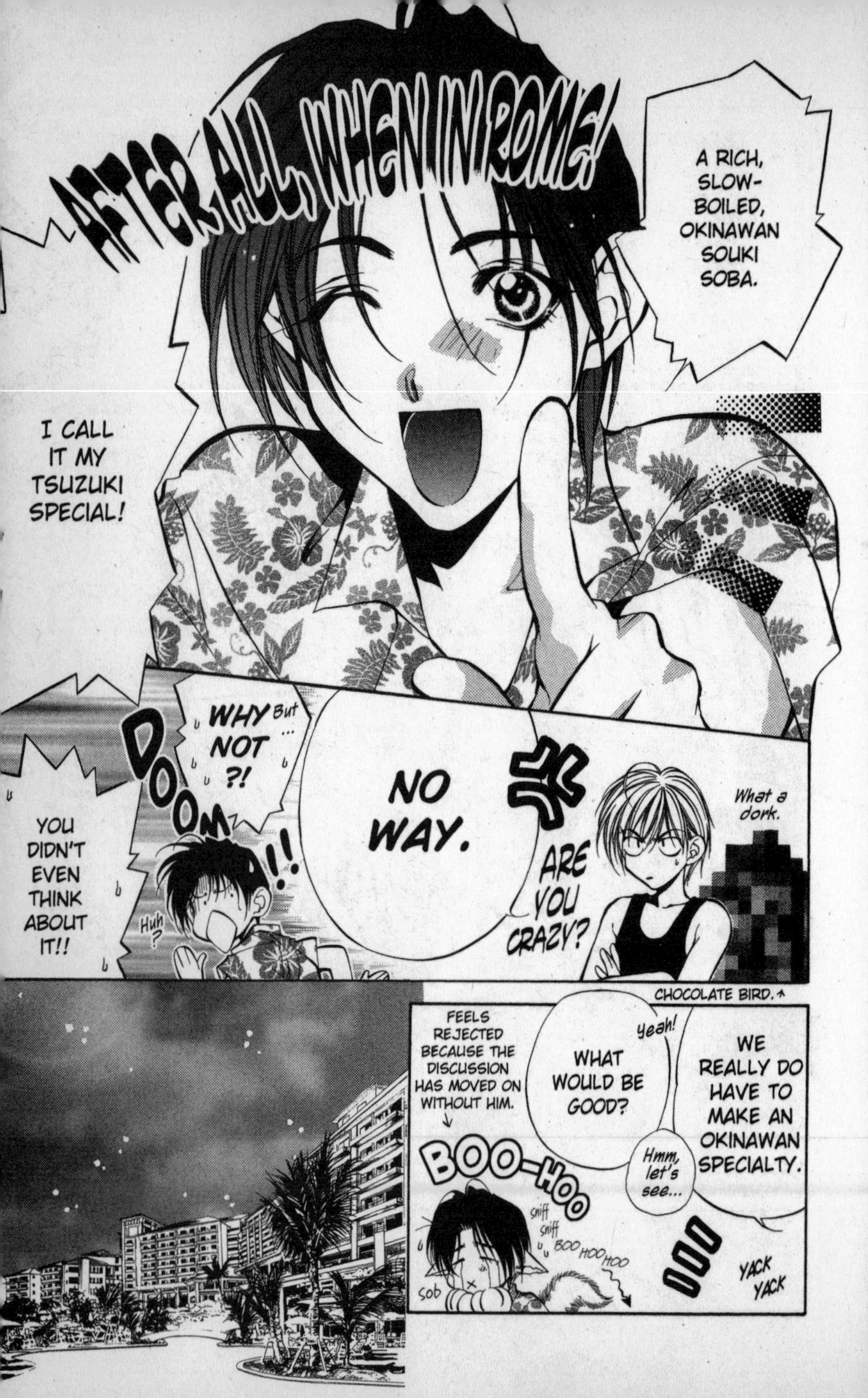
A RICH, SLOW-BOILED, OKINAWAN SOUKI SOBA.
AFTER ALL, WHEN IN ROME!
I CALL IT MY TSUZUKI SPECIAL!
What a dork.
ARE YOU CRAZY?
NO WAY.
WHY NOT?!
But...
DOOM!!
Huh?
YOU DIDN'T EVEN THINK ABOUT IT!!
CHOCOLATE BIRD.
WE REALLY DO HAVE TO MAKE AN OKINAWAN SPECIALTY.
yeah!
WHAT WOULD BE GOOD?
Hmm, let's see...
YACK YACK
FEELS REJECTED BECAUSE THE DISCUSSION HAS MOVED ON WITHOUT HIM.
BOO-HOO
sniff sniff
BOO HOO HOO
Sob

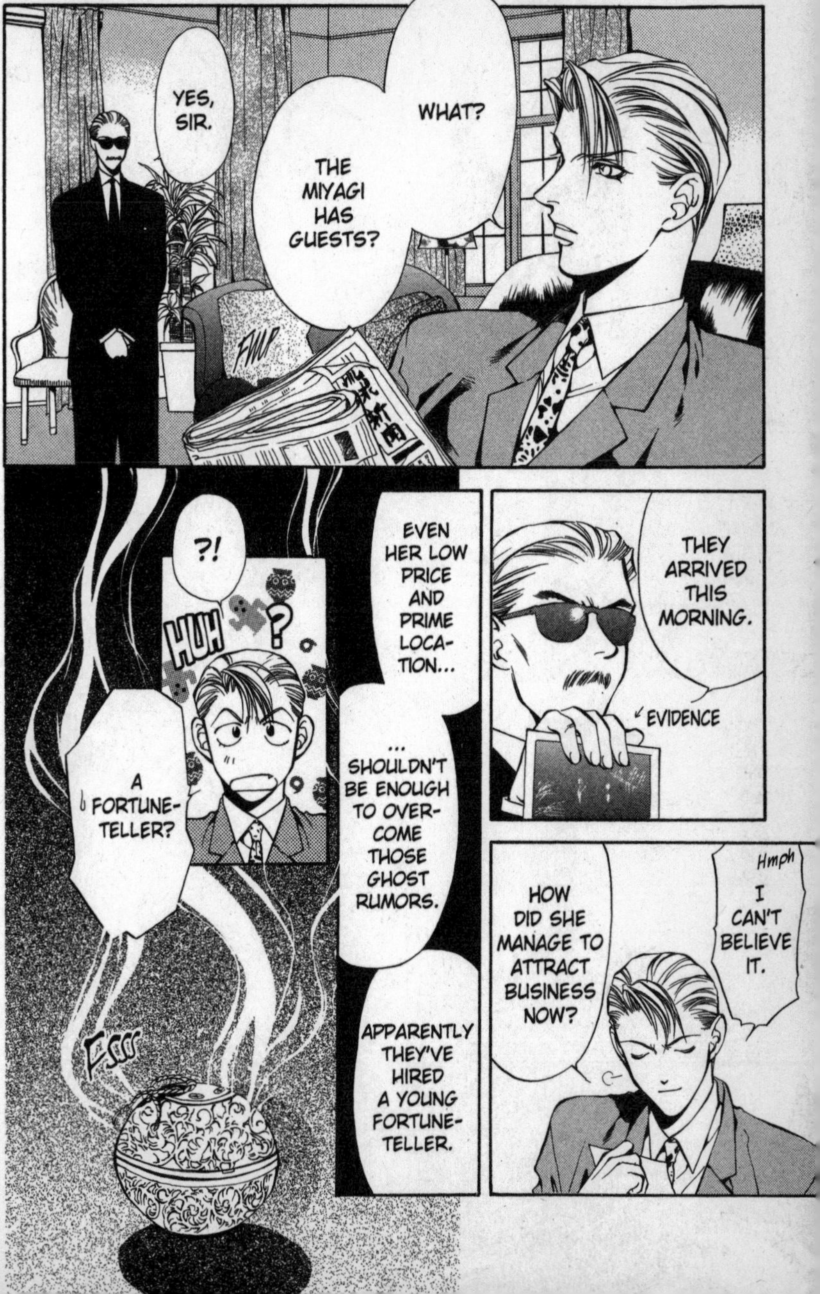
WHAT?
THE MIYAGI HAS GUESTS?
YES, SIR.
FWIP
THEY ARRIVED THIS MORNING.
EVIDENCE
Hmph
I CAN'T BELIEVE IT.
HOW DID SHE MANAGE TO ATTRACT BUSINESS NOW?
EVEN HER LOW PRICE AND PRIME LOCATION...
... SHOULDN'T BE ENOUGH TO OVERCOME THOSE GHOST RUMORS.
APPARENTLY THEY'VE HIRED A YOUNG FORTUNE-TELLER.
?!
HUH
A FORTUNE-TELLER?
FSSS

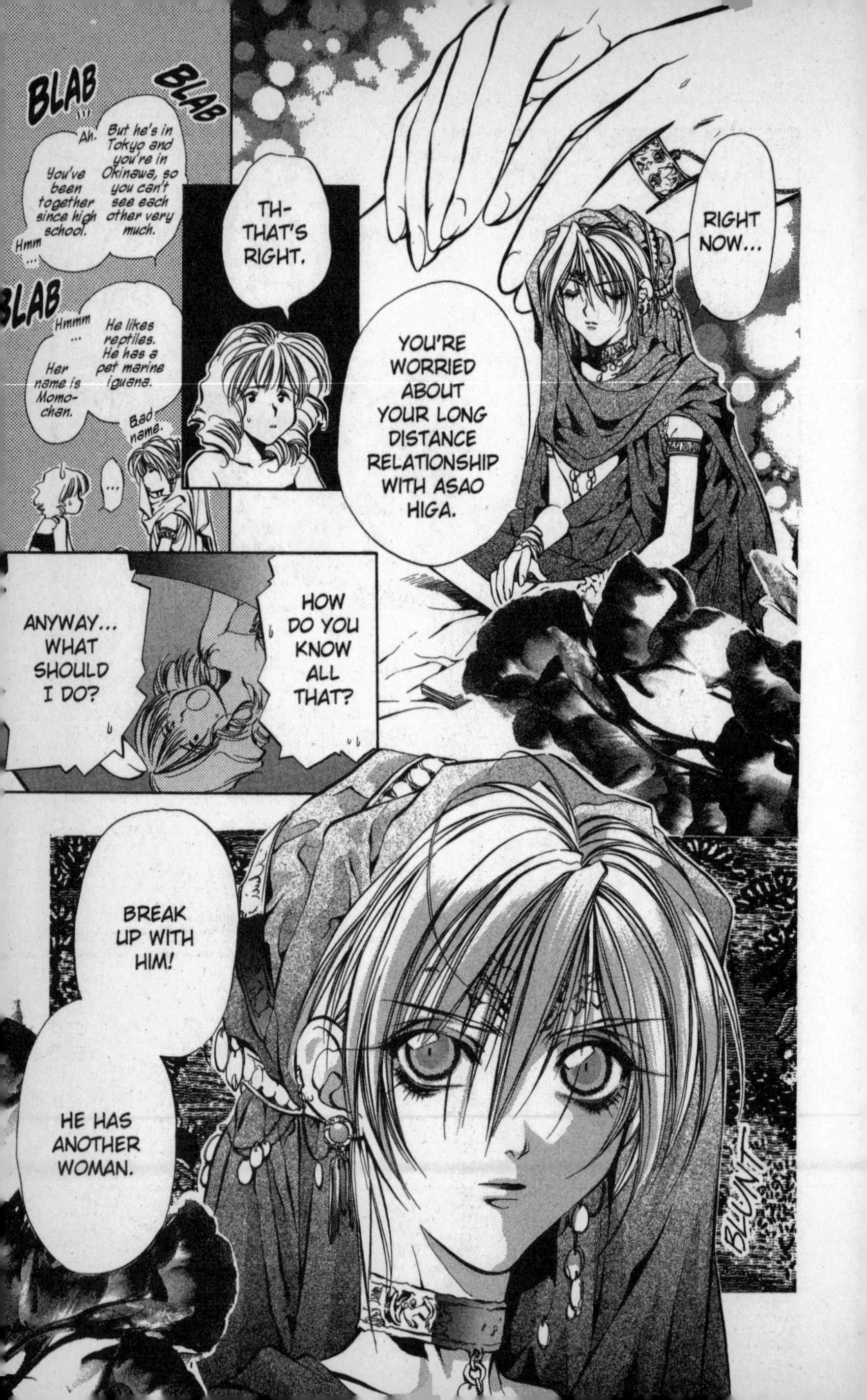
RIGHT NOW...
YOU'RE WORRIED ABOUT YOUR LONG DISTANCE RELATIONSHIP WITH ASAO HIGA.
TH- THAT'S RIGHT.
BLAB
BLAB
But he's in Tokyo and you're in Okinawa, so you can't see each other very much.
Ah. You've been together since high school.
Hmm...
BLAB
He likes reptiles. He has a pet marine iguana.
Hmmm... Her name is Momo-chan.
Bad name.
...
HOW DO YOU KNOW ALL THAT?
ANYWAY... WHAT SHOULD I DO?
BLUNT
BREAK UP WITH HIM!
HE HAS ANOTHER WOMAN.

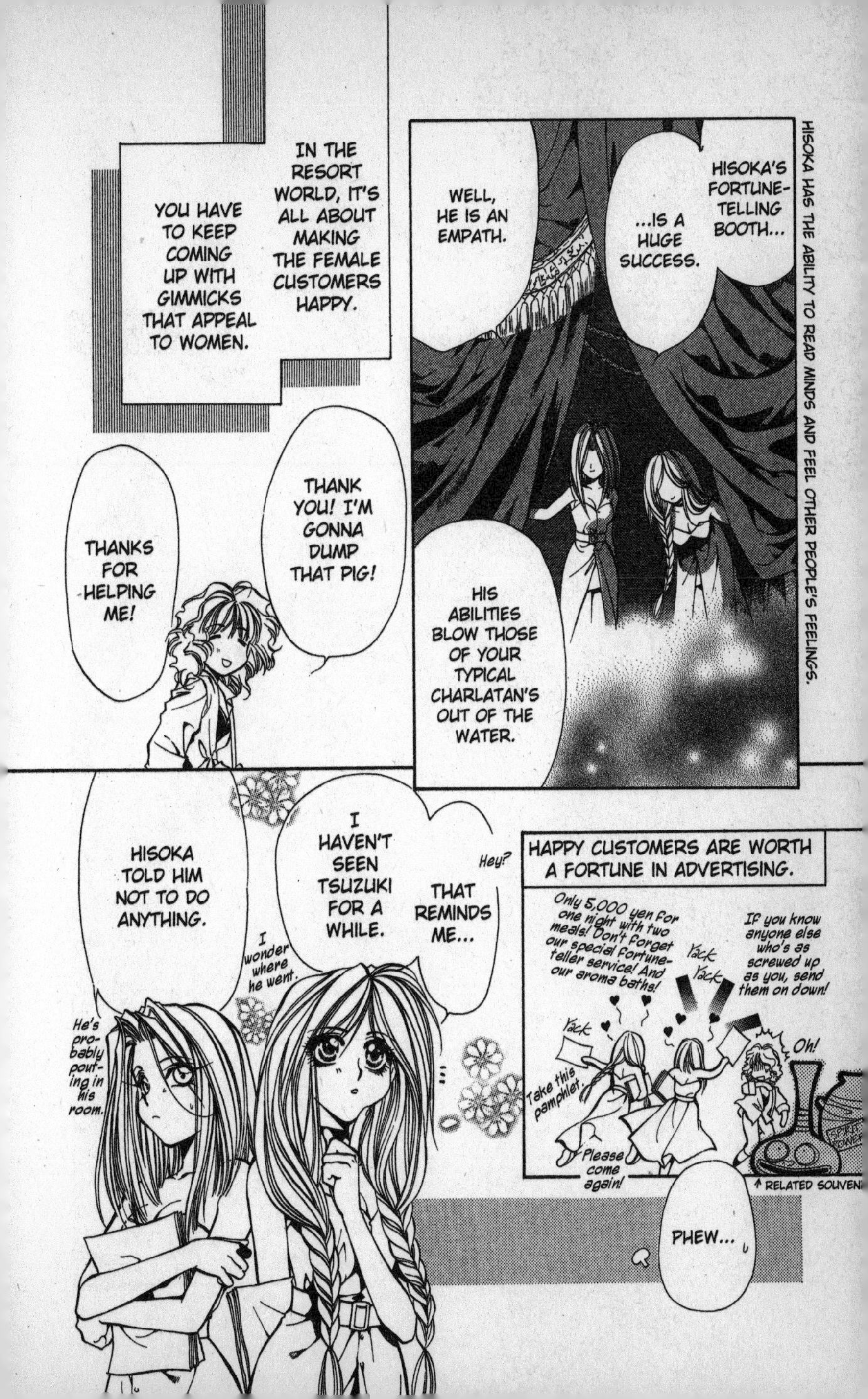
HISOKA HAS THE ABILITY TO READ MINDS AND FEEL OTHER PEOPLE'S FEELINGS.
HISOKA'S FORTUNE-TELLING BOOTH...
...IS A HUGE SUCCESS.
WELL, HE IS AN EMPATH.
HIS ABILITIES BLOW THOSE OF YOUR TYPICAL CHARLATAN'S OUT OF THE WATER.
IN THE RESORT WORLD, IT'S ALL ABOUT MAKING THE FEMALE CUSTOMERS HAPPY.
YOU HAVE TO KEEP COMING UP WITH GIMMICKS THAT APPEAL TO WOMEN.
THANK YOU! I'M GONNA DUMP THAT PIG!
THANKS FOR HELPING ME!
HAPPY CUSTOMERS ARE WORTH A FORTUNE IN ADVERTISING.
If you know anyone else who's as screwed up as you, send them on down!
Only 5,000 yen for one night with two meals! Don't forget our special fortune-teller service! And our aroma baths!
Yack Yack
Yack
Oh!
Take this pamphlet.
Please come again!
↑ RELATED SOUVENI
PHEW...
Hey?
THAT REMINDS ME...
I HAVEN'T SEEN TSUZUKI FOR A WHILE.
I wonder where he went.
HISOKA TOLD HIM NOT TO DO ANYTHING.
He's probably pouting in his room.

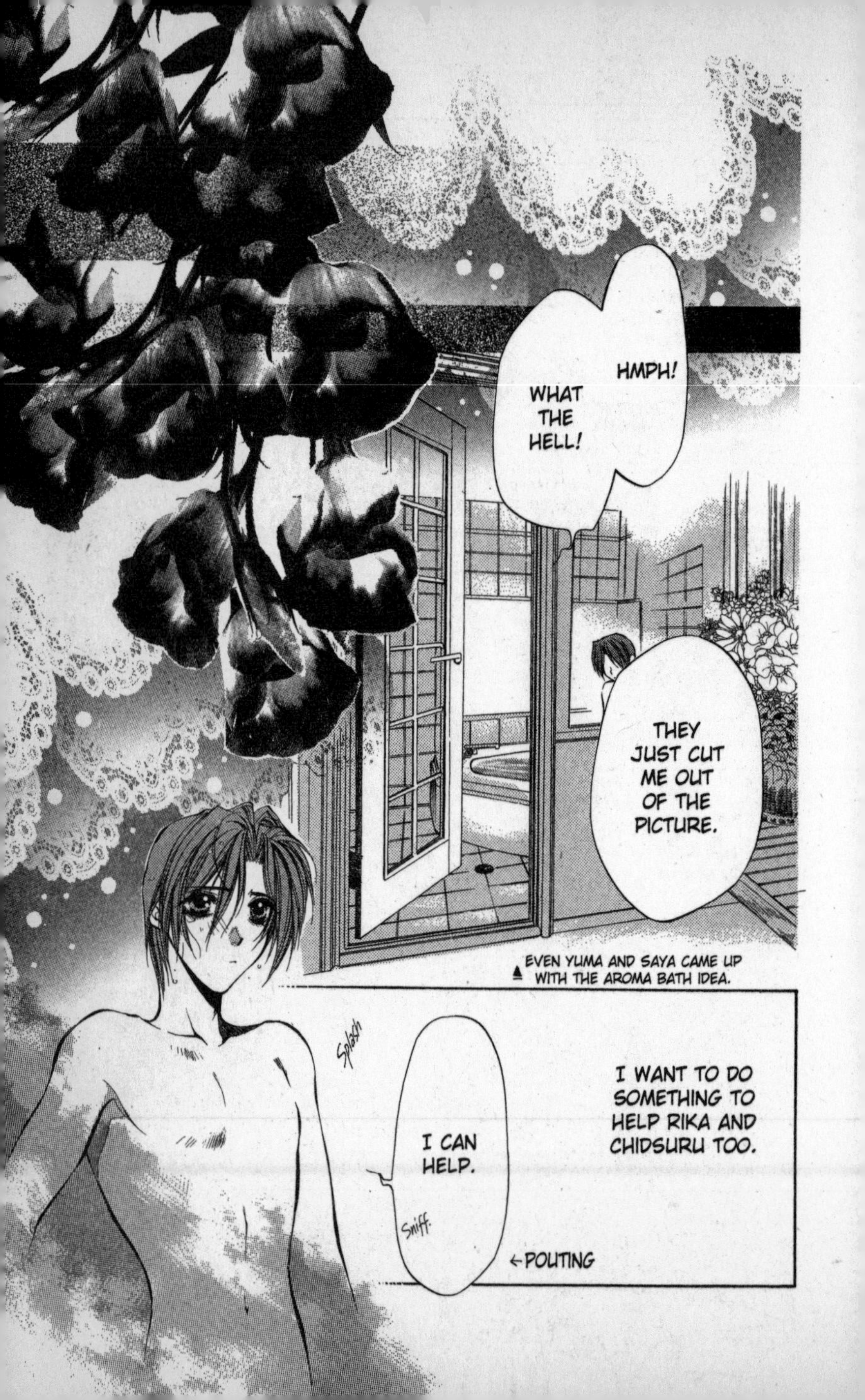
HMPH! WHAT THE HELL!
THEY JUST CUT ME OUT OF THE PICTURE.
EVEN YUMA AND SAYA CAME UP WITH THE AROMA BATH IDEA.
I WANT TO DO SOMETHING TO HELP RIKA AND CHIDSURU TOO.
Splash
I CAN HELP.
Sniff.
←POUTING

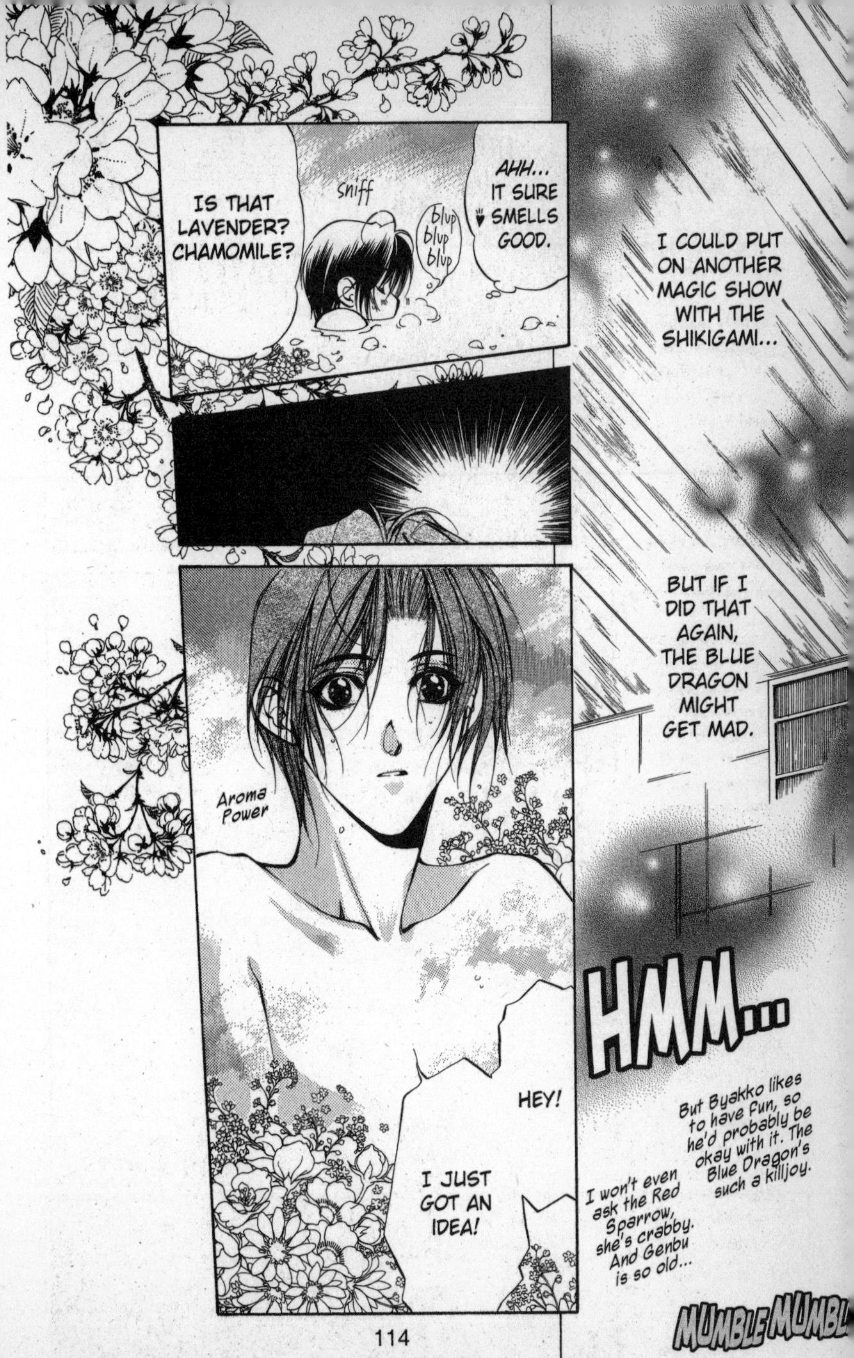
I COULD PUT ON ANOTHER MAGIC SHOW WITH THE SHIKIGAMI...
BUT IF I DID THAT AGAIN, THE BLUE DRAGON MIGHT GET MAD.
HMM...
But Byakko likes to have fun, so he'd probably be okay with it. The Blue Dragon's such a killjoy.
I won't even ask the Red Sparrow, she's crabby. And Genbu is so old...
MUMBLE MUMBL
AHH... IT SURE SMELLS GOOD.
blup blup blup
sniff
IS THAT LAVENDER? CHAMOMILE?
HEY!
Aroma Power
I JUST GOT AN IDEA!

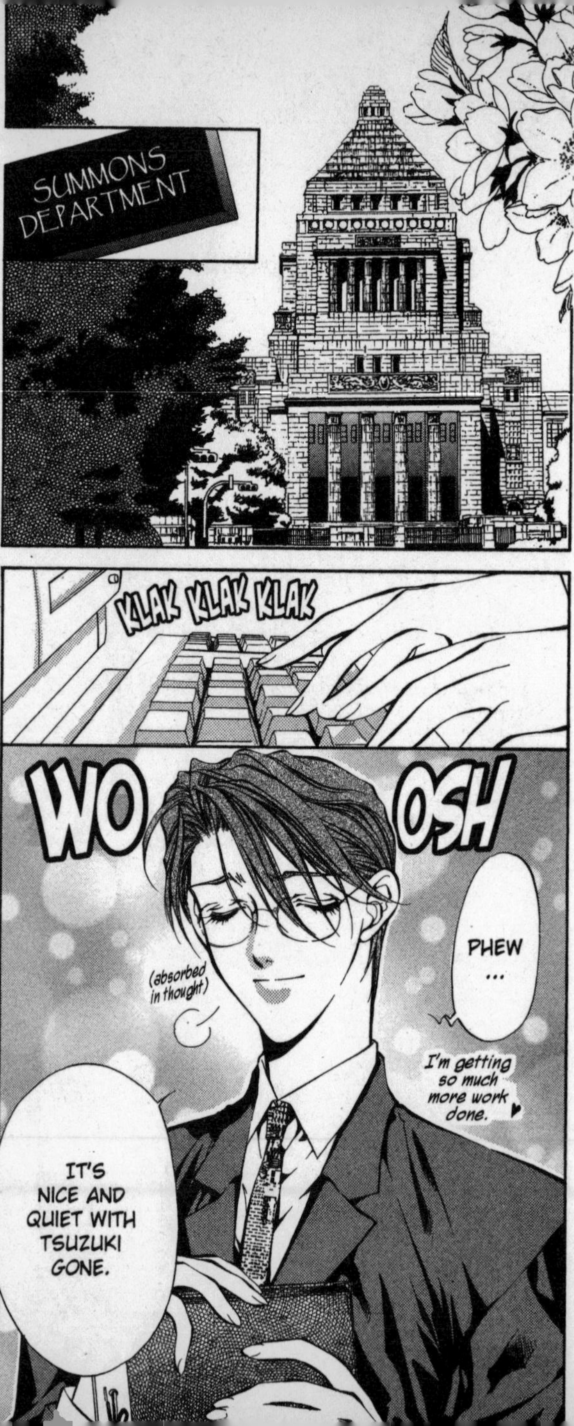
SUMMONS DEPARTMENT
KLAK KLAK KLAK
WOOSH
PHEW ...
I'm getting so much more work done. ♥
(absorbed in thought)
IT'S NICE AND QUIET WITH TSUZUKI GONE.

Lesson 3:
Choosing the proper stationery

I'm only speaking from my own tastes, but **simple is best!** I like simple brown paper with no design. Or animal prints and pretty photographs set in blue. Standard envelopes are okay, but nothing too weird.

The following are strictly forbidden.

- Free stationery from magazines
- Character stuff
- Artist's stuff
- Notebook paper and loose-leaf binder paper etc...

Please do not use these. Especially the **magazine freebies!!!**

Free stationery from magazines is really bad paper, and it collects dirt as it goes through the mail. By the time I receive it, it's in a bad way. It doesn't make me feel very good...

Lesson 4:
Things included with your letter

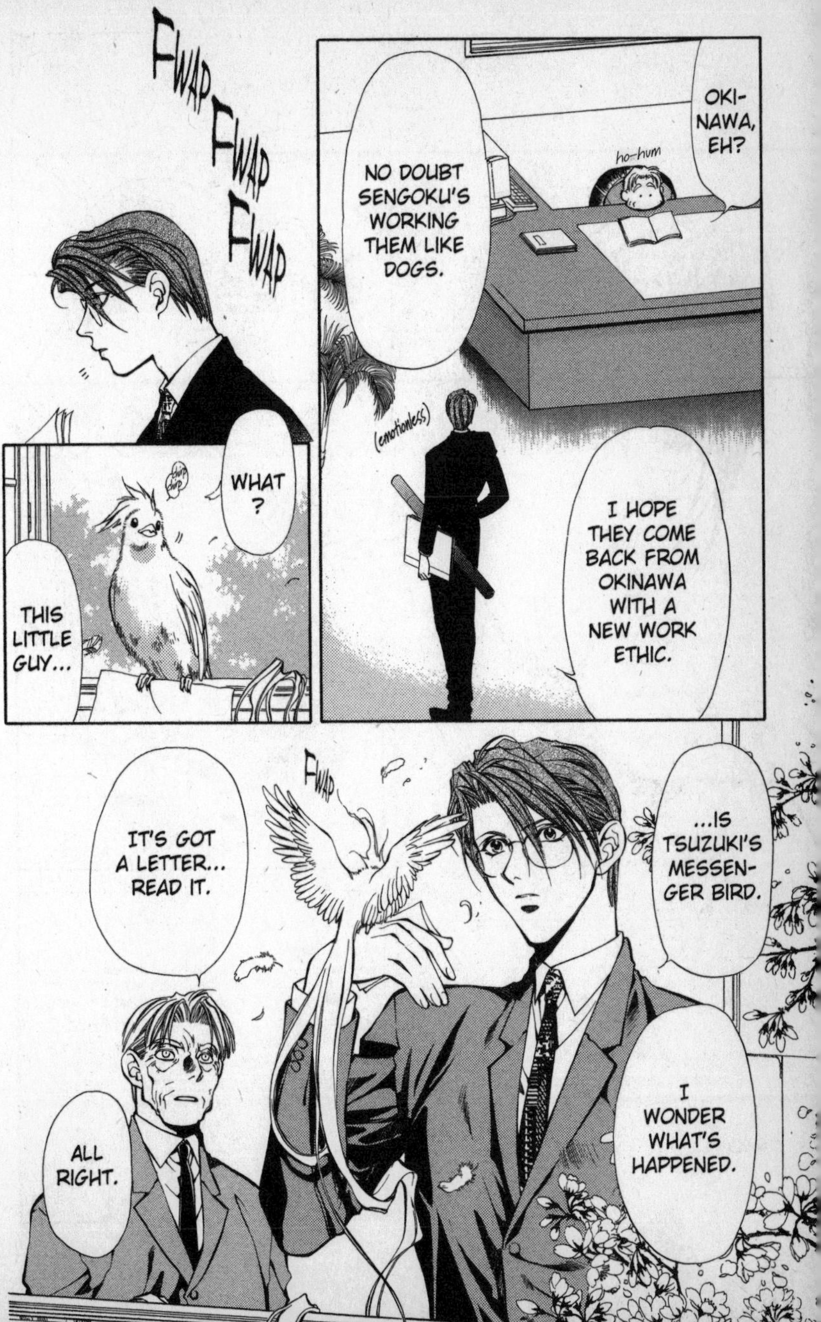
OKI-NAWA, EH?
ho-hum
NO DOUBT SENGOKU'S WORKING THEM LIKE DOGS.
(emotionless)
I HOPE THEY COME BACK FROM OKINAWA WITH A NEW WORK ETHIC.
FWAP FWAP FWAP
WHAT?
chirp chirp
THIS LITTLE GUY...
...IS TSUZUKI'S MESSEN-GER BIRD.
FWAP
IT'S GOT A LETTER... READ IT.
I WONDER WHAT'S HAPPENED.
ALL RIGHT.

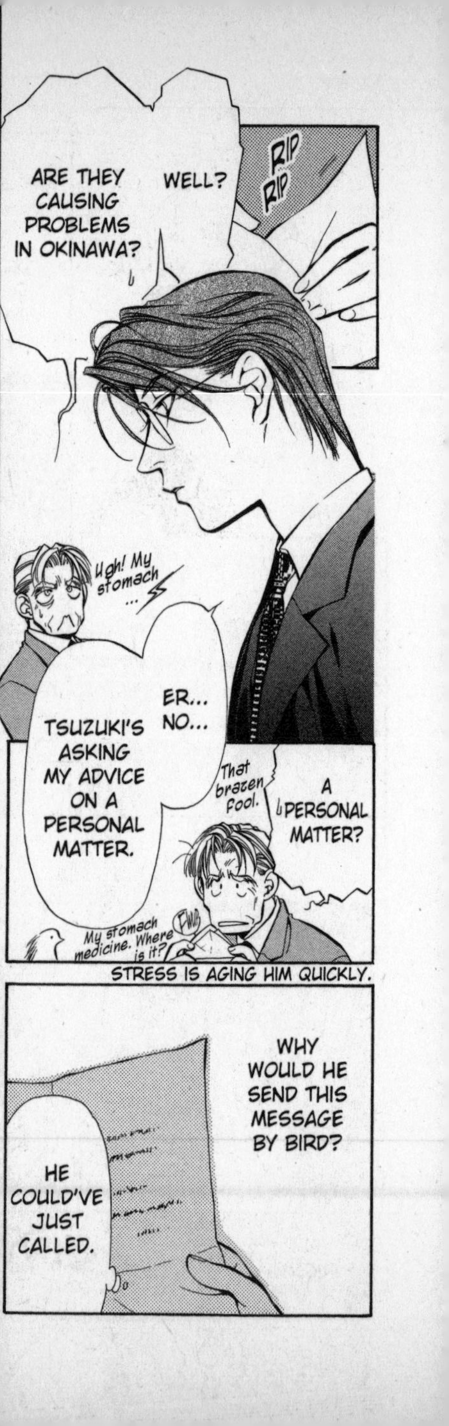
RIP RIP
WELL?
ARE THEY CAUSING PROBLEMS IN OKINAWA?
Ugh! My stomach ...
ER... NO...
TSUZUKI'S ASKING MY ADVICE ON A PERSONAL MATTER.
A PERSONAL MATTER?
That brazen fool.
My stomach medicine. Where is it?
STRESS IS AGING HIM QUICKLY.
WHY WOULD HE SEND THIS MESSAGE BY BIRD?
HE COULD'VE JUST CALLED.
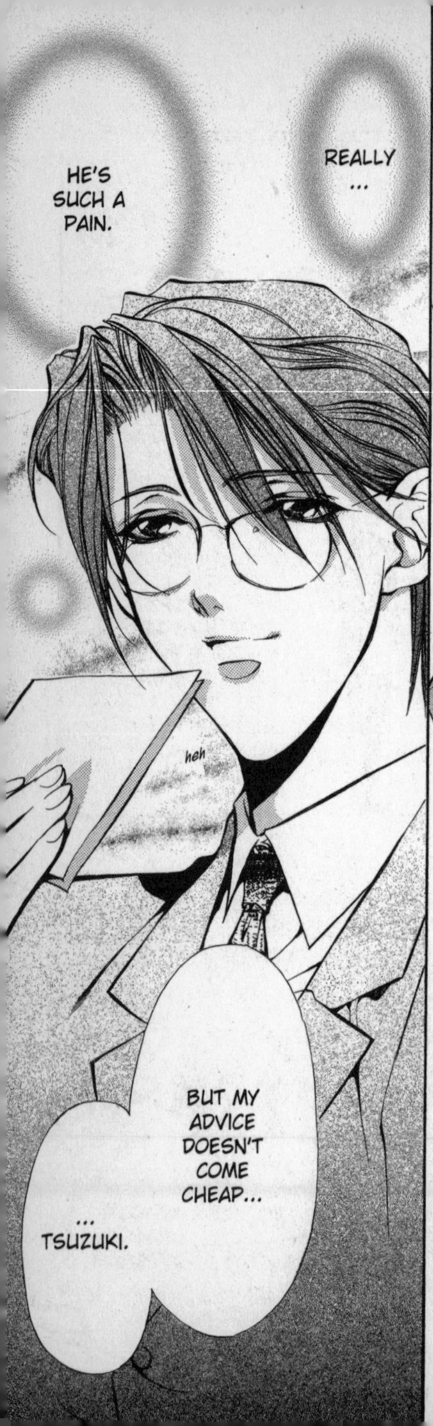
REALLY ...
HE'S SUCH A PAIN.
heh
BUT MY ADVICE DOESN'T COME CHEAP...
... TSUZUKI.

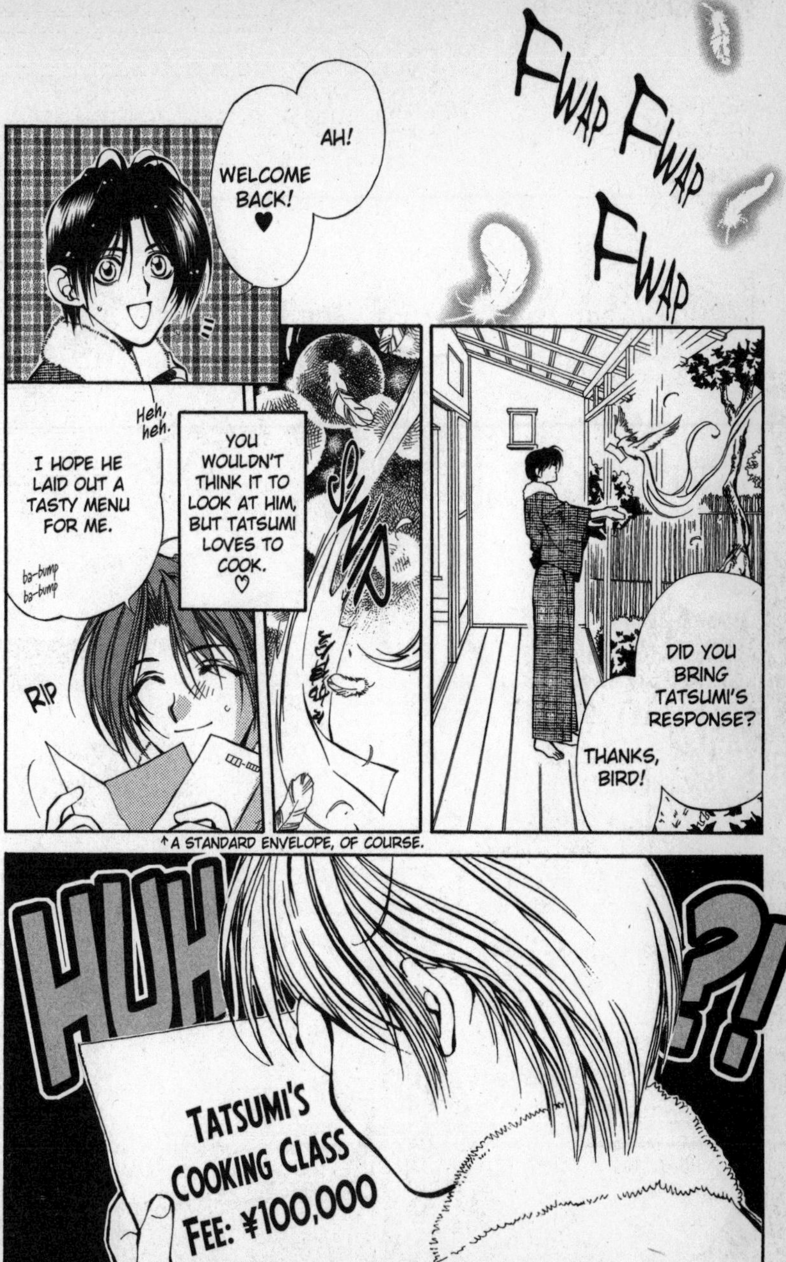
FWAP FWAP FWAP
AH! WELCOME BACK! ♥
DID YOU BRING TATSUMI'S RESPONSE?
THANKS, BIRD!
SWIP
YOU WOULDN'T THINK IT TO LOOK AT HIM, BUT TATSUMI LOVES TO COOK. ♡
Heh, heh.
I HOPE HE LAID OUT A TASTY MENU FOR ME.
ba-bump ba-bump
RIP
↑A STANDARD ENVELOPE, OF COURSE.
HUH...?!
TATSUMI'S COOKING CLASS
FEE: ¥100,000

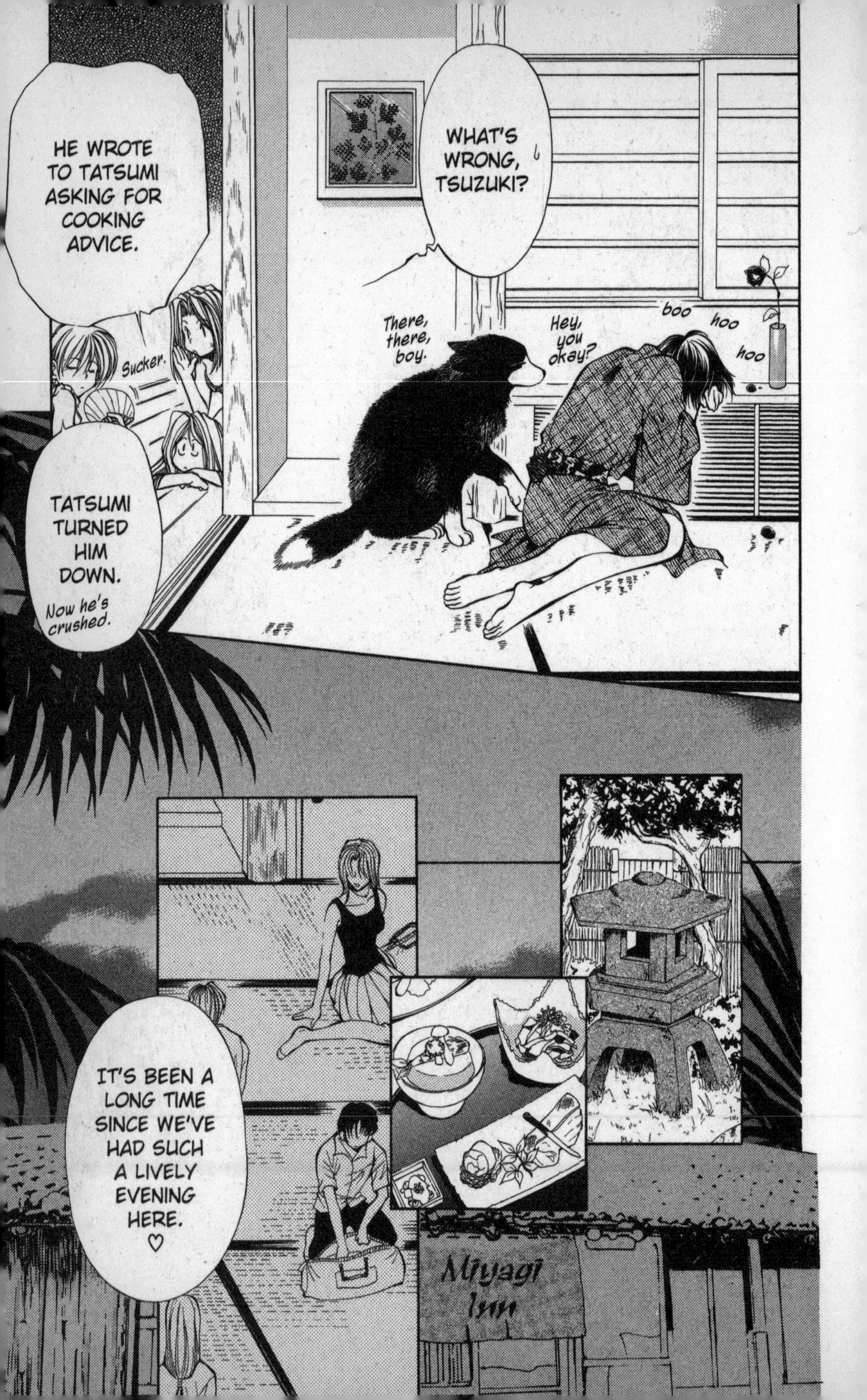
WHAT'S WRONG, TSUZUKI?
boo hoo hoo
Hey, you okay?
There, there, boy.
HE WROTE TO TATSUMI ASKING FOR COOKING ADVICE.
Sucker.
TATSUMI TURNED HIM DOWN.
Now he's crushed.
Miyagi Inn
IT'S BEEN A LONG TIME SINCE WE'VE HAD SUCH A LIVELY EVENING HERE. ♡

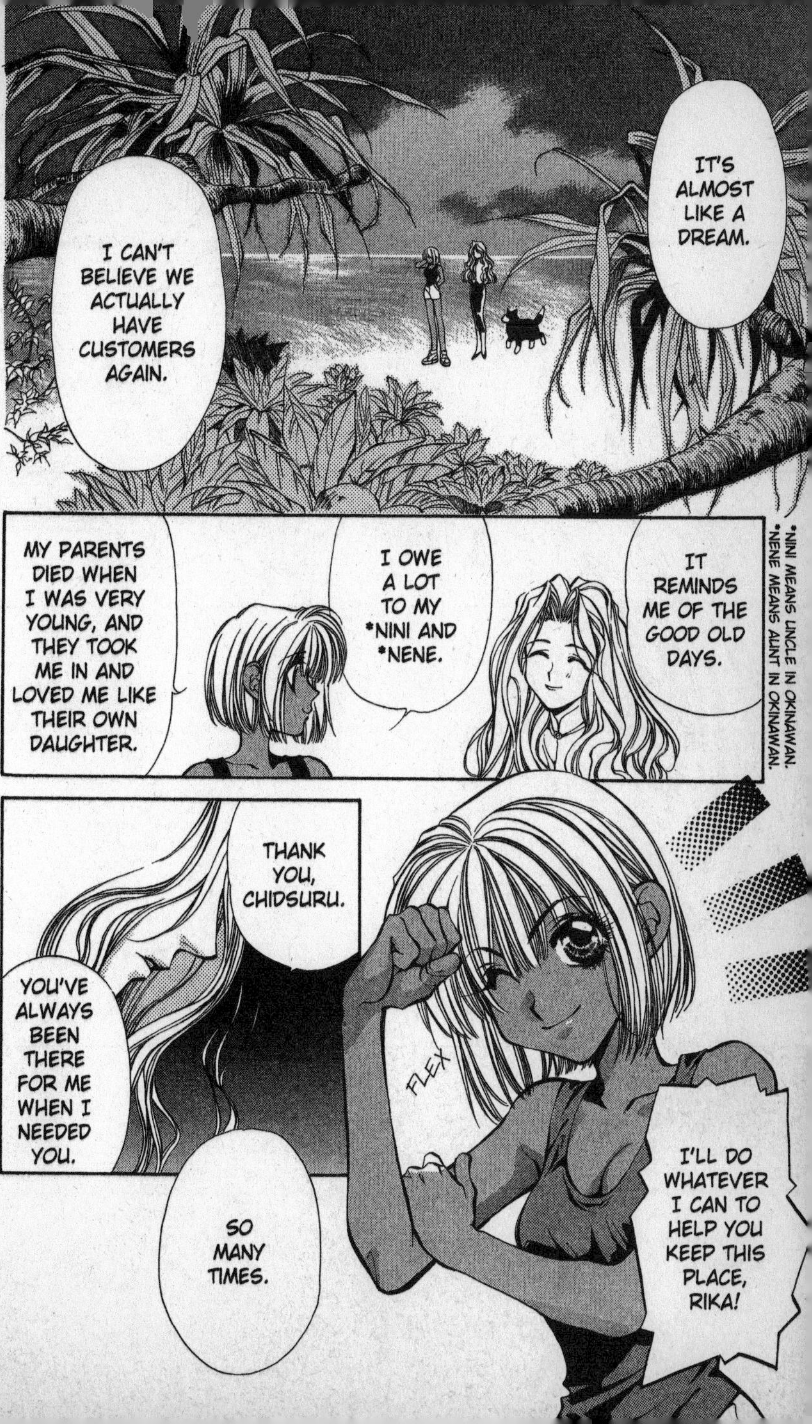
IT'S ALMOST LIKE A DREAM.
I CAN'T BELIEVE WE ACTUALLY HAVE CUSTOMERS AGAIN.
IT REMINDS ME OF THE GOOD OLD DAYS.
I OWE A LOT TO MY *NINI AND *NENE.
MY PARENTS DIED WHEN I WAS VERY YOUNG, AND THEY TOOK ME IN AND LOVED ME LIKE THEIR OWN DAUGHTER.
FLEX
I'LL DO WHATEVER I CAN TO HELP YOU KEEP THIS PLACE, RIKA!
THANK YOU, CHIDSURU.
YOU'VE ALWAYS BEEN THERE FOR ME WHEN I NEEDED YOU.
SO MANY TIMES.

*NINI MEANS UNCLE IN OKINAWAN.
*NENE MEANS AUNT IN OKINAWAN.

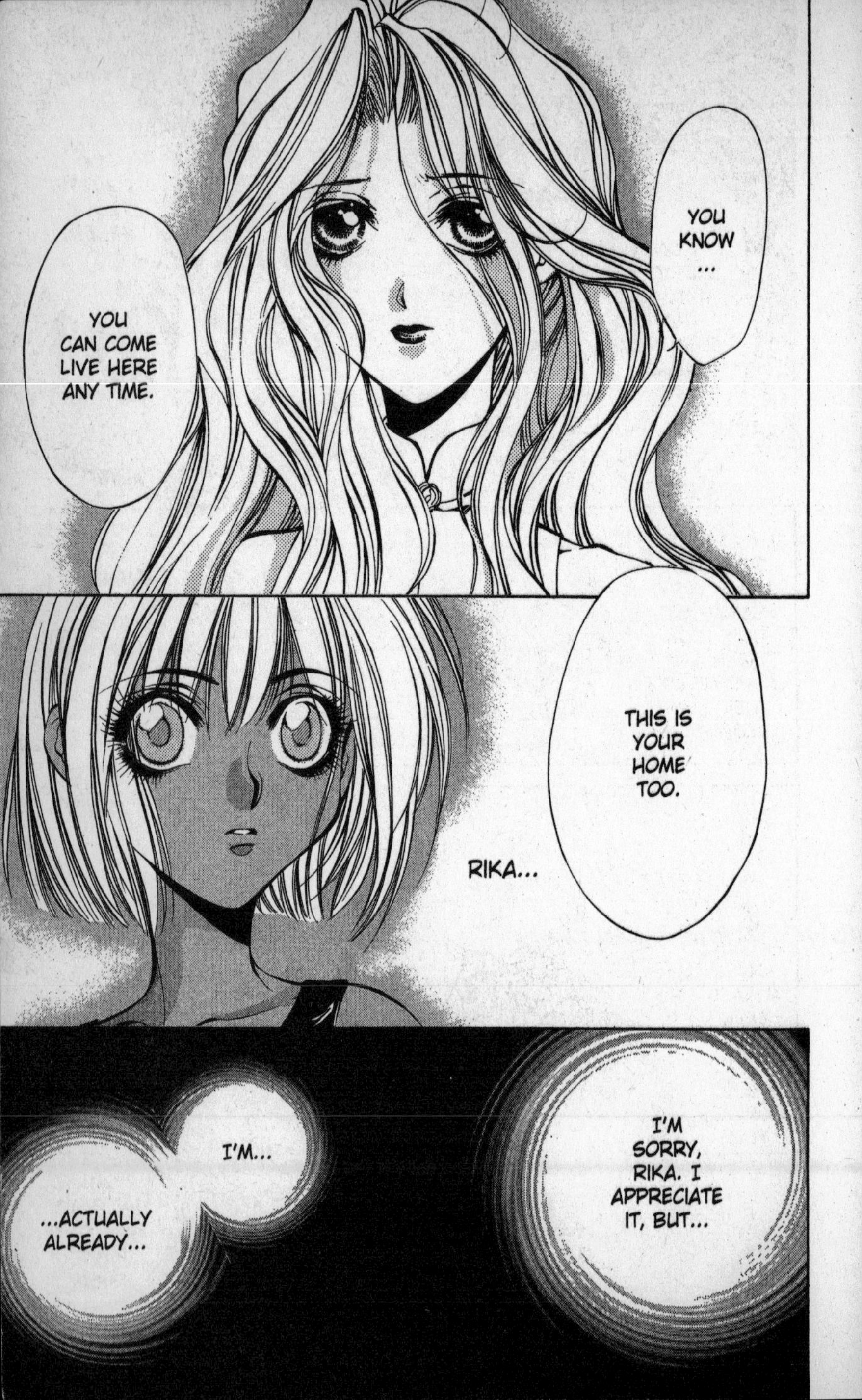
YOU KNOW ...
YOU CAN COME LIVE HERE ANY TIME.
THIS IS YOUR HOME TOO.
RIKA...
I'M SORRY, RIKA. I APPRECIATE IT, BUT...
I'M...
...ACTUALLY ALREADY...

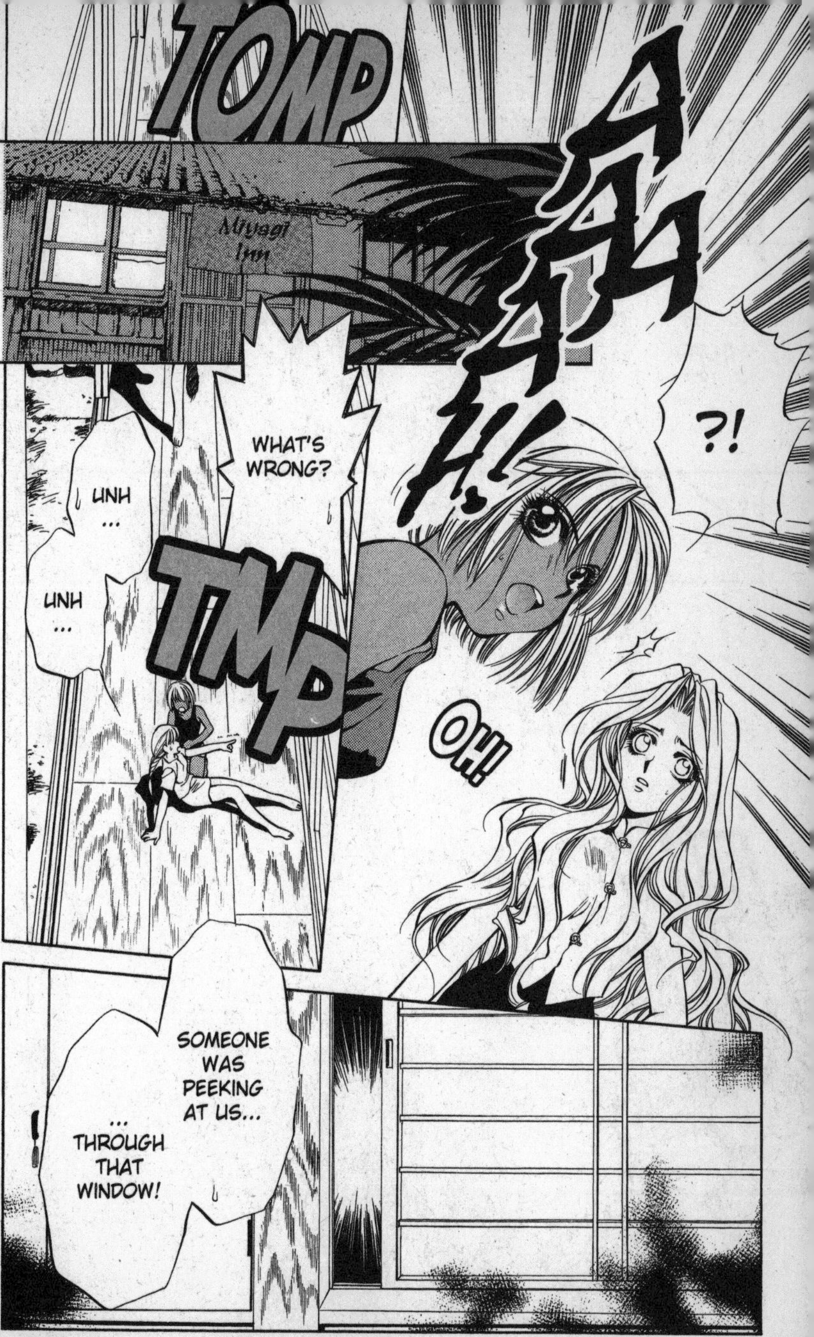
TOMP
Miyagi Inn
AAAAH!!
?!
TMP
OH!
WHAT'S WRONG?
UNH ...
UNH ...
SOMEONE WAS PEEKING AT US...
... THROUGH THAT WINDOW!

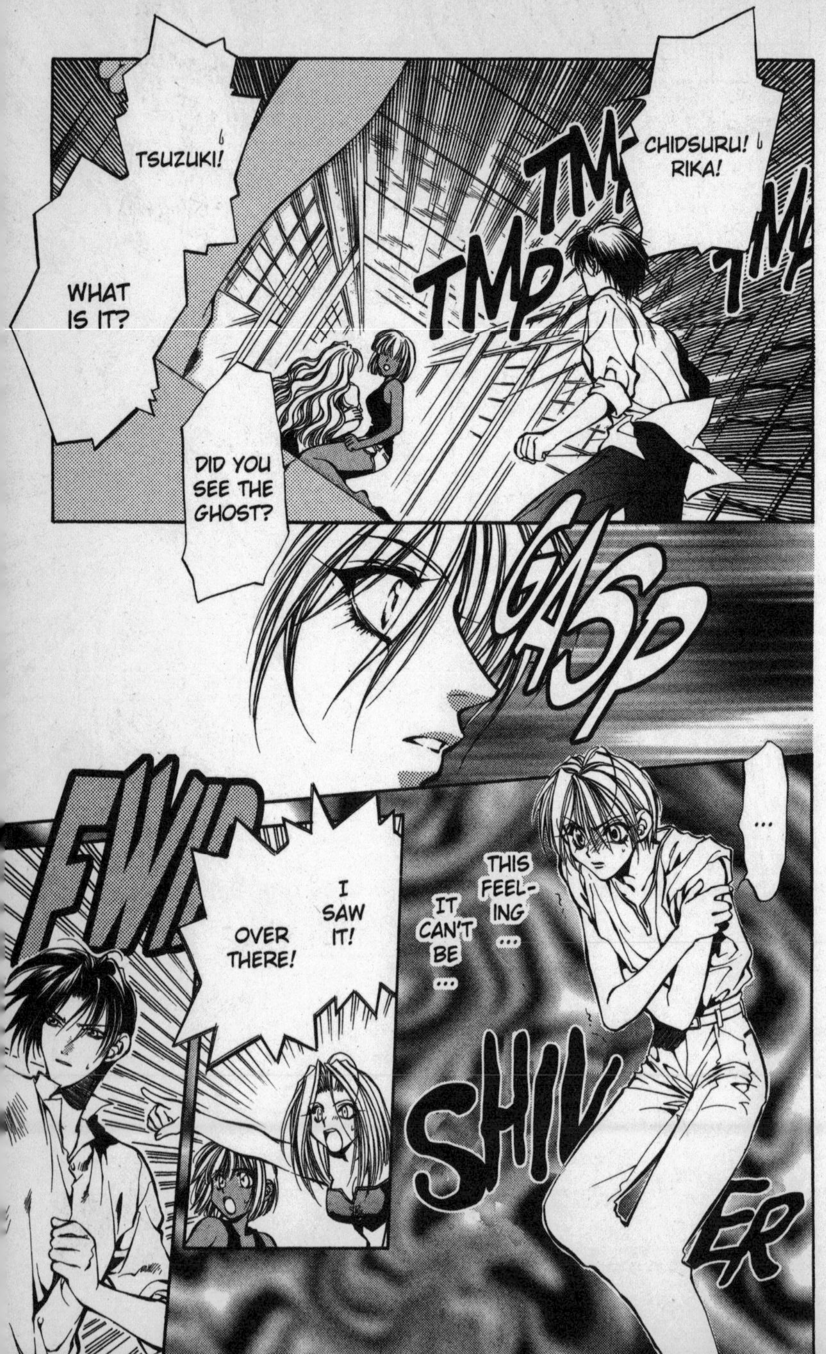
CHIDSURU! RIKA!
TMP
TMP
TMP
TSUZUKI!
WHAT IS IT?
DID YOU SEE THE GHOST?
GASP
...
THIS FEELING...
IT CAN'T BE...
SHIVER
I SAW IT!
OVER THERE!

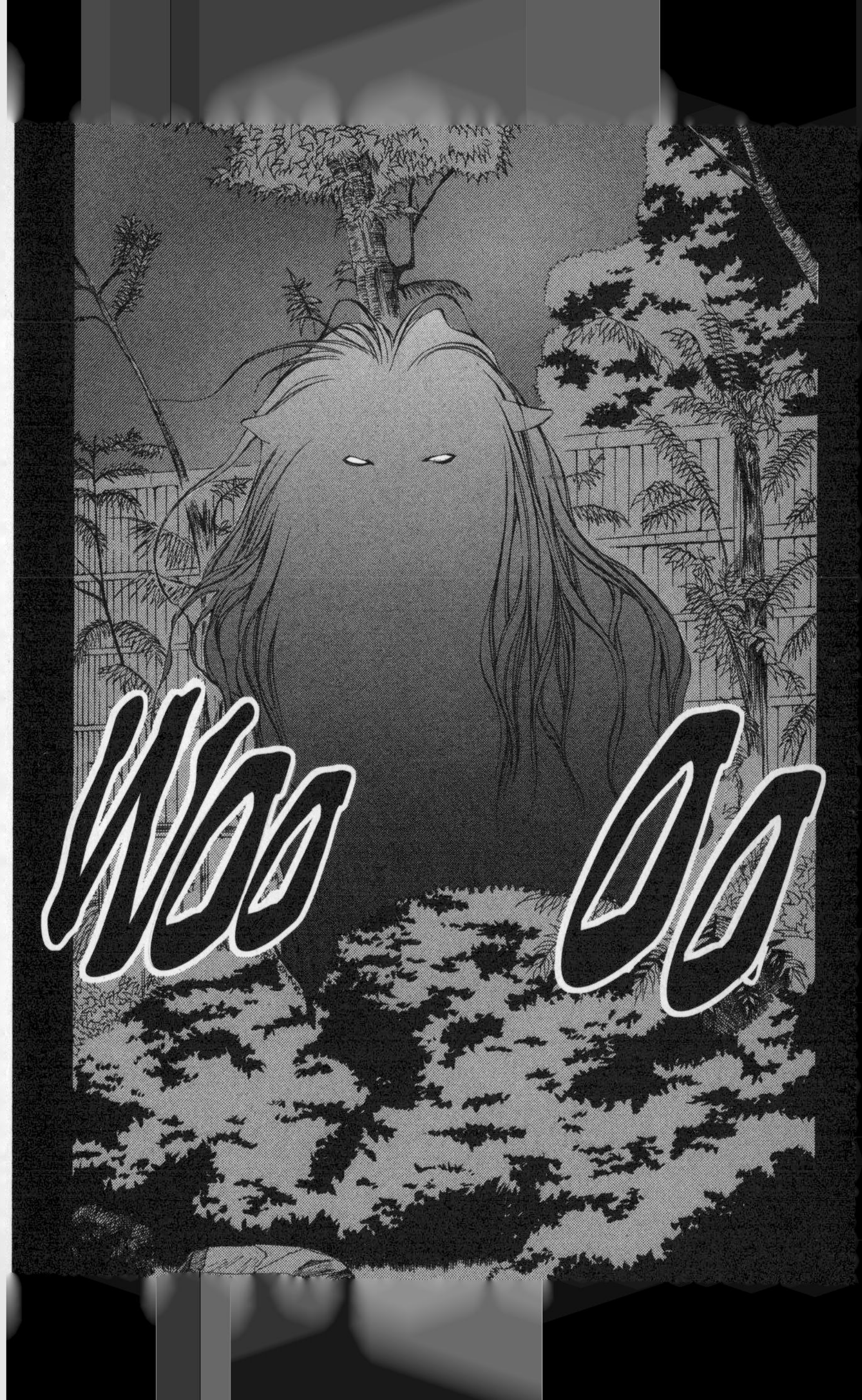
Woo oo

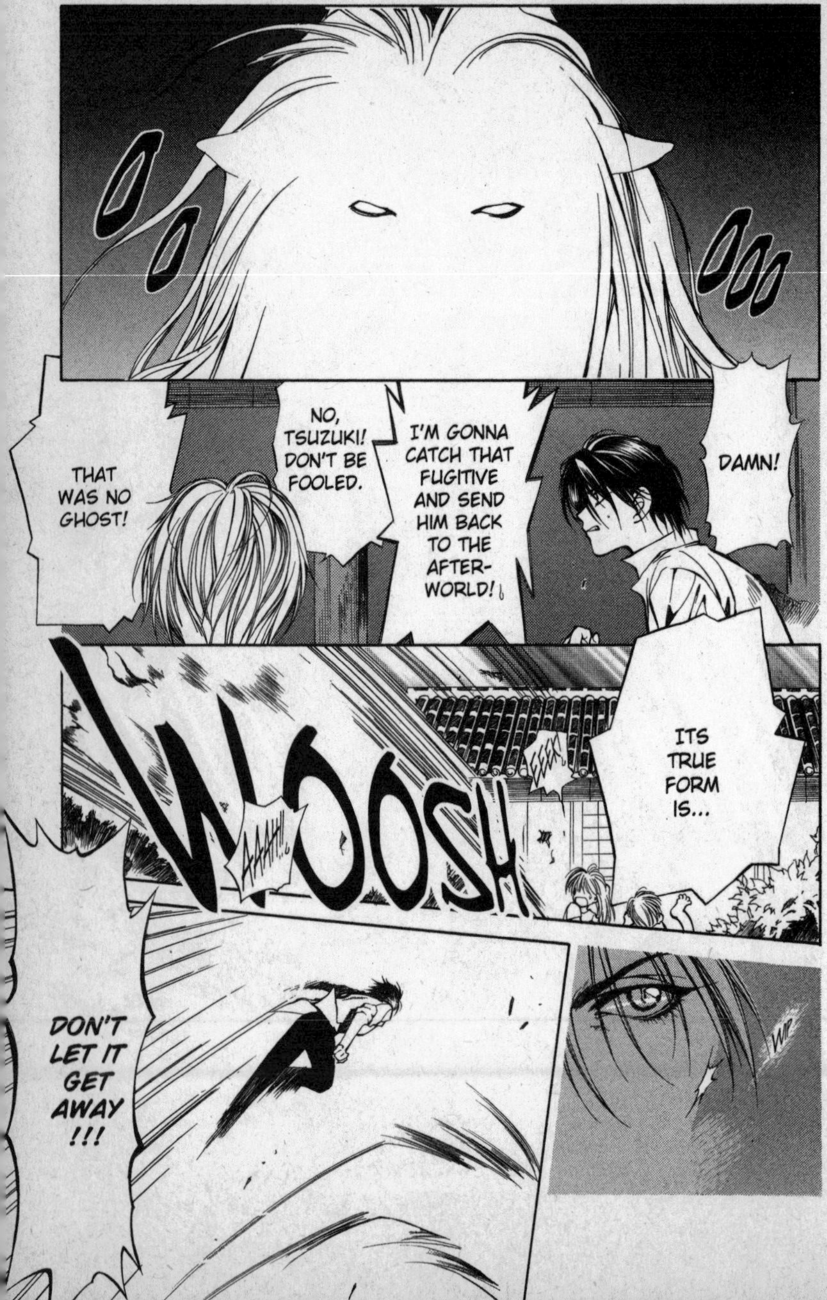
OOO
OOO
DAMN!
I'M GONNA CATCH THAT FUGITIVE AND SEND HIM BACK TO THE AFTER-WORLD!
NO, TSUZUKI! DON'T BE FOOLED.
THAT WAS NO GHOST!
ITS TRUE FORM IS...
EEEK!
WOOSH
AAAH!!
WIP
DON'T LET IT GET AWAY!!!

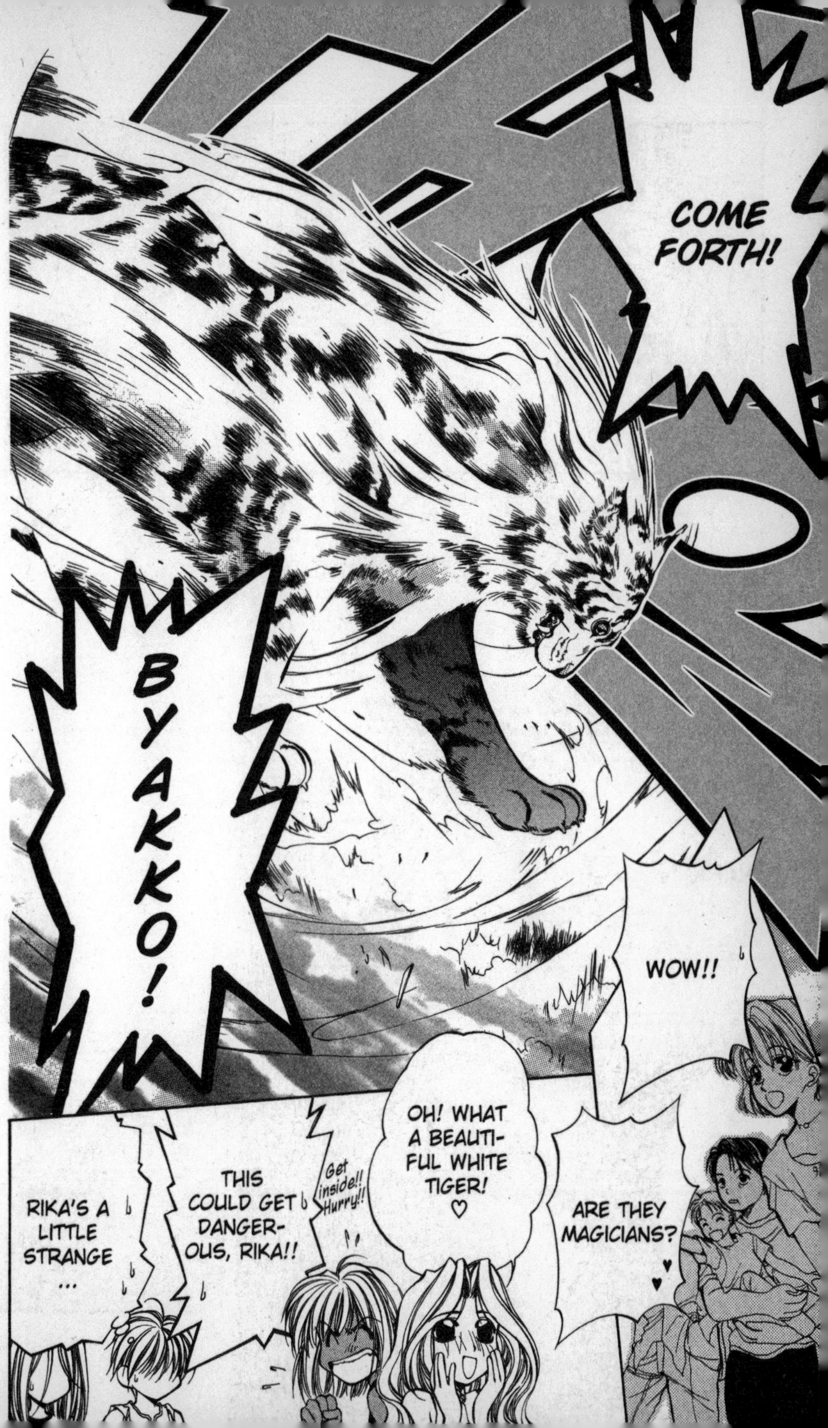
COME FORTH!
BYAKKO!
WOW!!
ARE THEY MAGICIANS? ♥
OH! WHAT A BEAUTIFUL WHITE TIGER! ♡
Get inside!! Hurry!!
THIS COULD GET DANGEROUS, RIKA!!
RIKA'S A LITTLE STRANGE ...

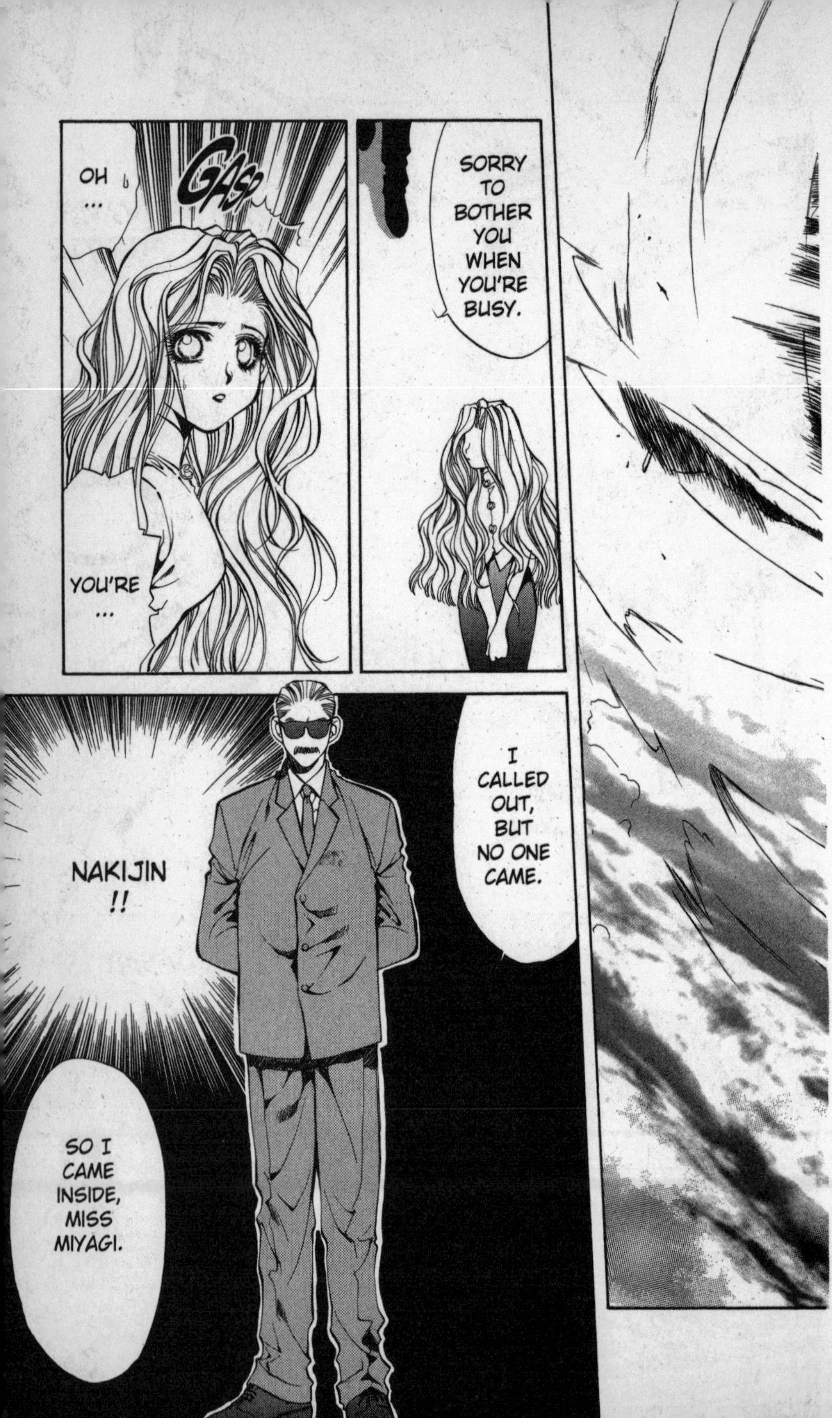
SORRY TO BOTHER YOU WHEN YOU'RE BUSY.
GASP
OH ...
YOU'RE ...
I CALLED OUT, BUT NO ONE CAME.
NAKIJIN !!
SO I CAME INSIDE, MISS MIYAGI.

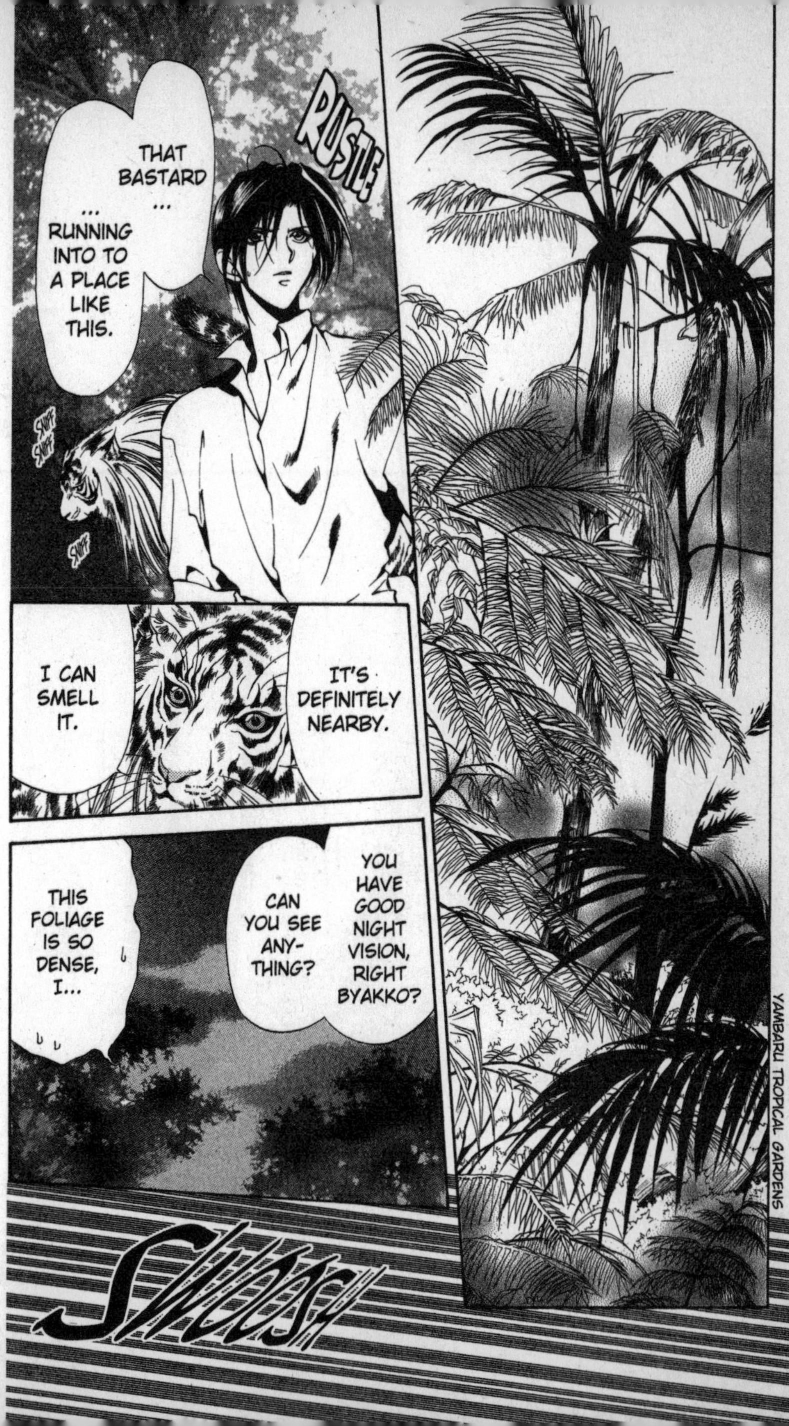
YAMBARU TROPICAL GARDENS
RUSTLE
THAT BASTARD ... RUNNING INTO TO A PLACE LIKE THIS.
SNIFF SNIFF
SNIFF
IT'S DEFINITELY NEARBY.
I CAN SMELL IT.
YOU HAVE GOOD NIGHT VISION, RIGHT BYAKKO?
CAN YOU SEE ANYTHING?
THIS FOLIAGE IS SO DENSE, I...
SWOOSH

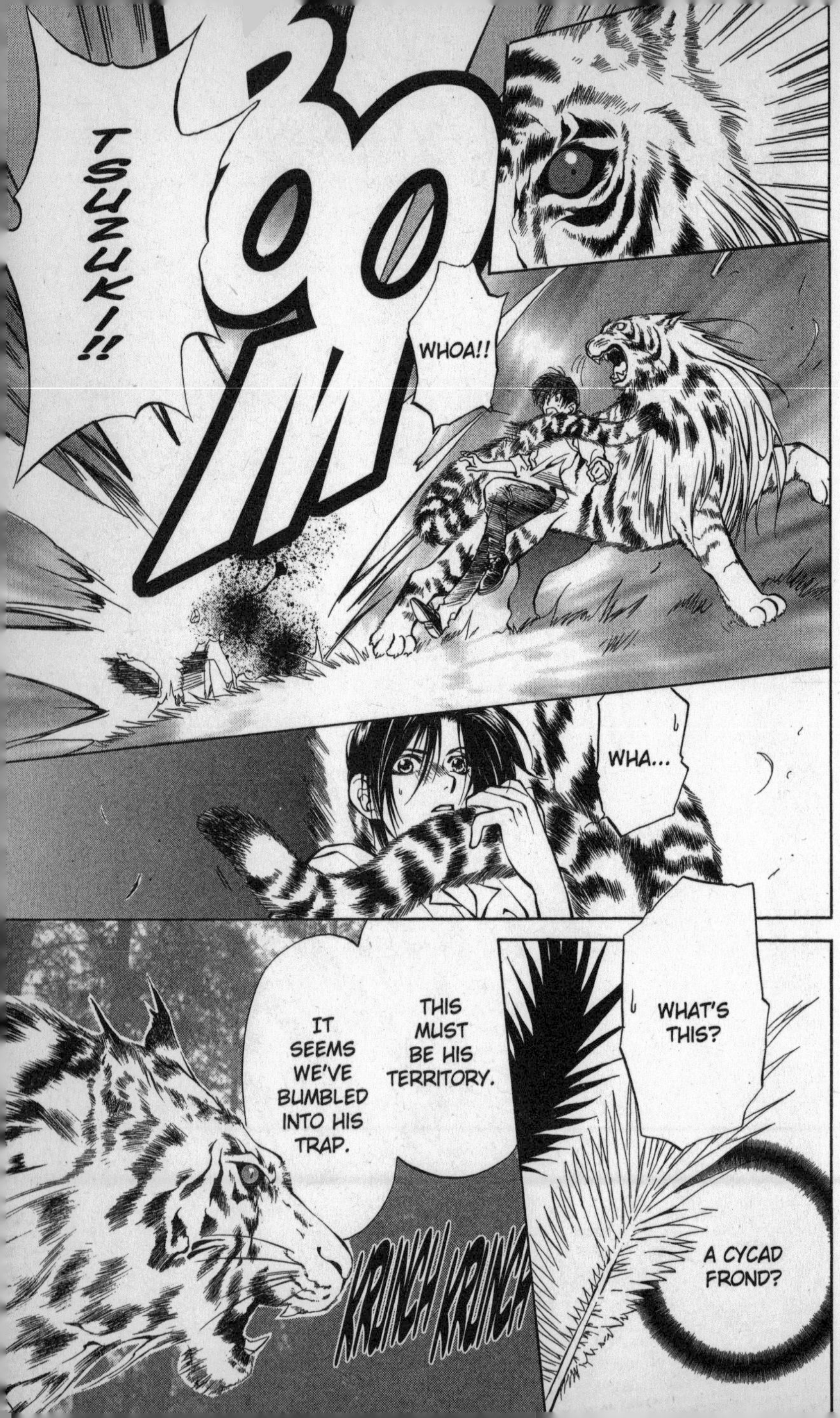
WHOA!!
ZOOM
TSUZUKI!!
WHA...
WHAT'S THIS?
A CYCAD FROND?
THIS MUST BE HIS TERRITORY.
IT SEEMS WE'VE BUMBLED INTO HIS TRAP.
KRUNCH KRUNCH

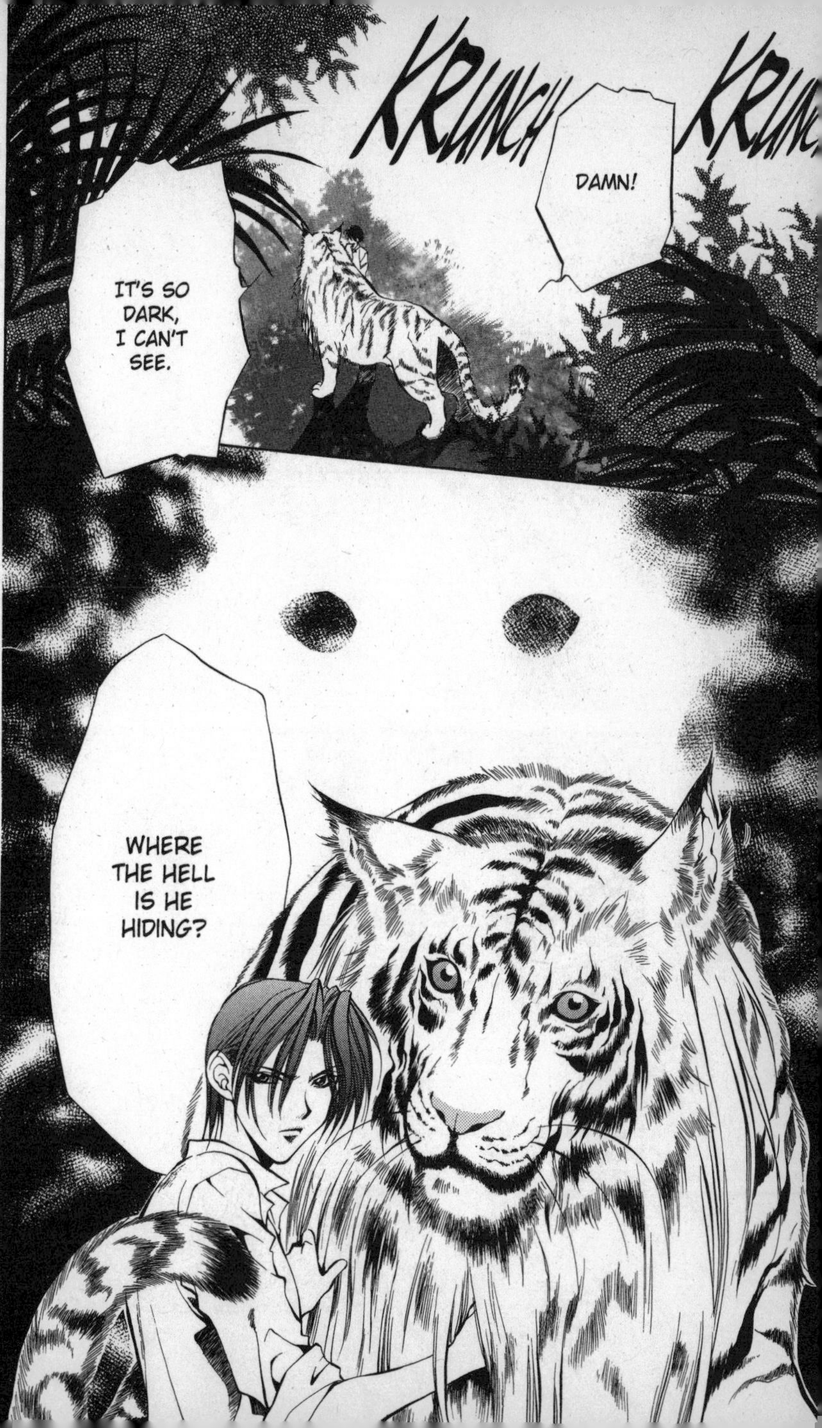
DAMN!
KRUNCH
IT'S SO DARK, I CAN'T SEE.
WHERE THE HELL IS HE HIDING?

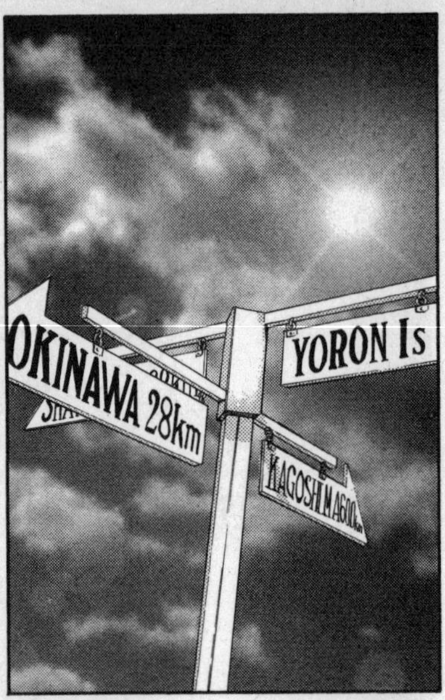
YORON Is
OKINAWA 28km
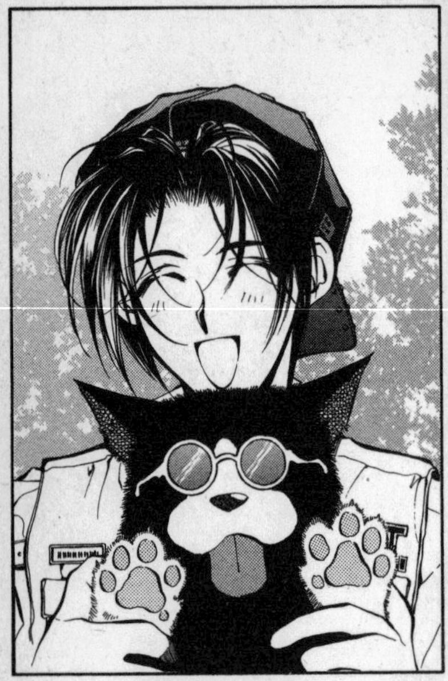
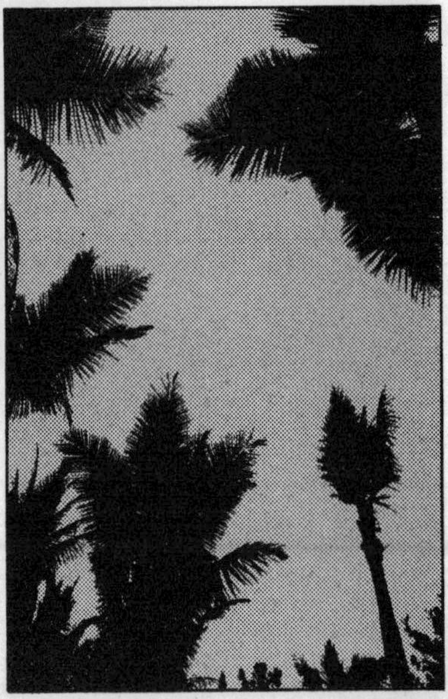
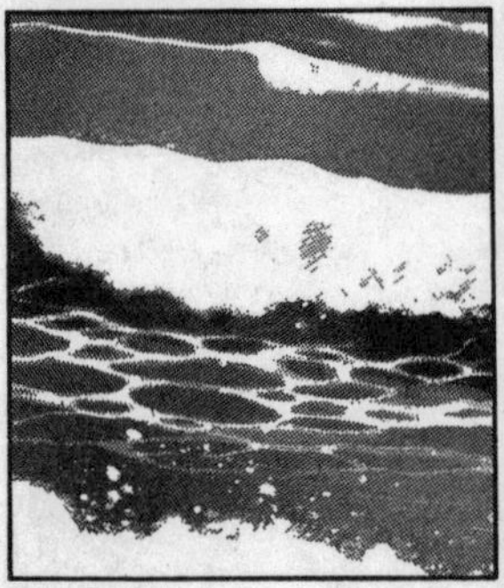

CHAPTER 17

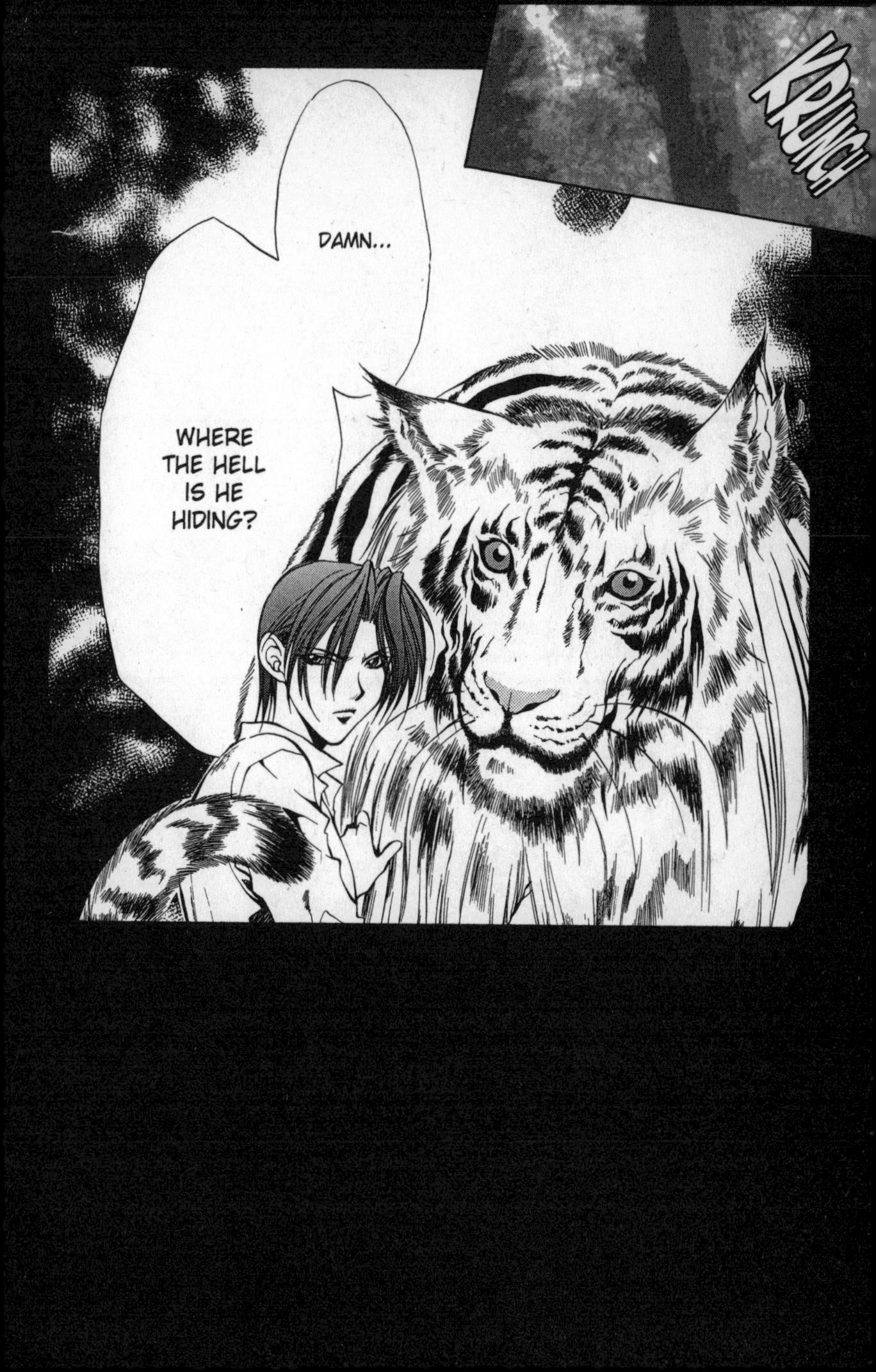
KRUNCH
DAMN...
WHERE THE HELL IS HE HIDING?

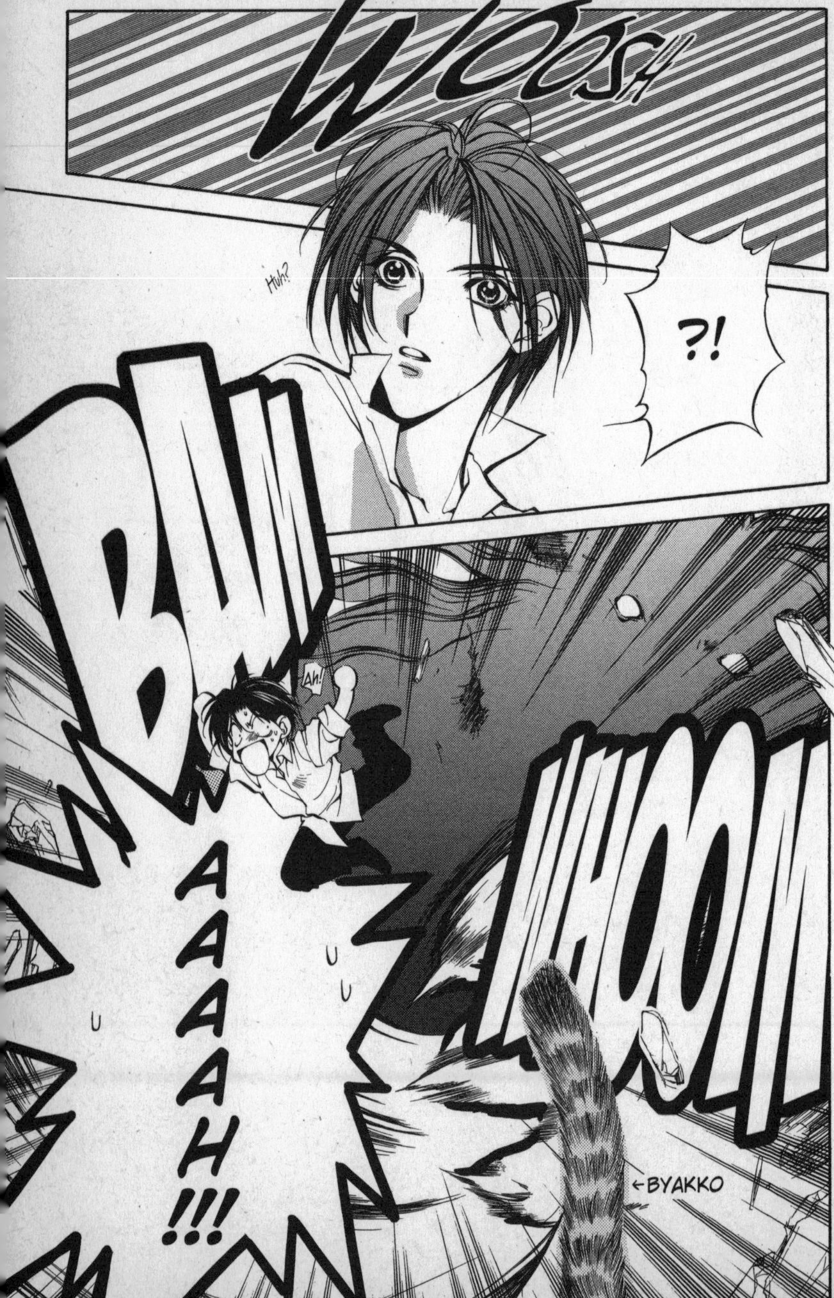
WOOSH
?!
Huh?
WHOOM
←BYAKKO
Ah!
BAM
AAAAAH!!!

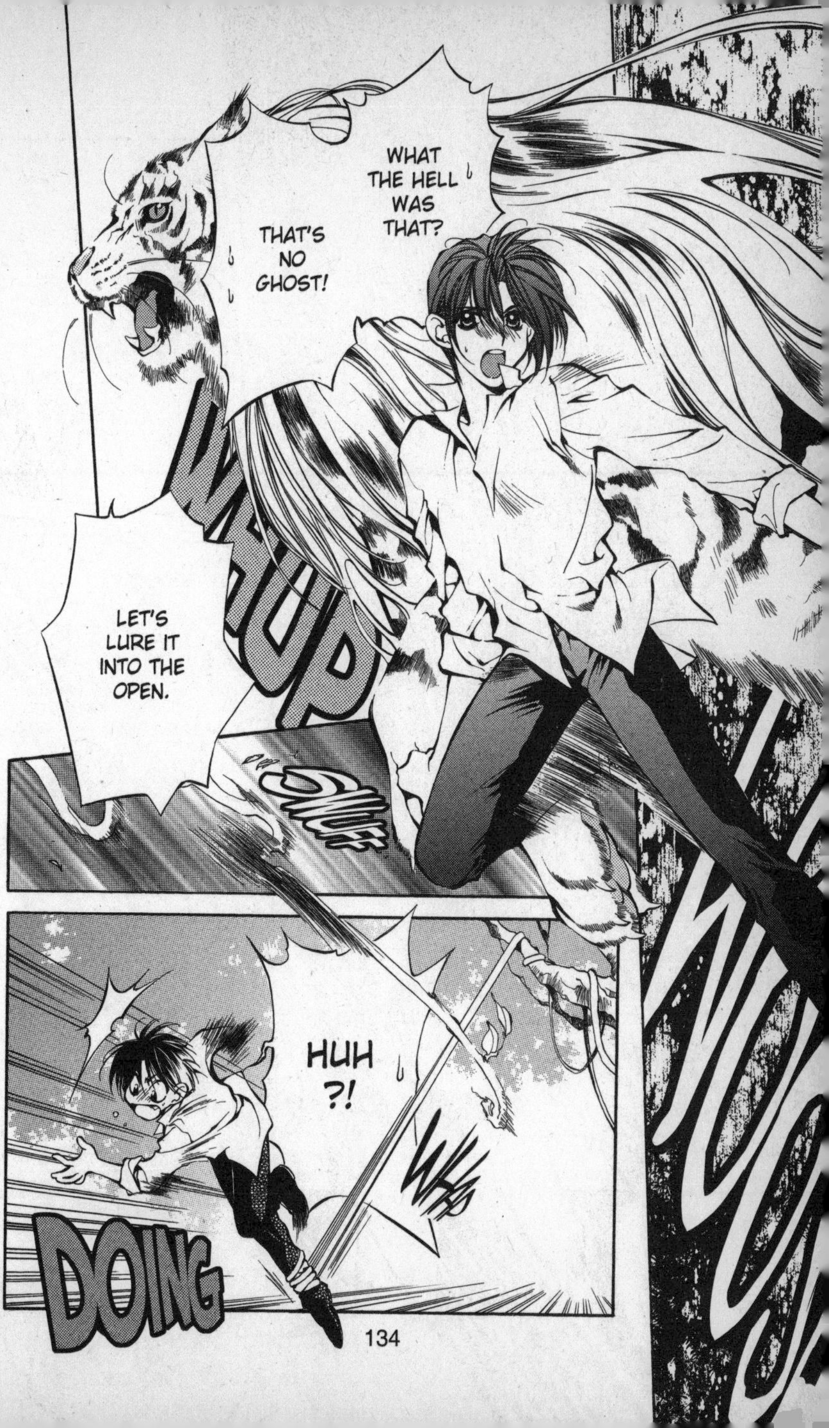
WHAT THE HELL WAS THAT?
THAT'S NO GHOST!
WHUP
LET'S LURE IT INTO THE OPEN.
SNUFF
HUH ?!
DOING

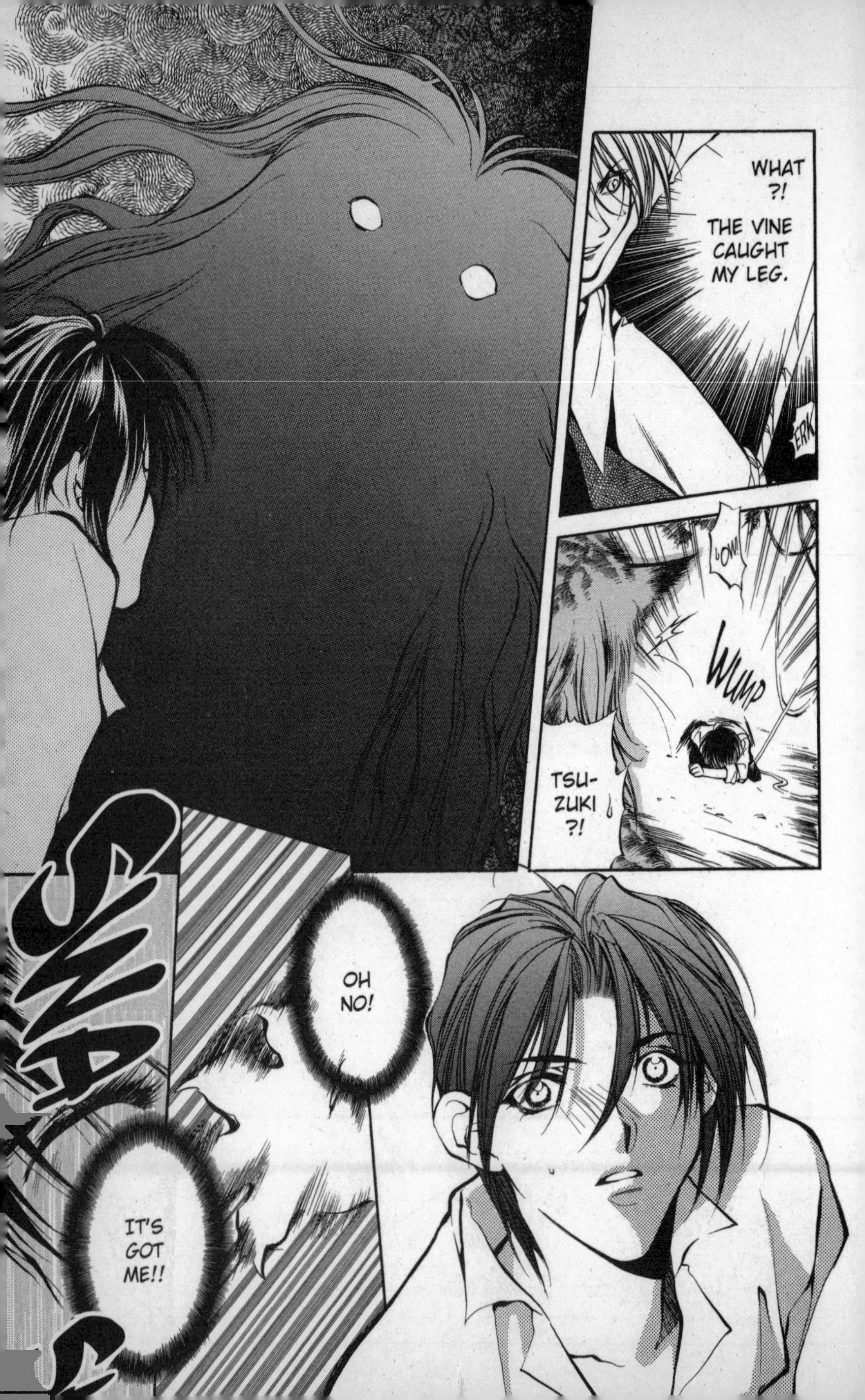
WHAT ?!
THE VINE CAUGHT MY LEG.
ERK
OW!
WUMP
TSU-ZUKI ?!
OH NO!
SNA
IT'S GOT ME!!

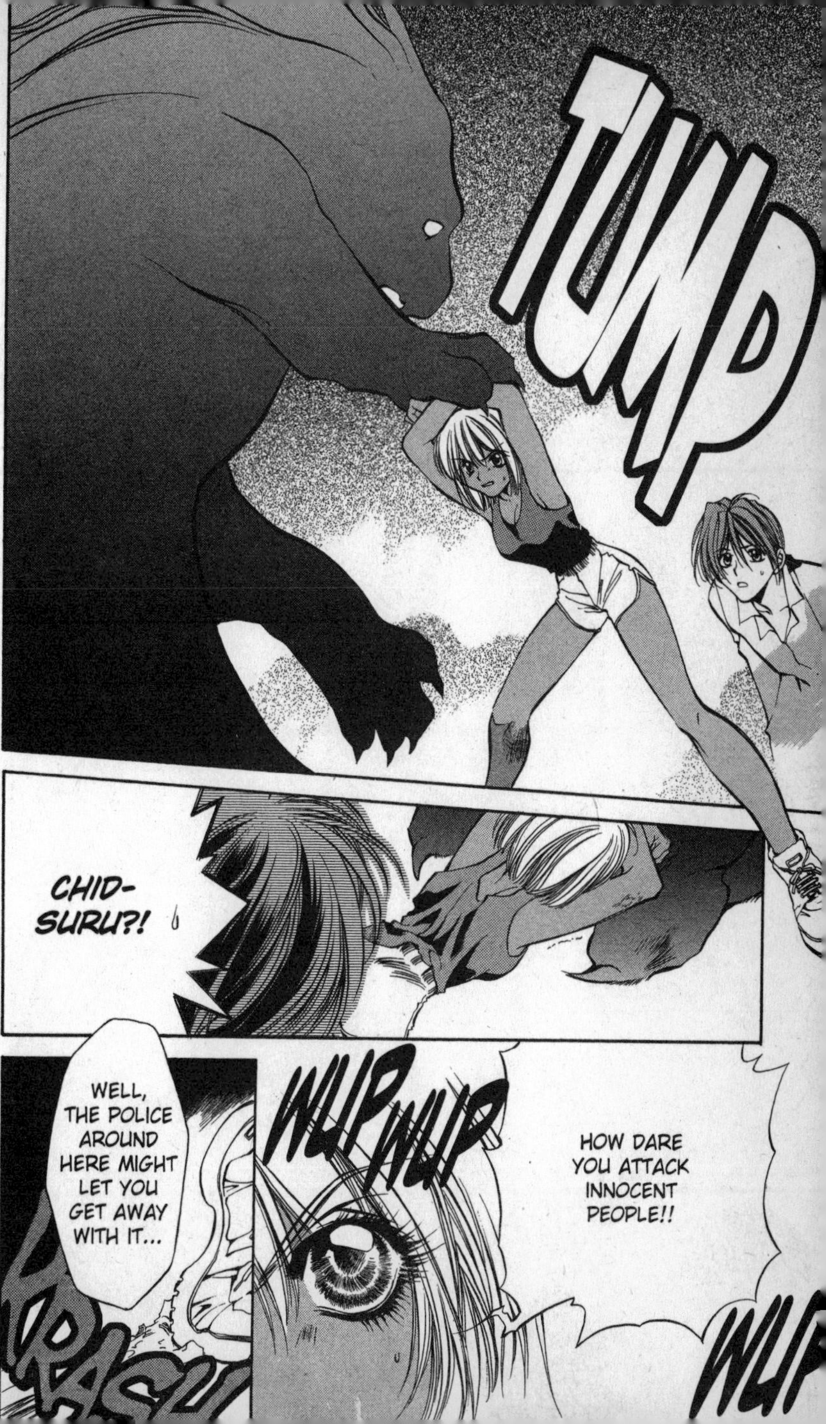
TUMP
CHID-SURU?!
HOW DARE YOU ATTACK INNOCENT PEOPLE!!
WUP WUP
WUP
WELL, THE POLICE AROUND HERE MIGHT LET YOU GET AWAY WITH IT...

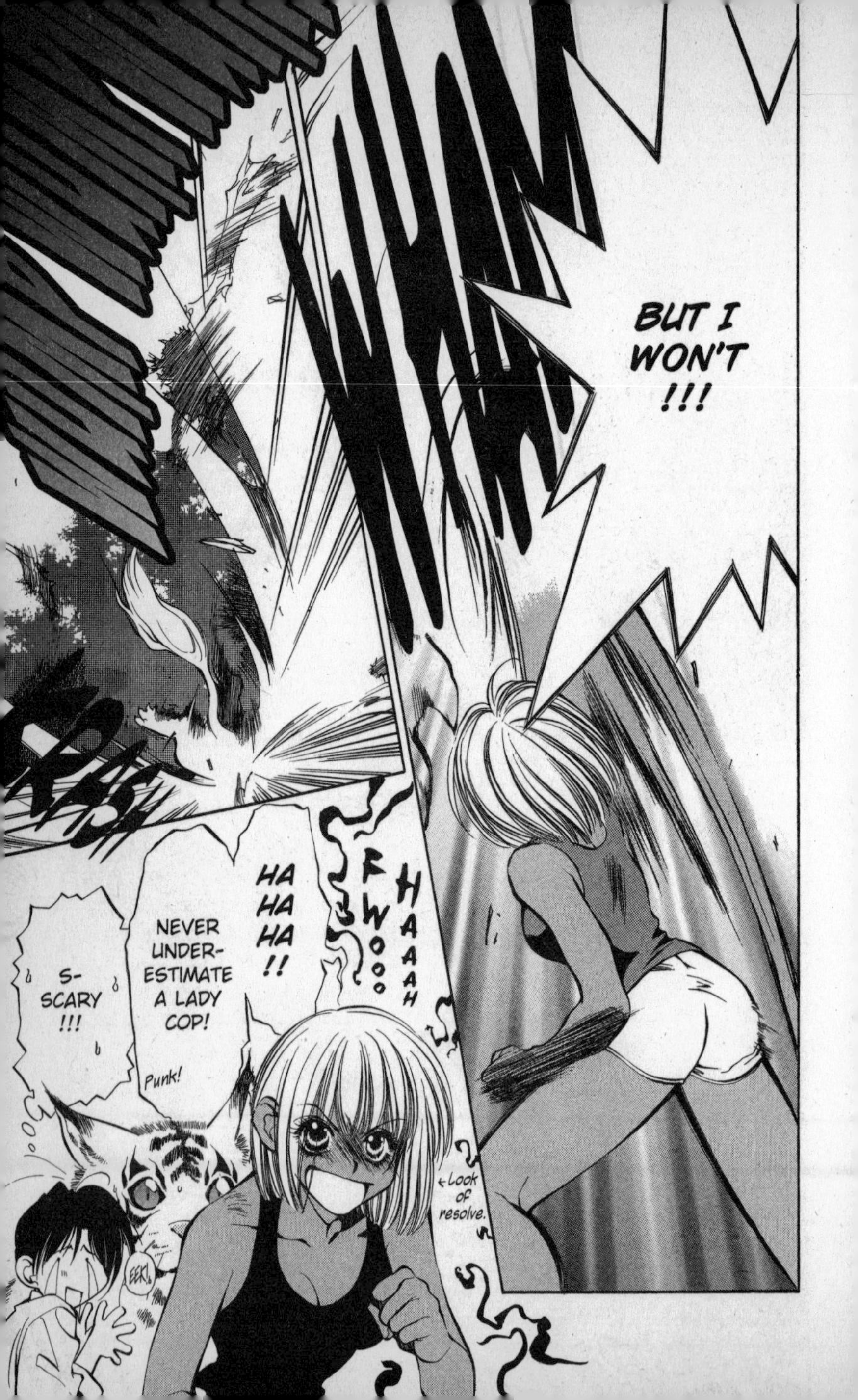
BUT I WON'T !!!
WHAM
KRASH
HAAAAH
FWOOO
HA HA HA !!
← Look of resolve.
NEVER UNDER-ESTIMATE A LADY COP!
Punk!
S-SCARY !!!
EEK!

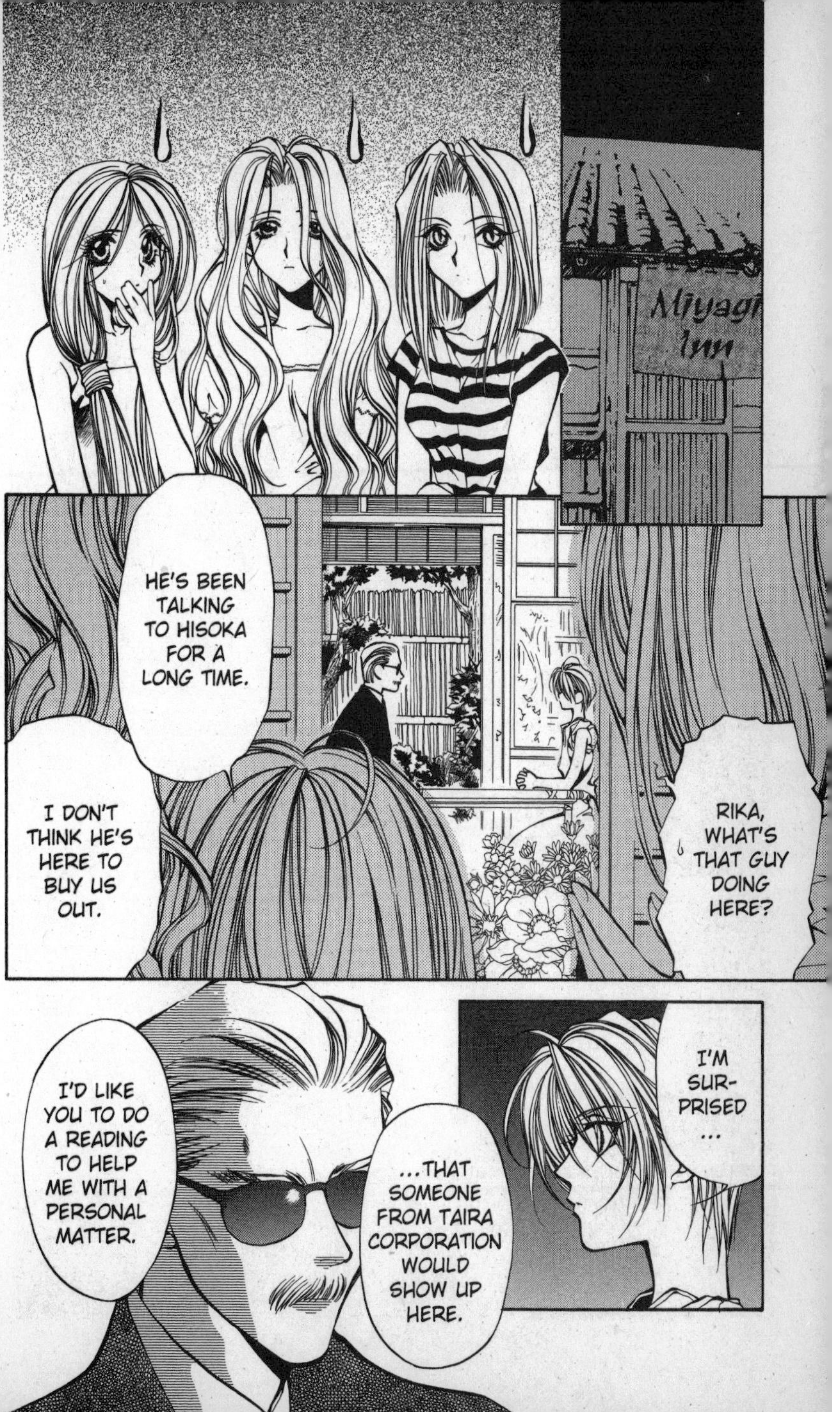
Miyagi Inn
RIKA, WHAT'S THAT GUY DOING HERE?
HE'S BEEN TALKING TO HISOKA FOR A LONG TIME.
I DON'T THINK HE'S HERE TO BUY US OUT.
I'M SUR-PRISED...
...THAT SOMEONE FROM TAIRA CORPORATION WOULD SHOW UP HERE.
I'D LIKE YOU TO DO A READING TO HELP ME WITH A PERSONAL MATTER.

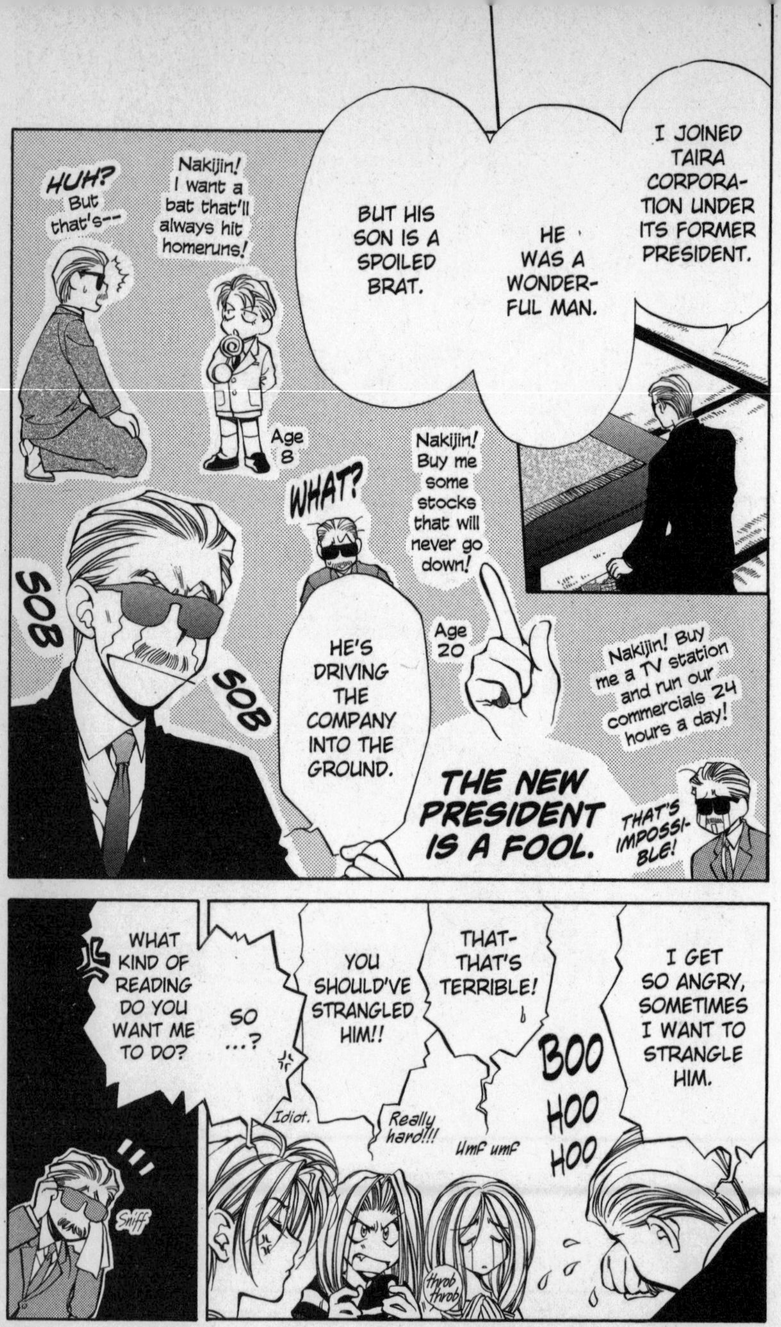
I JOINED TAIRA CORPORATION UNDER ITS FORMER PRESIDENT.
HE WAS A WONDERFUL MAN.
BUT HIS SON IS A SPOILED BRAT.
Nakijin! I want a bat that'll always hit homeruns!
HUH? But that's--
Age 8
Nakijin! Buy me some stocks that will never go down!
WHAT?
Age 20
Nakijin! Buy me a TV station and run our commercials 24 hours a day!
HE'S DRIVING THE COMPANY INTO THE GROUND.
SOB SOB
THE NEW PRESIDENT IS A FOOL.
THAT'S IMPOSSIBLE!
I GET SO ANGRY, SOMETIMES I WANT TO STRANGLE HIM.
BOO HOO HOO
THAT-THAT'S TERRIBLE!
Umf umf
YOU SHOULD'VE STRANGLED HIM!!
Really hard!!!
throb throb
SO ...?
Idiot.
WHAT KIND OF READING DO YOU WANT ME TO DO?
Sniff

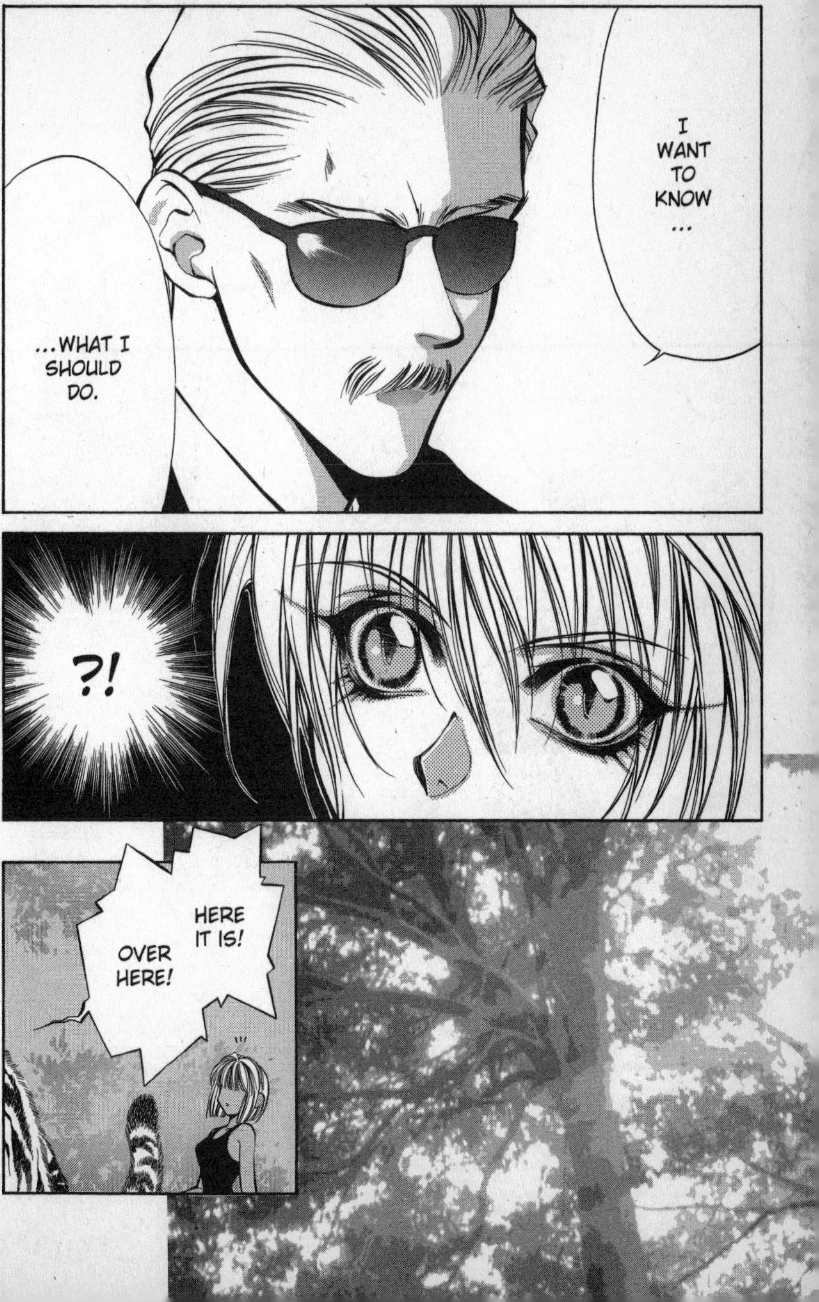
I WANT TO KNOW ...
...WHAT I SHOULD DO.
?!
HERE IT IS!
OVER HERE!

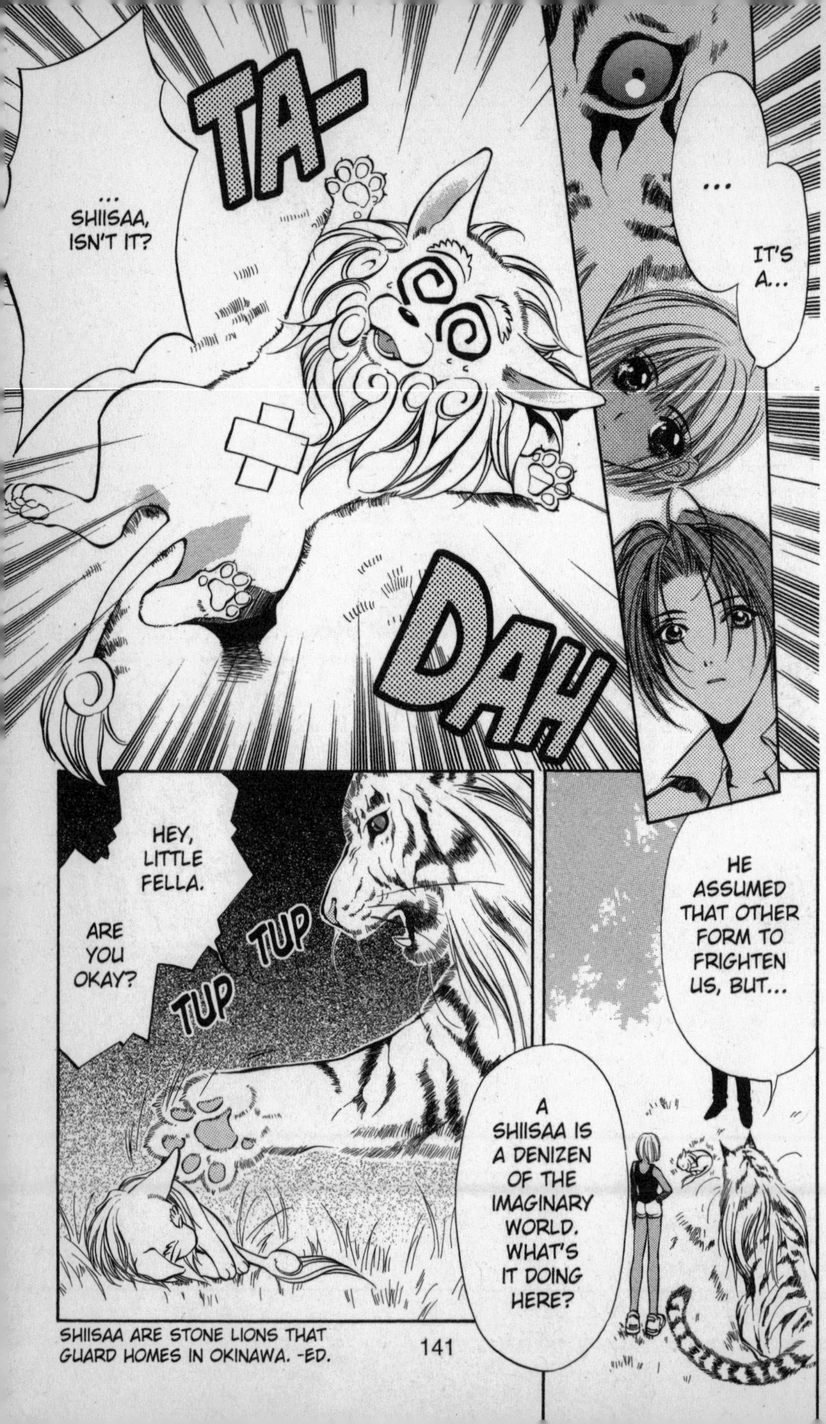

... IT'S A...
... SHIISAA, ISN'T IT?
TA- DAH
HE ASSUMED THAT OTHER FORM TO FRIGHTEN US, BUT...
A SHIISAA IS A DENIZEN OF THE IMAGINARY WORLD. WHAT'S IT DOING HERE?
HEY, LITTLE FELLA.
ARE YOU OKAY?
TUP TUP
TUP

SHIISAA ARE STONE LIONS THAT GUARD HOMES IN OKINAWA. -ED.

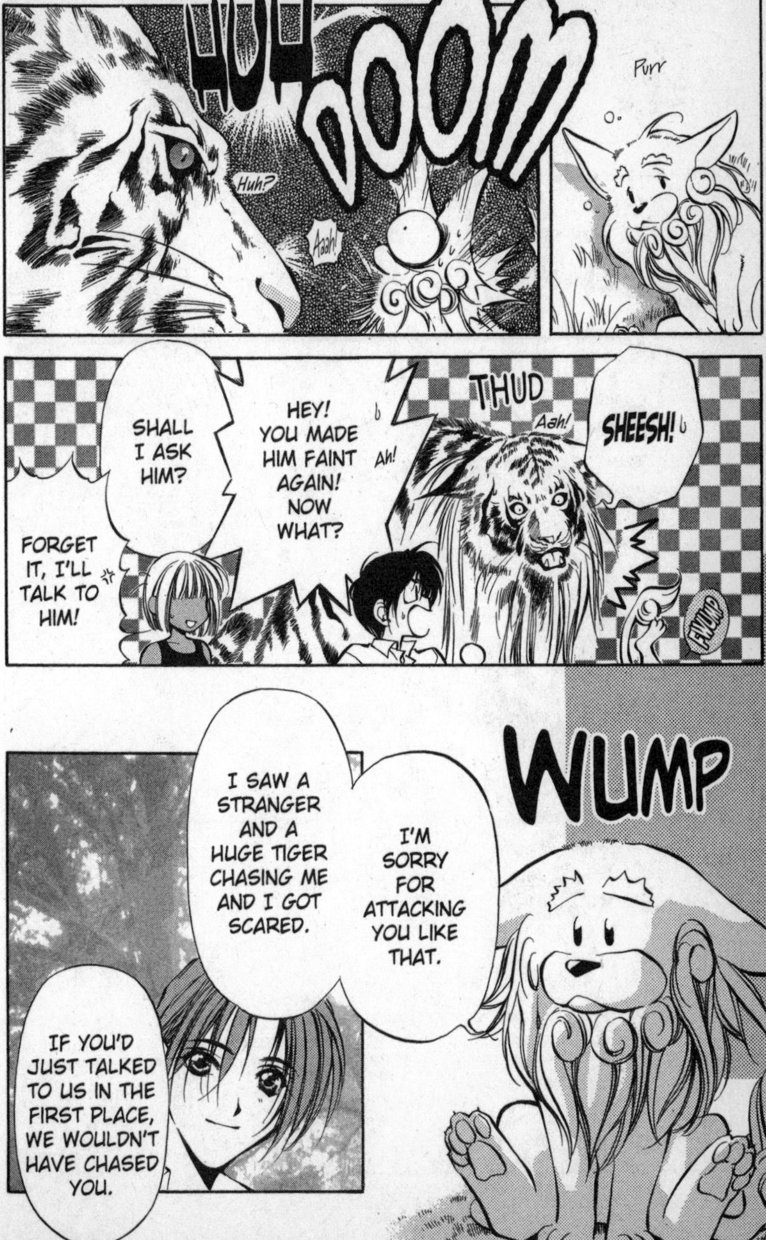
Purr
DOOM
HUH
Huh?
Aah!
SHEESH!
THUD
Aah!
FWUMP
Ah!
HEY! YOU MADE HIM FAINT AGAIN! NOW WHAT?
SHALL I ASK HIM?
FORGET IT, I'LL TALK TO HIM!
WUMP
I'M SORRY FOR ATTACKING YOU LIKE THAT.
I SAW A STRANGER AND A HUGE TIGER CHASING ME AND I GOT SCARED.
IF YOU'D JUST TALKED TO US IN THE FIRST PLACE, WE WOULDN'T HAVE CHASED YOU.

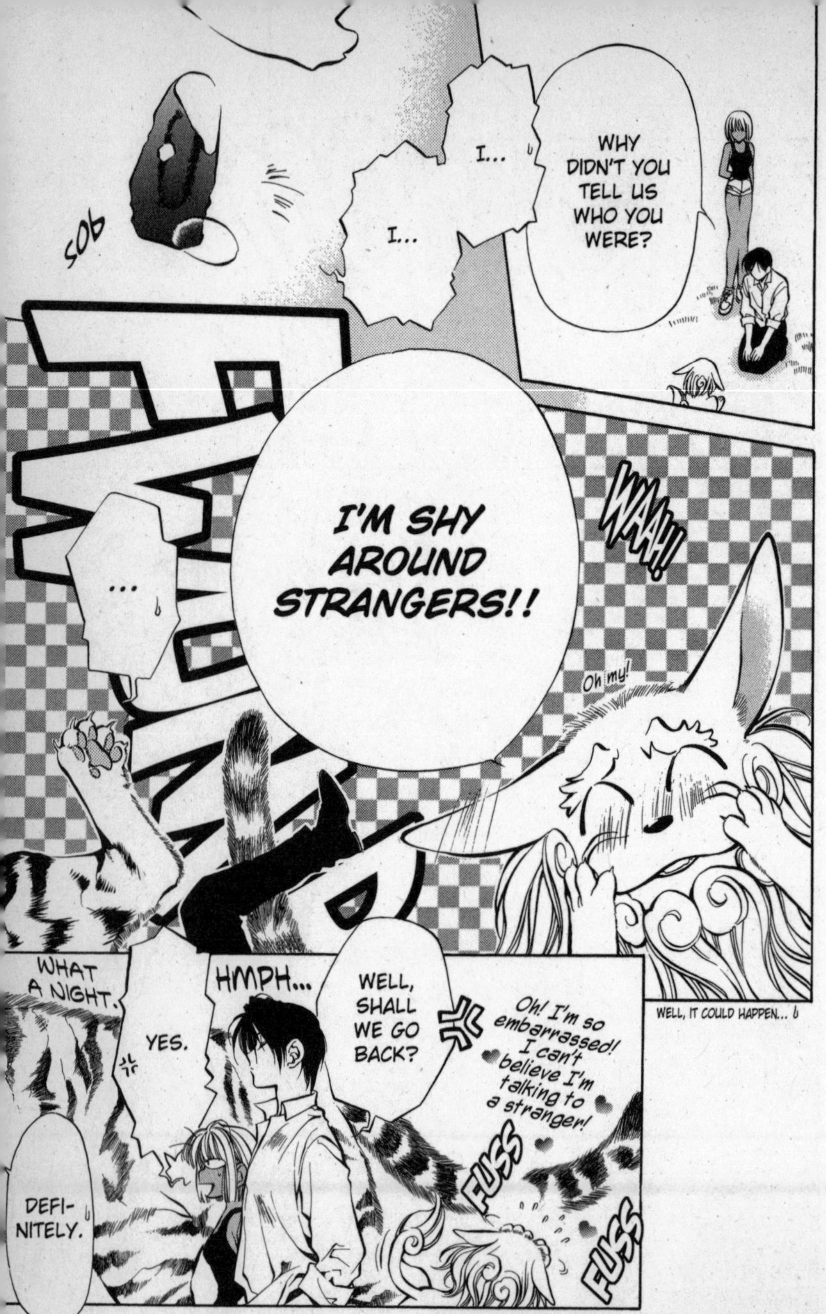

WHY DIDN'T YOU TELL US WHO YOU WERE?
I...
I...
SOB
I'M SHY AROUND STRANGERS!!
WAAH!!
Oh my!
...
WELL, IT COULD HAPPEN...
Oh! I'm so embarrassed! I can't believe I'm talking to a stranger!
FUSS
FUSS
WELL, SHALL WE GO BACK?
HMPH...
YES.
WHAT A NIGHT.
DEFI-NITELY.

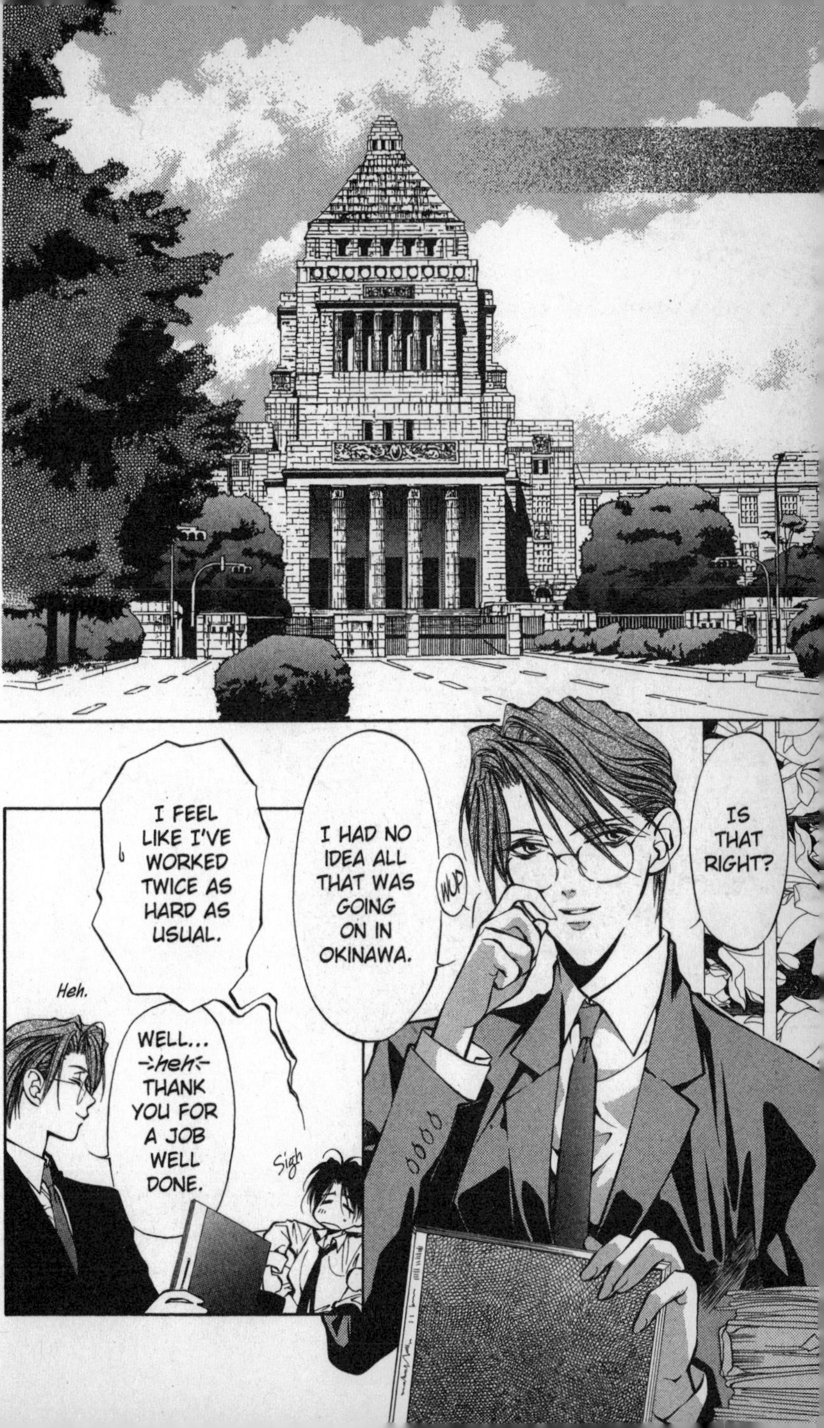
IS THAT RIGHT?
I HAD NO IDEA ALL THAT WAS GOING ON IN OKINAWA.
WUP
I FEEL LIKE I'VE WORKED TWICE AS HARD AS USUAL.
Heh.
WELL... -heh- THANK YOU FOR A JOB WELL DONE.
Sigh

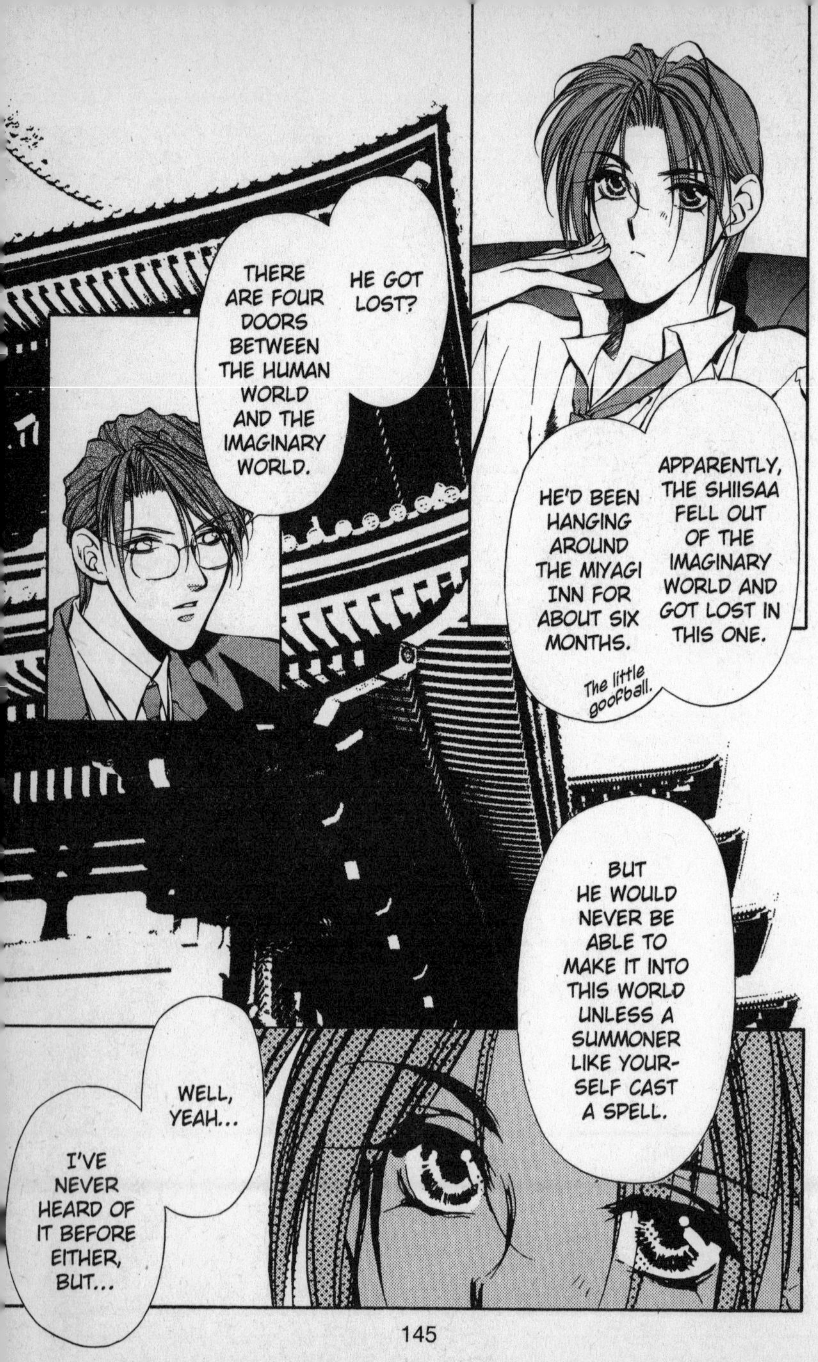
APPARENTLY, THE SHIISAA FELL OUT OF THE IMAGINARY WORLD AND GOT LOST IN THIS ONE.
HE'D BEEN HANGING AROUND THE MIYAGI INN FOR ABOUT SIX MONTHS.
The little goofball.
HE GOT LOST?
THERE ARE FOUR DOORS BETWEEN THE HUMAN WORLD AND THE IMAGINARY WORLD.
BUT HE WOULD NEVER BE ABLE TO MAKE IT INTO THIS WORLD UNLESS A SUMMONER LIKE YOUR-SELF CAST A SPELL.
WELL, YEAH...
I'VE NEVER HEARD OF IT BEFORE EITHER, BUT...

IT ONLY HAPPENS ONCE EVERY COUPLE OF CENTURIES.

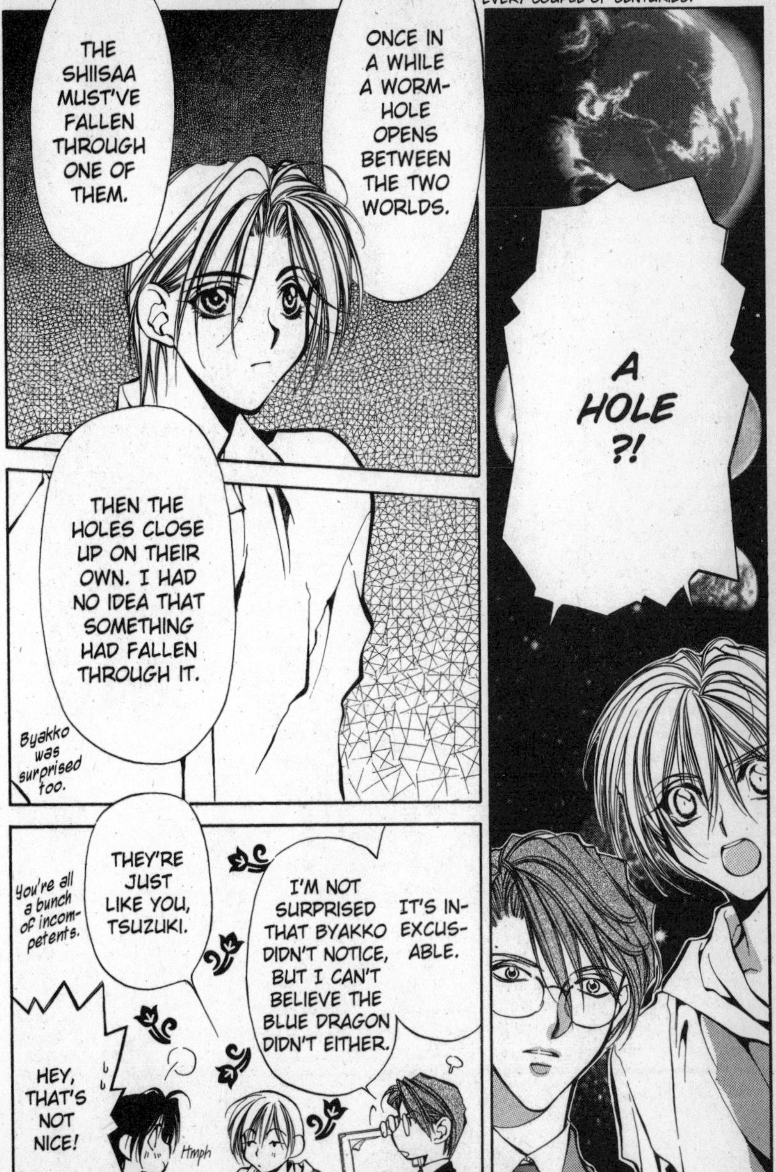
A HOLE ?!
ONCE IN A WHILE A WORM-HOLE OPENS BETWEEN THE TWO WORLDS.
THE SHIISAA MUST'VE FALLEN THROUGH ONE OF THEM.
THEN THE HOLES CLOSE UP ON THEIR OWN. I HAD NO IDEA THAT SOMETHING HAD FALLEN THROUGH IT.
Byakko was surprised too.
I'M NOT SURPRISED THAT BYAKKO DIDN'T NOTICE, BUT I CAN'T BELIEVE THE BLUE DRAGON DIDN'T EITHER.
IT'S IN-EXCUS-ABLE.
THEY'RE JUST LIKE YOU, TSUZUKI.
You're all a bunch of incom-petents.
HEY, THAT'S NOT NICE!
Hmph

HE MIGHT BE RIGHT. HA!

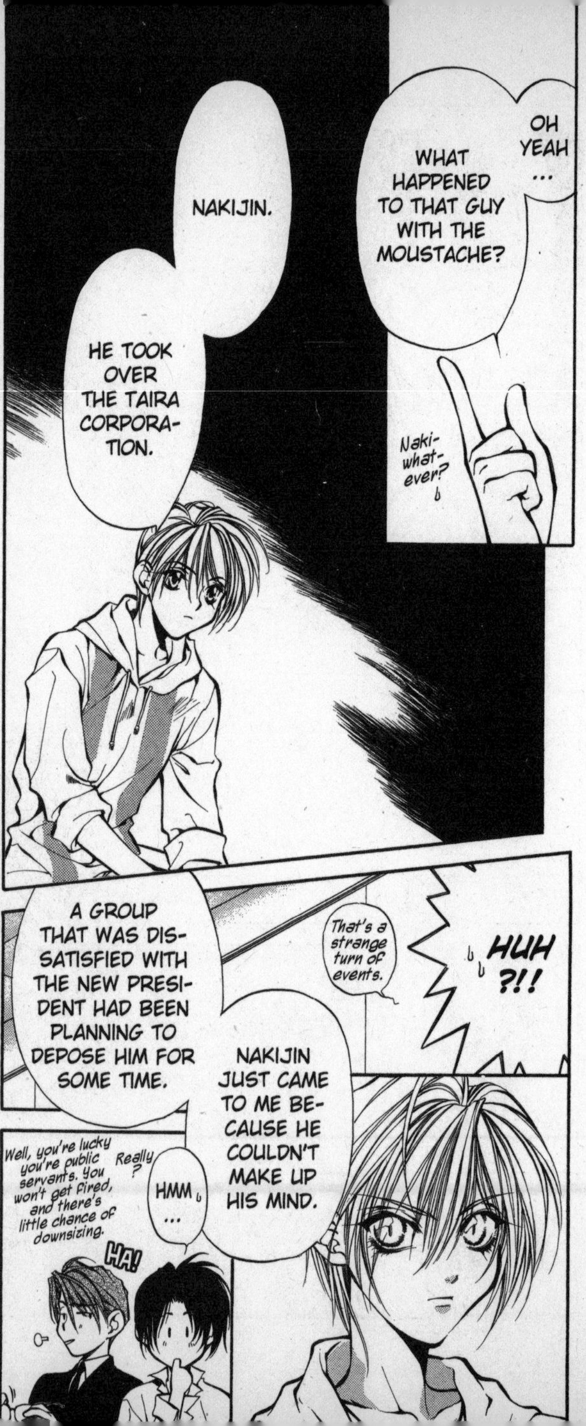
OH YEAH ...
WHAT HAPPENED TO THAT GUY WITH THE MOUSTACHE?
Naki-whatever?
NAKIJIN.
HE TOOK OVER THE TAIRA CORPORATION.
HUH ?!!
That's a strange turn of events.
A GROUP THAT WAS DISSATISFIED WITH THE NEW PRESIDENT HAD BEEN PLANNING TO DEPOSE HIM FOR SOME TIME.
NAKIJIN JUST CAME TO ME BECAUSE HE COULDN'T MAKE UP HIS MIND.
Really?
Well, you're lucky you're public servants. You won't get fired, and there's little chance of downsizing.
HMM ...
HA!

Lesson 4:
Things included with your letter

A lot of people include accessories with their letters. But I never wear accessories. If you really want to send something, please wrap it in bubble wrap (the kind that goes--Pop! Pop!), or in thick paper. Otherwise, the envelope ends up tearing, and the contents fall out before I get the letter. So please be careful.

I have a few other points to write about...

If you're going to use fanzine letterhead, please make sure you use the same paper for the whole letter. It's hard to read a letter where each page has different letterhead. Also, many people write me using pseudonyms. Please don't. There's no reason to hide your identity when you write to me. Finally, I prefer black and blue pens. Please don't use magic markers or felt tips.

THAT'S ALL! THE END!

WHEN FOLDING YOUR LETTERS, PLEASE PLACE ALL THE PAPERS TOGETHER AND FOLD THEM EITHER THREE OR FOUR TIMES. WHEN LETTERS ARE FOLDED IN A COMPLICATED WAY, IT MAKES THEM HARD TO OPEN.

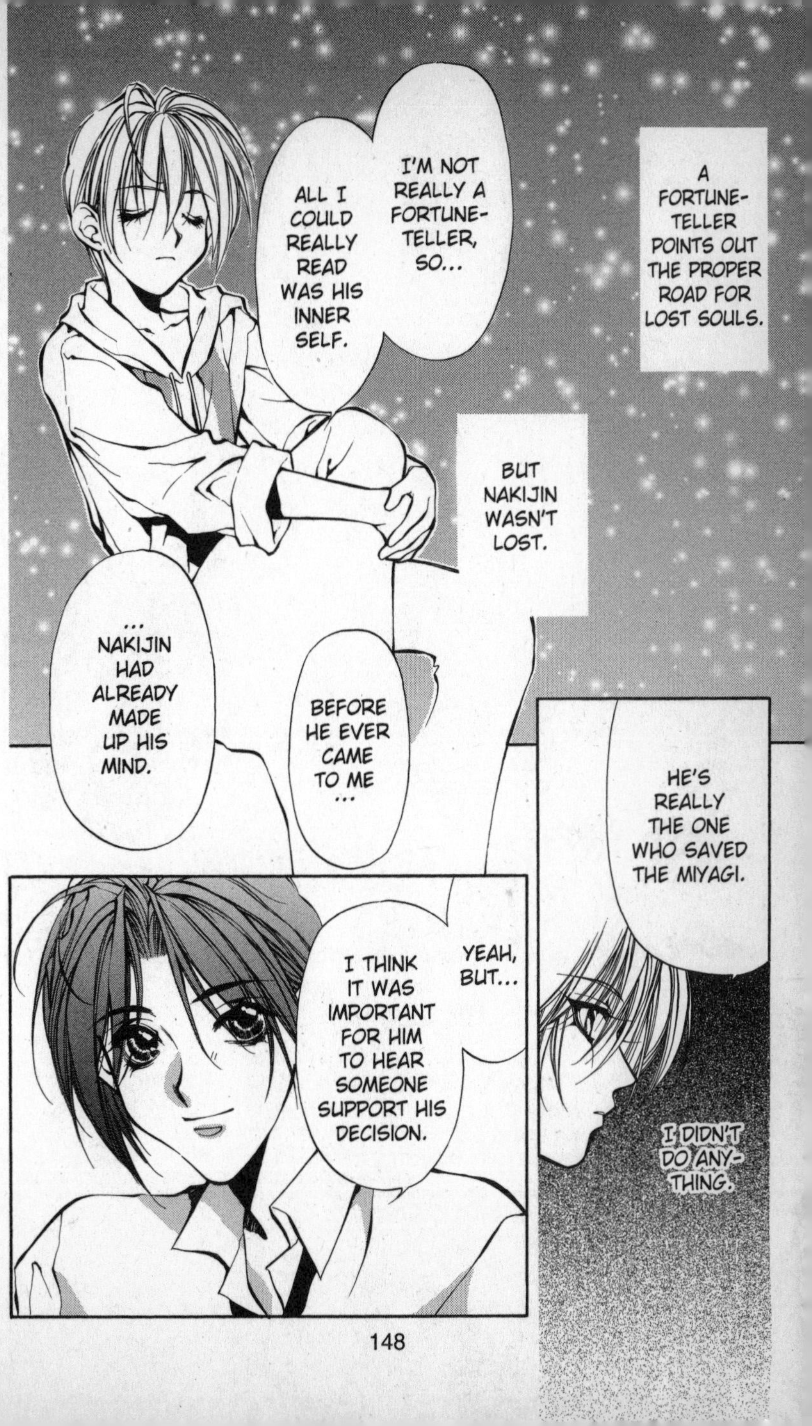
A FORTUNE-TELLER POINTS OUT THE PROPER ROAD FOR LOST SOULS.
I'M NOT REALLY A FORTUNE-TELLER, SO...
ALL I COULD REALLY READ WAS HIS INNER SELF.
BUT NAKIJIN WASN'T LOST.
BEFORE HE EVER CAME TO ME...
...NAKIJIN HAD ALREADY MADE UP HIS MIND.
HE'S REALLY THE ONE WHO SAVED THE MIYAGI.
I DIDN'T DO ANYTHING.
YEAH, BUT...
I THINK IT WAS IMPORTANT FOR HIM TO HEAR SOMEONE SUPPORT HIS DECISION.

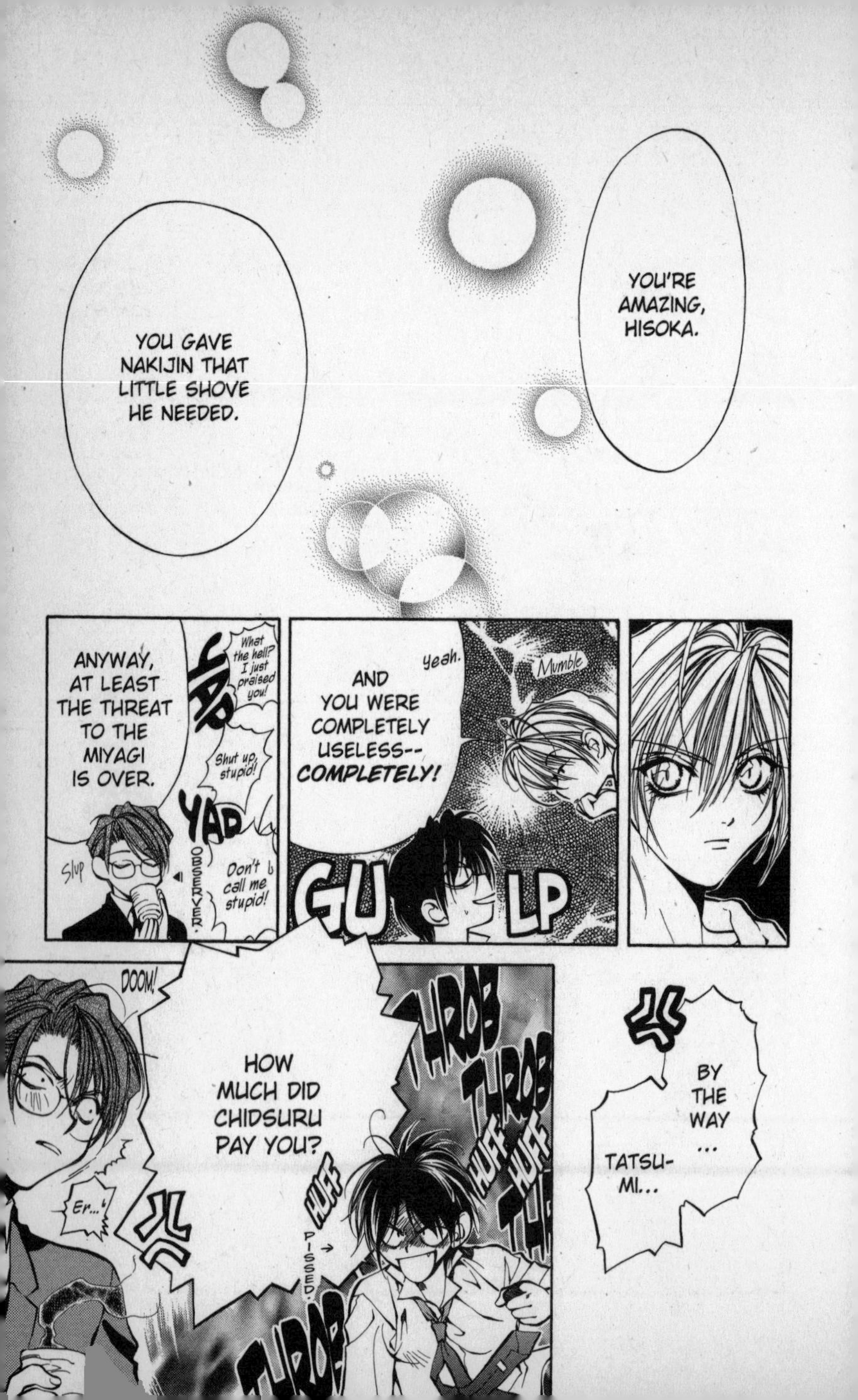
YOU'RE AMAZING, HISOKA.
YOU GAVE NAKIJIN THAT LITTLE SHOVE HE NEEDED.
Mumble
yeah.
AND YOU WERE COMPLETELY USELESS-- COMPLETELY!
GULP
ANYWAY, AT LEAST THE THREAT TO THE MIYAGI IS OVER.
What the hell? I just praised you!
YAP
Shut up, stupid!
YAP
OBSERVER.
Slup
Don't call me stupid!
BY THE WAY...
TATSUMI...
THROB
THROB
HUFF
HUFF
HOW MUCH DID CHIDSURU PAY YOU?
DOOM!
Er...
PISSED.
THROB

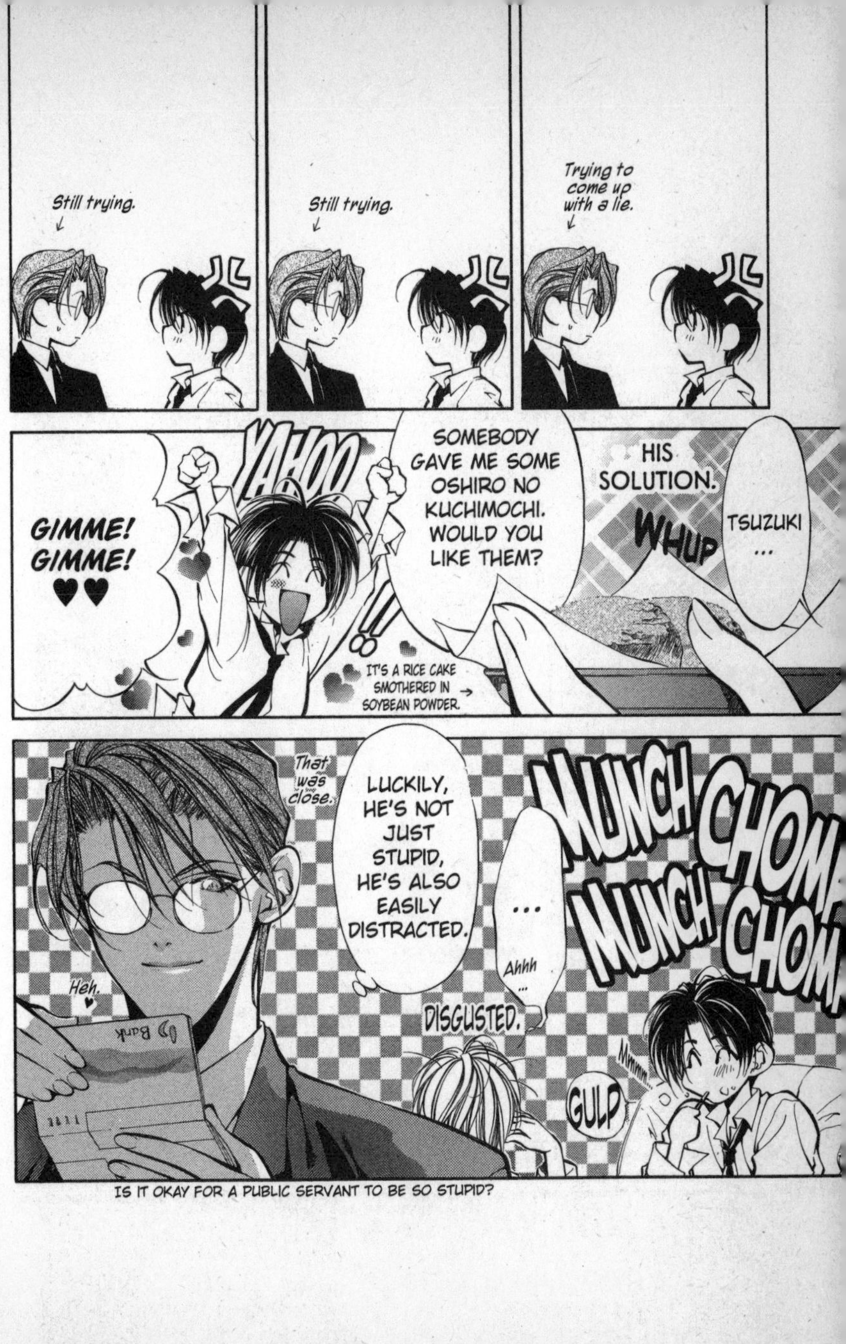

Trying to come up with a lie.
Still trying.
Still trying.
TSUZUKI ...
HIS SOLUTION.
WHUP
SOMEBODY GAVE ME SOME OSHIRO NO KUCHIMOCHI. WOULD YOU LIKE THEM?
YAHOO
GIMME! GIMME! ♥♥
IT'S A RICE CAKE SMOTHERED IN SOYBEAN POWDER.
MUNCH CHOMP
MUNCH CHOMP
...
Ahhh ...
DISGUSTED.
GULP
Mmmm...
LUCKILY, HE'S NOT JUST STUPID, HE'S ALSO EASILY DISTRACTED.
That was close.
Heh. ♥
Bank

IS IT OKAY FOR A PUBLIC SERVANT TO BE SO STUPID?

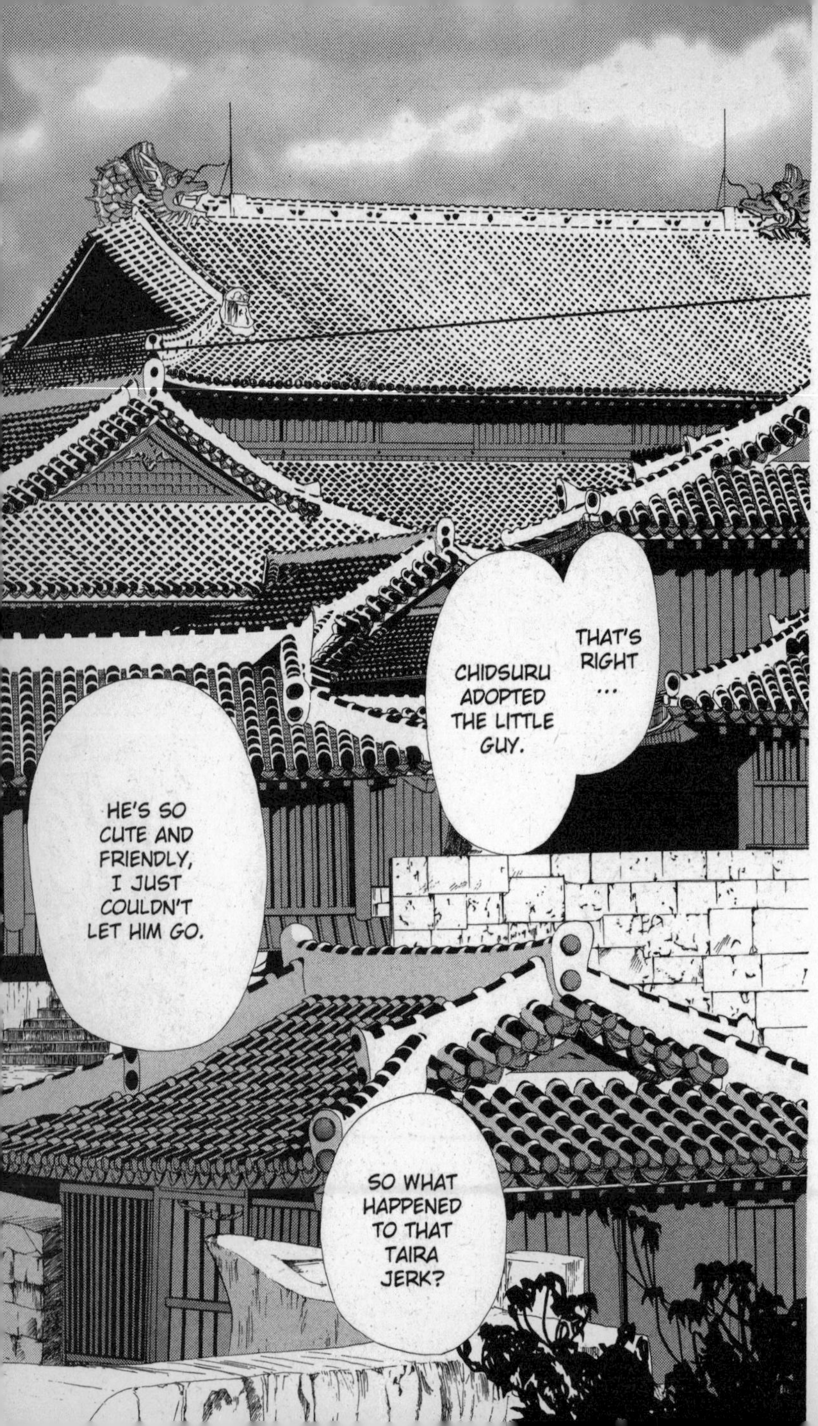
THAT'S RIGHT ... CHIDSURU ADOPTED THE LITTLE GUY.
HE'S SO CUTE AND FRIENDLY, I JUST COULDN'T LET HIM GO.
SO WHAT HAPPENED TO THAT TAIRA JERK?

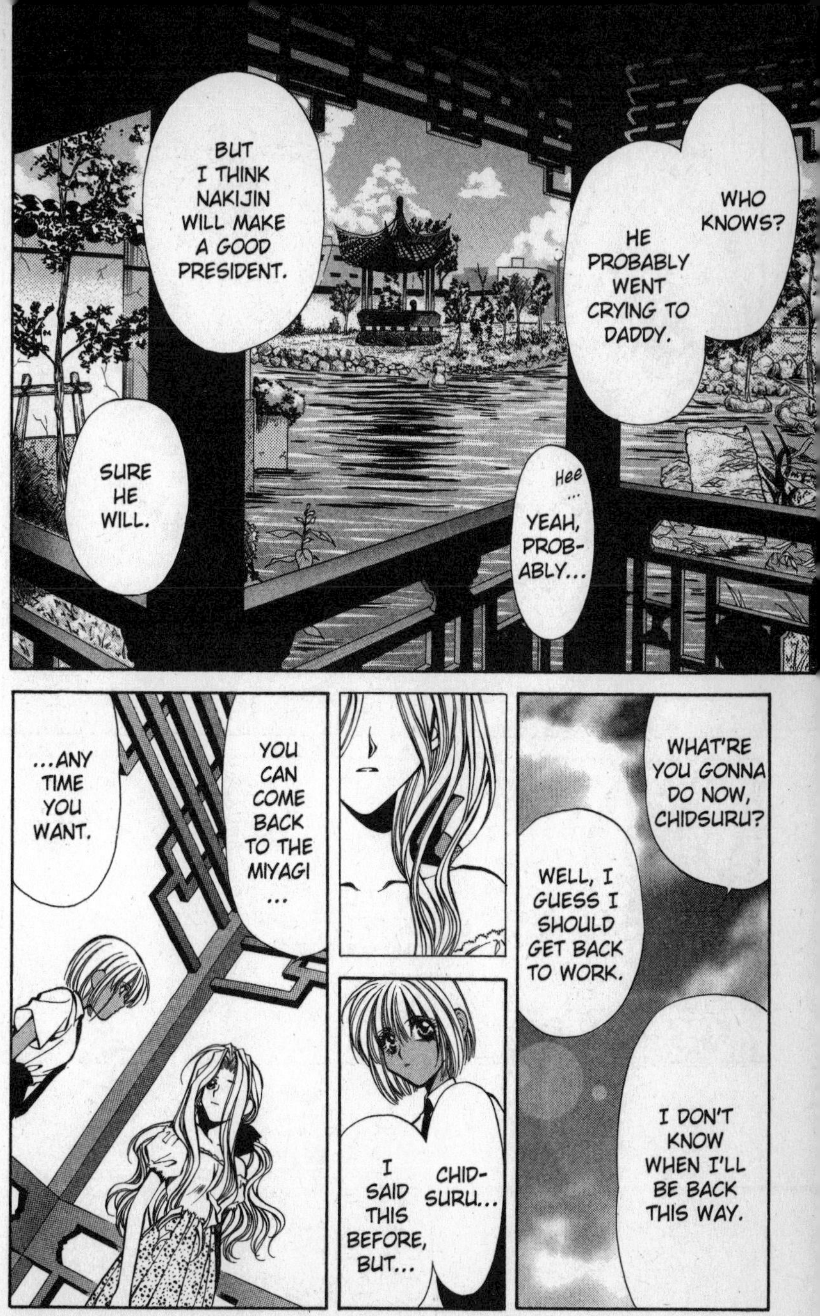
WHO KNOWS?
HE PROBABLY WENT CRYING TO DADDY.
Hee... YEAH, PROBABLY...
BUT I THINK NAKIJIN WILL MAKE A GOOD PRESIDENT.
SURE HE WILL.
WHAT'RE YOU GONNA DO NOW, CHIDSURU?
WELL, I GUESS I SHOULD GET BACK TO WORK.
I DON'T KNOW WHEN I'LL BE BACK THIS WAY.
CHID-SURU...
I SAID THIS BEFORE, BUT...
YOU CAN COME BACK TO THE MIYAGI...
...ANY TIME YOU WANT.

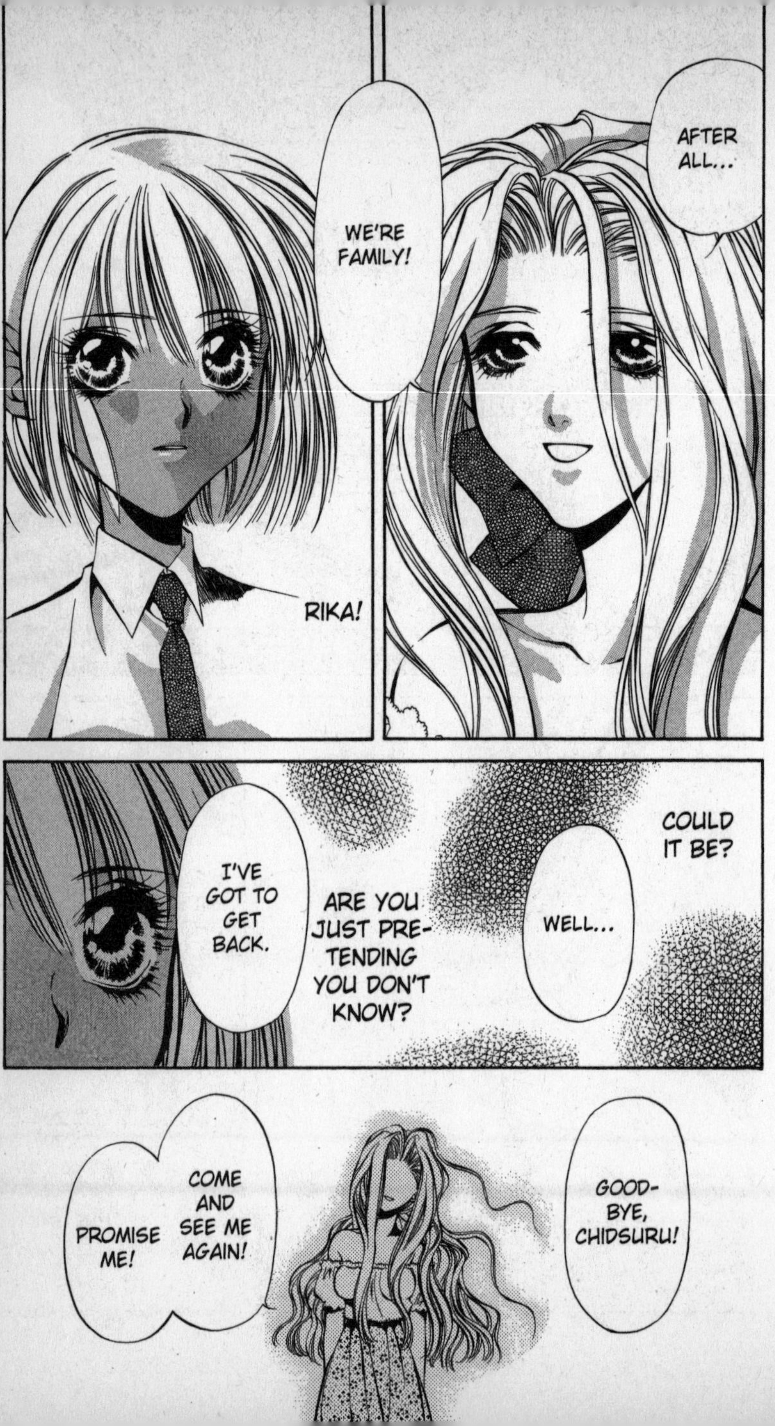
AFTER ALL...
WE'RE FAMILY!
RIKA!
COULD IT BE?
WELL...
ARE YOU JUST PRE-TENDING YOU DON'T KNOW?
I'VE GOT TO GET BACK.
GOOD-BYE, CHIDSURU!
COME AND SEE ME AGAIN!
PROMISE ME!

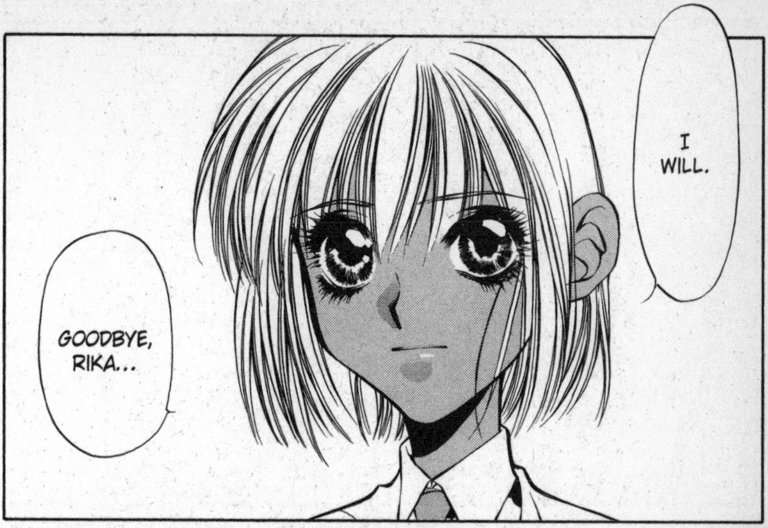
I WILL.
GOODBYE, RIKA...
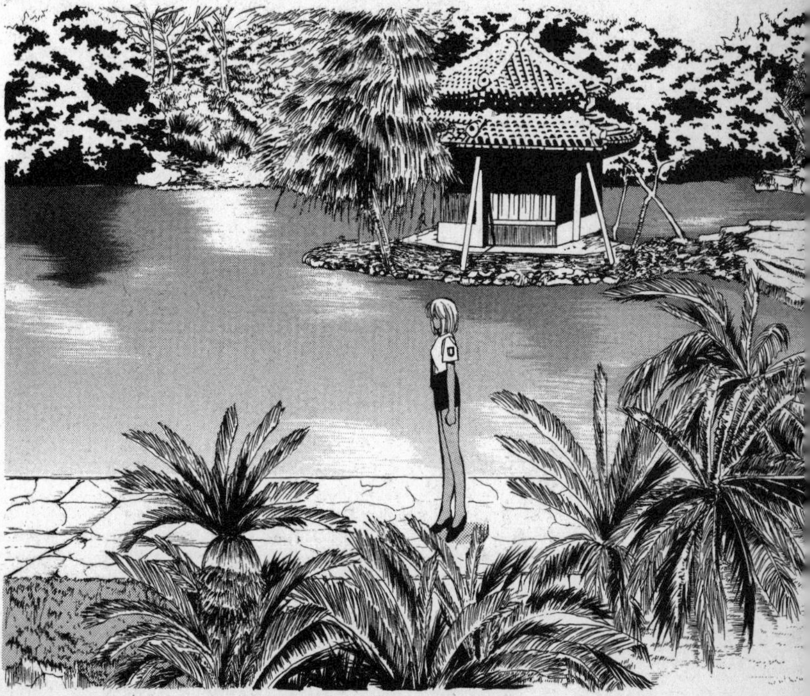

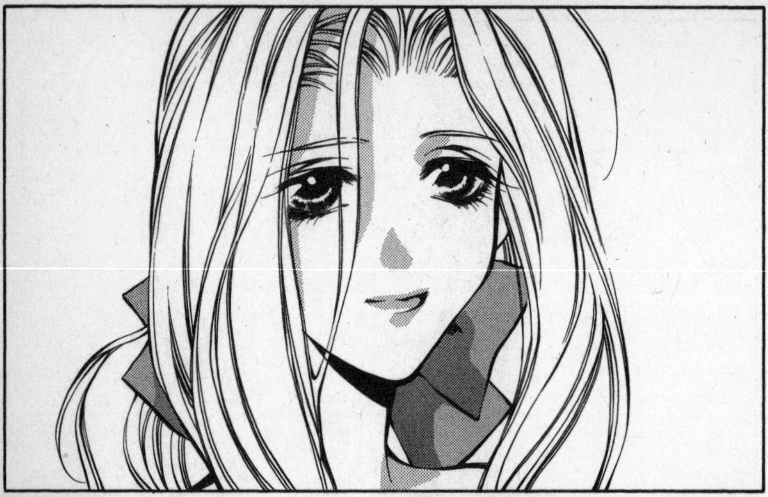

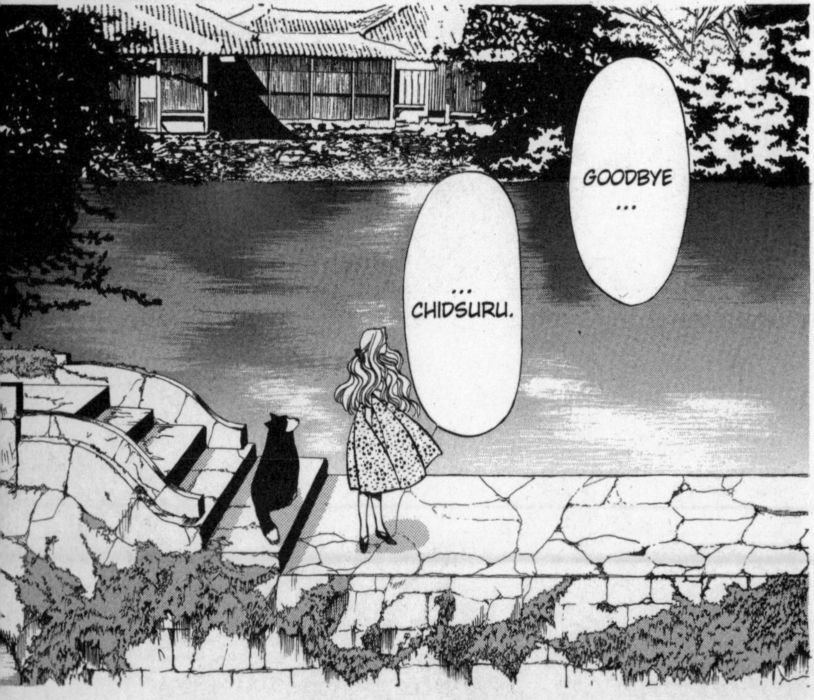
GOODBYE ...
... CHIDSURU.

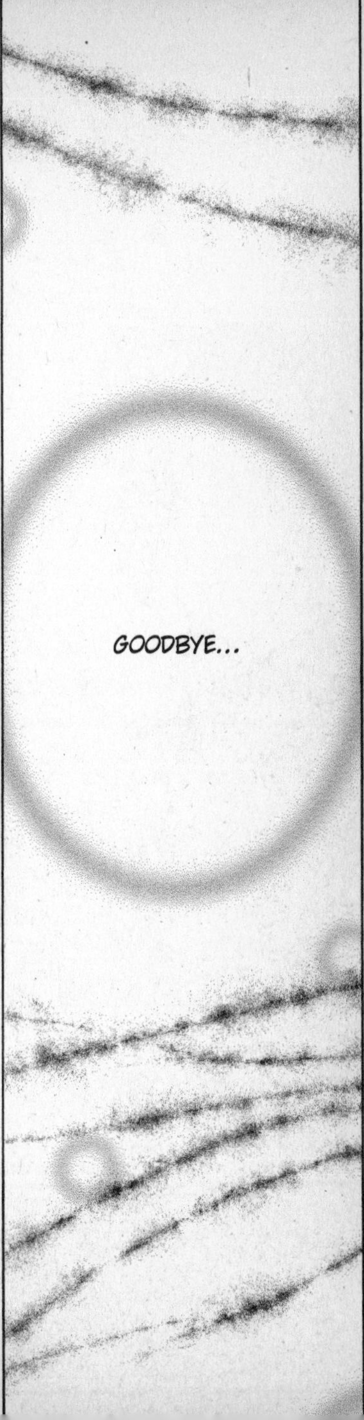
GOODBYE...

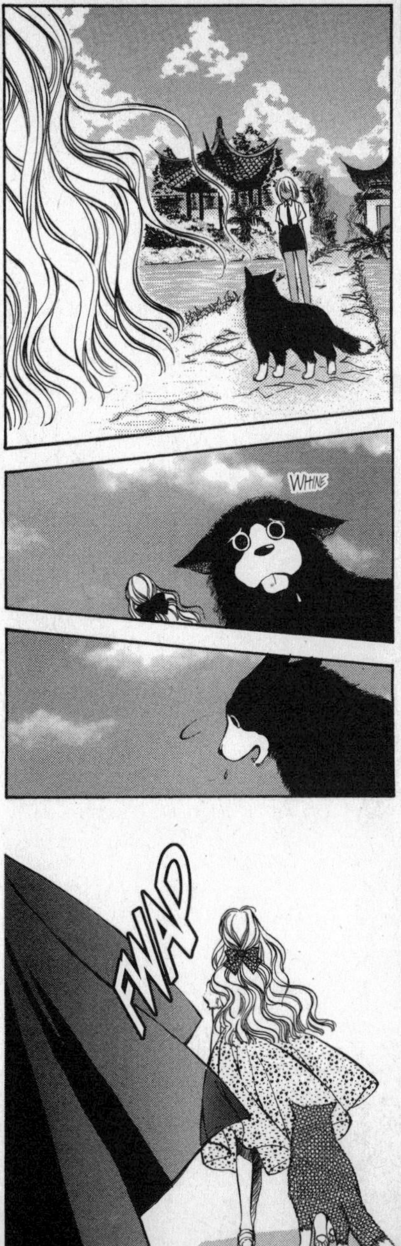
WHINE
FWAP

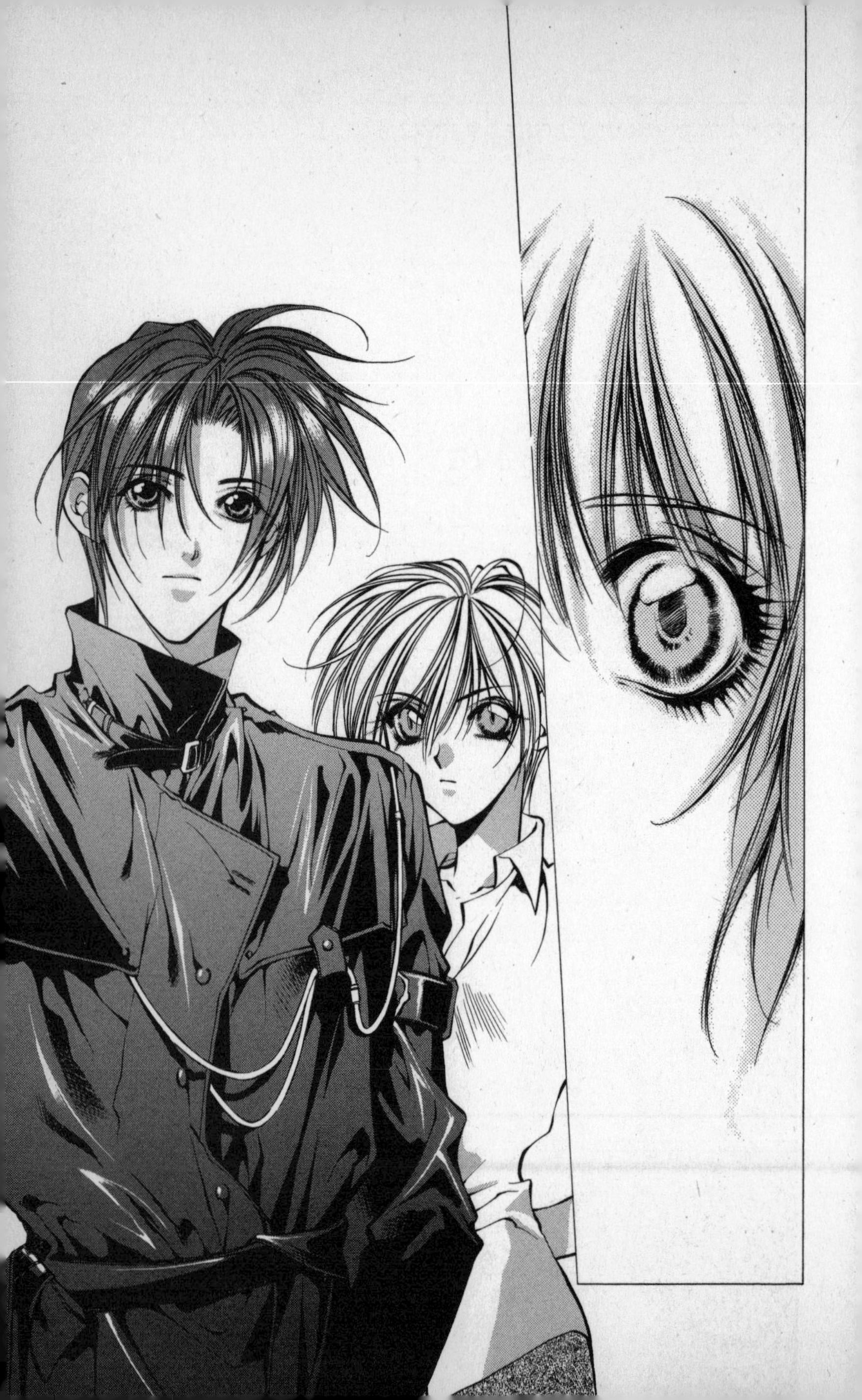

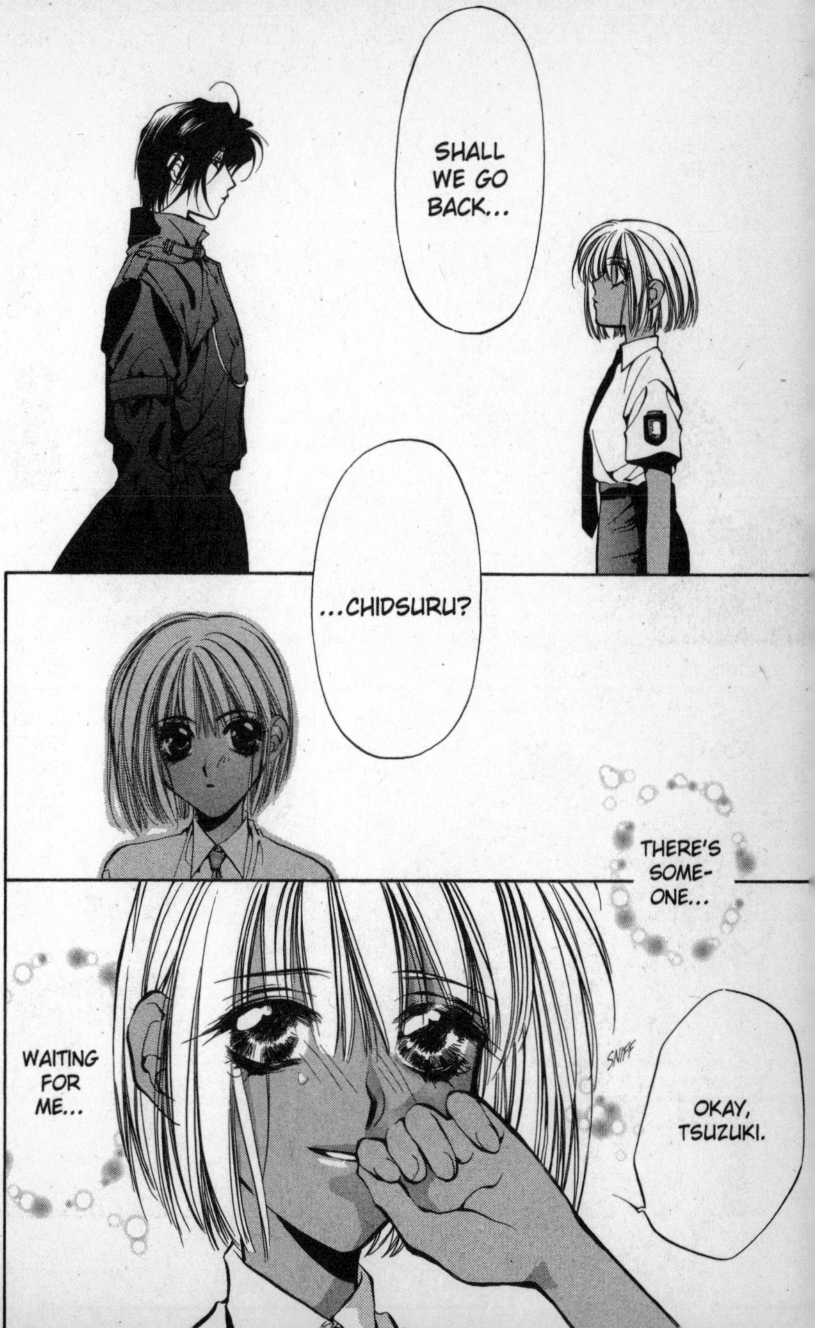
SHALL WE GO BACK...
...CHIDSURU?
THERE'S SOME-ONE...
OKAY, TSUZUKI.
SNIFF
WAITING FOR ME...

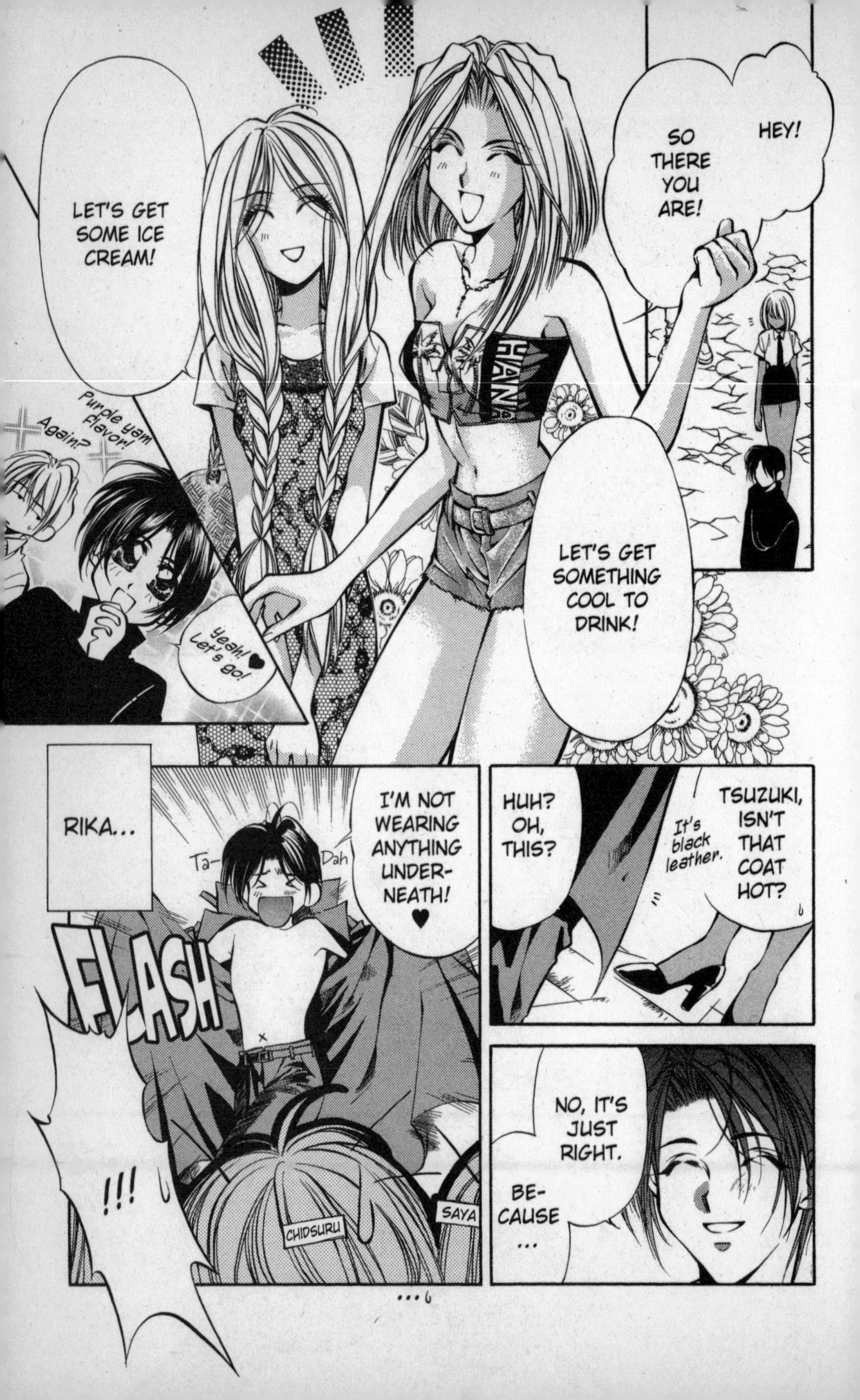
HEY!
SO THERE YOU ARE!
LET'S GET SOMETHING COOL TO DRINK!
LET'S GET SOME ICE CREAM!
Yeah! ♥ Let's go!
Purple yam flavor! Again?
TSUZUKI, ISN'T THAT COAT HOT?
It's black leather.
HUH? OH, THIS?
NO, IT'S JUST RIGHT.
BE-CAUSE ...
RIKA...
I'M NOT WEARING ANYTHING UNDER-NEATH! ♥
Ta-Dah
FLASH
!!!
SAYA
CHIDSURU

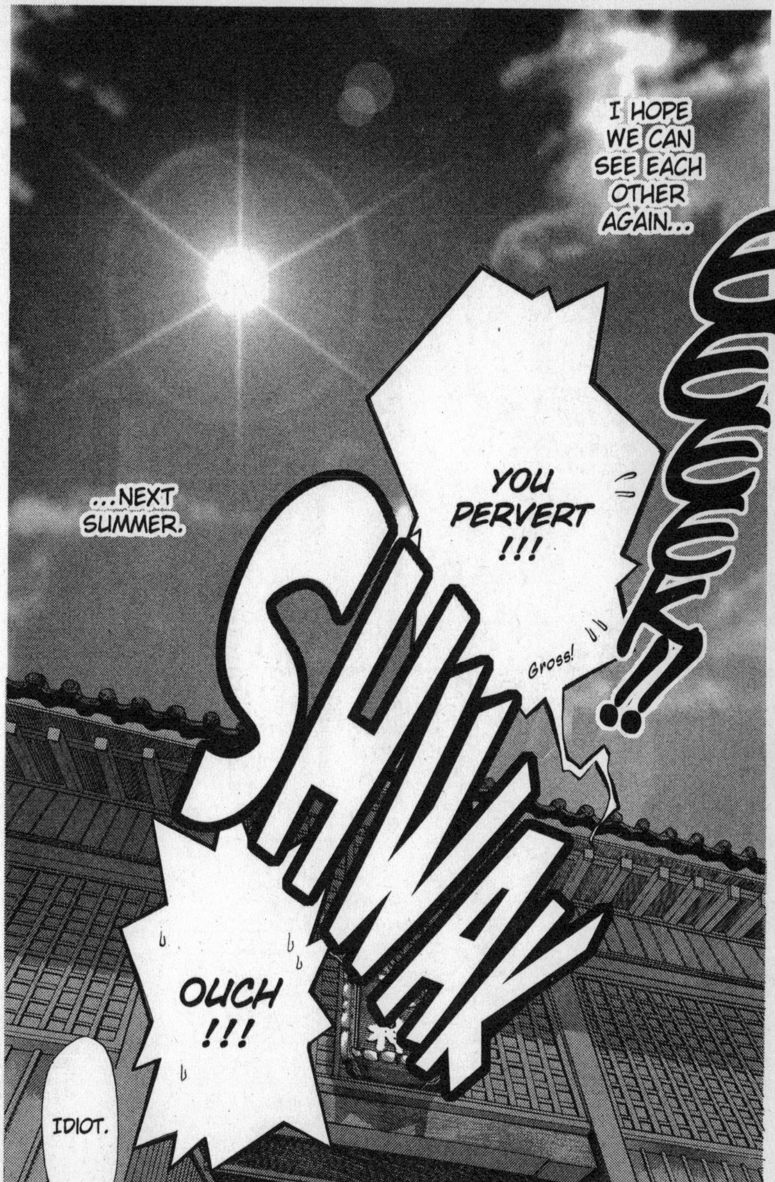
I HOPE WE CAN SEE EACH OTHER AGAIN...
...NEXT SUMMER.
YOU PERVERT !!!
Gross!
SHWAK
OUCH !!!
IDIOT.

END OF DESCENDENTS OF DARKNESS 6

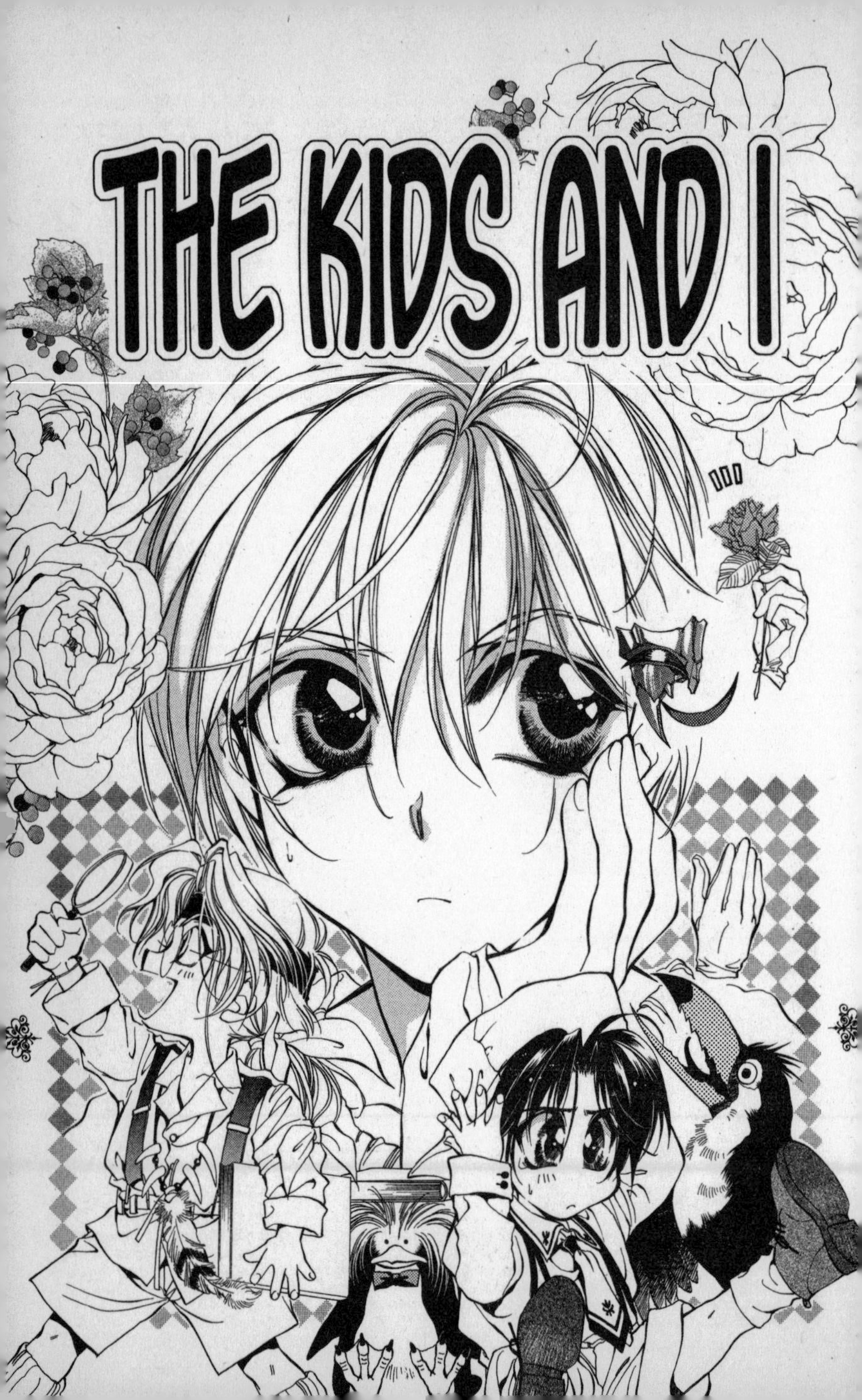
THE KIDS AND I

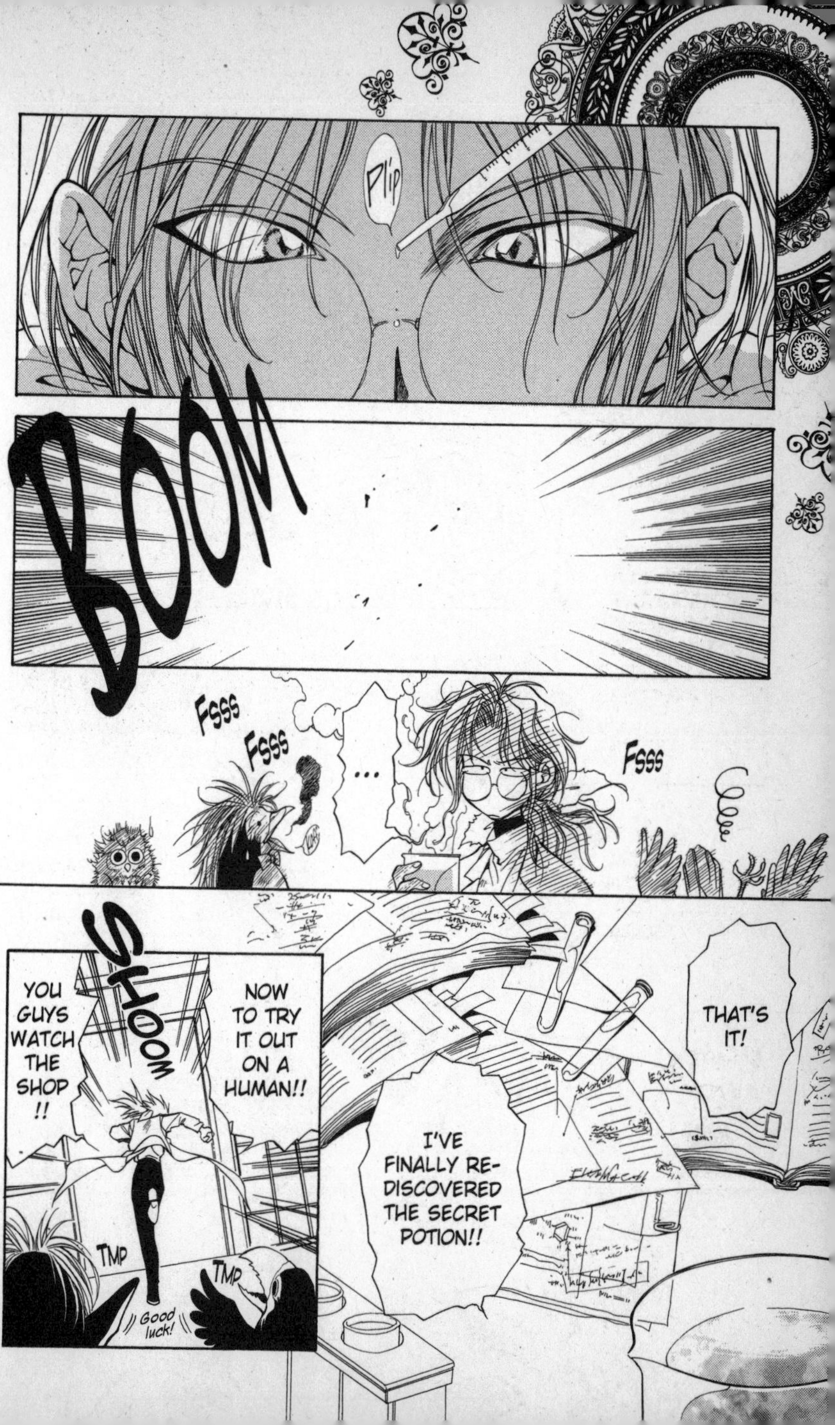
Plip
BOOM
Fsss
Fsss
...
Fsss
THAT'S IT!
I'VE FINALLY RE-DISCOVERED THE SECRET POTION!!
NOW TO TRY IT OUT ON A HUMAN!!
YOU GUYS WATCH THE SHOP!!
SHOOM
TMP
TMP
Good luck!

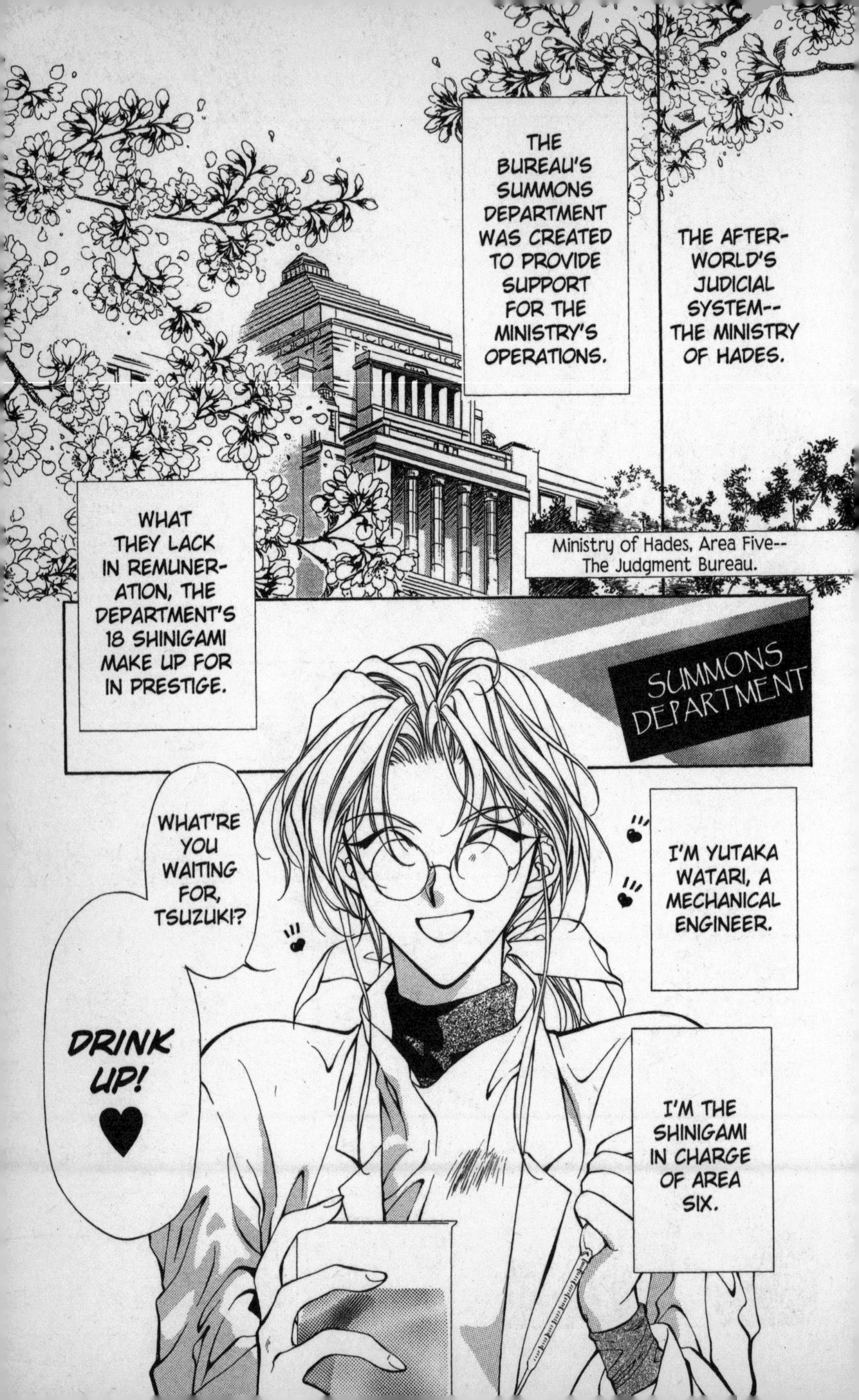
THE AFTER-WORLD'S JUDICIAL SYSTEM--THE MINISTRY OF HADES.
THE BUREAU'S SUMMONS DEPARTMENT WAS CREATED TO PROVIDE SUPPORT FOR THE MINISTRY'S OPERATIONS.
Ministry of Hades, Area Five-- The Judgment Bureau.
WHAT THEY LACK IN REMUNER-ATION, THE DEPARTMENT'S 18 SHINIGAMI MAKE UP FOR IN PRESTIGE.
SUMMONS DEPARTMENT
I'M YUTAKA WATARI, A MECHANICAL ENGINEER.
I'M THE SHINIGAMI IN CHARGE OF AREA SIX.
WHAT'RE YOU WAITING FOR, TSUZUKI?
DRINK UP! ♥

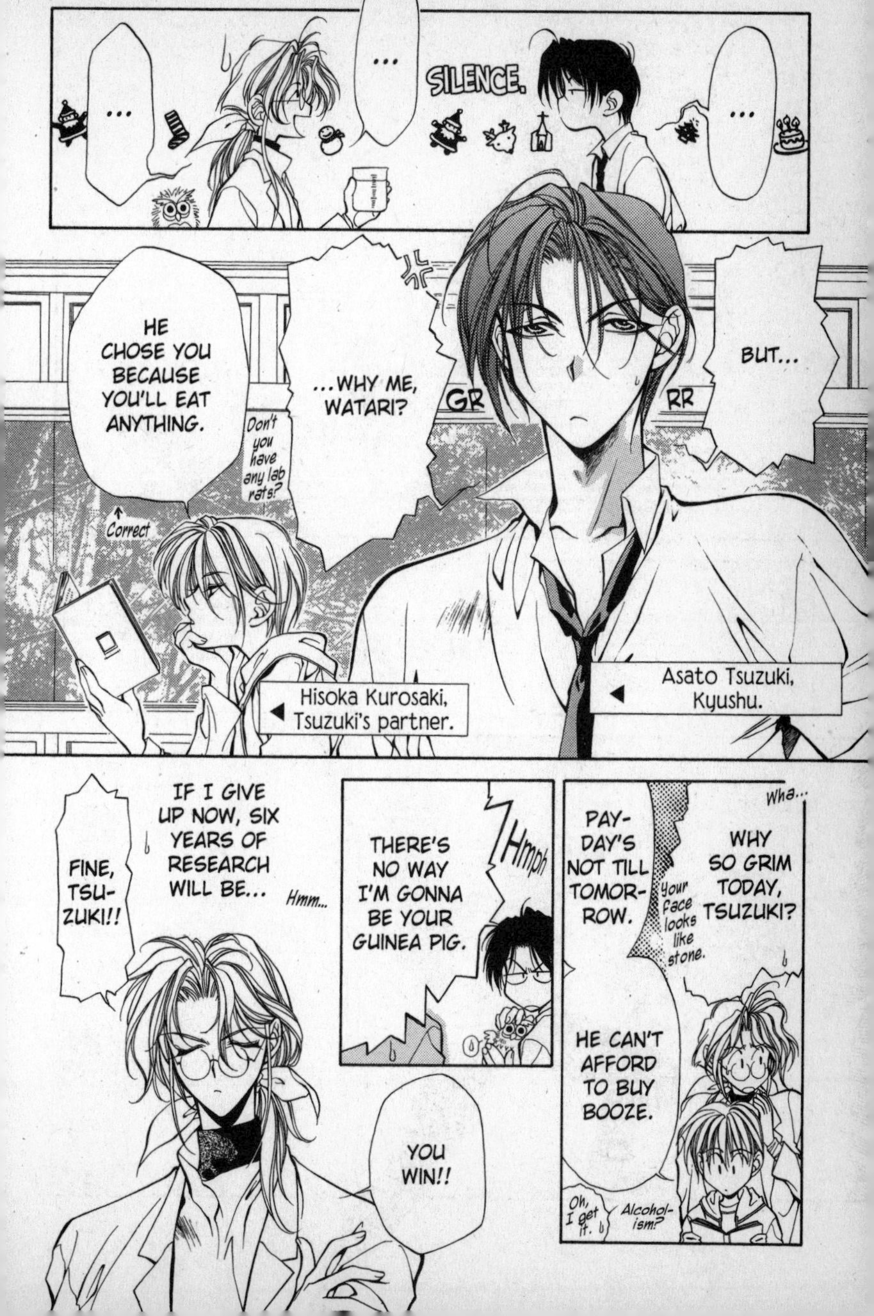

...
SILENCE.
...
...
BUT...
GR RR
...WHY ME, WATARI?
HE CHOSE YOU BECAUSE YOU'LL EAT ANYTHING.
Don't you have any lab rats?
Correct
Asato Tsuzuki, Kyushu.
Hisoka Kurosaki, Tsuzuki's partner.
Wha...
WHY SO GRIM TODAY, TSUZUKI?
Your face looks like stone.
PAY-DAY'S NOT TILL TOMOR-ROW.
HE CAN'T AFFORD TO BUY BOOZE.
Alcohol-ism?
Oh, I get it.
Hmph
THERE'S NO WAY I'M GONNA BE YOUR GUINEA PIG.
Hmm...
IF I GIVE UP NOW, SIX YEARS OF RESEARCH WILL BE...
FINE, TSU-ZUKI!!
YOU WIN!!

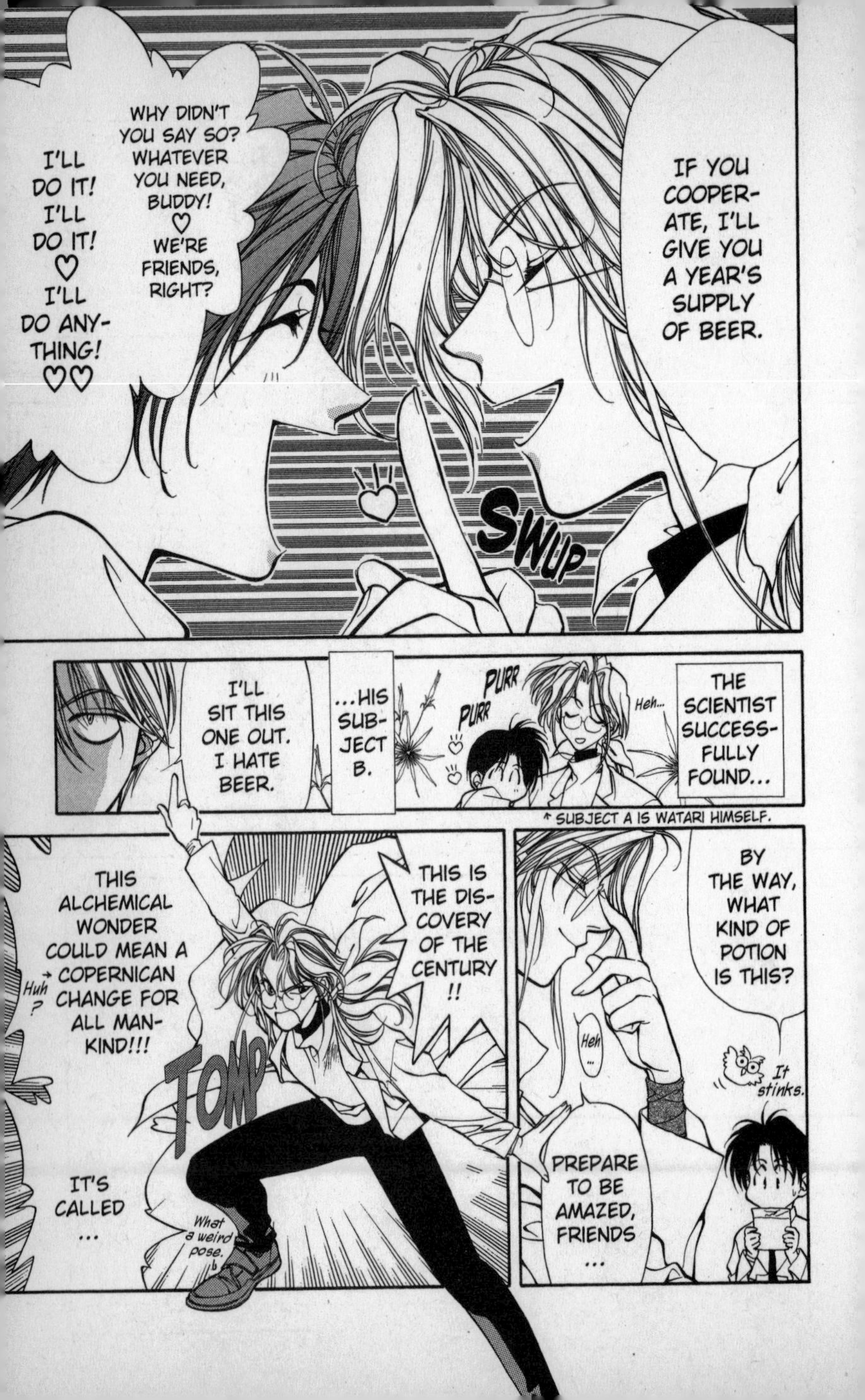

IF YOU COOPERATE, I'LL GIVE YOU A YEAR'S SUPPLY OF BEER.
WHY DIDN'T YOU SAY SO? WHATEVER YOU NEED, BUDDY! ♡ WE'RE FRIENDS, RIGHT?
I'LL DO IT! I'LL DO IT! ♡ I'LL DO ANYTHING! ♡♡
SWUP
THE SCIENTIST SUCCESSFULLY FOUND...
Heh...
PURR
PURR
...HIS SUBJECT B.
I'LL SIT THIS ONE OUT. I HATE BEER.
↑ SUBJECT A IS WATARI HIMSELF.
BY THE WAY, WHAT KIND OF POTION IS THIS?
It stinks.
Heh...
PREPARE TO BE AMAZED, FRIENDS...
THIS IS THE DISCOVERY OF THE CENTURY!!
THIS ALCHEMICAL WONDER COULD MEAN A COPERNICAN CHANGE FOR ALL MANKIND!!!
Huh?
TOMP
What a weird pose.
IT'S CALLED...

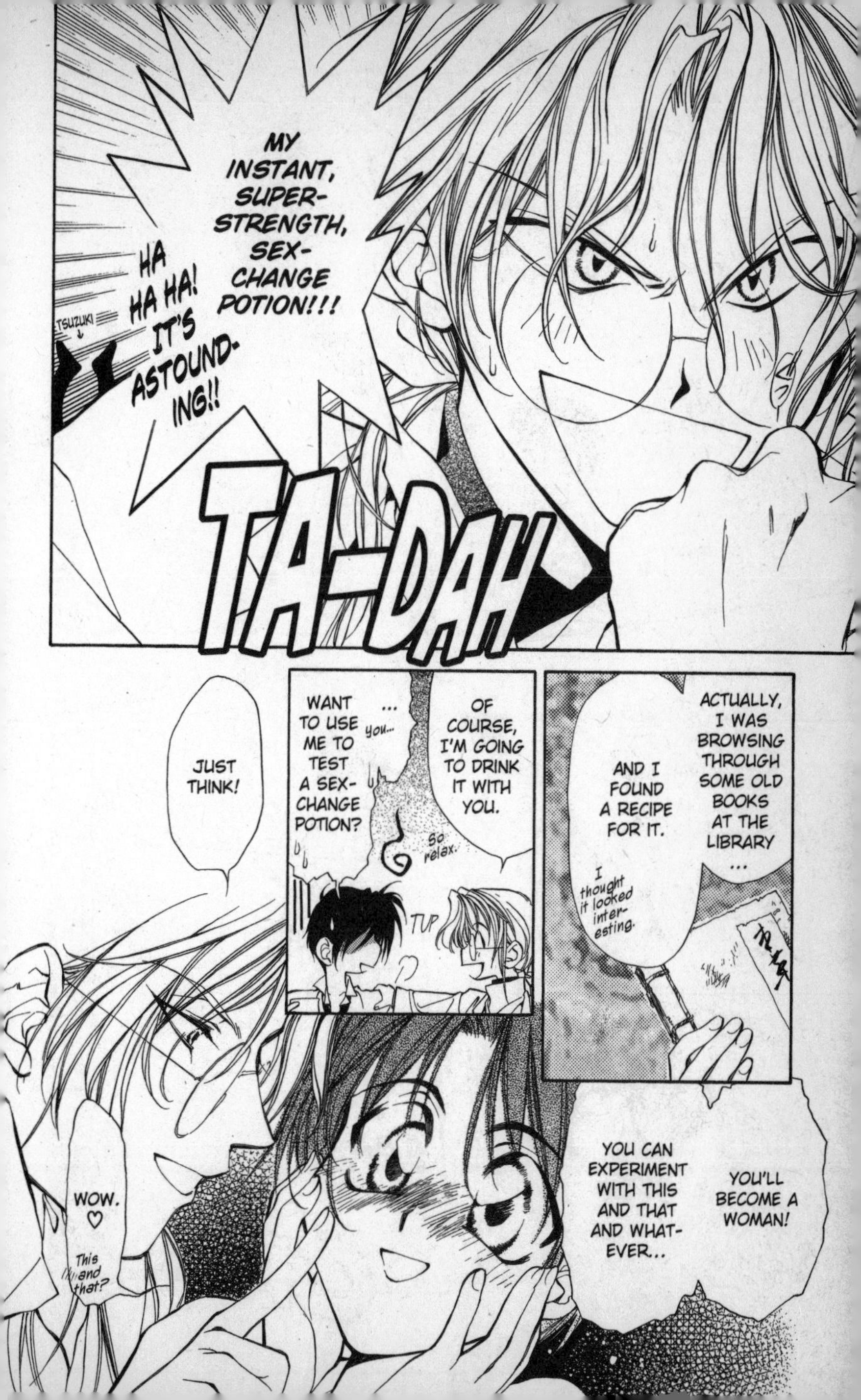
MY INSTANT, SUPER-STRENGTH, SEX-CHANGE POTION!!!
HA HA HA! IT'S ASTOUNDING!!
TSUZUKI
TA-DAH
ACTUALLY, I WAS BROWSING THROUGH SOME OLD BOOKS AT THE LIBRARY ...
AND I FOUND A RECIPE FOR IT.
I thought it looked interesting.
OF COURSE, I'M GOING TO DRINK IT WITH YOU.
So relax.
... you...
WANT TO USE ME TO TEST A SEX-CHANGE POTION?
TUP
JUST THINK!
YOU'LL BECOME A WOMAN!
YOU CAN EXPERIMENT WITH THIS AND THAT AND WHATEVER...
WOW. ♡
This and that?

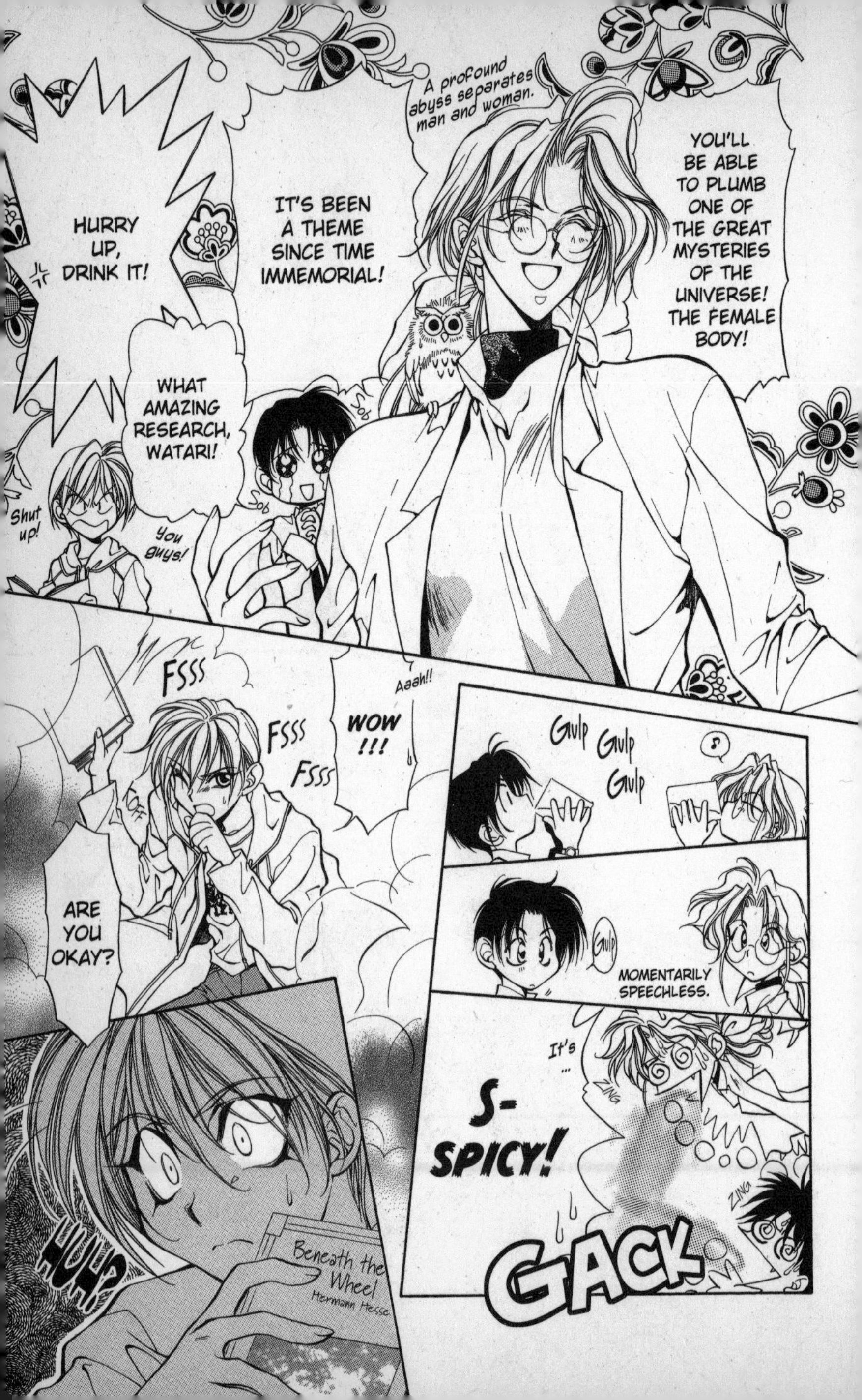
A profound abyss separates man and woman.
YOU'LL BE ABLE TO PLUMB ONE OF THE GREAT MYSTERIES OF THE UNIVERSE! THE FEMALE BODY!
IT'S BEEN A THEME SINCE TIME IMMEMORIAL!
HURRY UP, DRINK IT!
Sob
WHAT AMAZING RESEARCH, WATARI!
Sob
You guys!
Shut up!
Gulp Gulp Gulp
Gulp
MOMENTARILY SPEECHLESS.
It's ...
S- SPICY!
ZING
ZING
GACK
Aaah!!
WOW !!!
FSSS
FSSS
FSSS
KOFF
ARE YOU OKAY?
HUH?
Beneath the Wheel
Hermann Hesse

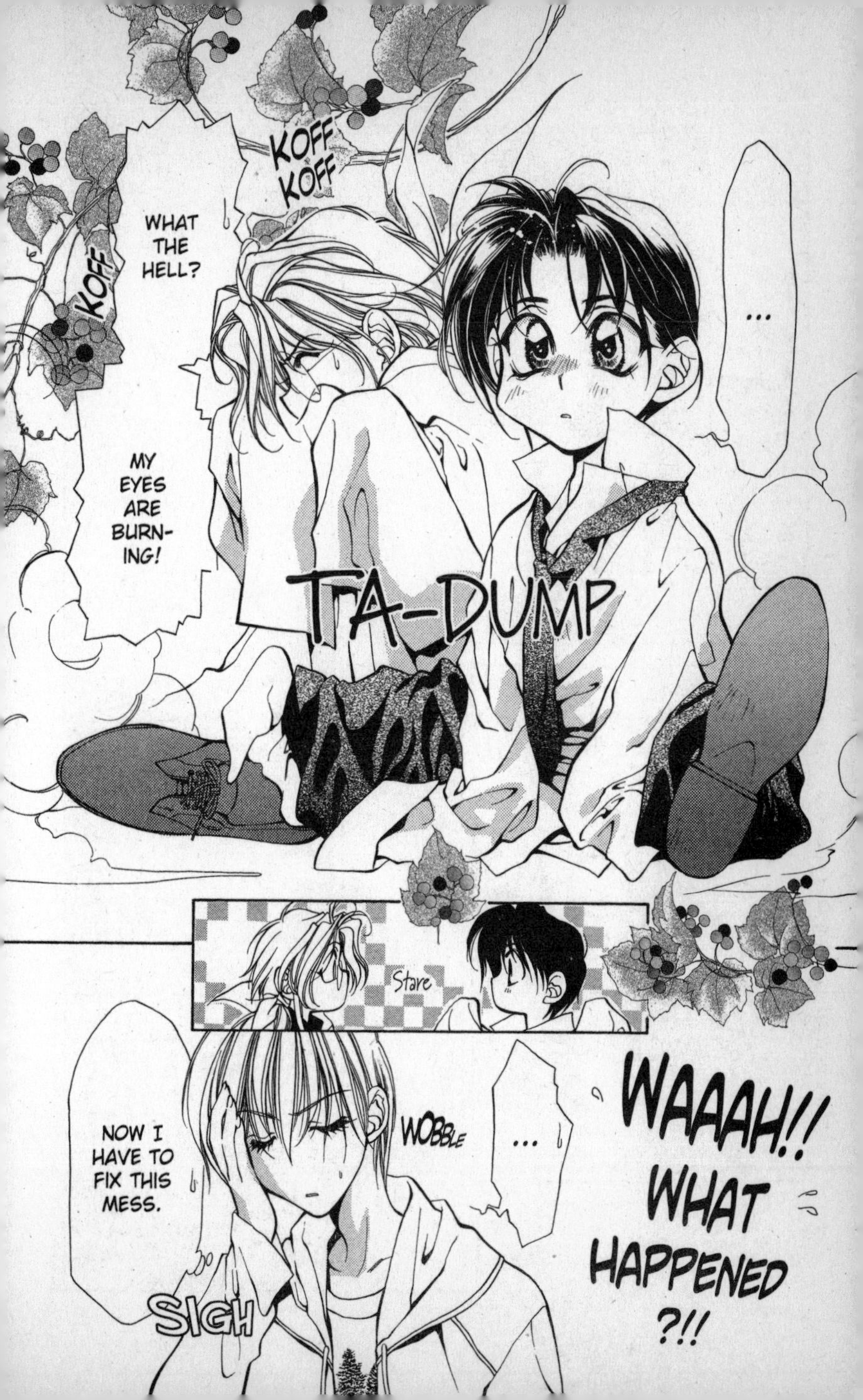
...
KOFF KOFF
WHAT THE HELL? MY EYES ARE BURNING!
KOFF
TA-DUMP
Stare
WAAAH!! WHAT HAPPENED ?!!
...
WOBBLE
NOW I HAVE TO FIX THIS MESS.
SIGH

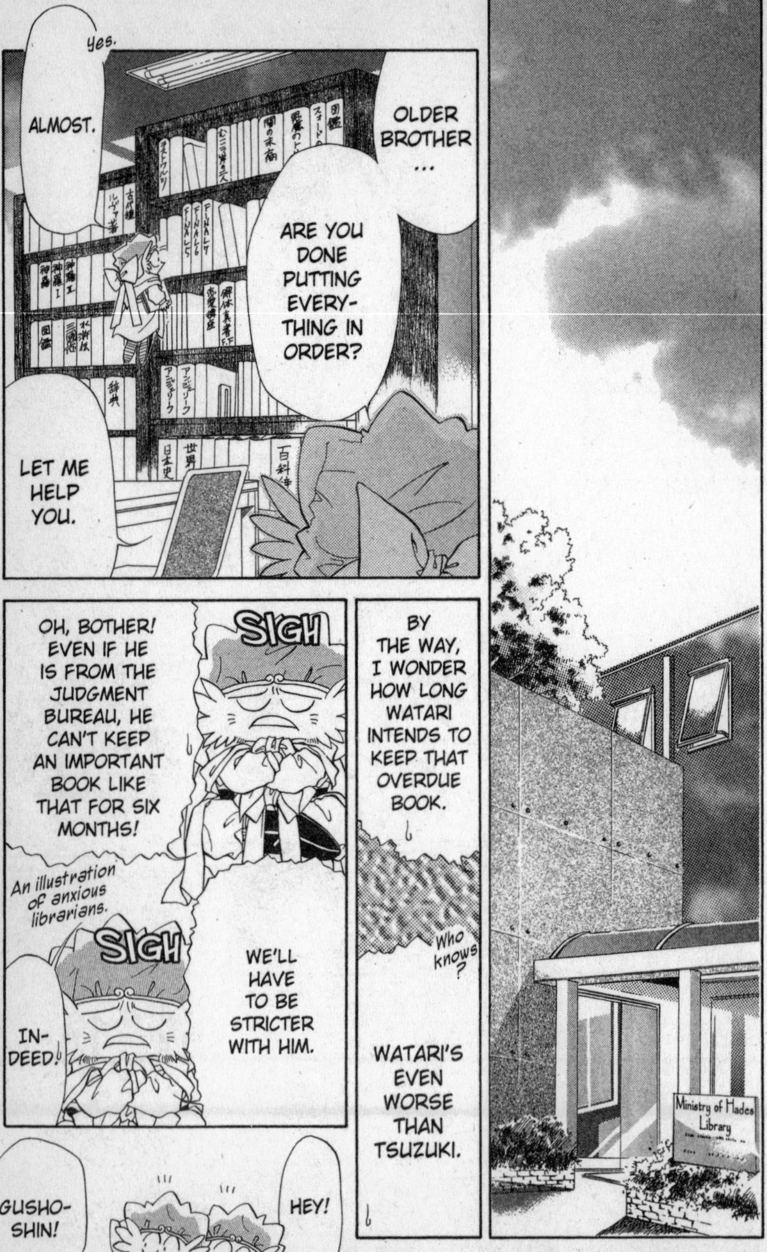
Ministry of Hades Library
OLDER BROTHER...
ARE YOU DONE PUTTING EVERY-THING IN ORDER?
yes.
ALMOST.
LET ME HELP YOU.
BY THE WAY, I WONDER HOW LONG WATARI INTENDS TO KEEP THAT OVERDUE BOOK.
Who knows?
WATARI'S EVEN WORSE THAN TSUZUKI.
SIGH
OH, BOTHER! EVEN IF HE IS FROM THE JUDGMENT BUREAU, HE CAN'T KEEP AN IMPORTANT BOOK LIKE THAT FOR SIX MONTHS!
An illustration of anxious librarians.
SIGH
WE'LL HAVE TO BE STRICTER WITH HIM.
IN-DEED!

ALWAYS RETURN YOUR LIBRARY BOOKS ON TIME.

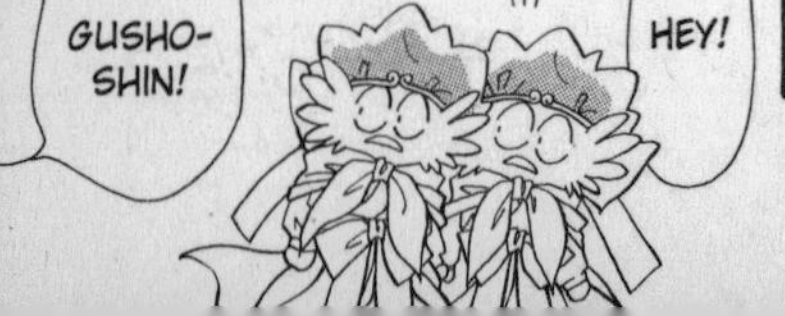
HEY!
GUSHO-SHIN!

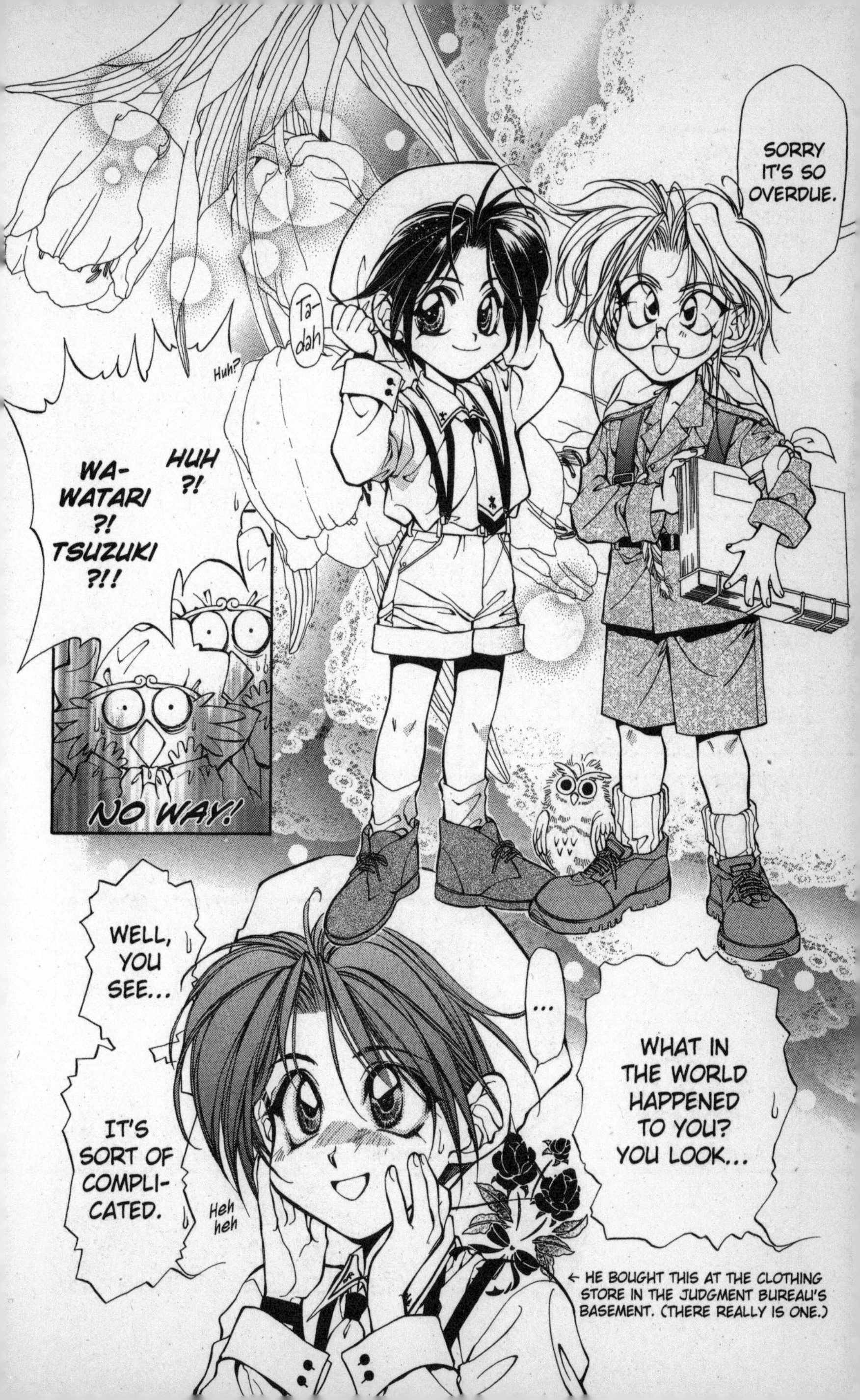
SORRY IT'S SO OVERDUE.
Ta-dah
Huh?
HUH ?!
WA-WATARI ?! TSUZUKI ?!!
NO WAY!
...
WHAT IN THE WORLD HAPPENED TO YOU? YOU LOOK...
WELL, YOU SEE...
IT'S SORT OF COMPLICATED.
Heh heh
← HE BOUGHT THIS AT THE CLOTHING STORE IN THE JUDGMENT BUREAU'S BASEMENT. (THERE REALLY IS ONE.)

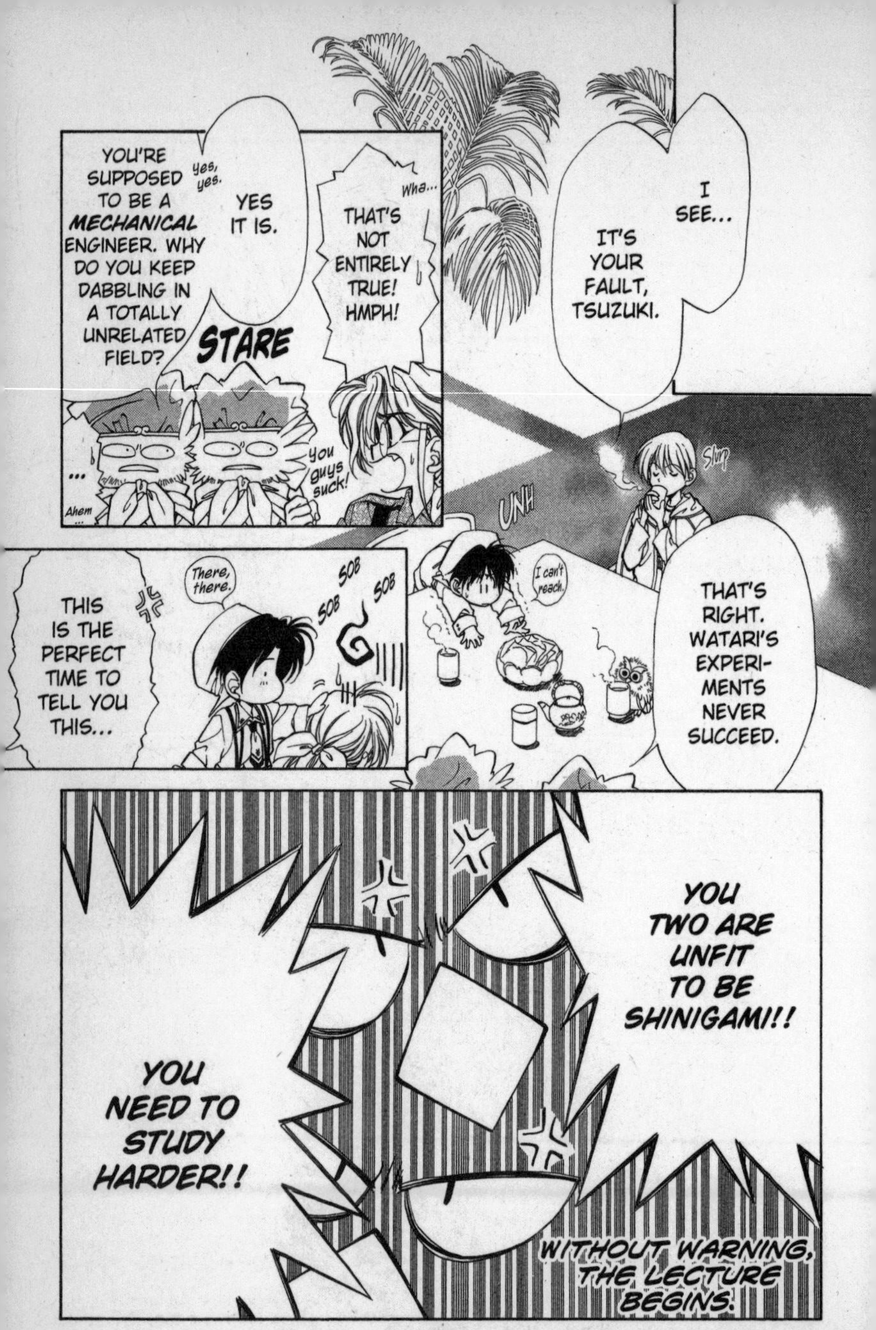
I SEE...
IT'S YOUR FAULT, TSUZUKI.
Slurp
UNH
I can't reach.
THAT'S RIGHT. WATARI'S EXPERIMENTS NEVER SUCCEED.
Wha...
THAT'S NOT ENTIRELY TRUE! HMPH!
YES IT IS.
Yes, yes.
YOU'RE SUPPOSED TO BE A MECHANICAL ENGINEER. WHY DO YOU KEEP DABBLING IN A TOTALLY UNRELATED FIELD?
STARE
You guys suck!
...
Ahem ...
SOB
SOB
SOB
There, there.
THIS IS THE PERFECT TIME TO TELL YOU THIS...
YOU TWO ARE UNFIT TO BE SHINIGAMI!!
YOU NEED TO STUDY HARDER!!
WITHOUT WARNING, THE LECTURE BEGINS.

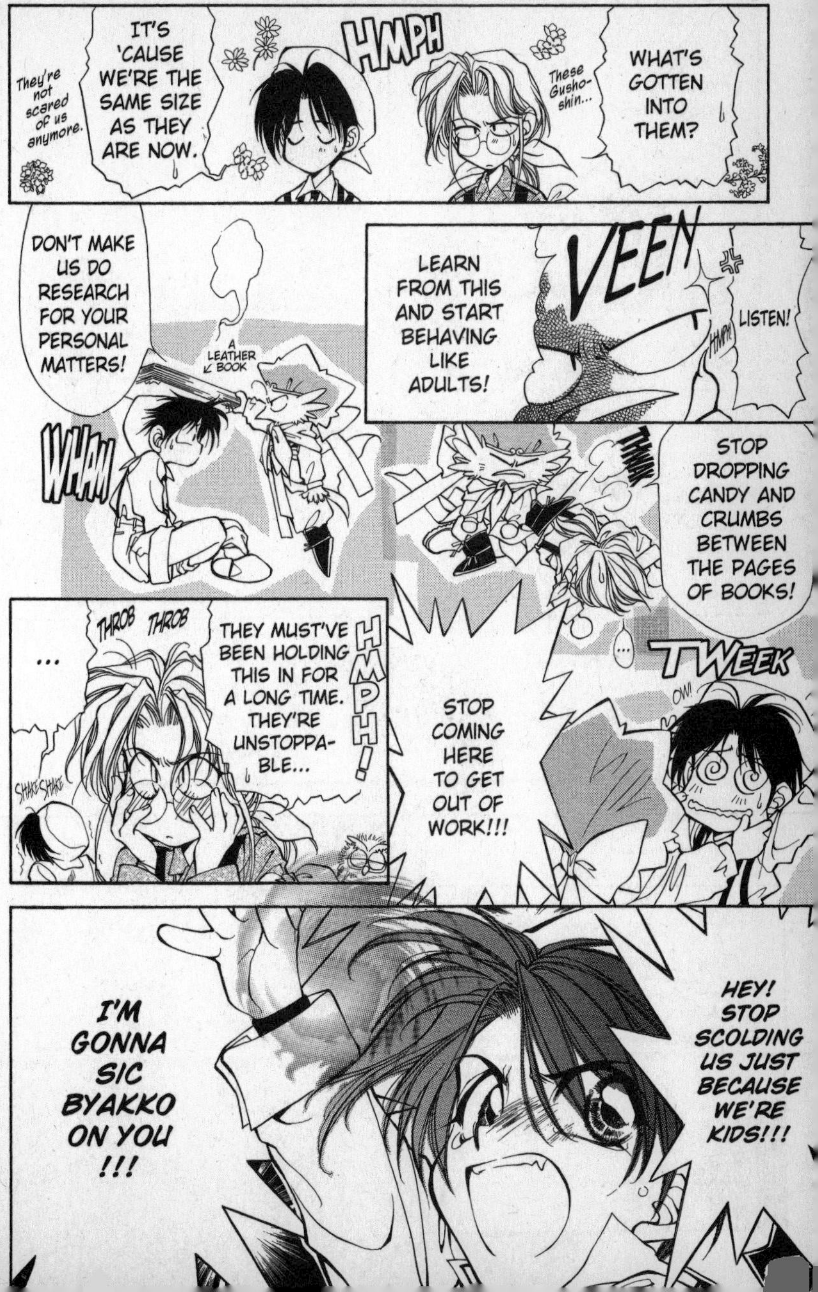
WHAT'S GOTTEN INTO THEM?
These Gusho-shin...
HMPH
IT'S 'CAUSE WE'RE THE SAME SIZE AS THEY ARE NOW.
They're not scared of us anymore.
LISTEN!
HMPH
VEEN
LEARN FROM THIS AND START BEHAVING LIKE ADULTS!
DON'T MAKE US DO RESEARCH FOR YOUR PERSONAL MATTERS!
A LEATHER BOOK
WHAM
STOP DROPPING CANDY AND CRUMBS BETWEEN THE PAGES OF BOOKS!
THWAK
...
TWEEK
OW!
STOP COMING HERE TO GET OUT OF WORK!!!
HMPH!
THEY MUST'VE BEEN HOLDING THIS IN FOR A LONG TIME. THEY'RE UNSTOPPA-BLE...
THROB THROB
...
SHAKE SHAKE
HEY! STOP SCOLDING US JUST BECAUSE WE'RE KIDS!!!
I'M GONNA SIC BYAKKO ON YOU !!!

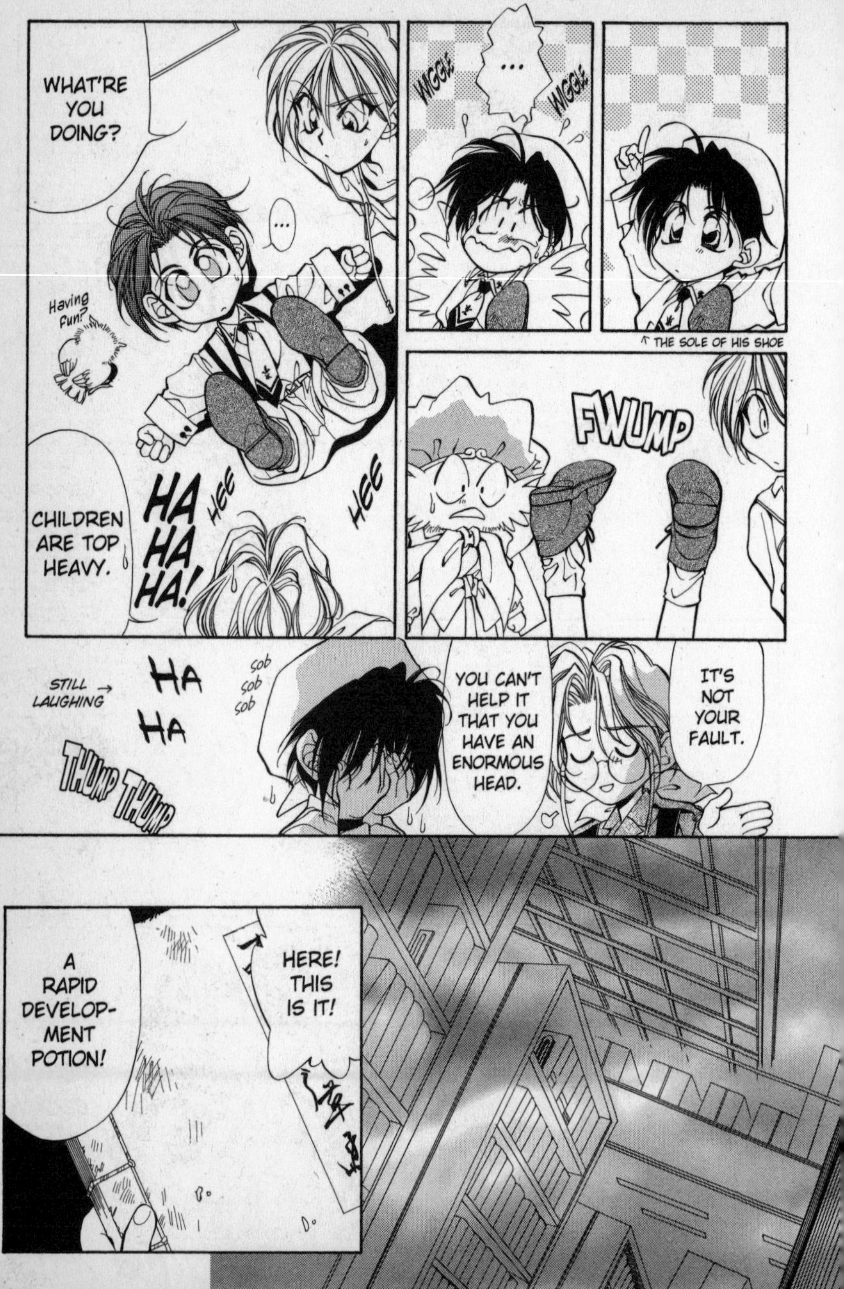
THE SOLE OF HIS SHOE
WIGGLE
...
WIGGLE
FWUMP
WHAT'RE YOU DOING?
...
Having Fun?
CHILDREN ARE TOP HEAVY.
HA HA HA!
HEE
HEE
IT'S NOT YOUR FAULT.
YOU CAN'T HELP IT THAT YOU HAVE AN ENORMOUS HEAD.
sob sob sob
HA
HA
STILL LAUGHING →
THUMP THUMP
HERE! THIS IS IT!
A RAPID DEVELOPMENT POTION!

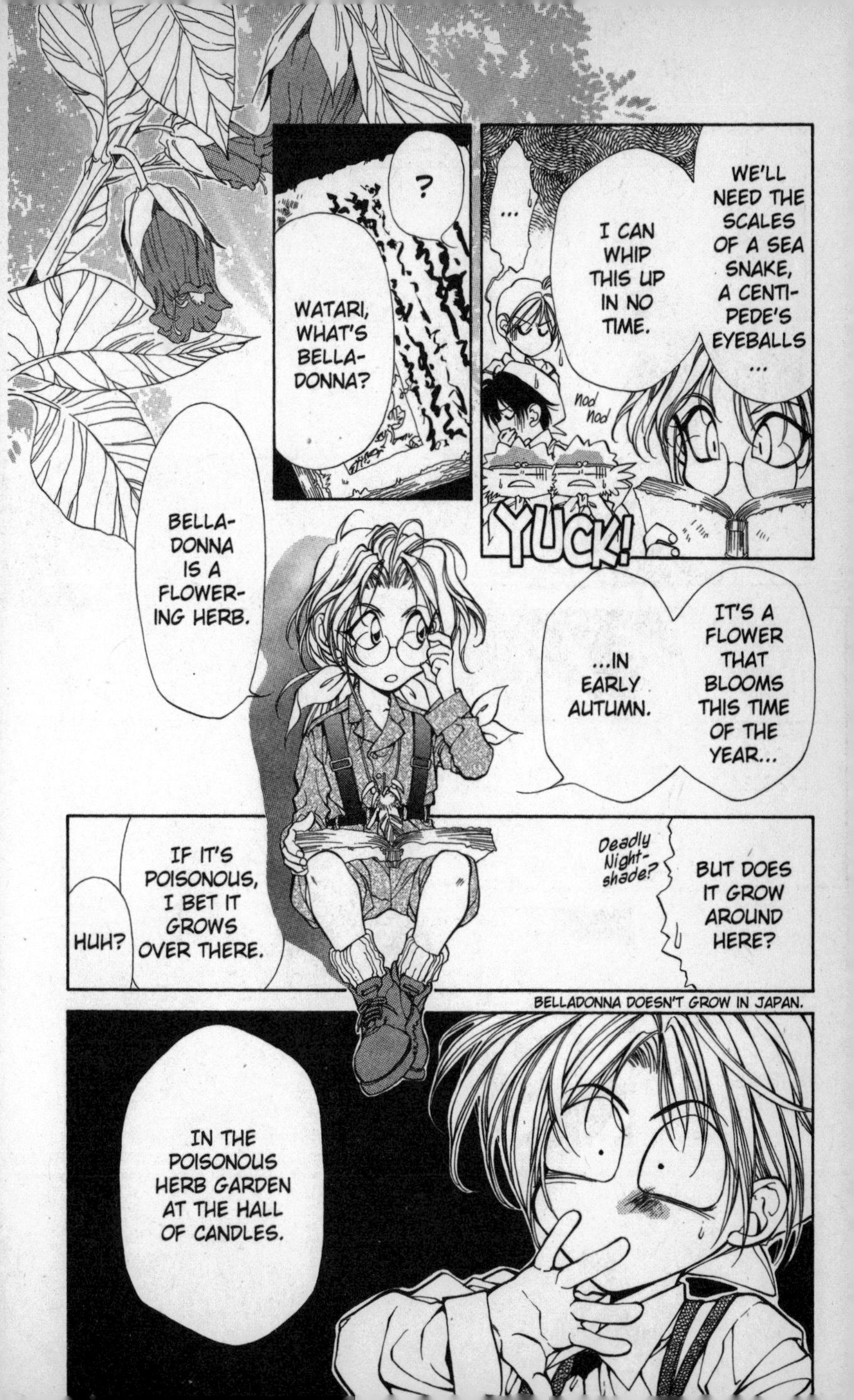

WE'LL NEED THE SCALES OF A SEA SNAKE, A CENTI-PEDE'S EYEBALLS ...
I CAN WHIP THIS UP IN NO TIME.
...
nod nod
YUCK!
?
WATARI, WHAT'S BELLA-DONNA?
BELLA-DONNA IS A FLOWER-ING HERB.
IT'S A FLOWER THAT BLOOMS THIS TIME OF THE YEAR...
...IN EARLY AUTUMN.
BUT DOES IT GROW AROUND HERE?
Deadly Night-shade?
IF IT'S POISONOUS, I BET IT GROWS OVER THERE.
HUH?
BELLADONNA DOESN'T GROW IN JAPAN.
IN THE POISONOUS HERB GARDEN AT THE HALL OF CANDLES.

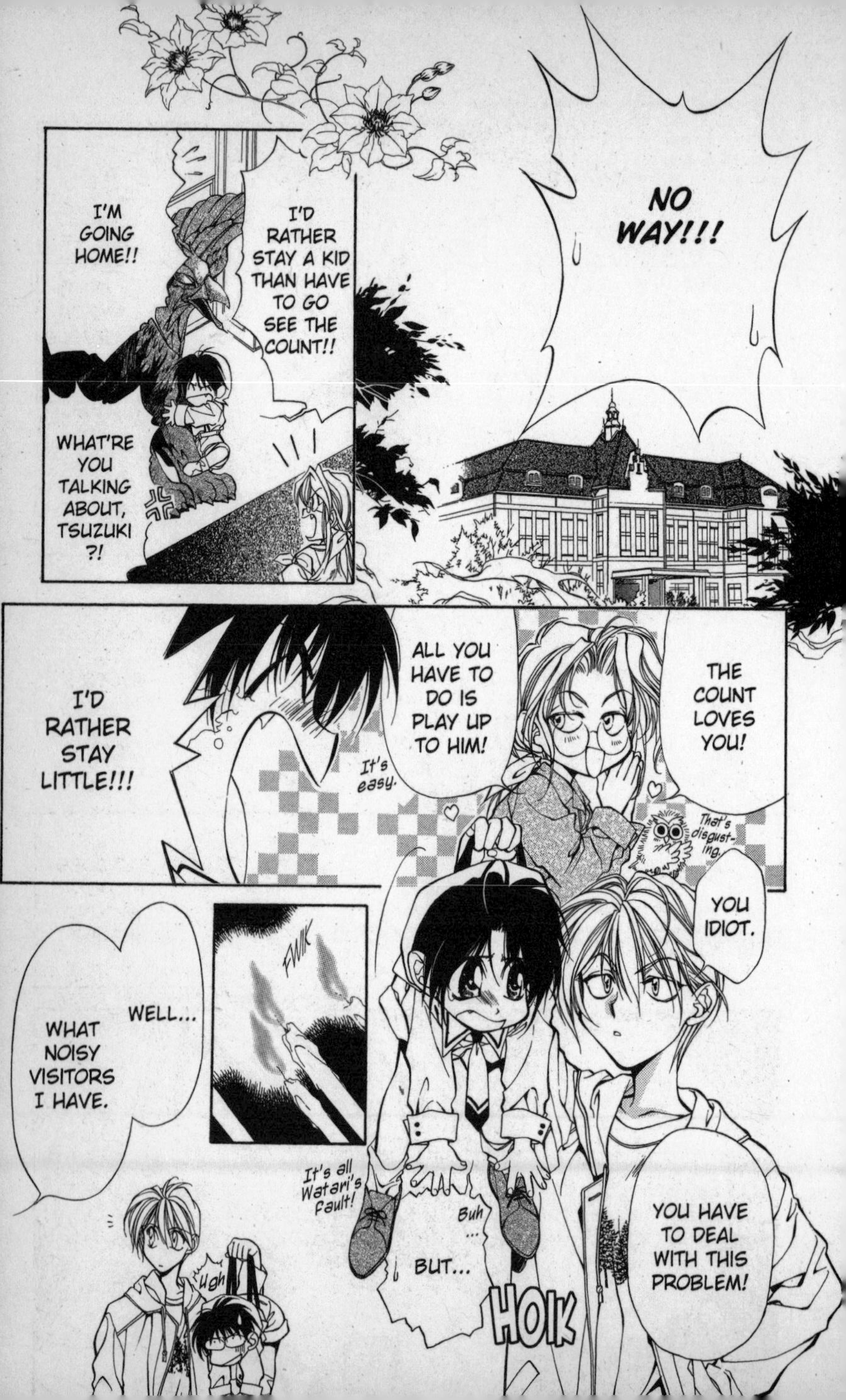
NO WAY!!!
I'D RATHER STAY A KID THAN HAVE TO GO SEE THE COUNT!!
I'M GOING HOME!!
WHAT'RE YOU TALKING ABOUT, TSUZUKI?!
THE COUNT LOVES YOU!
That's disgusting.
ALL YOU HAVE TO DO IS PLAY UP TO HIM!
It's easy.
I'D RATHER STAY LITTLE!!!
YOU IDIOT.
YOU HAVE TO DEAL WITH THIS PROBLEM!
HOIK
Buh...
BUT...
It's all Watari's fault!
Ugh
FWIK
WELL...
WHAT NOISY VISITORS I HAVE.

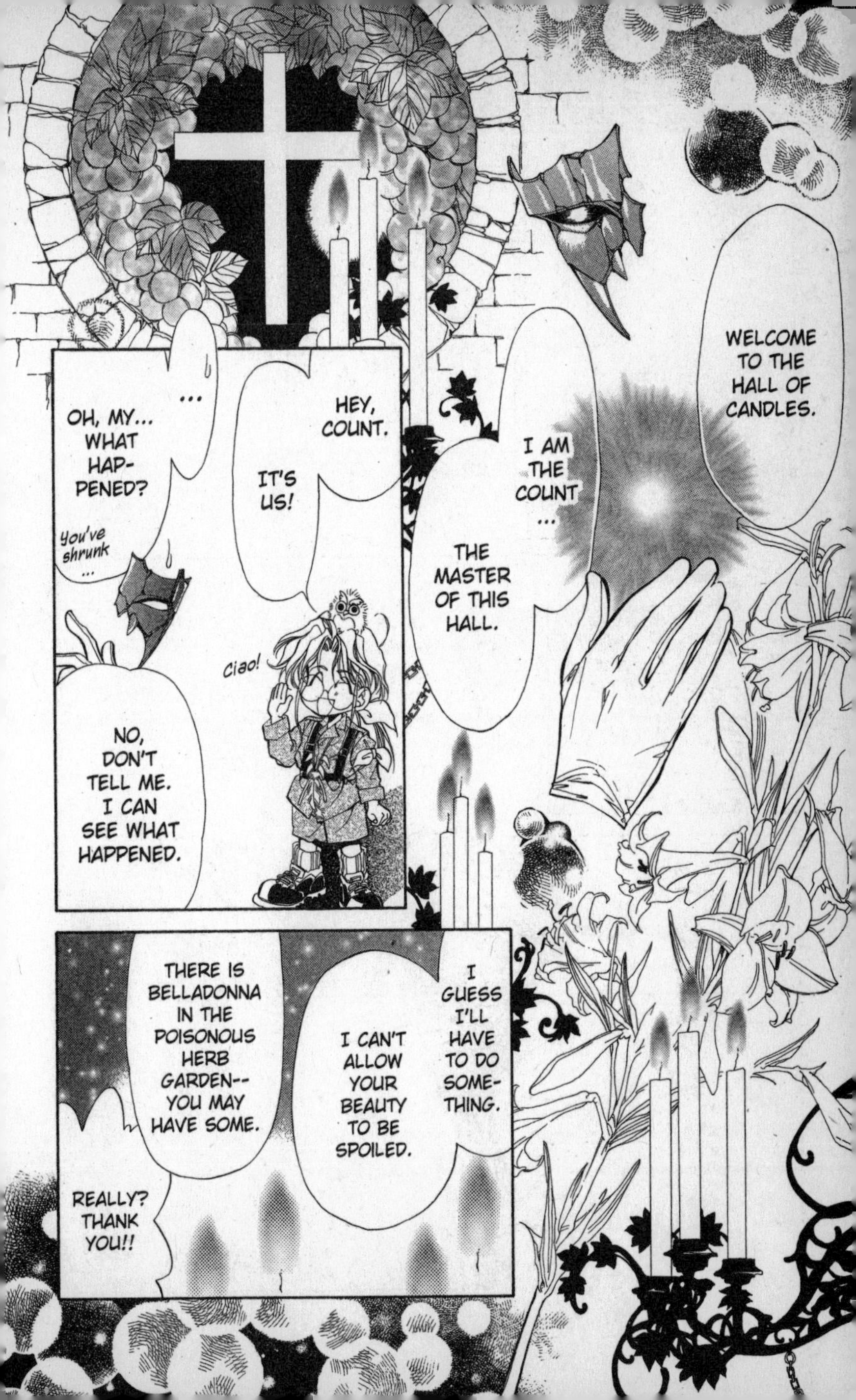
WELCOME TO THE HALL OF CANDLES.
I AM THE COUNT ...
THE MASTER OF THIS HALL.
HEY, COUNT.
IT'S US!
Ciao!
...
OH, MY... WHAT HAP-PENED?
You've shrunk ...
NO, DON'T TELL ME. I CAN SEE WHAT HAPPENED.
I GUESS I'LL HAVE TO DO SOME-THING.
I CAN'T ALLOW YOUR BEAUTY TO BE SPOILED.
THERE IS BELLADONNA IN THE POISONOUS HERB GARDEN--YOU MAY HAVE SOME.
REALLY? THANK YOU!!

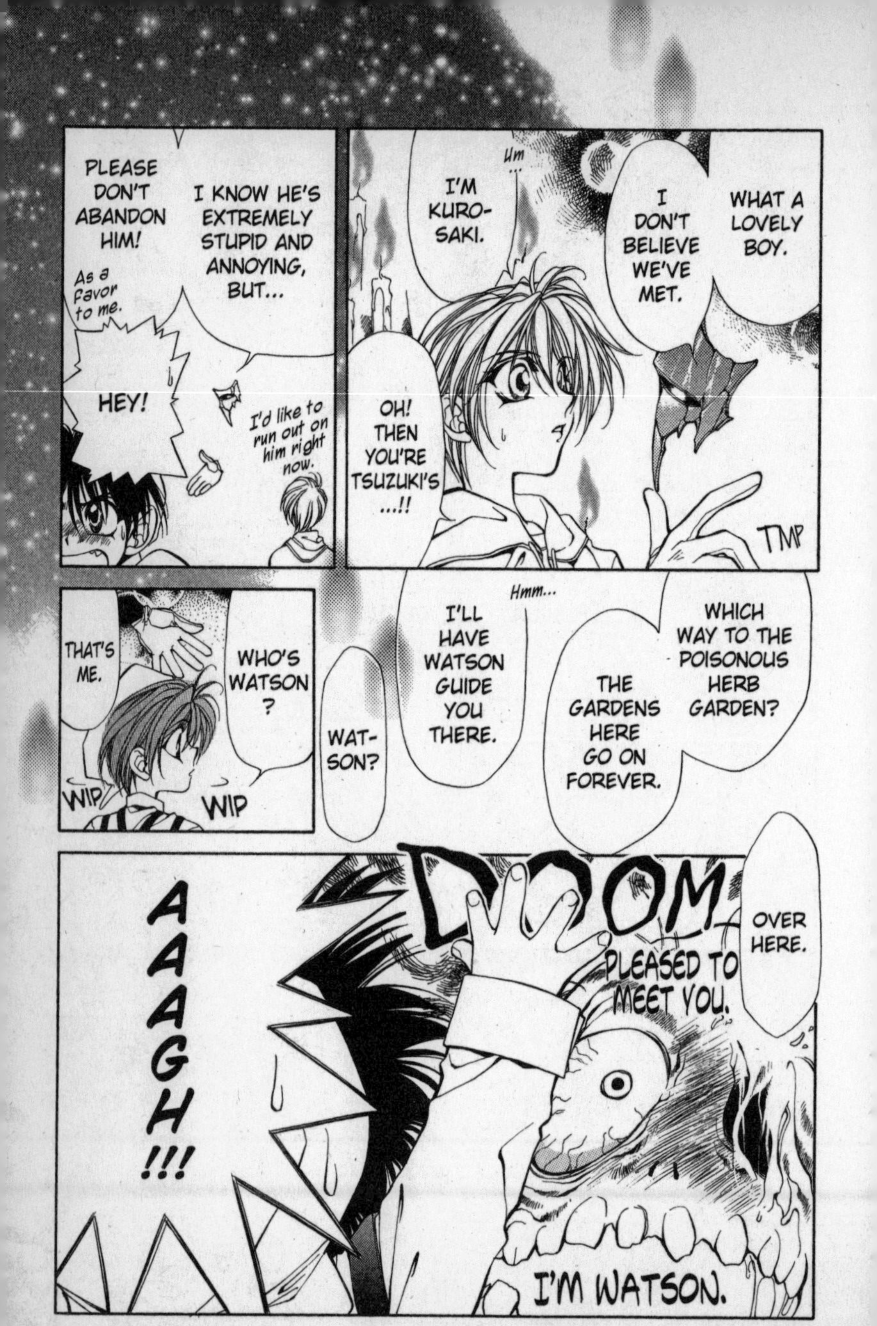

WHAT A LOVELY BOY.
I DON'T BELIEVE WE'VE MET.
Um...
I'M KURO-SAKI.
OH! THEN YOU'RE TSUZUKI'S ...!!
TMP
I KNOW HE'S EXTREMELY STUPID AND ANNOYING, BUT...
PLEASE DON'T ABANDON HIM!
As a favor to me.
HEY!
I'd like to run out on him right now.
WHICH WAY TO THE POISONOUS HERB GARDEN?
THE GARDENS HERE GO ON FOREVER.
Hmm...
I'LL HAVE WATSON GUIDE YOU THERE.
WAT-SON?
WHO'S WATSON?
THAT'S ME.
WIP
WIP
OVER HERE.
DOOM
PLEASED TO MEET YOU.
I'M WATSON.
AAAAGH!!!

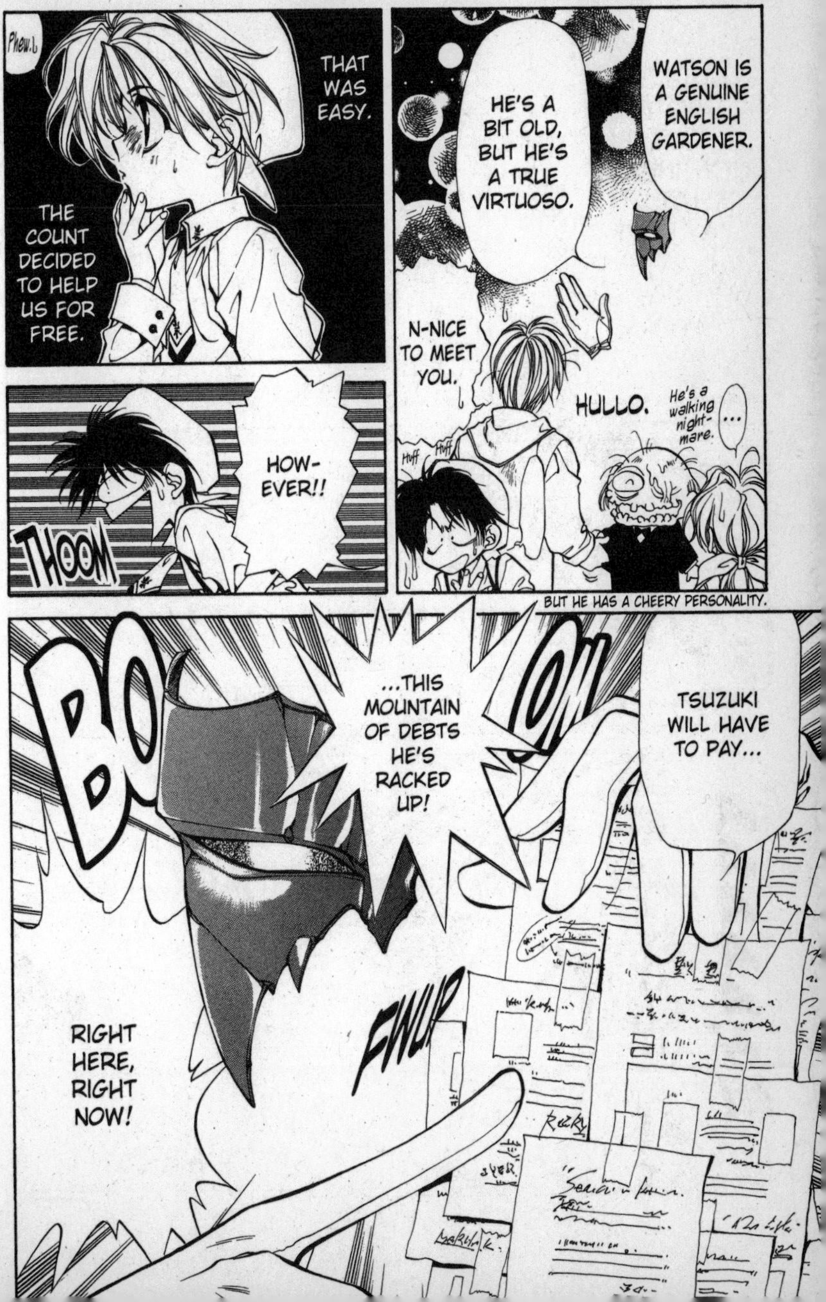
WATSON IS A GENUINE ENGLISH GARDENER.
HE'S A BIT OLD, BUT HE'S A TRUE VIRTUOSO.
...
He's a walking night-mare.
HULLO.
N-NICE TO MEET YOU.
Huff Huff
BUT HE HAS A CHEERY PERSONALITY.
THAT WAS EASY.
Phew.
THE COUNT DECIDED TO HELP US FOR FREE.
HOW-EVER!!
THOOM
TSUZUKI WILL HAVE TO PAY...
...THIS MOUNTAIN OF DEBTS HE'S RACKED UP!
BOOM
FWUP
RIGHT HERE, RIGHT NOW!

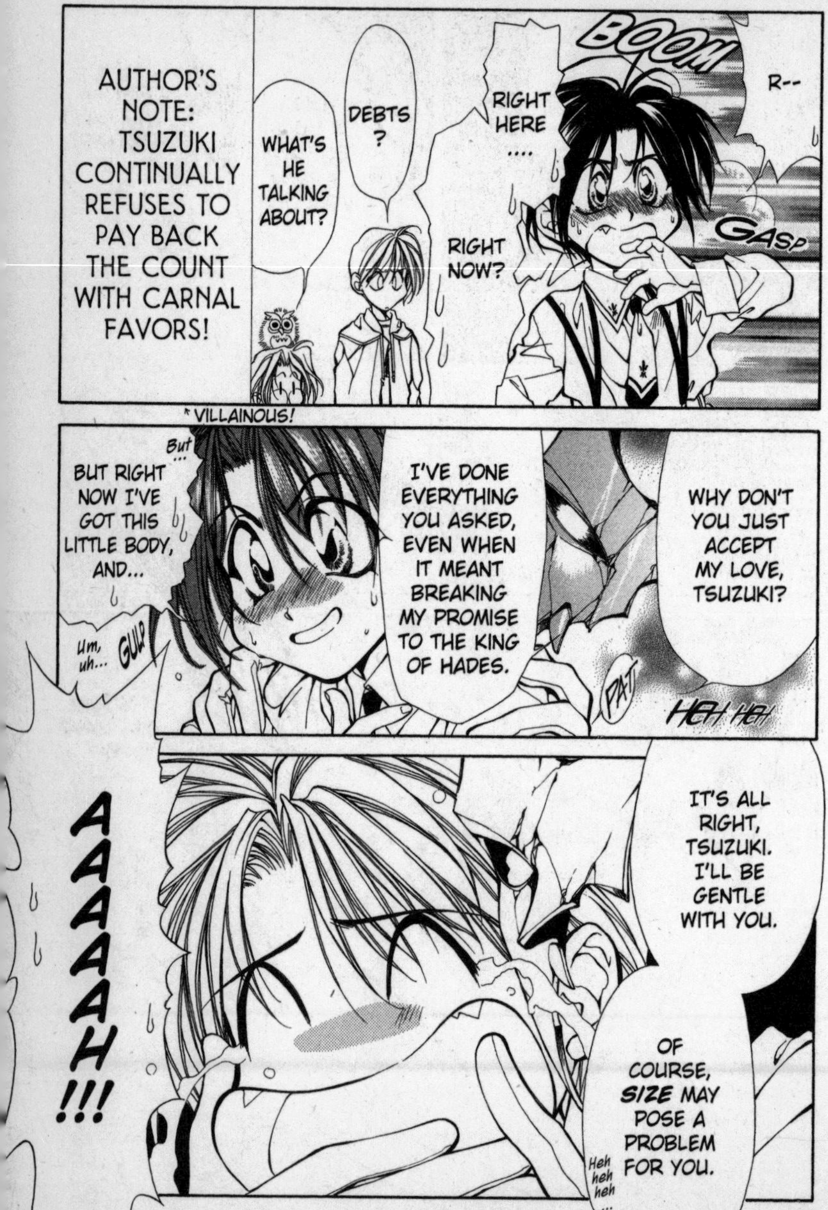
BOOM
R--
RIGHT HERE ....
GASP
RIGHT NOW?
DEBTS ?
WHAT'S HE TALKING ABOUT?
AUTHOR'S NOTE: TSUZUKI CONTINUALLY REFUSES TO PAY BACK THE COUNT WITH CARNAL FAVORS!
*VILLAINOUS!
WHY DON'T YOU JUST ACCEPT MY LOVE, TSUZUKI?
PAT
HEH HEH
I'VE DONE EVERYTHING YOU ASKED, EVEN WHEN IT MEANT BREAKING MY PROMISE TO THE KING OF HADES.
But ...
BUT RIGHT NOW I'VE GOT THIS LITTLE BODY, AND...
Um, uh...
GULP
IT'S ALL RIGHT, TSUZUKI. I'LL BE GENTLE WITH YOU.
OF COURSE, ***SIZE*** MAY POSE A PROBLEM FOR YOU.
Heh heh heh ...
AAAAAH!!!

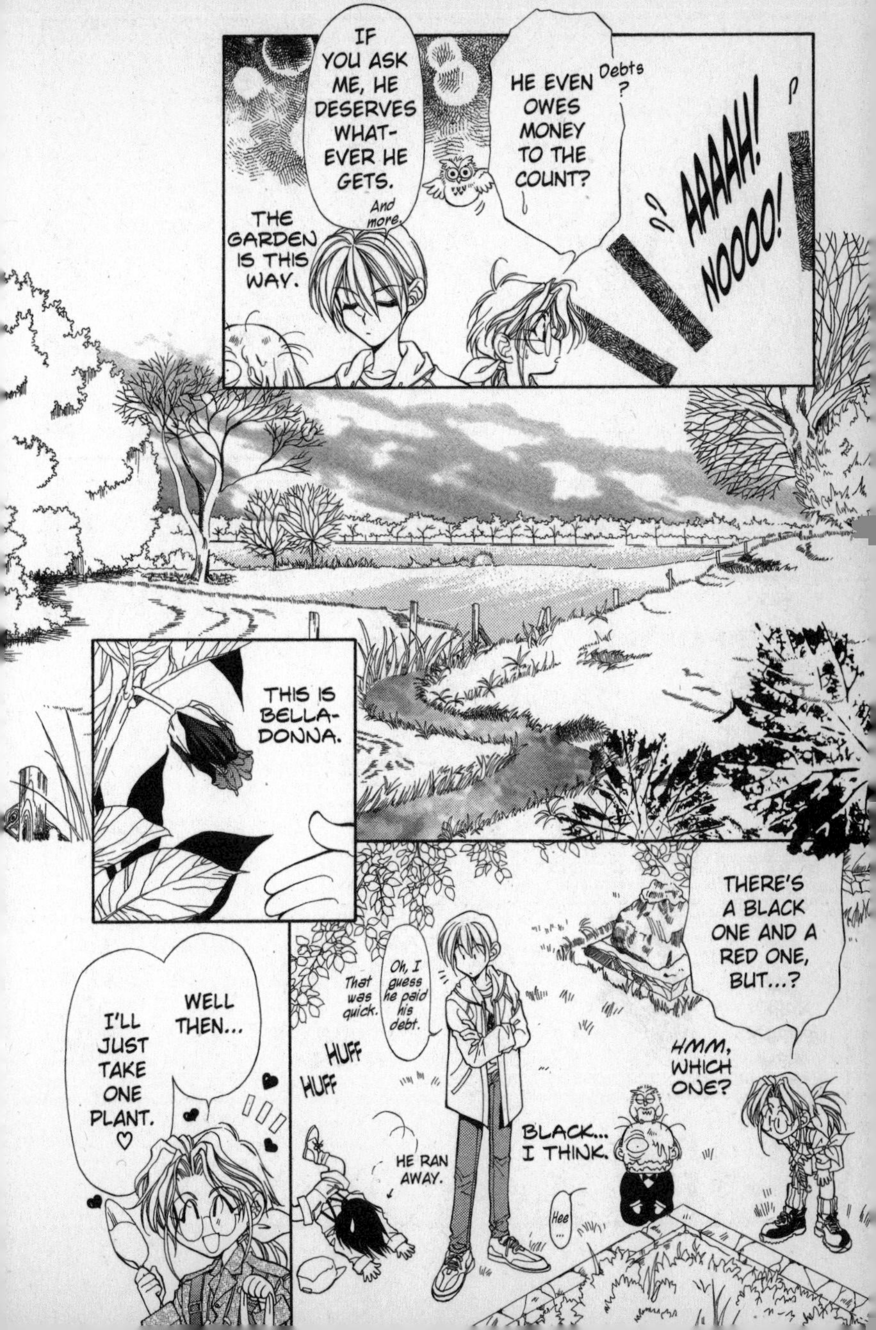
AAAAH! NOOOO!
HE EVEN OWES MONEY TO THE COUNT?
Debts ?
IF YOU ASK ME, HE DESERVES WHATEVER HE GETS.
And more.
THE GARDEN IS THIS WAY.
THIS IS BELLADONNA.
THERE'S A BLACK ONE AND A RED ONE, BUT...?
HMM, WHICH ONE?
BLACK... I THINK.
Hee...
Oh, I guess he paid his debt.
That was quick.
HUFF
HUFF
HE RAN AWAY.
WELL THEN...
I'LL JUST TAKE ONE PLANT. ♡

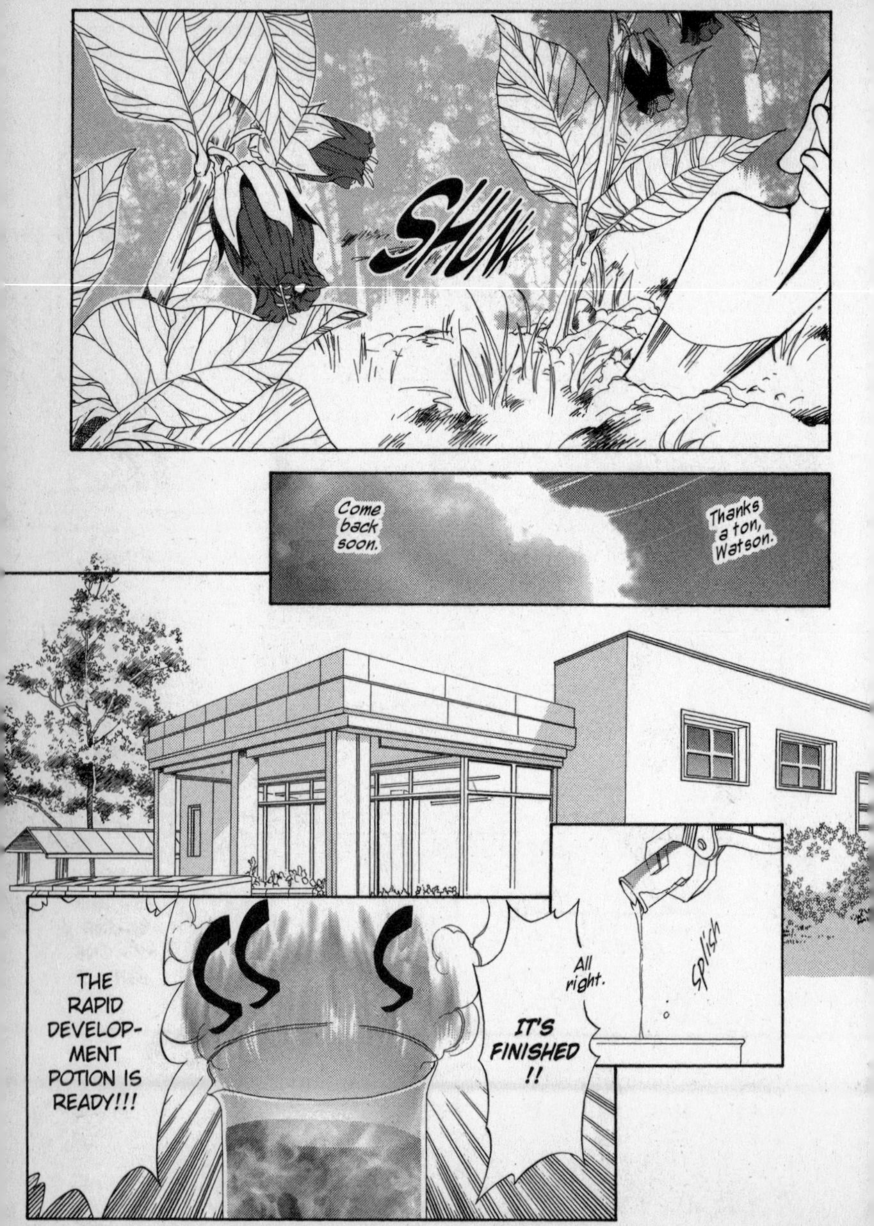
SHUN
Thanks a ton, Watson.
Come back soon.
splish
All right.
IT'S FINISHED!!
THE RAPID DEVELOPMENT POTION IS READY!!!

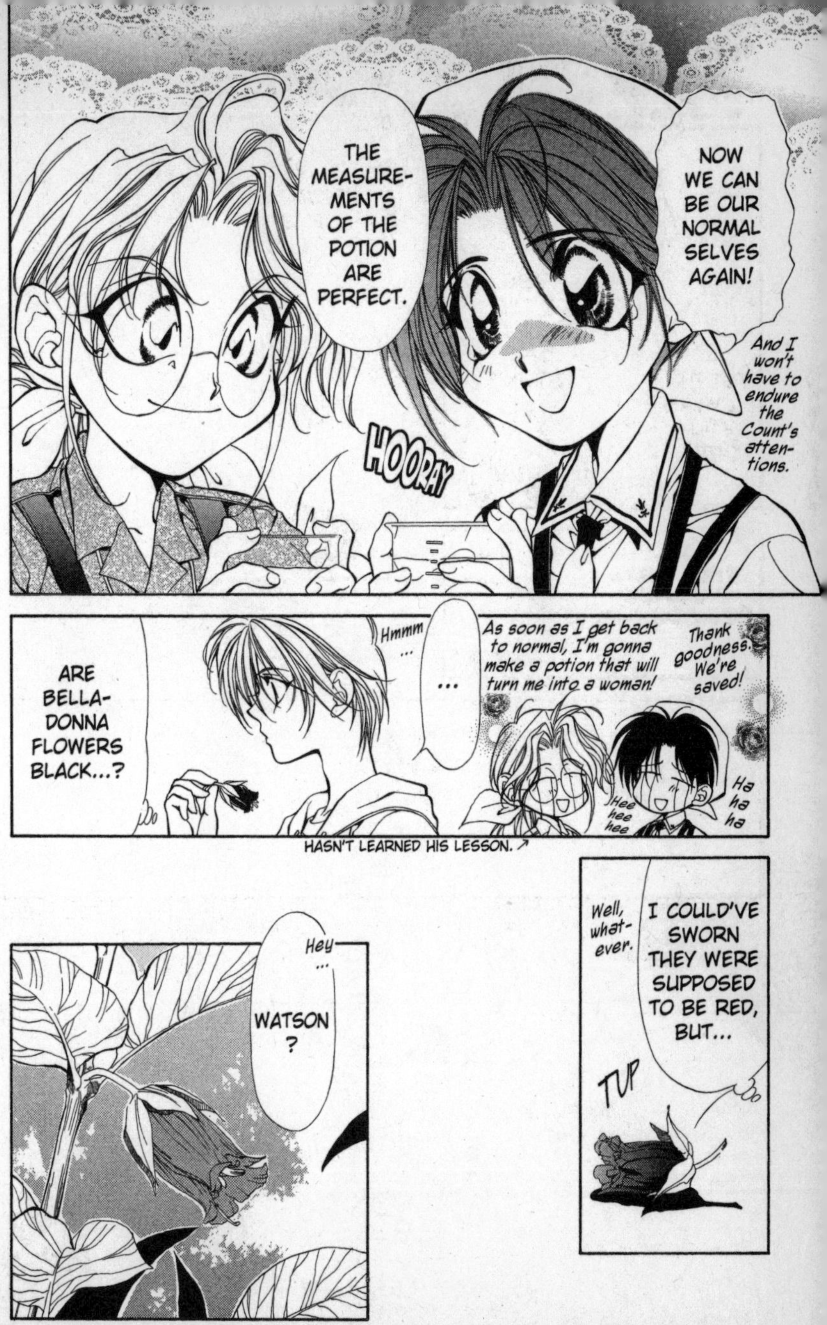
NOW WE CAN BE OUR NORMAL SELVES AGAIN!
And I won't have to endure the Count's attentions.
THE MEASURE-MENTS OF THE POTION ARE PERFECT.
HOORAY
Thank goodness. We're saved!
Ha ha ha
As soon as I get back to normal, I'm gonna make a potion that will turn me into a woman!
Hee hee hee
...
Hmmm ...
ARE BELLA-DONNA FLOWERS BLACK...?
HASN'T LEARNED HIS LESSON.
I COULD'VE SWORN THEY WERE SUPPOSED TO BE RED, BUT...
Well, what-ever.
TUP
Hey ...
WATSON ?

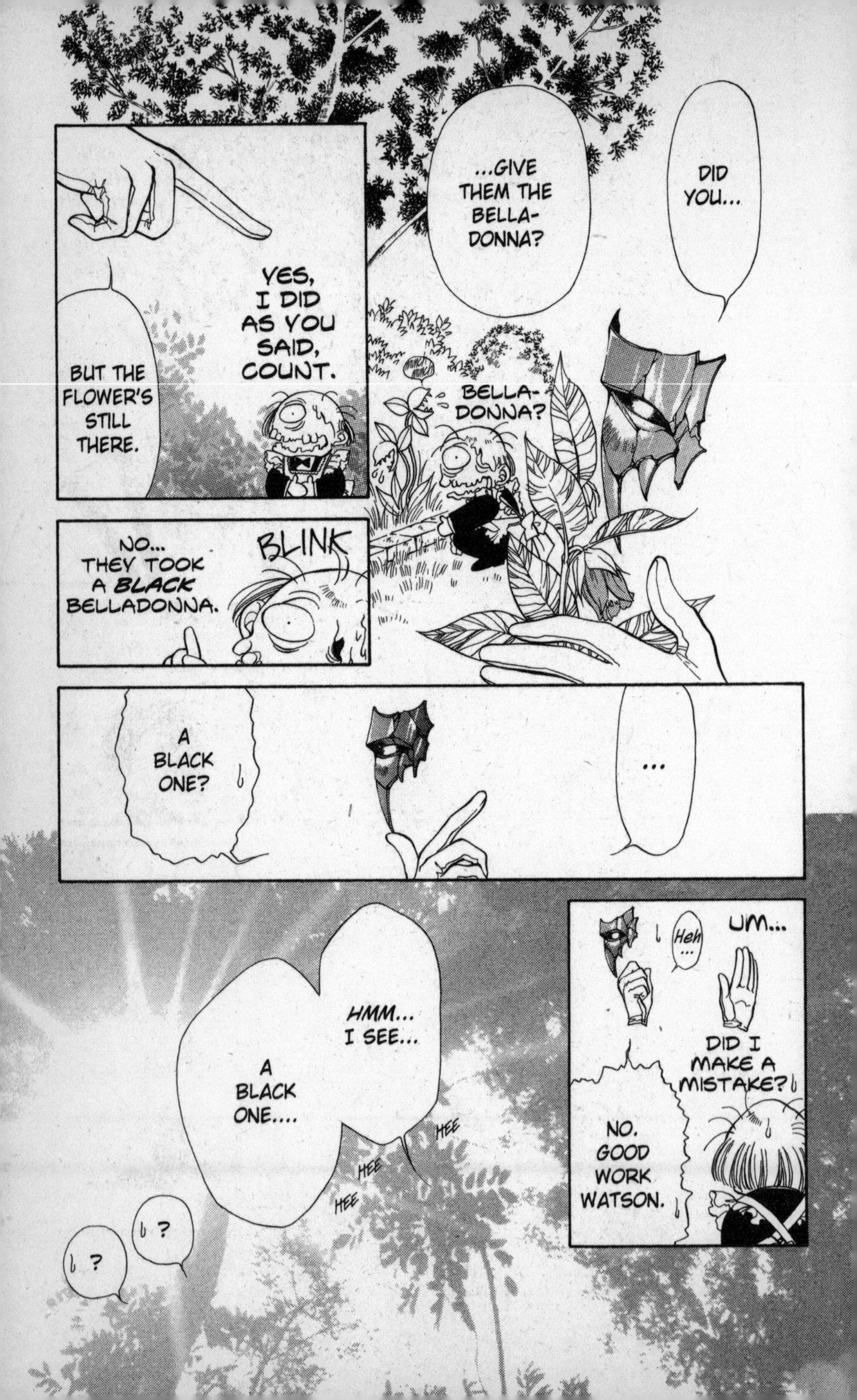
DID YOU...
...GIVE THEM THE BELLA-DONNA?
BELLA-DONNA?
YES, I DID AS YOU SAID, COUNT.
BUT THE FLOWER'S STILL THERE.
BLINK
NO... THEY TOOK A *BLACK* BELLADONNA.
...
A BLACK ONE?
UM...
Heh...
DID I MAKE A MISTAKE?
NO. GOOD WORK WATSON.
HMM... I SEE...
A BLACK ONE....
HEE
HEE
HEE
?
?

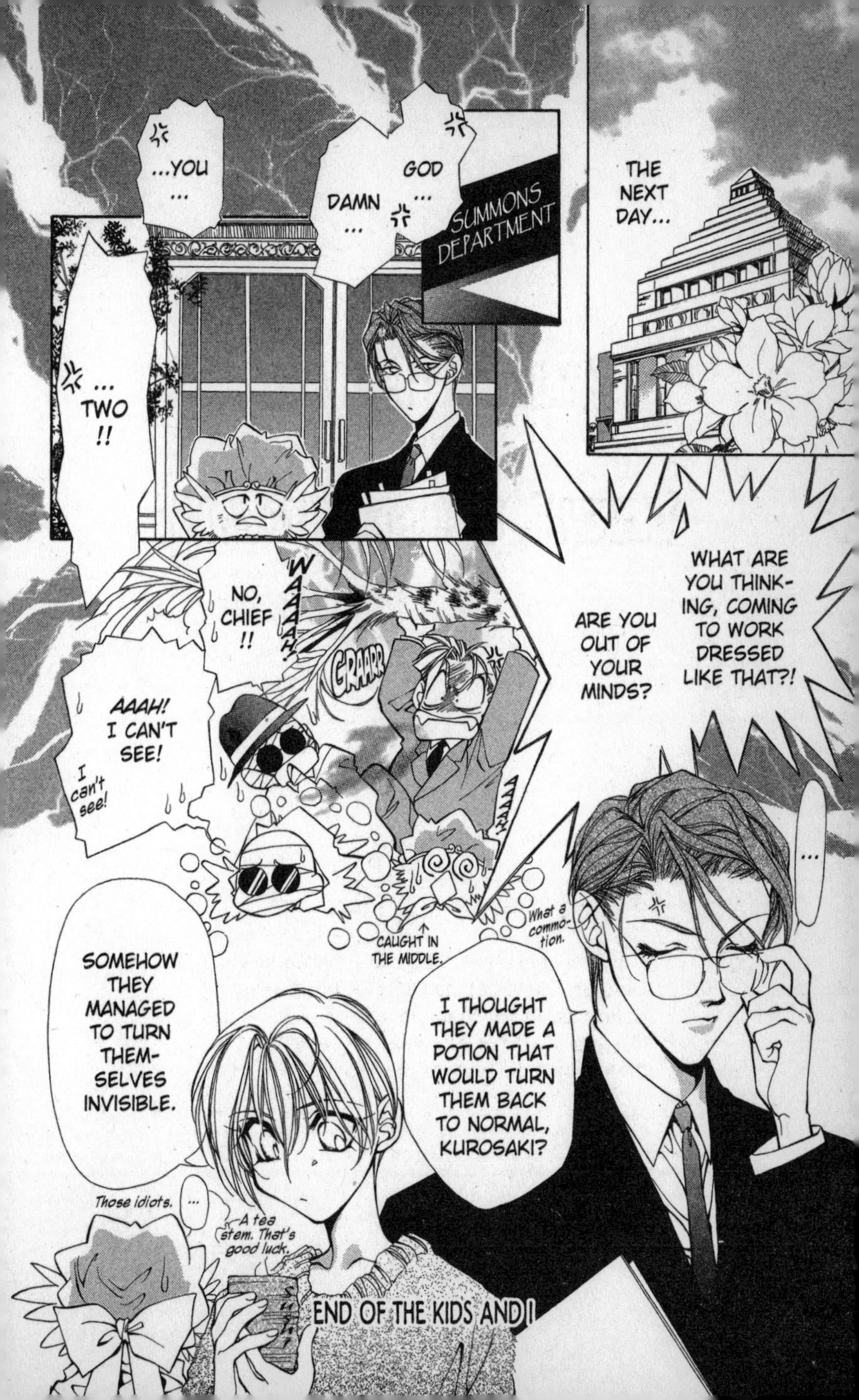

THE NEXT DAY...
SUMMONS DEPARTMENT
GOD ... DAMN ...
...YOU ...
... TWO !!
WHAT ARE YOU THINKING, COMING TO WORK DRESSED LIKE THAT?!
ARE YOU OUT OF YOUR MINDS?
WAAAAH!
GRAARR
NO, CHIEF !!
AAAH! I CAN'T SEE!
I can't see!
CAUGHT IN THE MIDDLE.
What a commotion.
...
I THOUGHT THEY MADE A POTION THAT WOULD TURN THEM BACK TO NORMAL, KUROSAKI?
SOMEHOW THEY MANAGED TO TURN THEMSELVES INVISIBLE.
...
Those idiots.
A tea stem. That's good luck.
END OF THE KIDS AND I

CHARACTER PROFILES
&
DESIGN ROUGH CUT SELECTIONS

I'm doing these special profiles for readers who were unable to get the CD. I included a few details about the characters that weren't in the CD, too. Those of you who are reading this at the bookstore…hurry to the register! Go! (Ha)

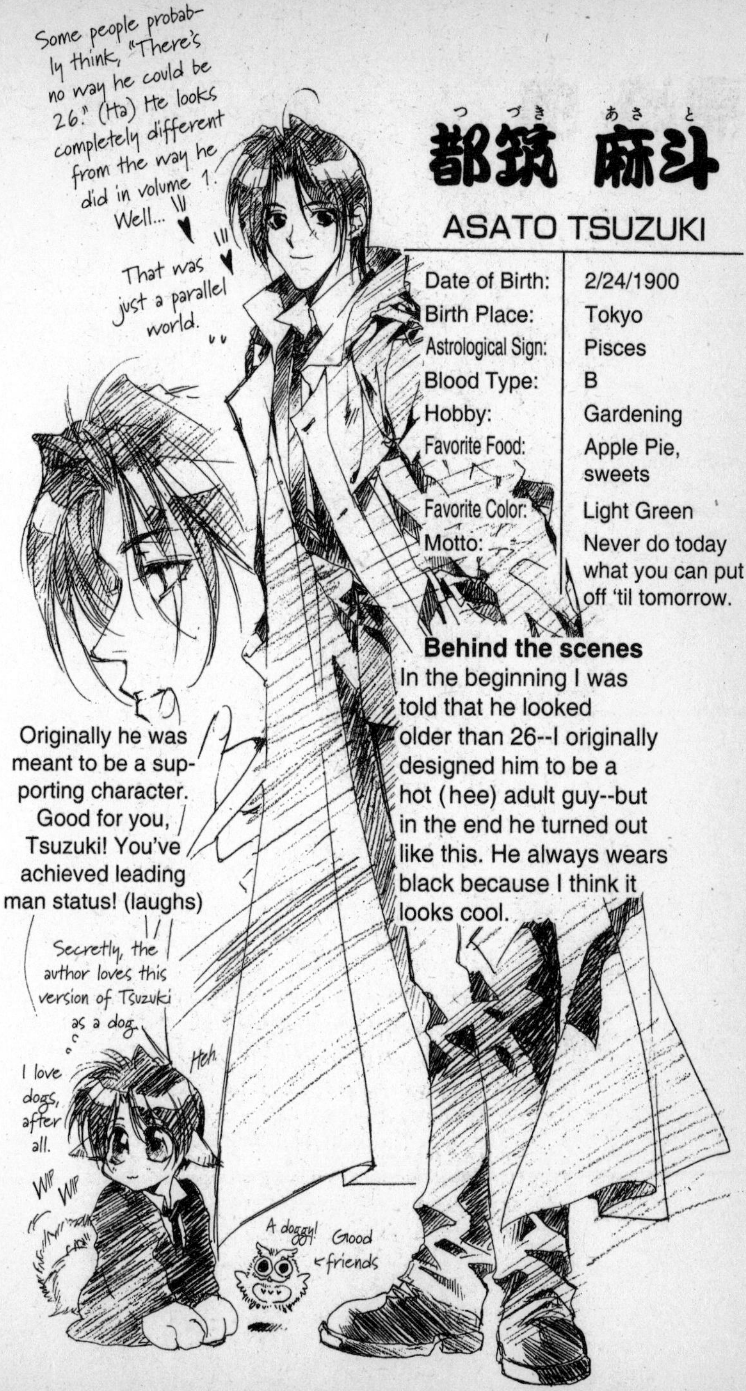

Some people probably think, "There's no way he could be 26." (Ha) He looks completely different from the way he did in volume 1. Well...
That was just a parallel world.
Secretly, the author loves this version of Tsuzuki as a dog.
Heh.
I love dogs, after all.
WIP WIP
A doggy!
Good friends

都筑 麻斗

ASATO TSUZUKI

Date of Birth:	2/24/1900
Birth Place:	Tokyo
Astrological Sign:	Pisces
Blood Type:	B
Hobby:	Gardening
Favorite Food:	Apple Pie, sweets
Favorite Color:	Light Green
Motto:	Never do today what you can put off 'til tomorrow.

Behind the scenes

In the beginning I was told that he looked older than 26--I originally designed him to be a hot (hee) adult guy--but in the end he turned out like this. He always wears black because I think it looks cool.

Originally he was meant to be a supporting character. Good for you, Tsuzuki! You've achieved leading man status! (laughs)

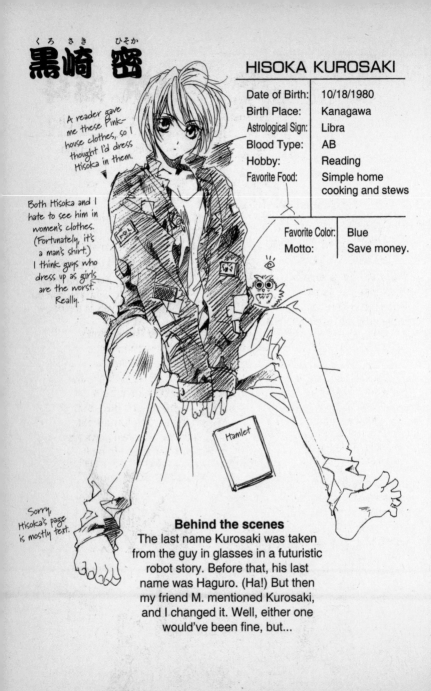

黒崎 密
くろさき　ひそか

HISOKA KUROSAKI

Date of Birth:	10/18/1980
Birth Place:	Kanagawa
Astrological Sign:	Libra
Blood Type:	AB
Hobby:	Reading
Favorite Food:	Simple home cooking and stews
Favorite Color:	Blue
Motto:	Save money.

A reader gave me these pink-house clothes, so I thought I'd dress Hisoka in them.

Both Hisoka and I hate to see him in women's clothes. (Fortunately, it's a man's shirt.) I think guys who dress up as girls are the worst. Really.

Sorry, Hisoka's page is mostly text.

Hamlet

Behind the scenes

The last name Kurosaki was taken from the guy in glasses in a futuristic robot story. Before that, his last name was Haguro. (Ha!) But then my friend M. mentioned Kurosaki, and I changed it. Well, either one would've been fine, but...

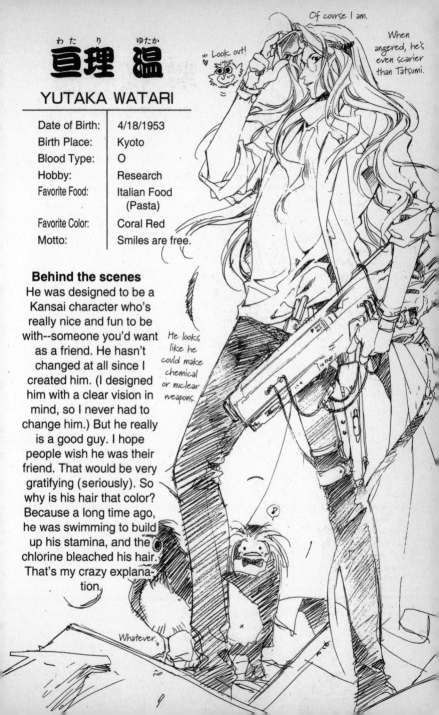

亘理 温
わたり　ゆたか

YUTAKA WATARI

Date of Birth:	4/18/1953
Birth Place:	Kyoto
Blood Type:	O
Hobby:	Research
Favorite Food:	Italian Food (Pasta)
Favorite Color:	Coral Red
Motto:	Smiles are free.

Behind the scenes

He was designed to be a Kansai character who's really nice and fun to be with--someone you'd want as a friend. He hasn't changed at all since I created him. (I designed him with a clear vision in mind, so I never had to change him.) But he really is a good guy. I hope people wish he was their friend. That would be very gratifying (seriously). So why is his hair that color? Because a long time ago, he was swimming to build up his stamina, and the chlorine bleached his hair. That's my crazy explanation.

Of course I am.

Look out!

When angered, he's even scarier than Tatsumi.

He looks like he could make chemical or nuclear weapons.

Whatever.

たつみ　せい いち ろう
巽 征一郎

SEIICHIRO TATSUMI

Date of Birth:	12/27/????
Birth Place:	N/A
Blood Type:	A
Hobby:	Counting money
Favorite Food:	Fried tofu soup
Favorite Color:	Globeflower green
Motto:	Time is money.

Behind the scenes

He started out as a nameless secretary. It's amazing how far he's come. He made his debut not as a secretary but as a Shinigami, but for some reason, he ended up a secretary. (Hee) I'm often asked if I got the name from a character in a certain novel, but I definitely did not. I actually got the name from a verse in the game hyakuninisshu. Seiichiro is the name of my friend M's little brother.

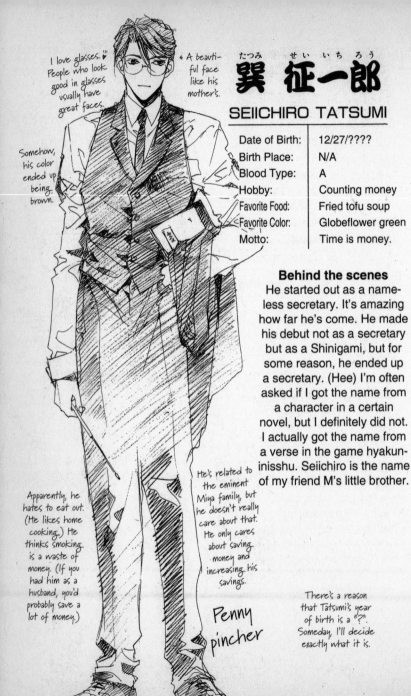

I love glasses.♥ People who look good in glasses usually have great faces.
← A beautiful face like his mother's.
Somehow, his color ended up being brown.
Apparently, he hates to eat out. (He likes home cooking.) He thinks smoking is a waste of money. (If you had him as a husband, you'd probably save a lot of money.)
He's related to the eminent Miya family, but he doesn't really care about that. He only cares about saving money and increasing his savings.
Penny pincher

There's a reason that Tatsumi's year of birth is a "?". Someday, I'll decide exactly what it is.

むらき　かずたか

邑輝 一貴

KAZUTAKA MURAKI

Date of Birth:	12/4/1964
Birth Place:	Tokyo
Astrological Sign:	Sagittarius
Blood Type:	A
Hobby:	Collecting antique dolls
Favorite Food:	Omelets
Motto:	It takes money to make money Or, Always keep doing what people don't like.

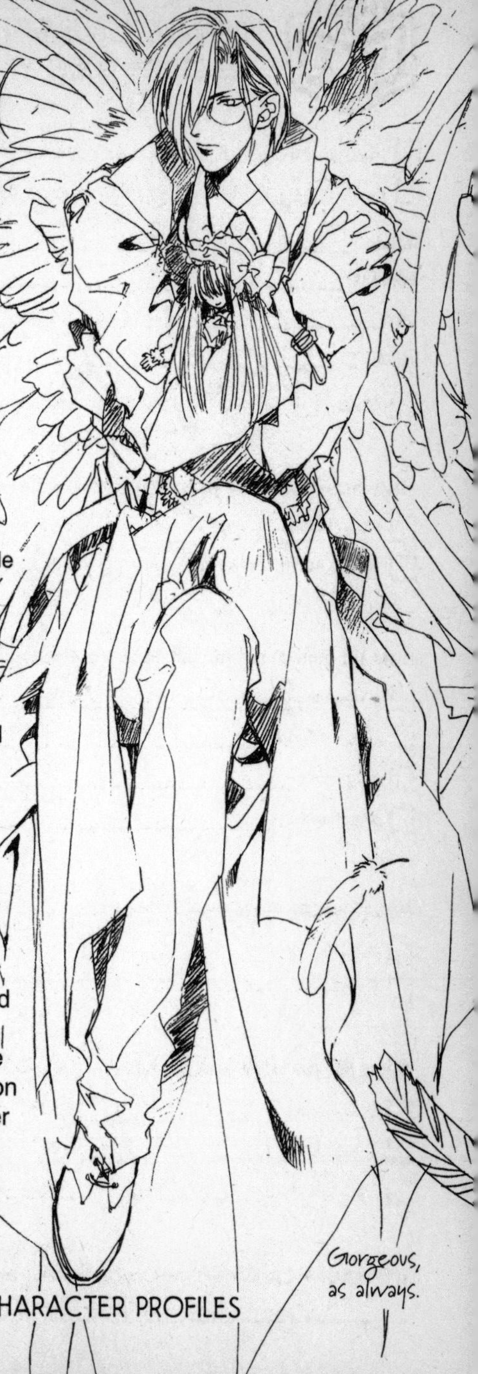
Gorgeous, as always.

Behind the scenes

I intended him to be a one-time villain in the Nagasaki story, so even I was surprised to see him become a regular character. I designed him as a foil for Tsuzuki, so he's rich and wears white, and has a cruel personality. By the way, Sakaki is the Doctor's butler, but also his mentor. (I was surprised when Morikawa did the voices of both Tatsumi and Sakaki in the CD.) As far as his hobby goes, apparently he inherited his mother's collection of antique dolls. This character reflects my love of doctors.

END OF CHARACTER PROFILES

COMPLETE OUR SURVEY AND LET US KNOW WHAT YOU THINK!

☐ Please do NOT send me information about VIZ products, news and events, special offers, or other information.

☐ Please do NOT send me information from VIZ's trusted business partners.

Name: _____

Address: _____

City: _____ **State:** _____ **Zip:** _____

E-mail: _____

☐ Male ☐ Female   **Date of Birth** (mm/dd/yyyy): ___ / ___ / ___   (Under 13? Parental consent required)

What race/ethnicity do you consider yourself? (please check one)

☐ Asian/Pacific Islander   ☐ Black/African American   ☐ Hispanic/Latino

☐ Native American/Alaskan Native   ☐ White/Caucasian   ☐ Other: _____

What VIZ product did you purchase? (check all that apply and indicate title purchased)

☐ DVD/VHS _____

☐ Graphic Novel _____

☐ Magazines _____

☐ Merchandise _____

Reason for purchase: (check all that apply)

☐ Special offer   ☐ Favorite title   ☐ Gift

☐ Recommendation   ☐ Other _____

Where did you make your purchase? (please check one)

☐ Comic store   ☐ Bookstore   ☐ Mass/Grocery Store

☐ Newsstand   ☐ Video/Video Game Store ☐ Other: _____

☐ Online (site: _____)

What other VIZ properties have you purchased/own? _____

_____

How many anime and/or manga titles have you ___
VIZ titles? (please check one from each column)

ANIME	MANGA
☐ None	☐ None
☐ 1-4	☐ 1-4
☐ 5-10	☐ 5-10
☐ 11+	☐ 11+

I find the pricing of VIZ products to be: (please check one)

☐ Cheap   ☐ Reasonable   ☐ Expensive

What genre of manga and anime would you like to see from VIZ? (please check two)

☐ Adventure   ☐ Comic Strip   ☐ Science Fiction   ☐ Fighting

☐ Horror   ☐ Romance   ☐ Fantasy   ☐ Sports

What do you think of VIZ's new look?

☐ Love It   ☐ It's OK   ☐ Hate It   ☐ Didn't Notice   ☐ No Opinion

Which do you prefer? (please check one)

☐ Reading right-to-left

☐ Reading left-to-right

Which do you prefer? (please check one)

☐ Sound effects in English

☐ Sound effects in Japanese with English captions

☐ Sound effects in Japanese only with a glossary at the back

THANK YOU! Please send the completed form to:

VIZ Survey
42 Catharine St.
Poughkeepsie, NY 12601

All information provided will be used for internal purposes only. We promise not to sell or otherwise divulge your information.